BRUTUS

BRUTUS

THE NOBLE CONSPIRATOR

KATHRYN TEMPEST

YALE UNIVERSITY PRESS
NEW HAVEN AND LONDON

For information about this and other Yale University Press publications, please contact:
US Office: sales.press@yale.edu yalebooks.com
Europe Office: sales@yaleup.co.uk yalebooks.co.uk

Set in Minion Pro by IDSUK (DataConnection) Ltd
Printed in Great Britain by TJ International Ltd, Padstow, Cornwall

Library of Congress Control Number: 2017948509

ISBN 978-0-300-18009-1

A catalogue record for this book is available from the British Library.

10 9 8 7 6 5 4 3 2 1

CONTENTS

ILLUSTRATIONS AND MAPS

Illustrations

Maps

PREFACE

> But on the day of Brutus' judgment, Caesar came without scroll or senate to declare verdict.
>
> 'You demean yourself, dear Brutus', he said almost gently, 'attempting suicide like this. But death for you, my friend, is not an option. You will live forever', eyes sad, 'in the shadow of my name.'
>
> And Brutus did live forever. He found himself not dead but filled with youth and eternity. Ashamed of his past, he travelled the worlds as Marcus, boundless centuries of world after world, from one galaxy to another, finding no peace.
>
> A shadow . . . If anyone spoke his name, it was in the same sentence as Caesar. Never just Brutus.
>
> — Eugene Bacon, 2015, 'Being Marcus', *New Writing* 12.3, 351

This extract from a short piece of fictional writing shows that the name of Marcus Brutus may suddenly pop up anywhere, even, as in this story, as a personal trainer at a fitness studio, somewhere on Earth in the twenty-first century. Condemned by Caesar's ghost to a lifetime of immortality, he has seen his reputation wax and wane throughout history. He has witnessed his own reception: as Caesar's assassin in Shakespeare and the eternal traitor chewed by Satan in Dante's *Inferno*, and he disdains it. 'History has forgotten the real Brutus', the reader is caused to reflect; the memory of his life has been eclipsed by that of Caesar. And here lies part of the problem in reconstructing a biography for Brutus; from the moment he stabbed Caesar, he has continued to capture the imagination of those who have studied him and his role in the assassination. Thus the judgments have all been pronounced with the clarity and bias that hindsight seemingly provides. Yet, despite his popularity in literature and history, biographical studies of Brutus have not been plentiful.

Already for Max Radin, writing *Marcus Brutus* back in 1939, the challenge was to present a living man and not a symbol. That man, in Radin's conclusion, was a conflicted personality; his desire to follow where Cato led forced him to pursue a career that was 'essentially repugnant' to him. We might disagree with the conclusion today, but still the approach was more imaginative than that of Gérard Walter's study (*Brutus et la fin de la République*), published in France the year before, which largely retold the story of Brutus from the ancient evidence, with little or no attempt to evaluate the material on which its conclusions were based. Since then, scholarship has moved on. Martin Clarke's *The Noblest Roman,* published in 1981, aimed to present an account of Brutus based on the ancient evidence, as well as to trace the course of his posthumous reputation. To this day, Clarke's work remains one of the best and most accessible books on the topic. But it is still too brief on certain points of detail, and especially so on the sources for studying Brutus' life, his political activity and ethical conduct. Appearing in the same year, Erik Wistrand's essay on 'The Policy of Brutus the Tyrannicide' went some way towards providing an explanation for the political agenda behind the assassination. However, for serious scholars of Brutus, the best contributions are only available to readers with some command of German.

Matthias Gelzer's 1917 entry for the *Real-Encyclopädie* presented a picture of Brutus which was particularly sympathetic to the times in which he operated. From this authoritative article, Brutus emerges as an essentially admirable man, yet one who had little political vision for the future. More apologetic still was Walter Stewens' 1968 essay on the political career of Brutus (*Brutus als Politiker*), which included an examination of the principles for which he had acted against Caesar. Prompted by what he saw as an unoriginal take on the life and career of Caesar's assassin, however, in 1970 Hermann Bengston produced his own collection of essays 'On the History of Brutus' (*Zur Geschichte des Brutus*). It did not claim to be a biography. Yet, in covering the sources for studying Brutus and by questioning a range of topics pertinent to an understanding of his life – that is, his relationship with Caesar, his conduct after the assassination, as well as the panegyric and propaganda surrounding him – it offered a far more penetrative analysis than anything that had gone before it.

In more recent decades, there have been several works which, although not dedicated to Brutus *per se*, have significantly advanced our understanding of him. Maria Dettenhofer's 1992 study on the 'lost generation' (*Perdita iuventus: zwischen den Generationen von Caesar und Augustus*) offers an important collection of mini-biographies of Brutus and a selection of his contemporaries. Essential for understanding the actions of Brutus in the aftermath of the assassination is Ulricht Gotter's *Der Diktator ist tot!* (1996). But still there has been a significant hiatus in the scholarly literature devoted to Brutus, and few scholars have recognised him as a subject worthy of study in his own right. Thus, it was several years ago, when I was working on Cicero, that I became interested in Brutus, a man with whom the great orator formed an unusual and at times fraught friendship. There and then I conceived the idea of writing a book on Brutus, and I was encouraged to undertake the present work by the absence of anything comparable either on the market or on library bookshelves. As I was putting the finishing touches to my own research, Kirsty Corrigan's *Brutus: Caesar's Assassin* (2015) appeared. Far from putting me off, however, it made me even more certain that a new study was worth the effort. Corrigan's book offers an engaging narrative of Brutus' life and times, which condenses a significant amount of ancient literature into a readable narrative. In what follows, on the other hand, I hope to add something different to that story.

To a considerable extent this book will examine how Brutus' life has been recorded and transmitted from antiquity to today; a central contention is that, to appreciate Brutus the man, we must really probe the sources we use, to understand who is speaking and why. From there, my aim is to make a significant contribution to the way we think about Brutus' life, as well as the conclusions we reach about how he conducted his political career. Even when some of the factual details might not in themselves be novel or surprising, I hope my analysis and evaluation of them will open up new approaches and different perspectives. To this end, this book will take an integrated approach to the topic, combining biographical exploration with historiographical and literary analyses. In so doing, it will offer a sense of who Brutus was and why he acted in the way he did, while simultaneously digging far deeper into the presentation of Brutus in the ancient evidence than has hitherto been attempted. As far as possible, then, it places his decisions and actions back into their real time, and it always prioritises an evaluation of the contemporary over later evidence for studying them. Wherever the evidence allows, Brutus is made to speak, argue and justify himself in his own words. Even when we do find ourselves having to rely on the works of later historians, I shall try to take us back to an understanding of them from the point of view of Brutus and his peers.

At the same time, this book does not shy away from the limitations of the biographical genre. It is enormously difficult to study the life of an ancient figure: in nearly all cases either the material is not there or it is too problematic to make the venture worthwhile. Yet, as Janet Nelson has succinctly argued in a comparable instance – that of early medieval biography and especially the case of Charlemagne – when there is a sufficient amount of a certain type of evidence, the task is worth the undertaking.[1] Not only does Brutus appear in a range of genres, we have some first-hand evidence written by Brutus himself. From his letters to Cicero, we can thus learn about what Nelson calls the subject's 'inner life': that is, the values he subscribed to or the beliefs he held in his lifetime. And from Cicero's letters more generally, as well as the later historians who wrote on the topic of the Roman Republic, we can establish ample links between Brutus' life and his historical context.

In fact, there is a huge amount of evidence from which to select, and the life of Brutus has been referenced in works spanning the centuries from his own day to the present. Modern scholars do not always agree on the particulars, or even the very large questions surrounding the times in which Brutus lived. Yet, insofar as this book aims to present the first critical analysis of Brutus' life and the sources that record it, I also want to make it accessible, regardless of the amount of knowledge with which the reader approaches this book. With this objective in mind, I have largely refrained from engaging in extensive debates in the main text. Key authors and thinkers will be referenced, but for those wanting to know why I have arrived at any particular conclusion, supplementary material has been provided at the end of the volume. In addition to the notes, I have also supplied a timeline (see Appendix 1) covering key dates to help guide the reader through this complex period.

I am particularly grateful to the friends and colleagues who took time out of their busy schedules to read through a draft of this book, or parts of it, especially Vicki Craig, Lisa Hau, Gesine Manuwald, Stephanie Tempest and Henriette van der Blom. Rosemary Barrow was there at the start, reading and helping me shape the proposal I put to Yale. Her premature death as I approached its completion was a blow and I only wish she could be here to see the final product. She would have especially liked the pictures, and in this connection, I am tremendously grateful to Si Sheppard and Hannah Swithinbank for sharing with me their personal photographs of Philippi and Rome. Kit Morrell, Christopher Pelling and Cristina Rosillo-López generously sent me material ahead of publication; at the same time, my project was buoyed up by discussions with Jaap Wisse, with whom I shared a lively debate over the date of Brutus' birth, as well as Kathryn Welch, whose ideas on Mark Antony have in turn caused me to think differently about a man so important and central to Brutus' life. As always, I owe much to Jonathan Powell, who offered sage advice and encouragement from start to finish.

The project benefited greatly from the financial assistance of the Leverhulme Trust, from which I received a grant to conduct research into the campaigns of Brutus in the east and the collection of letters I discuss in Chapter 7. While that project will be part of a fuller and separate inquiry, it has in turn fed into my discussions and appreciation of Brutus' activities in the Greek communities of Asia Minor between 43 and 42 BC. Likewise, I was fortunate to receive a term's leave from my own institution, the University of Roehampton, without which I might have lost the momentum needed to bring my thoughts to fruition.

During the process of writing, several chapters were tested on audiences at the Classical Association branches at Southampton and Roehampton, the University of Maynooth's classics seminar and the Association of Latin Teachers' annual conference. I am grateful to the organisers for inviting me, as well as to the participants on each occasion for asking probing and insightful questions. Heather McCallum, Rachael Lonsdale and Marika Lysandrou at Yale University Press were all unfailing in their support for the project – and very patient in awaiting its final delivery. I should also like to thank the three anonymous readers who offered excellent and much welcomed criticism, as well as Yale's copy-editor who saved me from several infelicities of expression. The book is a better product for all the input it has received, although it goes without saying that any errors which remain are entirely my own.

It remains to acknowledge that my greatest debt is without doubt to the friends and family who have supported me along the way: my mum, dad, sisters – and especially my husband, Tasos. The idea for this book came to me in 2011, at precisely the time he entered my life. Not only has he offered characteristic cheer throughout; he has provided sound advice, constructive ideas or just a pair of ears when I needed them most. Without him, neither the book, nor so much in life generally, would be quite the same.

London, January 2017

A NOTE ON THE TEXT

For ancient sources, the text and fragment numbering referred to throughout are those of the Loeb Classical Library (LCL) series, because it is assumed that they will be the editions most readily available to readers of this study. Unless otherwise noted in the main text, all translations are either my own or adapted from the editions I have consulted (see the list at the beginning of the Endnotes). I have sometimes deviated slightly from a strictly literal rendering of the Greek and Latin passages to ease the flow of the modern English; for the same reason, I have also adapted the punctuation to the needs of a modern reader.

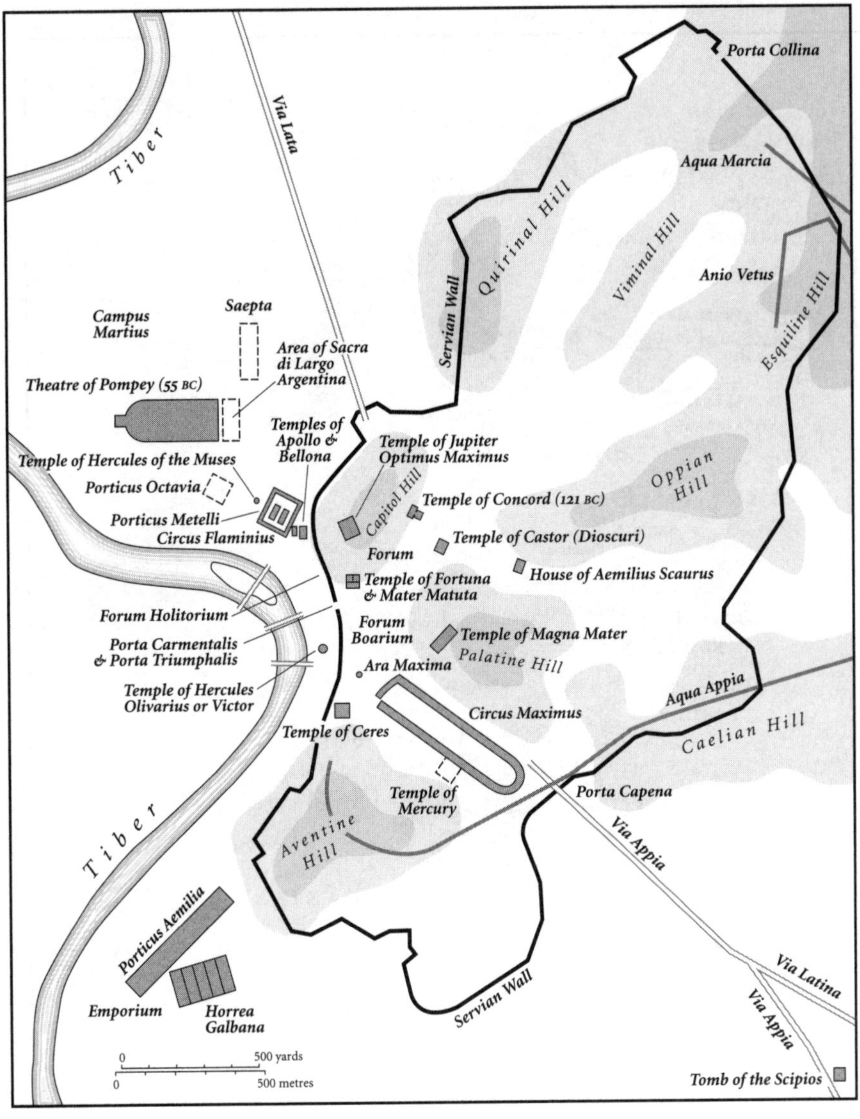

1. The City of Rome

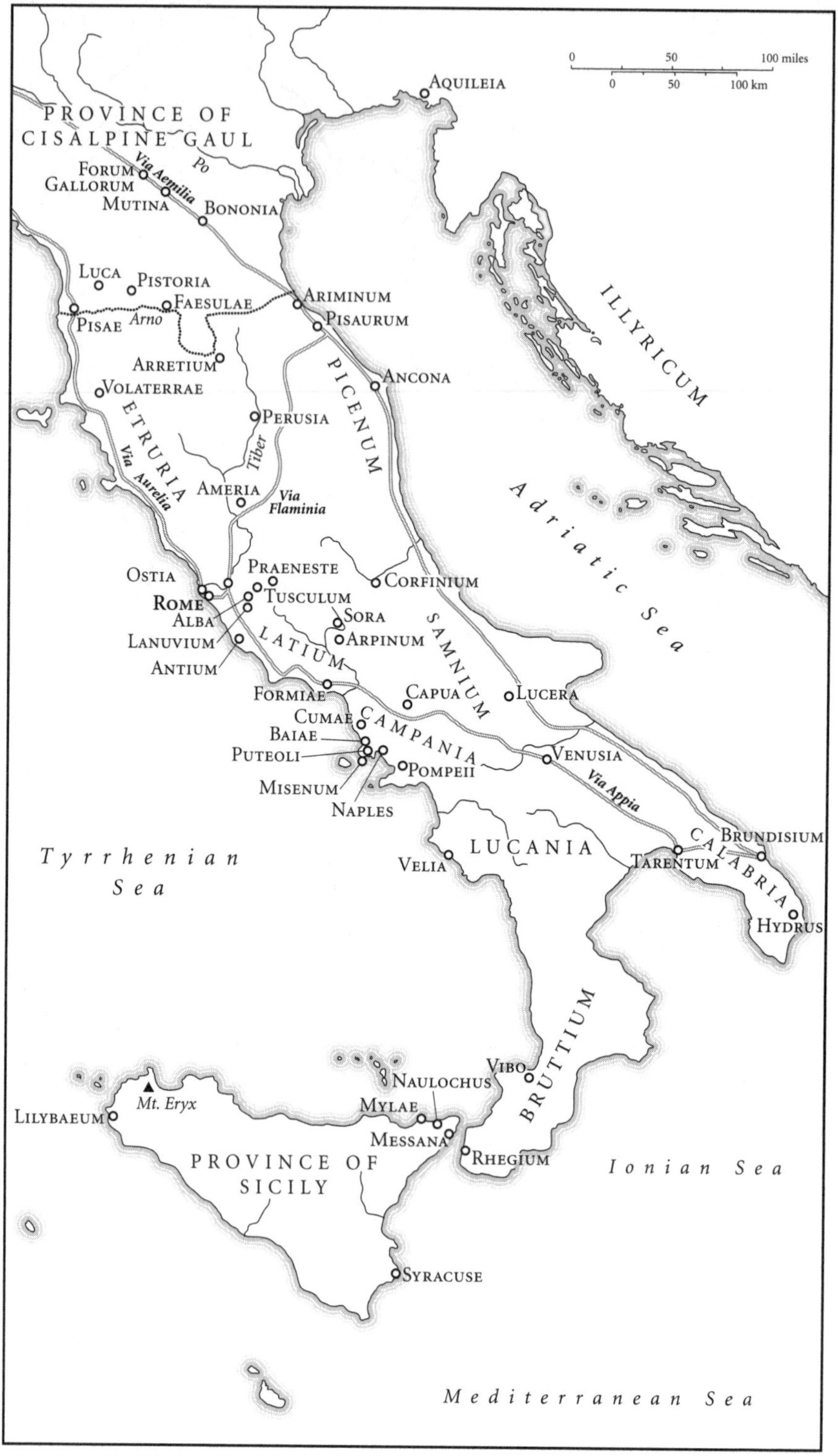

2. Italy in the Late Republic

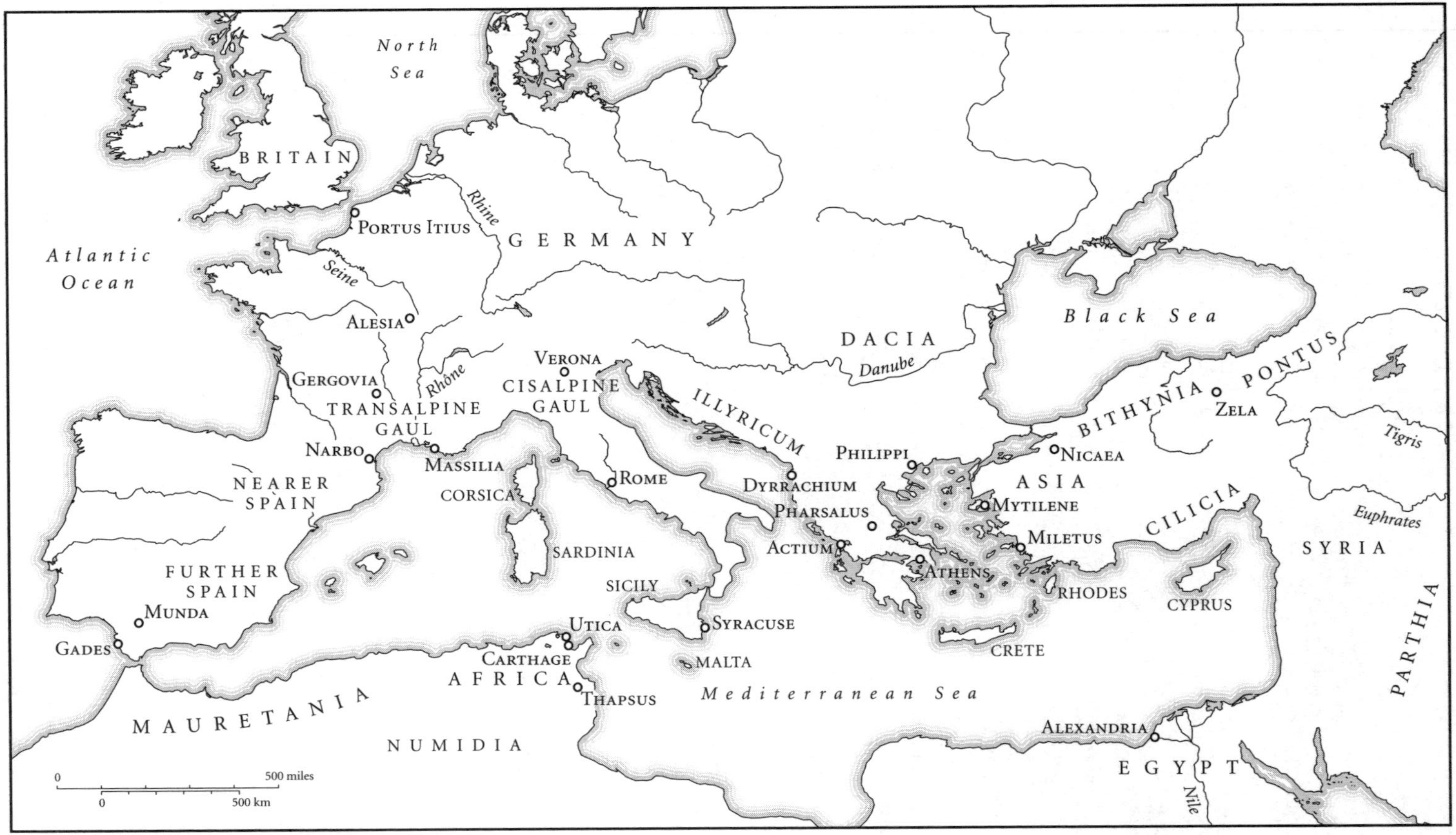

3. The Roman Empire in the First Century BC

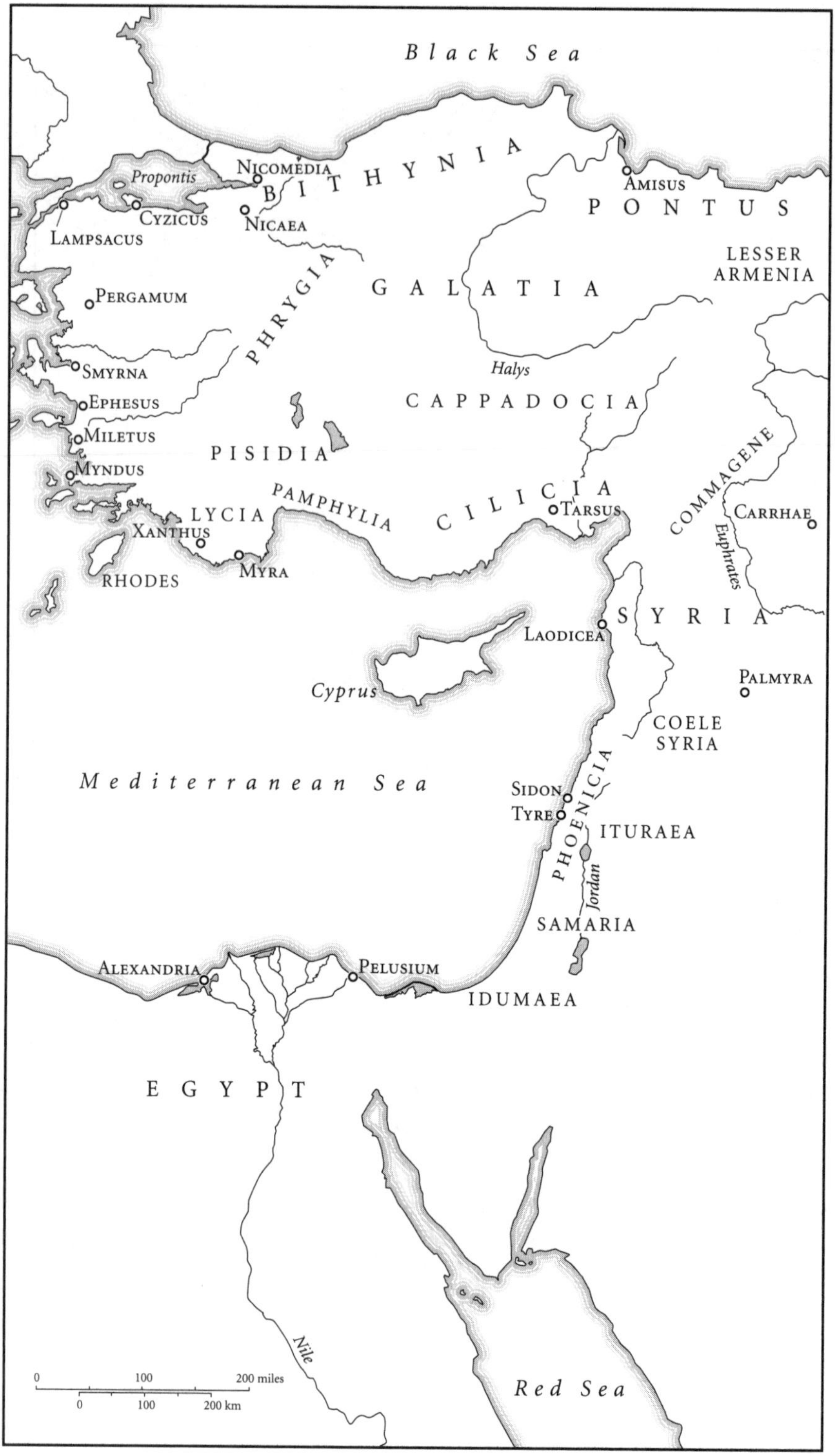

4. Provinces and Kingdoms of the East

INTRODUCTION

BRUTUS AND THE BIOGRAPHICAL TRADITION

The Ides of March

> If there be any in this assembly, any dear friend of Caesar's, to him I say that Brutus' love to Caesar was no less than his. If then that friend demand why Brutus rose against Caesar, this is my answer: not that I loved Caesar less, but that I loved Rome more. Had you rather Caesar were living, and die all slaves, than that Caesar were dead, to live all free men? As Caesar loved me, I weep for him; as he was fortunate, I rejoice at it; as he was valiant, I honour him: but, as he was ambitious, I slew him.
>
> — Shakespeare, *Julius Caesar*, 3.2.17–27

On 15 March 44 BC – a date known to the Romans as the Ides of March – a momentous occasion took place in the history of Rome: Julius Caesar was assassinated in a crowded meeting of the Senate. The story has been told many times before.[1] In the months leading up to his assassination he had accepted the title *dictator perpetuo* ('dictator for life'), as well as other honours and titles – both regal and divine – that were being heaped upon him. Now there was a rumour in the air that he would even be appointed king; a word, as we shall see, that was anathema to Roman political ideology. But, whatever title he took, one thing looked certain: Caesar was in no rush to abandon his power. In three days' time he was set to embark on his next great expedition – this time against Parthia. If he was successful, the campaign would bring Caesar the glory of another triumphal parade, another conquered nation, and even more personal wealth and power. Those who despised Caesar's domination now realised that there was only one way to free Rome from his grasp. They began to whisper about assassination and soon a conspiracy evolved; foremost among the plotters were Marcus Junius Brutus and Gaius Cassius Longinus.

On the morning of the assassination, Brutus and Cassius had arrived early. As praetors of the Roman Republic – the second highest magistracy after the consulship – they were responsible for overseeing and conducting matters of justice. While they waited for Caesar to arrive, they listened carefully to a number of disputes and applications presented before them: 'anyone who knew what was about to happen would have been amazed at the unshakeable calm and presence of mind which these men displayed as the critical moment drew near', adds the Greek biographer Plutarch, whose account of Brutus' life is the only one to survive from antiquity.[2]

Plutarch is right to draw our attention to this moment; that the conspiracy had even got this far is a wonder. More than once, however, the plotters' nerve was shaken. It was getting late in the day by Roman standards, almost eleven in the morning, and Caesar had still not appeared. Nicolaus of Damascus, who wrote an account of the conspiracy, tells us that Caesar had been delayed at home by a series of bad omens: his wife Calpurnia had been frightened by certain nightmares; the sacrificial victims were unfavourable. For both the Romans of Brutus' day and the writers who relayed these stories, it was the common belief that the gods manifested their will through natural phenomena. Hence, divinatory practices, known as auspices, were conducted to learn about the future or to seek approval from the gods by examining the entrails of animals. Birds, too, were seen as the transmitters of Jupiter's divine plan. Augurs and professional soothsayers (*haruspices* in the Latin) would be called upon to interpret these signs; it was a serious business and their warnings were not meant to be ignored. But a third conspirator, Decimus Brutus Albinus, who was also one of Caesar's most trusted friends, coerced him to leave the house: 'Will a man such as yourself place any trust in the dreams of a woman and the omens of brainless men?' he allegedly asked, adding that it would be considered an insult to the Senate if Caesar were to stay at home.[3]

Back in the complex of the theatre of Pompey, where the meeting was scheduled to take place, anxiety was mounting among the conspirators. A couple of times they either heard or thought they heard allusions made to the plot. Brutus too had received some unwelcome news from home: his wife Porcia had collapsed. But Brutus could not allow this news to distract him from his purpose. For Caesar was now on his way. And as the dictator of Rome disembarked from his litter – the sedan chair on which he travelled – the conspirators watched as Caesar was approached by a throng of men.

Among them was a soothsayer called Spurinna. A month earlier this man had approached Caesar and warned him 'to beware the danger that would not pass until the Ides of March', and now he approached him again. When Caesar saw Spurinna he laughed: 'The Ides of March have come', he said, mocking the prophecy he had been given. 'Indeed, they have come', replied Spurinna, 'but they have not yet gone.'[4]

In one hand, Caesar allegedly grasped a note that had been passed to him amidst the flood of petitions he received that morning; had he read it, this note might have saved his life, for it revealed details of the plot. But in a classic twist of dramatic irony, Caesar was too busy to notice it, and as he made his way into the Senate chamber the conspirators closed in around him. Tillius Cimber approached him first, pretending to plead for Caesar's mercy on behalf of his exiled brother. But then he wrenched the toga from Caesar's shoulders and thus provided the opportunity for attack. The first blow was struck by one of a pair of brothers called Casca who were both in on the plot; yet he misjudged his aim, so that for a while, at least, Caesar was able to fight back. At this point a wave of panic swept over the conspirators, and in the confusion that followed they even started stabbing each other; Brutus himself received a nasty wound to the hand. It was a bungled, bloody affair. Even so, Caesar did not stand a chance; he was like a wild beast caught in a trap – or so later accounts pictured it. Conspirators surrounded him on all sides.[5]

Plutarch adds that 'as he glanced around to see if he could force a way through his attackers, he saw Brutus closing in upon him with his dagger drawn'. Thereupon Caesar buried his head in his robe and yielded to the murderers' blows. Like Plutarch, most of our ancient sources attribute some importance to the sight of Brutus among Caesar's assassins. It was the playwright William Shakespeare who attributed to Caesar the famous dying words *Et tu, Brute?* ('And you, Brutus?') But a precedent for this claim can be found among our classical narratives, which Shakespeare must have known either directly or indirectly. For the historians Suetonius and Dio had both read earlier accounts in which Caesar had shouted in Greek, *Kai su, teknon* ('You too, child?'), fuelling speculations, as we shall see, that Brutus may have been Caesar's love child.[6]

Unsurprisingly, given the chaos of the event, the surviving accounts of the assassination contain several discrepancies; the details of who did what and when, for example, vary from one author to the next. But that is also because the majority of our sources were composed at least 150 years after the assassination; by then the story had been either simplified or expanded in the retelling. Inconsistencies include the number of wounds inflicted, which range from twenty-three to thirty-five; or how many conspirators were involved in the plot. Nicolaus of Damascus, who wrote our earliest surviving account, thought there were more than eighty conspirators, yet the Greek historian Appian could only list fifteen by name. Our sources are unanimous in placing Brutus and Cassius at the centre of the conspiracy, but opinions differ as to who the real leader was. The Greek historian Dio wrote that Brutus initiated the plot, and that it was he who recruited Cassius as his associate. But, more often than not, we see their names listed as 'Cassius and Brutus', suggesting that Cassius was the instigator. For Plutarch, however, this point was not enough to make him the real leader: even if Cassius had instigated the whole affair, he argued, it was the conduct and reputation of Brutus that drew men into the conspiracy.[7]

These differences are not in themselves too problematic; as Greg Woolf has explained, they may even be typical of the kinds of inaccuracies we often encounter in oral reports after a major traumatic experience.[8] And, besides, we can still reconstruct a fairly clear idea of what must have happened both on the Ides of March and in the days, months and even years afterwards. But they do remind us that there are limitations and indeed problems in dealing with the ancient sources of which the reader must remain aware. Two factors that are particularly worth bearing in mind as we read the ancient narratives are: first, that the authors can only be as reliable as their sources permit, and, second, they are people for whom the rule of the emperors was inevitable, the best form of government possible. Plutarch was not alone in concluding that 'the day of the Republic was past', and that 'it was necessary that the rule of a single man should take its place'. For later writers, Caesar was the heroic founder of Rome's monarchy and his murder was hence an atrocity. Writing in the third century AD, Dio begins his account with a strong condemnation of Caesar's assassins who were, by his verdict, jealous and hateful men.[9]

The effect this has on our assessment of and reaction to Brutus cannot be overestimated: much of what we think we know about the assassination and its perpetrators can only ever be tentative. Every piece of information must be read closely, in a manner that appreciates the bias and respects the individuality of its author or creator. But what is significant for our purposes is that the role of Brutus in the assassination – his motives, ethics and the principles for which he fought, right up until his death at the battle of Philippi – had already become the stuff of speculation and even legend by the time most of our sources were writing about him. Indeed, the largely mythologised accounts of Brutus often eclipse Brutus the man, and make it difficult to approach him as an historical figure. It is important to begin, then, by examining the nature of our ancient sources and the portrait of Brutus that emerges from them. By so doing, we witness the beginnings of the Brutus legend as it developed in the centuries immediately following his life.

After the Ides

The impression made by Brutus in his lifetime, and the conflicting way in which it was transmitted and received by later generations, is well illustrated in a passage by the Roman historian Tacitus, writing under the Emperor Trajan, over a century after Brutus' death. In his *Annals*, Tacitus records the details of the prosecution in AD 25 of Cremutius Cordus, who was brought before the Senate on a charge of treason and forced to commit suicide. Among the charges against him, Cremutius' enemies claimed that he 'had praised Brutus and called Gaius Cassius the last of the Romans'. In the defence speech attributed to him by Tacitus, Cremutius claims:

> I am accused of praising Brutus and Cassius, whose achievements have been recorded by many writers, and no-one has recalled them without honour. Livy, outstandingly and pre-eminently famed for his eloquence and reliability . . . nowhere calls Brutus and Cassius bandits and parricides (the descriptions now being used), but often as men of distinction. The works of Asinius Pollio give a glowing account of these same men; Messala Corvinus even boasted that Cassius was 'his general'.[10]

In short: Pollio, Messala, and Livy – all historians of the Augustan age whose verdicts on Brutus we sadly do not possess – had evidently treated the conspirators with respect.[11] But there was another train of thought in antiquity: one which was hostile towards Brutus and Cassius. For the prosecution had apparently called the two men 'parricides' and 'bandits'; they had murdered Julius Caesar, who was 'the father of his country' (*parens patriae*), and they had plundered the Greek east in their preparations for battle against his avengers. Their views, not to mention their motives for prosecuting Cremutius in the first place, suggest an atmosphere of intolerance under the reign of Augustus' successor, Tiberius. From this point of view, admiration of Brutus and Cassius was more sinisterly interpreted as a cry of protest against the imperial system.[12]

Further evidence of this hostile tradition can be found in the pages of Valerius Maximus and Velleius Paterculus – two more historians of the

Tiberian age, both of whom had pro-imperial tendencies. In Valerius' work *Memorable Doings and Sayings*, accusations of parricide are levelled against the assassins in two passages: first against Brutus and then Cassius. What is more, each is embedded within a broader series of narratives on omens and wonders; a hint to the fact that Valerius believed divine justice had overtaken the conspirators in the end. Apollo 'turned his darts against Brutus', he claims, while Caesar's divine spirit plagued Cassius by appearing to him at the battle of Philippi. According to this line of reasoning, their deaths were their just deserts for their 'sin' of killing Caesar.[13] Yet for Velleius, the error of the assassins lay in their ingratitude. Caesar had spared Brutus' life and the lives of many other defeated opponents after the battle of Pharsalus: 'Heavens above, what a reward this merciful man later received for his kindness to Brutus!' Velleius exclaims. In his verdict, Brutus would have been a far better man had the Ides not destroyed all his virtues at a stroke, and Valerius Maximus agrees: 'a single deed hurled his earlier virtues into the abyss and saturated all memory of his name with an unatonable curse'.[14]

By the time Brutus' biographer Plutarch was writing about him in the second century AD, these traditions were deep-rooted: 'the greatest charge brought against Brutus', he writes, 'is that although his life was saved by the kindness of Caesar, together with the lives of all the fellow captives for whom he wished to intercede, and although Caesar called him a friend and honoured him above many, he struck down his saviour with his own hand'.[15] Nor could Plutarch forgive another story he had read regarding his hero: namely, as we shall see, that Brutus promised to let his soldiers plunder the cities of Thessalonica and Sparta if they were successful against the forces of Octavian, Caesar's great nephew and adopted son. In a critical passage towards the end of his biography, it becomes apparent that Plutarch believes Brutus' character had deteriorated under the stress of war.[16] But, otherwise, Plutarch's account is largely eulogistic of Brutus: he decides to focus on his reputation for virtue – a reputation, as we have seen, that even Valerius and Velleius could not completely deny.

One reason for Plutarch's positive stance towards Brutus is that, as a Greek intellectual, he compiled his biographies by reading the literature that was available to him. In researching Brutus, he had thus read a number of earlier works, including those written by Brutus' friends and associates after his defeat at Philippi: memoirs written by Brutus' stepson Bibulus, for example, or biographies composed by his friends Empylus and Volumnius.[17] A second relevant point to mention, however, is that Plutarch's *Life of Brutus* is one of a larger series in which he paired famous Romans with their nearest counterparts in Greek history. It is worth bearing in mind when we read these works that ancient biographers did not necessarily approach their subjects in the same way as modern writers. While it would be unfair to claim that Plutarch did not pay attention to the historical context of the periods he studied, his approach was more often moralistic: he observed the lessons that could be learned from the past to draw up universal rules about virtue and vice.[18]

In this context it is significant that Brutus was paired with Dion, who lived in the fourth century BC, and was the brother-in-law of Dionysius II of Syracuse, whose tyranny Dion opposed and overthrew. In comparing the two men's respective struggles against tyranny, Plutarch focuses in particular on their adherence to Plato's philosophical teachings: Dion knew him in real life, whereas Brutus knew him through his works and by his attachment to the Old Academy. 'Both men were spurred on by one and the same training ground', adds Plutarch.[19] What is most commendable in Plutarch's eyes, then, is the fact both Brutus and Dion had put their philosophical ideals into practice. The result is that Plutarch's account is very selective and nearly always glorifies Brutus' actions. He comes across as the paragon of virtue, a philosopher in action, the noblest Roman of them all – themes that are echoed in the later traditions about Brutus, and especially in Shakespeare, who used a translation of Plutarch as his source.

For all these reasons, then, we have to treat this particular source with caution. But that does not mean that Plutarch's evidence is without value; on the contrary, its value is immense. To begin with, Plutarch's biography provides clues that will help us achieve a fuller picture of how Brutus was received by his contemporaries and later writers. At the same time, where comparative material exists, we can sometimes check Plutarch's work against it in order to assess his reliability. Glimpses of Brutus can be found, for example, in some of Plutarch's other biographies. For, in addition to Brutus, he wrote *Lives* of Cicero, Caesar and Mark Antony – all of whom knew Brutus well. Roughly contemporary with Plutarch was the Roman biographer Suetonius, who wrote the *Lives of the Twelve Caesars*, starting with an account of Caesar, *Divine Julius*, which included a long explanation of the conspiracy and Caesar's assassins. As secretary to the Emperor Hadrian, Suetonius had unrivalled access to the official records and he often includes information that corroborates or supplements the accounts of Plutarch.

The works of the imperial Greek historians provide another valuable perspective on Brutus' actions. Writing in the second century AD, Appian of Alexandria composed his *Civil Wars*, which provides the only full narrative account covering the period of Brutus' life. By zooming in on the period from 44 to 42 BC in particular, Appian's text is extremely important to anyone working on the events and personalities involved in the aftermath of Caesar's assassination. What is more, because his interest lies in the causes and casualties of civil wars, he tries to explain these events from a variety of perspectives. To this end, Appian draws on a range of earlier, often conflicting, sources. The result may not be the most historically consistent work we possess. But in transmitting the ideas and information he found in his own sources, Appian helps bring us into closer contact with the content of these lost works. It has often been noted, for example, that Appian pays more attention than other authors to the role and achievements of Cassius. His account thus balances out the picture presented by Plutarch, who draws a sharp contrast between Brutus and Cassius – always to the benefit of the former and the disadvantage of the latter.[20]

Larger in scope and later than Appian's work is Dio's *Roman Histories*, which covers the history of Rome from the legendary landing of Aeneas in Italy to the date of Dio's own consulship in AD 229. Despite its largely fragmentary state, the books which do survive (36–47) almost entirely cover the period of Brutus' adult life, starting from 68 BC. Using a more traditional annalistic framework than Appian, Dio too preserves detailed information on the events he describes, as he progresses through the evidence he found year by year. For the period from 44 to 42 BC, however, he breaks free from this pattern to concentrate in turn on the geographical zones in which the civil war was conducted. The overall picture is hence sometimes lost or distorted; the personalities of the people involved and their relationships with one another also fade into the background. But what is particularly interesting about Dio is that, despite some similarities, his work often differs from the account of Plutarch; a point which suggests he found some of his material in a different source tradition.[21]

From all of these accounts it is obvious how many more works of literature were available to the ancient authors than we possess today, in terms of both genre and number. Which returns us to one of the problems identified earlier: our primary sources are the secondary historians of their own day. They are not authorities on the topics they write about, but clever men with agendas of their own to pursue. Far more important for our purposes, and therefore placed at the heart of this study, is the contemporary evidence that survives. Coins, for instance, give us details of dates, careers and historical identities. However, by studying them closely, we can also see how Brutus and his supporters wanted to present and advertise their image and ancestry; they hence provide great insights into the slogans of self-fashioning and propaganda used by Brutus – as well as those employed by his political rivals.

By far the most influential informant for this period is Marcus Tullius Cicero. Today he is best known as Rome's greatest orator, but in addition to the speeches he published, Cicero composed numerous scholarly works on rhetoric, politics and philosophy, most of which still survive. A close reading of all these works can take us into the intellectual world of republican Rome and help us to understand better the values which men like Cicero and Brutus held dear.[22] Yet they also take us much closer to the historical Brutus than any other source permits us to get, allowing us to see him from different perspectives at various stages in his career.

For example, in 46 BC Cicero published a history of Roman oratory under the title *Brutus*, in which he gave Brutus a primary speaking part. While, naturally, we must take care not to read too much into the character of Brutus or be tempted to see in him a reflection of the historical man, still Cicero's *Brutus* provides some of our best evidence for Brutus' career and aspirations in the years prior to the Ides.[23] Yet Cicero was also a copious letter writer: more than 800 of the letters he wrote, plus about 90 that were sent to him, have survived. Among these we can read twenty-eight letters exchanged between Cicero and Brutus, from which something of the latter's living presence can be discerned.[24] Of immense importance here are the seven letters in the collection of Cicero's *Letters to Brutus* which were written to Cicero in Brutus' own hand, at a further stage of his life, in the period extending from late March to the end of July 43 BC, when Brutus prepared for war against Caesar's heirs. Not only was Brutus' life in terrible danger, but so was everything he had worked towards. We hear, from his own mouth, his worries, frustrations and plans at this critical point in history.

Further evidence for Brutus is contained within the letters written by Cicero to his closest friend and confidant, Titus Pomponius Atticus, which are often regarded as the most honest and frank of all Cicero's writings. For, although it is clear that towards the end of his life Cicero had envisaged that some of his letters should be made public, the *Letters to Atticus* is essentially a collection of private letters published only after Cicero's death by his freedman and secretary Tiro. These letters are hence particularly valuable because they contain Cicero's comments and reports about the people and events in his daily life. What is more, since they start in 68 BC and continue right up until November 44 BC, they cover the period from Brutus' entry into public life to well beyond the assassination of Caesar. From these we get a far more down-to-earth portrait of Brutus than anything given in the later, idealised accounts; we can also understand something of his lived experience in the brutal and bloody world of late republican Rome.

Yet Cicero's letters do come with an important caveat of their own with regard to using them as historical evidence; many scholars of the period still take the view that Cicero's statements to Atticus contain the unadorned truth, forgetting that the two men had their own ideas on how to deal with the disruptions of their day. In addition, the triangular relationship between Cicero, Brutus and Atticus – with Atticus in the centre – was almost certainly fraught with jealousies and disagreements. It is all too easy, then, to judge Brutus through Cicero's eyes and according to Cicero's own personal likes and dislikes about his younger contemporary. And from there it becomes difficult to remain objective when faced with the task of reading Brutus' own criticisms of Cicero in turn.

Writing in the early eighteenth century, for example, Conyers Middleton formed a highly unfavourable picture of Brutus for precisely this reason. The letters exchanged between Cicero and Brutus 'enable us to form the surest judgment of the different spirit and the conduct of the two men', he remarks in his *Life of Cicero*. To Middleton, Brutus seemed inconsistent: 'this inconsistency in his character would tempt us to believe that he was governed in many cases by the pride and haughtiness of his temper, rather than by any constant and settled principles of philosophy, of which he is commonly thought so strict an observer'.[25] These are harsh words indeed! But among those who were influenced by them was Edward Gibbon, who composed a short work entitled 'A Digression on the Character of Brutus', which was published posthumously in 1814. He agreed with Middleton: 'Neither as a statesman nor as a general did Brutus ever approve himself equal to the arduous task he had so rashly undertaken, of restoring the commonwealth; instead of restoring it, the death of a mild and generous usurper produced only a series of civil wars, and the reign of three tyrants whose union and whose discord were alike fatal to the Roman people.'[26]

From the moment he killed Caesar to the present day, then, Brutus' motives, dilemmas and his political policy after the Ides of March have sparked, and continue to stimulate, the imaginations of the historians, poets, playwrights and artists who have depicted this tumultuous event. Since the reception of Brutus in the western tradition – that is, his portrayal in art, literature, historiography and scholarship – is as much a part of his story as the man himself, it will necessarily form a part of this investigation. But already, from this initial survey of the ancient evidence, we can see that a number of key themes and questions have emerged from the works of those who have studied Brutus in any depth: was Brutus wrong to kill his benefactor – a friend and perhaps even (according to some) his father? Or was he right to place his duty to his country ahead of his own personal obligations?

Was Brutus a political failure, an idealist, or a fanatic to the cause of philosophy? Or, to put it another way, did the standards he had imposed upon himself in life drive him tragically towards a premature death? How we judge the question of the viability of the Republic, too, massively affects our political assessment of Brutus. If it was still possible to save the Republic, then his failure to restore it after the Ides may be blamed for its demise; but if it was already doomed, then his act was both politically out of touch and futile.

These are all big questions about Brutus' place in history which this book can pose, but it cannot conclusively answer. Still less can it pass moral judgment on Brutus or his deeds. Its aim in this respect is more limited: to expose readers to a range of points of view, to encourage them to enter into the debate themselves, and to review the historical evidence afresh for this complicated and complex character. In so doing, it also aims to make a significant contribution to the way we think about Brutus' life and political career, as well as to drive forward new ideas for how we interpret the evidence for studying it. As we go in search of Brutus, this book will take an approach that combines biography with historiography, in order to examine what we can learn not just about his life, but about how that life has been recorded and transmitted from antiquity to the present day.

In Search of Brutus

From the initial survey of the evidence presented above, it should be clear that a number of fundamental challenges face the biographer of Brutus. Precious little is known about his early life, for example; even his date of birth poses problems when we try to pin it down with any certainty. As Christopher Pelling has commented in one of his seminal studies on Plutarch, 'everybody notices when a great man dies; it is more difficult to notice when one is born, or when one is growing up'.[27] Thus, although this book follows the traditional birthdate of 85 BC, there are good reasons to think that Brutus may have been born several years after this date, perhaps in 79 or 78 BC.[28] Making precise claims about his age in relation to events and achievements is therefore impossible, and our reconstructions can only ever be hypothetical.

For the same reason, an obscure childhood is common among individuals whose exploits later became legendary; it will consequently come as no surprise that we do not know much about Brutus' youth, either. Yet there is another reason of which we should be aware: ancient political biography was not particularly concerned with the formation of character or childhood experiences. Authors like Plutarch were more interested in how a man lived his life, what traits he possessed, and what ethical considerations could be drawn from a careful examination of his conduct.[29] When we first meet Brutus in Plutarch's narrative, then, he is already well on his way towards a political career. We get a glimpse of his studies in philosophy and rhetoric, mainly because they serve to introduce the portrait of Brutus as a man whose actions were guided by studied principles. However, already by the third paragraph of Plutarch's *Life of Brutus* we find ourselves in the years of Brutus' adolescence, in 58 BC. By then, his life was more than half over.

Other sources provide us with a couple of further chance glimpses of Brutus prior to this date, which allow us to project back into the past and analyse his early years, as we shall see in Chapter 1, when we come to look at the world into which Brutus was born, as well as the expectations pinned upon a young boy of noble birth. However, even after Plutarch's narrative does pick up the thread of Brutus' entry into political life, the picture is never entirely complete, and this leaves large gaps in our knowledge. From 58 to 56 BC Brutus was away from Rome; when he does return to view, he shifts in and out of focus for the years 55–52 BC. Ever a shadow in his own biography, we lose sight of Brutus almost entirely in the main events leading up to Rome's civil war (51–50 BC). In Chapter 2, which covers these years, we thus have to fill out the outlines of Plutarch with some colourings from Cicero and other sources. In so doing, we can go some way towards completing the portrait of a man embarking on his political career in a society caught in the throes of revolutionary change.

The same is true, though to a greater degree, in Chapter 3. From Plutarch's narrative we can, at least, follow Brutus' decision-making processes at the beginnings of civil war in 49 BC, when he needed to decide whether to fight on the side of Pompey or Caesar. And there are some snippets of information regarding his actions in the civil war. But we lose any trace of Brutus in the year following his escape from the battle of Pharsalus in August 48 BC. Thereafter we can tentatively follow him as he spends the next two years working in Caesar's service (47–45 BC). We briefly see him operating in Asia in the summer of 47 BC and then serving as proconsul in Cisalpine Gaul (46 BC); he only returned to Rome in the spring of 45 BC whereupon he was appointed praetor for 44 BC. And then Brutus fell in with the conspiracy that defined the rest of his life: in killing Caesar, Brutus as a subject worthy of study was finally born.

It cannot be emphasised enough that up until the assassination of Caesar there is hardly anything that gives us any definite insight into Brutus' feelings or beliefs as a private person. The works of literature Brutus composed in the period after Pharsalus – *On Duties*, *On Virtue* and *On Endurance* – have all been lost, with the exception of a couple of tiny fragments. We can only rely on what we think we know about contemporary debates about tyrannicide and Brutus' own philosophical leanings to understand more about his ethics and motives leading up to the assassination (the subject of Chapter 4). Plutarch, Appian and Dio all help us fill some of the gaps here, but from this point in time onwards there is another fundamental challenge facing the historian: namely, the highly subjective nature of the ancient evidence. Because the story of Brutus' life was only compiled after his famous deed, he has been judged *ex post facto* either as a murderous traitor or as an honourable tyrannicide. As more than one scholar has reminded us, his biography has been aligned accordingly, almost as if his whole life was bound to culminate in the murder of Caesar.[30]

As a result of this sudden interest in Brutus, a huge amount of material survives from the period after the Ides of March up until his own death on the plains of Philippi in 42 BC. The precise details – dates, times and movements – continue to be muddled in our sources. But a broad understanding of the historical situation can largely be reconstructed from the histories of Appian and Dio, the relevant chapters of Plutarch, Suetonius and Nicolaus of Damascus, as well as from the fragments of other, less well-known, writers from antiquity. Closer in time, and critical for understanding the climate of fear in which Brutus was operating after Caesar's death, are the letters in which Cicero discussed the daily political changes of 44 BC (Chapter 5). In addition, we also have the letters Brutus exchanged with Cicero personally. Although the two men were not in contact during the critical months following Brutus' departure from Italy and his reappearance at the head of an army – that is, between August 44 BC and March 43 BC – the letters provide a useful, retrospective glimpse into Brutus' political policy for the period after Caesar's death, as well as his activities in the east as events spiralled towards civil war (Chapter 6).

In all then, for the forty years or so that Brutus was alive, we only really have hard historical evidence covering the last two of them in any depth; scarcely enough to be able to reconstruct a plausible biography in modern terms. But what might seem like a dearth, perhaps because of his great name and famous legend, is in fact more than we have for most figures from the period. And to complain about what we do not have is to miss a far more important point: a staggering amount of material survives from the Roman world from which we can reconstruct a fairly comprehensive image of the culture and society in which Brutus lived, as well as how he operated within the changed political climate that engulfed Rome during his lifetime. Provided the limitations of the evidence are kept in mind, it is also possible to discern something of the characteristics of Brutus as a man and as a political personality.

Consequently, although this book covers what we know about Brutus' ancestry and childhood, and concludes with his death, it does not aim to be a straightforward biography; nor does it provide a linear historical narrative of his every alleged move. Instead, in each chapter there is an attempt to understand central aspects of Brutus' lived experience from a selection of different perspectives, such as his political profiling, professional rise, his friendships and relationships, as well as his elevation to power under Caesar and beyond that to the assassination and Brutus' command of an army against Antony and Octavian. My own account of Brutus' life and career will also build on several themes that have dominated recent scholarly approaches to the literary tradition and political culture of Rome: self-fashioning and the genre of life-writing, as well as emotions and the shaping and creation of memory.

How far all of this can help us discover the 'real' Brutus is debatable. As we shall see in Chapter 7 when we deal with the accounts of Philippi, the nature of our source material has been largely responsible for a kaleidoscopic range of views as to Brutus' personality and career. Certainly, we can get very close to the way Brutus wished to be perceived by his contemporaries and remembered by future generations; we can also sketch a clear picture of his strengths and weaknesses in the eyes of others. To be faithful to Brutus, however – the historical person we can never truly know – the real task is to engage with the evidence for his life, to tease out the themes and biases of our source material and to make sense of the results. To anticipate my conclusions towards the end of this study (Chapter 8), it would be dangerous to claim we can see Brutus for the man he actually was; even to his contemporaries he was an unfathomable character. But a far more interesting tale is waiting to be told about how the story of Brutus' life has been interpreted and transmitted from antiquity to the twenty-first century.

CHAPTER 1

BECOMING BRUTUS

Image and Identity

In the centre of Mediolanum in Cisalpine Gaul (ancient Milan) there once stood a bronze statue of Brutus, probably erected in his own lifetime. The Emperor Augustus, upon seeing it, was said to have frowned at the effigy of his former enemy; after all, Augustus was Caesar's great-nephew and adopted son, and Brutus had killed Caesar. Yet for others, the statue was laden with symbolism. Brutus was 'the founder and defender of our laws and liberties', cried one impassioned advocate towards the end of the first century BC, as he pointed to the statue and lamented the state of Italy, where he thought freedom of expression was being curtailed. From this point of view, the assassination had been a glorious deed: philosophy and principles had joined forces with military strength to remove a dictator. This had been Brutus' particular achievement: to be remembered not just as a man of action, but as a man of virtue. Of all the men who colluded to kill Caesar, it was said that Brutus was the only noble conspirator.[1]

Throughout his life, Brutus' reputation was important to him.[2] Thus, although the bronze statue from Mediolanum has not survived, we have other images which help us construct a clear idea of how Brutus broadcast his identity as a defender of liberty.[3] Of these representations, the most fascinating has to be that struck onto the obverse of a coin which was issued in late 43 or early 42 BC to celebrate the Ides of March (Plate 1). It shows a man approaching maturity but still relatively youthful, with a full head of thick, slightly curly hair, and a short beard on his chin. Beneath a straight forehead are his deep-set eyes, prominent nose, well-defined cheeks and full, pursed lips. Steely faced and resolute, this Brutus stares coldly into the future as he begins a new chapter in the history of Rome's civil wars and bloodshed; his military status and intentions are highlighted by the title of *imperator* ('commander'), abbreviated to 'IMP' on the surrounding legend. Described by Barry Strauss as having 'leading-man looks', 'intelligence' and a 'forceful personality', to some historians Brutus' low forehead and heavy bones are features which betray his narrow mind and obstinacy. He is simultaneously 'young and old'. 'It is not easy to think of him as the bold and inspiring leader in the fight for freedom', concluded the art historian Jocelyn Toynbee.[4]

Yet, if such efforts to tease out Brutus' leadership skills and personality from a portrait seem to us a pointless exercise in physiognomy, we should begin by remembering that image was, as it remains today, a forceful mode of visual communication. Roman portraits – whether in the form of sculpted busts, statues, or minted on coins – did not just depict a man's physical appearance; they could advertise his ancestry, political agenda, offices and achievements to a far wider audience than the written or spoken word. Far from the idealised statues of Classical Greece, Roman republican portraits aimed at verism: images were made to appear true to life and were intended to reflect the real character of the man represented. Writing at the turn of the first and second centuries AD, Pliny the Younger – a Roman orator, author and magistrate – suggested that such portraits aimed to encapsulate their subject's moral and ethical qualities too, and that it was not unusual for a man's features to be highlighted or even improved upon to this end.[5] It is hence no simple matter of enquiry to start by focusing on how Brutus is represented in his portraiture. In fact, it takes us into the heart of his political and social milieu: a man's image reflected the way he perceived, fashioned and advertised his self-identity.

To discern the full extent of the message the coin was intended to convey, however, we need to look at both sides. For on the reverse is a menacing depiction of two daggers on either side of a *pileus*: the cap of liberty customarily awarded to slaves when they had earned their freedom. Underneath it, the legend 'EID[ES] MAR[TIAE]' – an archaic spelling of the Ides of March – made the jubilant reference to Caesar's assassination all too clear. Already in antiquity, the coin and its symbolism were famous. As the historian Dio comments: 'Brutus stamped upon the coins which were being minted in his own likeness a cap and two daggers, indicating by this and by the inscription that he and Cassius had liberated the fatherland.'[6] The imagery on this coin consequently points to the powerful rhetoric surrounding the death of the dictator. For the victory cry of his assassins was *libertas* ('freedom'); Brutus and Cassius claimed to have liberated Rome from the tyranny of Caesar.

One thing we should note immediately, however, is that there is an unnerving contradiction between the message and the mode of Brutus' coin portrait. Until Julius Caesar's image had appeared on denarii in the year 44 BC, no Roman coin had ever featured the image of a living man before. The introduction of portrait coinage reflected the unique position of power Caesar had achieved in his lifetime: the very same position of power for which he had been murdered. If Dio saw the irony of Caesar's murderer minting coins in his own likeness, while supposedly championing the liberation from tyranny, he did not say it explicitly. Then again, it was not the first time Brutus had engaged in such an act of propagandistic self-fashioning: *libertas* and the freedom from tyranny were at the core of Brutus' public profile, the roots of which stretched much further back in time than the death of Caesar. We might ask: who were his models? Which historic and current events made strong impressions on Brutus? What were his ultimate goals? Why such deep animosity towards tyranny? We shall consider these questions throughout the course of this chapter. But what is important to highlight right at the beginning of any study of Brutus is that he was always the architect of, and not simply the slave to, his reputation.

Brutus' Claim to Fame

What inspired Brutus in the creation of his public image was that his family could boast a connection with *libertas* that went right back to the legendary tales of Lucius Junius Brutus and the expulsion of the kings, said to have ruled Rome from its foundation under Romulus in 753 until 510 BC. For tradition had it that Lucius Brutus had deposed Rome's seventh and final king, Tarquinius Superbus, and driven him and his clan, including his sons, out of Rome. Our fullest treatment of this story comes from Livy (*c.* 59 BC–AD 17), who adds that Rome now took her first step towards political liberty.[7] Power over Rome's affairs was thereafter concentrated in the hands of the aristocratic families, while two annually appointed magistrates, later referred to as 'consuls', shared the responsibility for directing the Senate on a monthly basis.[8] Lucius Brutus was the first man to hold this office in 509 BC – or so the story went. And while 'the people were still greedy for the new taste of liberty', Livy tells us he took an important step: 'he made them swear an oath that they would suffer no man to be king at Rome'.

It was this moment in the historical tradition that was used to explain Rome's long-standing hatred of the title *rex*, the Latin word for king, as well as the political monopoly such a man could establish: a *regnum*.[9] Lacking a precise political vocabulary, later Romans described this development by the term *res publica* (meaning something like 'the public business'), from which we get 'republic' – a word used today to refer both to the constitutional arrangement Rome set in place and to the long period of history it spanned (roughly 509–31 BC). It was an imprecise label and ideas over how the *res publica* should be managed were hotly contested in the period of the late Republic.[10] What is more, the Romans never wrote down their constitution, so it was a flexible and dynamic system whose institutions evolved over time. Broadly speaking, however, the main pillars of the *res publica* were the Senate, the executive magistracies, and the popular assemblies. It was a partnership in power between the government and those they governed, best encapsulated in the motto *SPQR – senatus populusque romanus*, or 'the Senate and the people of Rome' (see Plate 2).[11] The association between a more open political system and the expulsion of the kings by Lucius Brutus hence did much to link ideas of *libertas* with *res publica,* and these stories were used to significant effect by our Brutus, especially in the years after Caesar's assassination.[12]

To be sure, Livy's accounts of the early history of Rome need to be treated with a healthy degree of caution. Not only was he writing over five centuries after the events he describes, the historical material with which Livy was working was itself inherently problematic.[13] Yet the veracity of the tales need not concern us too much here; the fact is that exemplary anecdotes formed the stuff of Roman literature and history, both in the oral and written traditions. Heroes and villains, virtues and vices, patriots and traitors were all showcased as a means of presenting lessons on how (or how not) to behave: they were called *exempla* and Roman citizens of all classes would have had these stories at their fingertips.

Even before our Brutus made a feature of his ancestry, the story of Lucius Brutus and the expulsion of the kings had been staged in dramatic productions which did much to reinforce its currency in the popular imagination.[14] A bronze statue of the original Brutus was placed among the images of the seven kings of Rome on the Capitoline Hill (Plate 3), his drawn sword 'indicating how steadfast he was in deposing the Tarquins', according to Plutarch.[15] Funeral processions, too, included spectacular displays of famous families, with actors representing the deceased man's ancestors, adorned in their historical insignia of office.[16] The story goes that, probably in 91 BC, an otherwise unknown Marcus Brutus was shamed in court when the funeral entourage of another member of the clan happened to pass by in close proximity. For his opponent, the famous orator

Lucius Licinius Crassus, seized the moment and lambasted this Brutus, precisely because he was unworthy of his family name.[17]

A Roman noble, in other words, was expected to live up to and even emulate the deeds of his forebears; at the same time, the legends of great families gave significant authority to the individual households who inherited them. Admittedly, not all members of the Junii Bruti after Lucius chose to follow in his footsteps or to flag allegiance to their exemplary ancestor. Yet our Brutus was particularly proud of his claim to fame and the unique reputation it conferred upon him as a defender of the Roman Republic. As a result, he actively sought to nurture a very specific public profile.[18]

To begin with, Brutus had a family tree composed for the central hall, or *atrium*, of his house by the great antiquarian Titus Pomponius Atticus, the friend he shared with Cicero. On his father's side (the Junii Bruti), it traced his family right back to its alleged origins under Lucius Brutus. But on his mother's side of the family, too (the Servilii), Brutus had an ancestor of whom he could boast: the republican hero Servilius Ahala, who was famous for killing Spurius Maelius in 439 BC on the grounds that he was aspiring towards tyranny.[19] It must have been a great work of art to judge from Cicero, who had seen the family tree in one of Brutus' villas. But the grandeur of the *atrium* was further enhanced by wax masks of Brutus' ancestors – the *imagines* traditionally on show in the halls of aristocratic families. Cicero had seen these too, he claims, and they included representations of both Lucius Brutus and Servilius Ahala.[20] As the first room a visitor would have entered, the *atrium* must have made an overwhelming impression. As much as any of the other steps Brutus took to promote his famous reputation, his house was a projection of his political identity.[21]

It was probably for this reason, and especially in the wake of Caesar's murder, that some of Brutus' enemies denied his claim to descend from the Lucius Brutus who had liberated Rome in 509 BC. The original Brutus was a patrician, they pointed out: a member of one of the few privileged families who could trace their lineage back to the original senators (*patres*) who had advised Romulus. On the other hand, our Brutus and his paternal ancestors were from plebeian stock, just like most people. More problematic still, however, was the legend that Lucius Brutus had killed his sons and, with them, his whole family line; so there was no way Brutus could be linked to him unless one got creative with the past.[22] Yet before we get too distracted by the question of whether Brutus *was* related to the legendary hero, we should note that it seems to have been an accepted fact in the intellectual circles of Brutus' day that family histories were often distorted, embellished or even completely fabricated.[23] Nor did it really matter for Brutus that the Junii Bruti were of plebeian status and not patrician. What is more important for our purposes is the fact that he embraced this aspect of his heritage above any other consideration. For the name came with serious political cachet, and it gave Brutus an enviable advantage which he used to pronounced effect throughout his career.

In short, the family *exempla* Brutus chose to advertise acted almost like a political pledge: candidates in electoral campaigns were more often judged on the virtues and achievements of their ancestors than on any political programme.[24] But to understand precisely what it was about Lucius Brutus that made him such an appropriate role model let us return to Livy. For, as hinted at above, the story does not end with the expulsion of the kings and the institution of a new form of government. Rather, in Lucius Brutus' year of office, Livy tells us that Brutus' two sons were implicated in a plot to restore the ejected Tarquinii to Rome, and that they were consequently stripped, flogged and beheaded at their father's command: 'All the while it was the father, his face, and expression that everyone watched, it was a father's heart that was swelling as he administered the public penalty.'[25] Macabre as it sounds, the execution of his sons contributed to the legendary status of Lucius Brutus who consequently embodied and projected the ideals of the Roman republican aristocracy: the victorious triumph over monarchical despotism, the upholding of constitutional government and individual self-sacrifice for the good of one's country. These were the very ideals that were championed after the Ides of March too: by promoting his claim to fame both before and after the assassination, Marcus Brutus gave an intensely clear statement of what he stood for.

The World of Brutus' Childhood

It would be a mistake to think, however, that the governance of Brutus' day bore much resemblance to the institutions established in that earlier period of history.[26] Instead, there were many twists and turns in Rome's constitutional journey and it was already heading into another new era when Brutus was born. Although, as we have seen, the exact date of Brutus' birth has been disputed, the fact remains that it coincided with one of the most turbulent periods of Rome's history. In the years 91 to 82 BC alone, somewhere in the region of 200,000 men were killed, as two of Rome's most powerful men – Gaius Marius and Lucius Cornelius Sulla – fought for military and political supremacy.[27] It was Rome's first civil war but the emergence of Sulla as a victor had a tremendous and devastating impact on the world into which Brutus was born.

'The *res publica* was on the point of utter destruction', wrote Sulla, in one of the only fragments to remain from his memoirs.[28] But the truth was that neither Marius nor Sulla had ever played by the existing rules of the political game, which soon received detailed revision in Sulla's hands. For as soon as the Marian faction had been defeated, Sulla established himself as the dictator of Rome – an archaic post he revived and went on to hold for an unprecedented period of eighteen months. During this time, the republican system of government received one of its most dramatic transformations in its over 400 years of history.

Without a doubt, the figure of Sulla cast a long shadow over Roman history for reasons other than his constitutional reforms. For one thing, Sulla had demonstrated the immense potential of the army to influence political action, when he became the first man to march his soldiers on Rome and forced the Senate to give him command in a war in the east. And for another, he instituted the horrific practice of proscriptions: a series of rewards and incentives offered to any man who would kill his foes and bring him their heads. Sulla's was a reign of terror, and so it was remembered. Yet the measure that had the most direct effect on Brutus' generation was the reforms Sulla made to the constitution of Rome, as he sought to draw up new rules for the *res publica*. For the changes Sulla made to the staffing and management of the law courts, the size and function of the Senate, the roles of the magistrates and other officials, as well as the level of popular participation in political affairs, all drastically altered the way public life operated in Rome. It is not the place here to chart the many, detailed reforms that Sulla passed, or to speculate on his motives for doing so; others have written on those topics elsewhere.[29] But what is important is to assess the impact these reforms had on the political culture which Brutus and his peers later entered, and to question how they might have affected Brutus' own tendencies and strategies in the years to come.

It will be enough, for now, to focus on the reforms Sulla made to the Senate, the elite body which stood at the heart of Roman political life. Although the Senate's role was, in theory, to act as an advisory board, in practice its authority was vast: decisions in the Senate, reached by a majority verdict, could have the force of law provided they were not vetoed by one of the ten tribunes appointed annually to act in the interests of the people. In the years before Sulla the Senate had comprised 300 members. However, many had since died in the calamity of the civil wars and its ranks were greatly reduced. In 81 BC Sulla therefore doubled the number of senators, to perhaps as many as five or six hundred, taking his new recruits either from the rank of the equestrians – the wealthy middle class of Romans – or from the distinguished families of Italian towns.[30] *Prima facie* it looked as though Sulla was aiming to strengthen the Senate and to restore its traditional authority. But, as one scholar has succinctly reminded us, 'there is almost nothing you can do to an exclusive and aristocratic body which is worse than flooding it with new members'.[31] Indeed, as closer inspection reveals, the reforms Sulla made to the Senate led to dire longer-term consequences, and especially to increased competition at the top.

Admittedly, aristocratic competition had always formed a central element of republican political culture.[32] The way it worked was that honour was bestowed upon politicians by the electorate who voted for them; it is no accident that the so-called 'ladder of offices' which formed the career path for aspiring politicians is rendered in the Latin as the *cursus honorum*. Thus, senators vied to surpass their peers in the accumulation of respect, influence and authority: a goal best summed up by the term *dignitas*, which translates as something like 'worth' or 'esteemed standing'. To this end, a man started his senatorial career as a quaestor (a largely administrative office) and passed through various other magistracies in turn: from the optional post of aedile, responsible for putting on the games and overseeing the city's food supply, to the two prize goals of the praetorship and consulship which bestowed the office-holder with *imperium* – the right to command an army – and an enormous amount of executive power. At each stage a senator was striving and competing against his peers: 'to reach the summit of riches and power of things', as Brutus' contemporary, the Roman poet Lucretius, later expressed it.[33]

None of this changed under Sulla's reforms; yet several important modifications he made to the rules did increase the level of competition to an unhealthy degree. First, in the years before Sulla, censors had performed the task of regulating the number of senators, both by appointing new members and by expelling those whom they deemed to have fallen below the expected standards. But from now on, anyone who held the junior office of quaestor automatically became a senator for life. Furthermore – and this is the second important reform – Sulla increased the number of quaestors from around eight to twenty.[34] By making the quaestorship an automatic gateway to the Senate and by setting the number of annually appointed quaestors higher, Sulla saw a way to maintain a healthy quorum in the Senate. However, what frustrated some senators' ambitions further was that Sulla imposed or reinstated minimum age limits on office-holding, and he revived previous laws enforcing a period as a private citizen between posts. The result was a much more definitive and hierarchical pyramid of offices, which decreased in opportunities the higher a man climbed.

One positive effect of this reform was that the bar on repeat office-holding arguably reduced competition by preventing the kind of personal power that his enemy Marius, seven times consul, had managed to accrue. But the problem was that there was little flexibility in the system: a quaestor had to be at least thirty years of age to embark upon his career; if he wanted to be aedile, a man had to wait until he was thirty-two. And finally, there were the praetorships and the consulships, which a man could hold aged thirty-nine and forty-two, respectively. Presumably, of course, not all senators would have wanted to progress all the way up the *cursus honorum*. But for those who did make it to the higher offices of the praetorship and consulship, the rewards were vast: 'rank, prestige, splendour at home, a reputation and esteem abroad, a purple-bordered toga, an ivory curule seat, marks of distinction, the rods of office, an army, commands and provinces', as Cicero famously enumerated them in 66 BC.[35] In addition to this more respectable list of gains, for the men who made it to these positions, great wealth could also be accrued from the booty of war or the exploitation of provincials in Rome's expanding empire.[36]

Yet, following the reforms of Sulla, such prizes and opportunities became even more elusive: for out of the twenty quaestors appointed in any given year, only eight could go on to become praetors. Furthermore, although Sulla had actually raised the number of praetorships available from six to eight, there were still only two consulships available. There was always the chance that death or disgrace might remove some of the competition and hence ease the bottleneck. But, otherwise, it was at the top of the ladder that the competition was particularly fierce: whereas in previous years one in three praetors would have gone on to become consul, from the 80s BC onwards the chances were one in four. For the senators who had made it this far, it mattered that they should try to achieve their consulship in the earliest year allowed to them by law. To fail in this goal once was humiliating; to fail at the polls twice would be deemed a signal disgrace for a man like Brutus.[37]

On the one hand, of course, Brutus was extremely fortunate in that he had the more conventional and privileged start to life when it came to his own career: wealth and a distinguished family name. He was one of the nobility – the *nobiles*, from the Latin word for 'well-known', who could point to at least one ancestor who had held the consulship in the past.[38] Yet, on the other, the pressure for young *nobiles* to continue the successes of their families was intense. Even though his family could hope to provide him with the aristocratic connections on which the power of an individual *nobilis* was habitually founded, a political career could be shaped by any number of additional factors: from military service to skill in speech, as well as an ability to use charm, largesse and bribes.[39] What became important over time was that a man knew how to use his assets to best effect, but first he had to acquire the right skills to succeed. Before we can go on to examine his entry into public life, then, we first need to set the scene in Rome and later Athens, where the young Brutus spent his early years and received his education; in so doing, we can also begin to trace some of the likely influences that shaped Brutus during his formative years.

Early Years and Education

If the reforms of Sulla were to have an overbearing impact on Brutus' later career, a more immediate consequence of the dictator's reforms hit a lot closer to home. For, although Brutus' father (henceforth the elder Brutus) had somehow survived the years of civil conflict, it was not long before factional fighting claimed his life, too. Marius had died early in 86 BC, and Sulla – having resigned the dictatorship in 79 BC – died in early 78 BC. However, within a year of the former dictator's death, one of the consuls, Marcus Aemilius Lepidus, sought to take up the cause of those who had lost their civil or political rights under Sulla's reforms. His aims hinted at populism, enough for his opponents in the Senate to argue that Lepidus was planning to overthrow the Sullan *res publica*.[40] And soon enough he was proclaimed a national enemy, as were his main allies, including the elder Brutus, who was stationed as a commander of the power base Lepidus had created in Cisalpine Gaul.[41]

We probably only know the details of the elder Brutus' death because the responsibility for it rested with one of Rome's most famous characters: Gnaeus Pompeius Magnus (Pompey the Great, as he is better known), whose fame was on the rise at the time of the revolt.[42] Five years earlier, at the age of just twenty-three, Pompey had raised three private legions which he used to support Sulla in the civil war; now, in 78–77 BC, Pompey ostensibly continued to fight in defence of the Sullan *res publica*. Yet it was under this banner that he first forced the elder Brutus to surrender and then had him treacherously murdered. It was a monstrous act, and one which caused the young Brutus to harbour a deep and profound hatred towards Pompey which lasted well into his adulthood; as we shall see in Chapter 3, at the outbreak of the next civil war, the death of the elder Brutus was bandied about by the opposing side as just one of several reminders of Pompey's reputation as a 'teenage butcher'.[43] In the meantime, without a father to call his own, Brutus was drawn into the family of his mother, Servilia, who belonged to the patrician family of the Servilii.

As a skilful political player in her own right, Servilia was possibly the largest single influence on Brutus for most of his life; however, as a widow from a good family, she did not remain unmarried for long.[44] Her next husband, and hence Brutus' stepfather, was Decimus Junius Silanus, who in 62 BC rose to the consulship, and by whom she had three daughters – Brutus' half-sisters. In time, their marriages were to have the effect of increasing Brutus' own political circle: one married Publius Servilius Isauricus, consul in 48 BC; another was the wife of Marcus Aemilius Lepidus, consul in 46 BC and later one of the triumvirs; while the third married Gaius Cassius Longinus, praetor in 44 BC, and Brutus' co-conspirator in the assassination of Caesar. But Silanus himself does not seem to have had much sway over his stepson and, indeed, he died at some date around 59 BC, when Brutus was only just starting on his political career.

It was probably at about this time that Brutus was adopted by one of Servilia's male relatives.[45] Adoption in ancient Rome did not resemble what we think of as adoption today; often, it was a political or familial transaction designed to pass down the name, property and religious rites to the next generation.[46] In the case of Brutus, it was the legacy of the once illustrious Servilii Caepiones that was being preserved. Marcus Junius Brutus thus legally became known as Quintus Servilius Caepio Brutus, although he hardly used his legal name, and nothing is really known about his adopted father. If we are looking for a male relative to identify as a father figure to Brutus we may well find ourselves disappointed. Even his famous relative Marcus Porcius Cato, the half-brother of Servilia, who is often suspected of having some guidance over Brutus' education, does not seem to have influenced Brutus that much in his earliest years.[47] As will be argued in the next chapter, Cato certainly helped Brutus on his way, but he did not steer the younger man's ideas, alliances or political decisions in any discernible fashion. It was only once Cato had died that Brutus saw the potential in following in his uncle's footsteps.

Instead, there would have been other influential factors in Brutus' early life apart from his immediate family. We know that as a boy Brutus studied grammar alongside Cassius with Staberius Eros, a teacher who offered his services free of charge to children who had lost their fathers in the Sullan proscriptions. Several scholars have taken this last fact to suggest that Brutus was exposed to the pitfalls of absolute power from his youth, which is not altogether impossible. A famous anecdote about Cassius might even be adduced to support this idea; for the story goes that as a schoolboy Cassius fought the son of Sulla, Faustus, after Faustus used his father's position to intimidate other youngsters.[48] These vignettes help build the image of two young men who attached importance to the value of liberty from an early age; or they may tell us more about Cassius' political inclinations than Brutus'. Either way, we have to be careful here: to make such an argument runs the risk of circularity – a case of the answer begging the question. As it stands, the evidence for the rest of Brutus' education at Rome is very scant.

He learned Greek and Roman rhetoric, but we do not know the name of the rhetor who taught him.[49] And we can only assume that at the age of around fifteen or sixteen, when he had ceremoniously put aside his boyhood clothing and replaced it with the toga of manhood, he would have frequented the Forum to watch the famous orators of his day in action: a kind of 'apprenticeship of the Forum', termed a *tirocinium fori* by modern scholars. If we can tentatively date Brutus' own *tirocinium fori* to the 60s, he would surely have witnessed Cicero performing in a number of high-profile trials: extortion in the provinces, a military offence, and a complicated inheritance suit are just some of the famous cases Cicero conducted in these years.[50] And many other trials would have been held in the permanent courts established by Sulla to deal with cases of murder and poisoning, forgery, electoral bribery, theft, assault, extortion and treason. This was an education in itself. The trials he watched would have exposed Brutus to the problems of the society he was about to enter, but he could simultaneously learn the art of practical oratory by observation.

Such training was important because appearing in the law courts was a sure means of attracting attention and making important political allies. Indeed, many of Rome's most famous statesmen made their names by speaking in the courts, as Brutus too would go on to do.[51] And thereafter a would-be politician's influence and rise through the ranks often depended on his ability to give an effective oratorical performance, both in public assembly meetings and within the exclusive meetings of the Senate. But when a young man made his first public appearance as an orator, the expectation was that he knew the art of speaking already. To this end, Brutus' informal *tirocinium fori* would have been supplemented with rigorous training in the arts of rhetoric and oratory: the theory and the practice of public speaking respectively.[52]

As part of his rhetorical education, Brutus would have studied the famous speeches composed by the fourth-century BC Athenian orators (the 'Attic orators'), the works of Lysias, Aeschines, Demosthenes, Isocrates and Hyperides – which can still be read today – seem to have figured highly on the curriculum.[53] Reading the speeches of the Attic orators helped Brutus form his own (highly developed) opinions on oratory and they also shaped his personal practice. Later in life, for example, he criticised a passage from Demosthenes' otherwise highly acclaimed speech *On the Crown*; likewise, he did not share Cicero's high opinion of Isocrates. Rather Brutus preferred a more natural style of speech characterised by iambic endings, the rhythm of speech found most commonly in ancient Greek drama, and especially in passages that involved speeches or line-by-line dialogue. Aristotle had said that iambic rhythm was native to everyday Greek speech and that people might even produce lines of this verse unintentionally, mid-conversation and without thinking. Thus Cicero criticised Brutus' style because it was too 'leisurely' and 'disjointed'. Yet, to judge from his response, Brutus considered his own manner of speech the manlier of the two: Cicero's oratory, he said, was 'delicate and effeminate'.[54]

Brutus would have also studied model speeches composed by Roman orators, and it is possible in this context that he read the works of his distant ancestor, Cato the Elder – his uncle's great-grandfather. Somewhere in the region of 150 of Cato's published speeches were available in Brutus' day. And fragments of seventy-nine of these still survive today to corroborate what we know of him; namely, that he promoted himself as a man of virtue and austerity, as a defender of old-fashioned Roman values.[55] The emphasis on this last feature was what the Romans called the *mos maiorum* – 'the custom of the elders' – and we have already seen the important place such elders occupied in republican culture and society. Throughout his life the younger Cato used his famous ancestor as a role model for his own political conduct, and we can only speculate as to whether his influence rubbed off on Brutus too.[56] Either way, however, the devotion to the *mos maiorum* was endemic among the upper classes of Roman society, to whom innovation and changes to the *status quo* generally seemed anathema. Instead the Romans championed conformity, deference, and a continuation in tradition.[57] This would have been another factor drilled into Brutus by his family and teachers alike.

One final element of the general rhetorical education must not be overlooked in building an impression of the young Brutus' development. The budding orator, of course, needed to practise and for this he used preliminary exercises called the *progymnasmata*. Our only surviving evidence for the *progymnasmata* comes from the late first century AD onwards, but the contents of these exercises date back to at least the Hellenistic age of Greek history (323–31 BC).[58] They were thus a Greek educational tool, the aim of which was to build up to a speech using stock themes and patterns of argument that could be adopted and adapted as part of the orator's later repertoire. As such, their contents reflect the concerns of the Hellenistic world – tyrants and pirates holding chief place among them – but these could readily be fitted to Roman situations. Indeed, so potent a tool was the exercise that

Cicero tells us he practised his declamations even as an adult.[59] This point should cause us to reflect on our idea of what an oratorical education meant and its implications for studying Brutus: it was not just about mastering a finite set of skills. Rather, the rhetorical training which started at the time of a man's youth was part of a longer process of 'fine-tuning', an evolving artistic accomplishment, so to speak. As will be argued in Chapter 4, we should not neglect the significance of Brutus' rhetorical education when we examine his motivations and conduct in 44 BC. For just as the tyrant was a stock figure in these declamatory exercises, so too was the tyrannicide: the man who sees the tyrant's death as a liberation and decides to do what is best for his country. From a young age, then, Brutus' mind would have been trained on the question of what it meant to kill a tyrant.[60]

To cap it all, Brutus' education was further polished when he went to complete his studies abroad, as was becoming customary for young Romans of wealth, aspiration and potential.[61] In Athens and Rhodes, he received further oratorical training with Pammenes and Empylus: the former, according to Cicero, was by far the greatest orator of his day; the latter became a lifelong friend to Brutus, and was the author of one of the (lost) biographies of him. But by far the biggest influence on the formation of Brutus' character was the study of philosophy in which he engaged there. Thus, Plutarch tells us that as a young man he attended lectures in all the major schools of philosophy: Academic, Peripatetic, Epicurean and Stoic. Yet he adds that it was the Academic tradition Brutus favoured most, and especially the so-called 'Old Academy' of Antiochus of Ascalon, which promoted a return to the original doctrines of Plato.

True as this may be, there is also a strong chance that Plutarch has exaggerated the extent to which Brutus adhered to the one school of thought.[62] All we know for sure is that Antiochus himself had died by the time Brutus went to Athens, and that he instead took up with Aristus, Antiochus' brother and successor to the headship.[63] Cicero tells us that, in Athens, Brutus attended Aristus' lectures for quite some time, and that later he invited the philosopher into his household at Rome and regarded him as a close friend.[64] However, while he certainly tended towards the Academic school, Brutus also incorporated elements of Stoicism into his philosophical outlook; not because he was imitating Cato, but because Brutus was a critical and independent-minded philosopher in his own right. In time, he too became an author of some note, and his published works were still available to read over a century after his death.

Brutus' reputation as a lover of Greek literature, culture and especially philosophy has long been used as means of explaining his later reasons for leading the conspiracy against Caesar. And certainly, as we shall see in both Chapters 4 and 5, the tools of philosophical reasoning can take us a long way towards understanding how Brutus might have made sense of the times in which he found himself. But there was a lighter side to Brutus' character and learning, too: he dabbled in writing poetry, he was a keen collector of art, and he could weave quotations from Greek literature into his daily exchanges with like-minded peers.[65] These were all signs of the good education and upbringing which would stand Brutus in good stead as he looked ahead to his preparations for a political career. Shared cultural learning was also a factor that features in Roman definitions of friendship. Brutus' love of the Greek world united him with and made him appreciated by men such as Atticus and Cicero; erudite conversation would have been a part of his charm.

As we shall see, Brutus only counted Cicero among his friends later in life, and even then their relationship was strained. However, Atticus was almost certainly a guiding influence on Brutus as he progressed into his manhood, and he deserves special mention here. As a member of the equestrian order, Atticus did not hold political office at Rome and he was not a member of the Senate. But as a political adviser and a man with a sharp sense for business and investments, his influence was second to none. He remained a constant and loyal friend to Brutus and Servilia, and he may even have helped them manage their finances;[66] however, it was not a one-sided relationship. As a 'natural statesman' – to borrow Cicero's description of his friend[67] – Atticus must have seen something worth cultivating in the young Brutus: he was a man who bore all the marks of a winning horse, one which Atticus deemed it to his advantage to back.

The End Goal

By the end of the 60s, contemporary observers might have said that Brutus had it all going for him – as indeed he did. For Brutus' entire education and upbringing had been geared towards this one goal: personal advancement and the continuation of the family name, Servilius Caepio Brutus, as it legally became at around this time.

However, the situation facing Rome when Brutus came to embark on his career was fraught with tension. Even though most of Sulla's laws had been either repealed or modified in the decade following his dictatorship, still the reform allowing for the election of twenty quaestors per year stood in place, which in turn refreshed the annual pool of competition. Moreover, the fact that Sulla had flooded the Senate with new members created a far sharper distinction between the older and the more recent senatorial families in later generations: a 'two-tiered Senate', in which the *nobiles* continued to dominate the consulship while many others did not progress much further than the quaestorship.[68]

For those excluded from the inner circle of the old political elite, and especially for the 'new men' (*novi homines*) who lacked senatorial ancestors altogether, there were significant struggles to be faced in the competition for high office; some *nobiles* jealously guarded the honours to which they felt entitled by birth, for example, and they challenged the ambitions of would-be climbers. At the opposite end of the spectrum, a great expectation was placed upon the younger generation of *nobiles* to continue the achievements of their forebears. Yet, for these men, factors such as poverty, an ancestor's disrepute or an early death in the family (as in the case of Brutus' own father) might intensify the pressure or make success harder to come by. Before we trace Brutus' first foray into political life in the next chapter, then, it will serve us well to examine some of the challenges a young *nobilis* might have expected to face. Such a focus is important because a concentration on Brutus' privileged position has traditionally clouded our appreciation of his responses to the political circumstances under which he conducted his career.[69] At the same time, however, it will enable us to shed further light on some of the ways in which politics actually worked in Rome.

To begin with, although the *res publica* was configured as a sharing of power between the Senate and the people, Rome had never been a democratic city-state. Nor, however, was it entirely oligarchic. On the one hand, the *nobiles* held sway over domestic politics by virtue of their individual and collective authority (*auctoritas*), as well as the merits they inherited from their ancestors; Brutus, from this perspective, stood to gain. Yet, on the other, a powerful system of checks and balances on Rome's magistrates meant that the political elite was to some extent constrained by the need to obtain popular approval: magistrates needed to win elections, and they had to present legislation to be passed in the popular assemblies. In this context, no one would deny the advantage of inherited status, not least because the voting system itself was weighted in favour of the wealthiest members of society. But it is important to point out that success at the polls was not automatic: no one ever inherited the consulship. To succeed in attaining office hence required ceaseless and considerable industry in courting the people who voted – that is, all adult male citizens over the age of seventeen.

It is difficult to quantify precisely how much the Roman people at large participated in and influenced the politics of the late Republic at any given time. Yet recent studies have at least demonstrated that the popular will was a real force to contend with in the quest for power and influence.[70] Thus, politicians often broadcast their names as advocates in the courts; at the same time, they might address the crowds in public meetings (*contiones*, singular *contio*) in a bid to win support in the run-up to votes on legislation. The games and the theatres, too, became hugely influential both in the pursuit and testing of a senator's political popularity. More recently, Cristina Rosillo-López has argued for the importance of public opinion as a political mechanism, operating through a blend of oral and written media: the circulation of rumours and gossip, as well as pamphleteering, posters and graffiti, should all be factored into any assessment of how the mass and elite interacted in Rome. And, in time, we shall see Brutus using and being affected by exactly this kind of information exchange.

However, the principle of popular sovereignty is best evidenced in the office of the tribunate: the ten tribunes of the plebs who were elected annually to represent the people in its negotiations with the Senate. In the early history of the Republic, this office had been conceived as a means of protecting ordinary citizens against overbearing magistrates and arbitrary punishment; in return, the tribune was regarded as sacrosanct, and it was forbidden to inflict any damage on his person. Yet, over time, it had evolved so that the tribunes gained new powers: the right to propose legislation which was binding on the whole people, for example, or to veto decrees of the Senate which went against the plebeians' interests. Even though the original distinction between the patrician and plebeian families had lost its importance by the first century BC, still the office persisted and it became an incredibly powerful tool with which to challenge the authority of the *nobiles*, the political elite of which Brutus was a part.

Not all tribunes, of course, used the office to resist the *nobiles* or to champion the interests and rights of the people; indeed, many holders were themselves from distinguished families (it was only patricians who were barred from holding the post). Yet those who did were labelled 'demagogues' (*populares*), and they were perceived as a threat by the men who favoured the traditional authority of the Senate: the self-styled 'best men' (the *optimates*) or the 'good men' (*boni*) who supported them. On a side note, it is important to understand that these terms – *boni* and *optimates* versus *popularis* (sing.) and *populares* (pl.) – did not constitute political 'parties' in any modern sense; likewise, it is difficult to rank the activities of Rome's politicians on any modern left-to-right scale.[71] However, the tendency of some tribunes to champion the rights of the people led to a rise of populist activity, which propelled the *libertas* of the people and the *auctoritas* of the Senate – two ideals traditionally seen as a guarantee of political stability – into a state of conflict which reached its peak in the first century BC.

What this meant in practice was that, although his privileged heritage and impressive connections continued to count heavily in Brutus' favour, it was the use to which he put these advantages that was going to be important in the scramble for high honour. For in the atmosphere of competition that prevailed over the late Republic, as families of the patrician aristocracy and the noble-plebeian households fought against men with little or no family history of participation in the Senate, 'packaging the past' became 'an enduring concern', as Catherine Steel has succinctly put it.[72] When we remember the image Brutus presented of himself on his coin, as well as the message he spread after the assassination of Caesar, the importance of his claim to fame should by now be clear.

But if, in this chapter, we have started by tracing the legend that stood behind Brutus' name, let us now turn, in the next, to examine how he fashioned his own identity by rehearsing and recycling the ingredients that had made Servilius Ahala and especially Lucius Brutus so renowned. In so doing, we shall see how Brutus used his ancestry to negotiate the political tensions of his day; at the same time, we shall watch him adapt his strategy, to position himself and become a Brutus for his age, as three of the most powerful men in Rome pooled their interests and placed themselves above the principles of the free *res publica*.

CHAPTER 2

INDEPENDENT OPERATOR

The Changed Nature of Politics

> When I consider your case, Brutus, I am filled with sorrow. You were a young man racing ahead to the applause of all when across the path as it were of your chariot came the misfortunes of our country.
>
> — Cicero, *Brutus*, 331

While Brutus had been away studying in Athens and Rhodes, those living in Rome witnessed major political upheavals which were to have a grave effect upon Brutus' early career. Later in life, when Cicero looked back on the opportunities that would ordinarily have been available to Brutus, he could only remark with regret how the younger man's progress had been hampered by the political circumstances under which he conducted his career: namely, the domination of Pompey and Caesar in the 50s, as well as the outbreak of civil war in 48 BC. Before then, he had been 'a young man racing ahead to the applause of all' – or so Cicero wrote in the history of oratory he both dedicated to and named after Brutus in 46 BC. For Brutus' heritage and connections gave him a political advantage which men like Cicero, a 'new man', could only dream about. Furthermore, his studies had equipped him with the skills deemed necessary to succeed in political life: 'a tongue sharpened by rhetorical training as well as an eloquence enriched by a profound culture', as Cicero put it.[1] But these were not ordinary times, and the 'rules' of the political game changed dramatically during the course of Brutus' rise to manhood; however much Cicero tells us he 'raced ahead' in his early career, Brutus still encountered hurdles along the way.

As we saw in the last chapter, even though much of Sulla's legislation had been dismantled in the decade immediately following his dictatorship, still the competition culture of the 70s persisted and even intensified as individual senators and their factions fought for control over Rome's affairs. Yet amidst all their manoeuvrings, one figure had emerged as the leading man of the day: Pompey the Great – Brutus' personal enemy. His spectacular military successes had seen him awarded two triumphs before he was even a senator, and then, in 70 BC, he was elected consul at the age of just thirty-six. Not only was Pompey too young for the post when he assumed it, he had not even held any prior magistracies on the *cursus honorum*. But that did not matter to the electorate at Rome. As was often the case with great military generals, Pompey had become the people's darling, and the Senate presumably felt compelled to oblige.[2]

Although Brutus' activities are not documented during the years of Pompey's meteoric rise to power, it presumably irked the young man to see his father's killer become a national hero. For, during the 60s, Pompey enjoyed further successes when he swept the Mediterranean clear of piracy, before concluding the war against the Pontic king Mithridates VI – an enemy who had posed the greatest threat to Rome's security since the days of Hannibal. When the great general returned to Italy towards the end of 62 BC, he was one of the richest and most popular men in Rome. He celebrated a third triumph in 61 BC, boasted that he had nearly doubled the state income from the eastern provinces, and further swelled the Roman treasury with cash and booty worth 480 million sesterces.[3] On top of that he had increased his own personal wealth exponentially. Yet, by 59 BC – the year in which Brutus first entered the political arena – the opposition to Pompey had greatly increased, and this soon led to rumours of a conspiracy against his life. Something had gone terribly wrong.

Part of the problem was that, because of his phenomenal and unconventional successes, the atmosphere within the Senate was one of growing hostility towards Pompey. Individual jealousies and personal quibbles doubtless played their part. Yet, as a protégé of Sulla, and as a military man whose career bore striking *popularis* resemblances to that of Marius, Pompey must have seemed to combine in his character the most threatening traits of these two warlords. He was consequently more than a personal enemy to Brutus; Pompey was a political force to be feared among the inner circle of the Senate, and especially by the so-called *optimates* who were now grouped around Cato. Whatever Pompey's real motivations or conduct may have been, senators with any sense of self-preservation must have worried deeply about where all this would lead. Thus, in the years that followed Pompey's return to Rome, the Senate resisted any move that would help strengthen his hand further, which included delaying the ratification of Pompey's eastern settlements after the Mithridatic war.

By far the greatest factor in the demise of Pompey's popularity, however, was that at some point, probably in 60 BC, Pompey agreed to join forces with Marcus Licinius Crassus and Gaius Julius Caesar in an informal coalition commonly dubbed the 'First Triumvirate'.[4] For his part, Crassus had been left humiliated when the Senate refused to support him in a matter pertaining to the equestrians; Caesar, too, had been frustrated when the Senate forced him to choose between a triumph and campaigning for the consulship, when he wanted both at the same time. And by then, Pompey had lost patience with the Senate's refusal to comply with his wishes. Yet between them they saw a way to get everything they wanted. Backed by Pompey and Crassus, Caesar was elected consul for 59 BC, with Marcus Calpurnius Bibulus as colleague. But soon he was acting independently to push through legislation to satisfy his allies, and together – our sources tell us – the three men controlled decision-making processes by force and violence and with ruthless contempt for the traditional institutions.[5]

Exactly when all these secret arrangements between the three men took shape is not known. The compact between them even came as something of a surprise to Cicero, who always had his ear to the ground otherwise. But it all became very obvious by May 59 BC, when Pompey announced his marriage to Caesar's daughter, Julia. 'We must expect the worst', Cicero told Atticus: 'it is clear that he is preparing to take absolute power.'[6] For, although later writers could joke that the year 59 BC was the consulship of Julius and Caesar – in reference to the sidelining of his consular colleague, Bibulus – it is clear that those living at the time saw Pompey as the senior partner in the alliance.[7] Even the ordinary people of Rome, who had been great supporters of Pompey just a few years before, were reported to have shown their disapproval of him when they enthusiastically applauded an actor who jibed, 'At our peril are you Great', with an obvious pun on Pompey's *cognomen*, 'Magnus'.[8]

But what part did Brutus play? And how did he react to these early manifestations of autocracy? Fortunately for us, Cicero's letters of this period provide a convenient window from which we can view these developments, as well as a vantage point we can use to position Brutus within the ever-changing landscape of Rome's political affairs. For, in June 59 BC, just a month before the popular outcry at the theatre, Cicero had written:

> The whole situation has come to the point where there is no longer any hope, neither among the private citizens nor even the magistrates, that we shall ever be free again. But amidst the oppression, the freedom of speech is greater than it was – at least in small gatherings or over the banquet tables. Anxiety is beginning to conquer fear, but still an air of desperation prevails.[9]

There are certainly details in the letters from this period that invite explanation. It is helpful to know, for example, that Cicero's despair was intensified by the personal danger he sensed approaching, and which culminated in his exile the following year. But, however much his gloomy outlook was influenced by his own situation, still we see that the catchwords of 'liberty' and 'freedom' were being mentioned that summer. What was needed in this climate was a new Lucius Brutus or another Servilius Ahala, Cicero had been heard to say, evoking the names of our Brutus' famous ancestors.

The Vettius Affair

Such, then, were the broad developments leading to Brutus' first appearance in our contemporary evidence: the 'Vettius affair', so called because the central figure was a certain Lucius Vettius. As a man with a track record in the shady business of informing, four years earlier this same Vettius had provided Cicero with information about a revolutionary uprising led by the disgruntled patrician Lucius Sergius Catilina.[10] But, now, either in the July or August of 59 BC, he had been involved in the plans for a new conspiracy: this time, to attack Pompey in the Forum when the gladiatorial games were taking place.[11] Vettius claimed that some senior political figures were involved in the plot, including the consul Bibulus, who was to provide Vettius with a dagger. Otherwise, the men involved in the conspiracy were largely of the younger generation, led by Gaius Scribonius Curio. And Brutus too, as we shall see, was said to have occupied a prominent role in the planning. It is hence important to provide some details of the conspiracy, so that we can better understand Brutus' alleged involvement and, from there, tease out some possible implications for reconstructing his early political affiliations.

There is not the space here to chart all the twists and turns of this mysterious incident, or to explain how Vettius turned from being a participant in the conspiracy to an informer against it.[12] Instead, let us pick up at the point when he presented his accusations to the Senate. Unfortunately for Vettius, no one believed him and all he accomplished for himself was a sentence in

Rome's dingy prison, since he had confessed to carrying a weapon – a criminal offence under the Plautian law on violence, the *lex Plautia de vi.*[13] Yet it is here that the plot thickens, becoming more interesting still. For the next day, Vettius was summoned to appear in a second meeting, this time a *contio*. However, as Cicero explained to Atticus, there was a noticeable difference in the testimony Vettius provided on this second occasion:

> To begin with he removed Brutus' name from his speech entirely, after he had named him so bitterly in the Senate. It was clear that a night as well as a nocturnal intervention had come to pass. Then, he added the names of men to whom he had not even attached the slightest hint of suspicion in the Senate.[14]

Even Cicero was not safe from attack this time; for, although Vettius had not named him explicitly, he did blame a certain 'eloquent ex-consul' for filling the young men's heads with ideas of tyrannicide.[15]

And so it seemed to Cicero as if Vettius had been 'primed and prepared' for his appearance on the *rostra* – the elevated platform from which speakers addressed the people in *contiones* of this sort. And it is hard to disagree. The addition of some names, as well as the removal of Brutus' own, certainly suggest that some person or people had interfered; hence Cicero's derogatory comment that 'a night as well as a nocturnal intervention had come to pass'. The affair between Brutus' mother Servilia and Caesar had been a topic of common gossip for some time, such that Cicero could joke that some pillow talk might have persuaded Caesar to intervene with Vettius on Brutus' behalf.[16]

Could Caesar have been persuaded by his lover to remove Brutus' name from Vettius' hit list? Or was it possible that Caesar had used the opportunity to damage the political reputations of his political opponents – men to whom Vettius 'had not even attached the slightest hint of suspicion in the Senate' the day before? It is impossible to know, and indeed our sources present a mixed bag of evidence for the conspiracy, how it unfolded, and who was behind it all.[17] But what is important to note is that, throughout his letter to Atticus, Cicero continually evaluates and tries to make sense of the event, because it reminds us that – although our only contemporary evidence – it contains the musings of someone who does not quite have the full information available to him.

Cicero's own hypothesis was that Caesar had stage-managed the whole sordid affair from the beginning – perhaps, it has since been suggested, as a means of casting suspicion over the rising star of Curio, or of making sure that Pompey remained conscious of his precarious position. Either way, our most consistent accounts of the event – Cicero, Suetonius and Plutarch – all appear to agree, with only varying details, that the alleged assassination was a sham rather than a real plot, and that its bogus exposé was intended to bring shame upon those it implicated. Despite the best efforts of several modern scholars to tease out further clues, however, the event remains as elusive now as it was at the time.[18] For the intriguing chain of events set in motion by Vettius' accusations came to a sudden halt when the informer was found strangled in prison in mysterious circumstances.

And yet Vettius' observations do, at least, provide signs as to Brutus' political activity and the circles in which he was moving at the time of the affair. We may remember that, in his original statement to the Senate, Vettius had pinpointed a 'band of young men' as the engineers behind the plot and that he had identified Curio as their ringleader. This much we know is true: by June 59 BC Curio was indeed the man leading the protest movement against the triumvirs, an act of defiance for which he was winning a lot of political support. Cicero had observed this too, and he even explained the situation in a letter to Atticus: 'The only one to speak or offer open opposition is young Curio. He gets hearty rounds of applause, a most flattering amount of general salutation in the Forum, and a great many other signs of support from the good men.' At the recent games, when Pompey had been jeered at, Curio had been enthusiastically greeted by the crowds.[19]

What is more, Curio had even visited Cicero that month and declared that he 'hated proud kings.' 'The youth are inflamed and cannot bear the current state of affairs,' Cicero added. None of this should be taken to suggest that Cicero had been inciting the young men towards tyrannicide – as Vettius alleged. But it may give a flavour of the kind of activities the unscrupulous informer had been collecting as evidence against the men he targeted. That the band of young men may have had something afoot is by no means impossible; even Cicero does not reject the possibility, although an ironic aside hints that Cicero did not place much hope in any such ventures: 'a fine situation we're in now, if our hope rests on them!' he despairingly joked to Atticus.[20]

Yet, whatever the young men were, or were not, planning is of secondary interest to the fact that Brutus was not merely identified as a minor player in the act; as Cicero explicitly states, Vettius had named him in very bitter terms (*acerrime*, in the Latin). If we can accept this much as true, the fact that Brutus could be found among, or even closely identified with, the group of young men formed around Curio's leadership is worthy of comment. As one of the 'goateed' and fashionable young men of his generation (to borrow

Cicero's description of him), Curio operated according to a rather different political code to Brutus, who appeared to maintain a conservative and deferential attitude towards the Senate and republican institutions. Brutus' uncle Cato, for one, had clashed with Curio politically, and so we can imagine he would have disapproved entirely of his nephew's early connections.[21] Consequently, the alliance suggests that Brutus was not influenced by Cato's opinion at this, still early, stage in his career. He appears to have been more of a pragmatist, and as such he was prepared to transcend personal differences for what he perceived to be the greater political advantage. His concerns were those shared by the younger generation; the men who hated 'proud kings.'[22]

An Eastern Interlude

Curio, Brutus and the other Roman youths were not the only ones dissatisfied by the new 'regime' imposed by Pompey, Caesar and Crassus. For, in the years preceding the Vettius affair, further opposition had come from the influential circle surrounding Brutus' uncle, Cato. Indeed, by 59 BC, Cato – despite the fact he did not hold high office – had become one of the most dominant figures in the Senate. Thus, he had numerous times spoken out in the Senate and blocked measures that favoured the ambitions of the three. So far had he pushed his opposition to them that even Cicero, who otherwise held a large amount of respect for Cato, once famously criticised him for speaking 'as if he is living in Plato's Republic, not in the sewers of Romulus.' But stories of his manoeuvring and timewasting tactics mask a more serious point about Cato: his reputation as the Senate's champion meant that Cato represented a challenge to those who wished to play a different political game.[23]

One of these men was the notorious tribune of 58 BC, Publius Claudius Pulcher – better known simply as Clodius, the adopted plebeian version of his name – who devised an ingenious method for removing Cato from Rome as soon as he entered office. First, he set up a special command to organise the annexation of Cyprus, which Rome had decided to add to its empire; then he gave the honour of administering it to Cato.[24] This was a tactical move: Clodius knew Cato would thus be bound to leave Rome. Hence, the manoeuvre was part of a much larger strategy to help Clodius push through his controversial reforms. More important for our purposes, however, is the fact that Brutus went with Cato. In a period, as we have seen, in which many of his peers found their ambitions thwarted, thanks to Cato's reputation Brutus received his first official assignment and the chance for personal advancement.

Plutarch includes a brief account of this mission in his *Life of Brutus* which can be pieced together and summarised as follows: Brutus, he tells us, accompanied Cato as far as Rhodes, but upon falling ill he went to Pamphylia to recuperate while Cato dealt with business on the island. From there, Cato sent a certain Canidius (perhaps the tribune L. Caninius Gallus) to negotiate a surrender with Ptolemy of Cyprus.[25] However, his task was greatly facilitated when the king took his own life. Cato quickly summoned Brutus to sail to Cyprus and told him to take charge of removing the king's treasure, a job he did not trust Canidius/Caninius to perform. But Plutarch tells us that Brutus was reluctant to go: to begin with, he thought Cato was being unfair towards his friend. Then he adds that, 'as a young man devoted to his studies', Brutus also considered such administrative matters 'unworthy of him'. But, if there is any truth in the story, he soon gave in to his uncle's demands, taking us to the swift conclusion to this narrative. Brutus quickly converted the treasures of the king into money that the Roman treasury needed and thereby won Cato's praise for his efficiency.[26]

But what are we to make of Plutarch's account here? On the one hand, it is often cited as proof that Brutus was trustworthy in the handling of public finances. On the other, the vaguely critical remark that he considered the task 'unworthy of him' suggests a reluctance to undertake public duties, and perhaps even a lack of responsibility – an accusation which Plutarch seems to deflect by twice referring to his immature age at the time. When read in conjunction with Plutarch's version of the same mission in his *Life of Cato the Younger*, however, we have cause to question the veracity of the tale; for there it is Cato, not Brutus, who painstakingly converted the treasure to cash before conveying it back to Rome.[27] This does not necessarily mean that we should write Brutus out of the picture entirely. However, as John Moles has pointed out before me, Plutarch's account of Brutus' role has almost certainly been exaggerated.[28]

Yet, the passage in Plutarch's *Life of Brutus* is interesting for another reason largely overlooked by Brutus' biographers: his disapproval of Cato's distrust of Canidius/Caninius, who he thought had been 'shamefully cast aside' by his uncle. For Cato's grave suspicions of even his closest friends during his term of office gave ammunition to his detractors, a point of view which is also attributed to Brutus here.[29] It is highly likely that the distancing of Brutus from Cato at work in this passage, especially when taken in conjunction with the emphasis on Brutus' reliable handling of monies in the provinces, points to Plutarch's use of a source that was friendly to Brutus. This suggestion will become more significant in what follows, when we have had a chance to analyse some of Brutus' less creditable dealings in provincial affairs. For now, however, the obvious point should not be passed over in silence: he was not, as an ancient commentator later styled him, merely 'an imitator of his uncle Cato' (*auunculi Catonis imitator*).[30] As this episode reveals, even when he was working closely alongside his uncle, Brutus was a man with views and a *modus operandi* independent of Cato.

Establishing a Name, Establishing Networks

We do not know exactly when Brutus returned to Rome; at this point Plutarch's account fast-forwards from 58 BC right through to 49 BC, and there are no narrative treatments of Brutus in our other sources either. However, Brutus was likely to have been back in Italy by early 56 BC, possibly by February.[31] Thereafter, although we have a significant gap in the biographical tradition, enough contemporary evidence survives to help us piece together a largely coherent picture of Brutus' activities in the years missing from Plutarch.

To begin with, there are the coins Brutus had minted in either 55 or 54 BC in his capacity as *triumvir monetalis*, one of three annually appointed moneyers responsible for the production of coinage.[32] As a post normally held by young men at the beginning of their political careers, it offered more than the average opportunity for ambitious upstarts, for Romans elected to this position in Brutus' day frequently issued coins that commemorated their ancestors' achievements.[33] We have already seen something of how a man's family *exempla* could act almost as a pledge in electoral campaigns, and to this end Brutus had probably been broadcasting his claims to fame from the moment he entered the political stage. But as a *triumvir monetalis*, and as he looked ahead to the elections for the quaestorship, Brutus could now publicise his name and its legendary associations to a wider audience.

Two of the coin types Brutus issued survive to reveal something of his political profiling in these years. For on the first coin (Plate 4), he struck the image of Libertas, the goddess of liberty, which he connected on the reverse to his legendary ancestor, Lucius Junius Brutus. A closer look at the imagery, however, may tell us something more precise about Brutus' political message, when we notice that the original Brutus is shown in the full regalia of his ancient office, together with his public officers – the *accensus* who preceded him and two lictors behind. The emphasis is hence on the official responsibility of magistrates in general, and on the Brutus clan specifically, to act as guarantors of *libertas*. Looked at from this perspective, then, Brutus' attempts to associate his name with the famous Liberator of 509 BC may be related, and indeed even a response, to the much wider political development we traced in Chapter 1: the rise of populism and its exponents' powerful anti-establishment rhetoric.[34]

As a result, not only does this coin provide important evidence for the role of *libertas* in Brutus' reputation prior to the Ides; it impresses and advertises Brutus' own view of *libertas* as anchored in the traditions of the past and the institutions of the *res publica*. And yet, insofar as he claimed to descend from the founder of the *res publica* – the man who first gave political freedom to the urban populace at Rome – Brutus presented himself as the real champion and true friend of both the Senate and the people: in other words, he claimed to speak to both sides of the so-called *optimates–populares* divide. But there is more. For, if this first coin jogged memories of the ancient constitution, its origins and the value of *libertas*, then a second coin he issued was a more threatening reminder of what happened to those who transgressed these ideals. Because on this coin (Plate 5), Brutus stamped the portraits of both his famous ancestors, Lucius Junius Brutus and Servilius Ahala, and in so doing he glorified their parts in Rome's historical resistance to tyranny.

It was a bold political strategy: just a year or two before, in April 56 BC, the unpopular coalition between Pompey, Caesar and Crassus had been reaffirmed in a meeting at Luca, in northern Italy, from which the three emerged stronger than before, with a renewed agreement to work together for their better advancement. Caesar's military command in Gaul had been extended for a further five years, while it had been agreed that Pompey and Crassus would jointly hold the consulship in 55 BC; the year after that, they too were to hold strategic and lucrative commands. In 55/54 BC, then, the regime of the three showed no signs of abating and their stranglehold over electoral procedures was causing competition for office and political violence to erupt at an unimaginable level. And so, by circulating these coins, Brutus was not just tapping into a nostalgic longing for the old *res publica*; he was delivering a direct and powerful message to the triumvirs and their allies, whose grip over Roman political life had crippled the free institutions and the authority of the Senate.[35]

Yet the coins of Brutus were only one part of his political self-fashioning and the steps he was taking to shore up his position in the 50s BC. Next, there was the matter of his marriage to Claudia, the daughter of Appius Claudius Pulcher, which probably took place in 54 BC.[36] Little is known of Brutus' first wife; however, more than enough is known about her father for us to understand that this was a marriage of some political convenience for Brutus. Not only was Appius the consul of 54 BC; he was also a leading member of the aristocratic Claudii – a patrician clan famous for its arrogance. To judge from contemporary encounters with him, and especially Cicero's own impressions, Appius seems to have been no exception to the stereotype of the Claudii: at times, he was quite impudent and quarrelsome, unshakeable even when caught red-handed in a shameless action. Among Appius' close circle were his younger brother Clodius, the hugely influential popular politician who, as a tribune of the plebs, had packed Cato off to Cyprus a couple of years before, as well as Pompey, whose eldest son married another of Appius' daughters at around the same time.[37]

These descriptions of Appius Claudius and his circle might make Brutus' decision appear an odd move to begin with, especially when we remember his hatred for Pompey and know in hindsight that he positively welcomed the death of Clodius two years later. But, as a man of culture and literary pursuits, and a member of the college of augurs, Appius seems at least to have had some admirable qualities. Besides, he did, as Cicero had to admit, have all the advantages of birth, rank, riches, talent, children and relatives.[38] Like Brutus' own family, Appius was one of the *nobiles*. And so, by marrying into Appius' family, Brutus expanded his access to a powerful network and reaffirmed the impressive political position he had established for himself. In the short term, however, the alliance was soon quickly repaid when Brutus accompanied his father-in-law as a member of his staff in the province of Cilicia.

We shall return to Brutus' activities in Cilicia in the next section because, as we shall then see, they demand to be treated separately. For now, however, it remains to follow the manner of the appointment because it is often connected to another significant landmark in Brutus' political career: his election to the quaestorship and first senatorial appointment, probably in 53 BC.[39] As so often, the precise details elude us, but a tantalising glimpse into the circumstances of Brutus' appointment is provided by the fourth-century AD writer known as Pseudo-Aurelius Victor, who compiled a catalogue of short biographies of famous men. In his entry on Brutus, he writes: 'as quaestor he [Brutus] refused to go to Gaul, because he [Caesar] was despised by all good men'.[40] Instead, our source tells us, Brutus went to Cilicia with Appius. But what did Brutus' refusal to serve under Caesar mean? Was this an act of political opposition – a further demonstration of Brutus' strong feelings against the regime of the three?

In a detailed study of the political choices facing the younger generation in the late Republic, Maria Dettenhofer has refuted this suggestion. To begin with, she points out, Brutus' gripe was with Pompey, not Caesar. Then, she argues, there were economic considerations; for a man like

Brutus, Gaul may have been less appealing than Cilicia, where there were rich pickings to be made without engaging in military warfare. On top of that, she adds consideration of what his political associates, and especially Appius Claudius, would have thought of Brutus had he thrown in his lot with Caesar.[41] But this only means that Brutus' decision could be more positively reconstructed as family loyalty to his new father-in-law, rather than as opposition towards Caesar. And so, the fact remains that Caesar's invitation to Brutus must have left the younger man in an awkward position.

For even if we accept that Brutus was more ill-disposed towards Pompey than Caesar (and there are good reasons for thinking he was), he *had* nevertheless taken a very public stance in support of liberty and against the domination of the three; such that would not easily have been squared with service to Caesar. At the same time, the senior politician had gone out of his way to court Brutus and to offer him a significant opportunity. Quaestors were normally appointed to their posts by lot; it was only by a special arrangement with the Senate that a quaestor could be assigned to a specific province 'without a lot' (*sine sorte*, in the Latin).[42] Caesar's offer to him was hence an honour. As several contemporary sources emphasise, the relationship between a governor and his quaestor was assured by an unbreakable bond of trust.[43] Furthermore, it was important to Caesar that he should gain the support of the most promising representatives of the younger generation, and indeed he made a habit of promoting the careers of talented young men.[44] In short: it matters little whether Brutus' refusal was, or was not, an act of determined opposition; for, either way, it remained a rejection of a close political alliance. How Caesar reacted to Brutus' decision we do not know. But, in this period of promoting his name and networks, Brutus evidently knew where his best prospects lay.

An Eastern Scandal

Now that he was a senator of Rome, Brutus doubtless had a firm eye on the future, but a future in Roman politics required vast amounts of personal wealth.[45] As he looked ahead to the remaining offices on the *cursus honorum*, Brutus had electoral campaigns to conduct, games to put on for the people, not to mention his own living costs to support. He was already a wealthy man to judge from what we know of him; he had estates at Tusculum, Circeii, Antium, Cumae, Astura and Lanuvium.[46] But it is highly likely that Brutus had also been in the business of lending money at Rome from as early as 58 BC, and that he expanded his commercial interests to

Cyprus when he accompanied Cato there. As one of the only ways a senator could gain profits from trade, lending money and making a profit on the capital represented a lucrative business opportunity.[47] His appointment to Appius Claudius' cohort in 53 BC thus offered Brutus more than just an official appointment in the service of the *res publica*; it gave him a chance to check in on his investments.

However, we only hear about this stage of Brutus' career because two years later Cicero was appointed to take over from Appius Claudius as the governor of Cilicia; and when he did, it revealed, in Cicero's eyes, disconcerting evidence about the young man's business dealings. The story behind Brutus' eastern scandal consequently spreads over three different periods of activity: it has its roots in Brutus' connection with Cilicia and Cyprus going back to 58–56 BC, his stint on Appius Claudius' staff in 53 BC, and Cicero's own administration of the province between 51 and 50 BC. To understand the chain of events that follows, it is best to begin at the point when Brutus' transactions were discovered, by following the 'narrator' and our source for the information, Cicero, who left Rome unwillingly to serve as governor of Cilicia in 51 BC. At the risk of anticipating my conclusion, however, we should be careful not to take everything Cicero says of Brutus at face value.

Cicero knew from experience that the administration of a province held many temptations for a governor and his staff: in his earlier career, as quaestor, he had served in Sicily; as an advocate in the law courts he had both prosecuted and defended men on charges of extortion; and he had given plenty of words of advice to his brother on the subject of provincial management when Quintus Cicero had been stationed in Asia Minor between 61 and 58 BC.[48] For, away from the controlling eye of Rome, the governor had a very considerable degree of freedom in how he managed affairs. There were no permanent members of staff, apart from the garrison troops, and each new governor brought out the men he needed with him. An entourage of reliable men could be a pillar of strength to a moderate governor; on the other hand, under a less scrupulous or a weak leader, their behaviour could wreak havoc.

As a result, Cicero vowed to govern the Cilicians with justice and clemency; he intended to practise self-control and to make sure his staff behaved too. More than anything, Cicero wanted to offer a model example of provincial government, and he certainly did not want to provide ammunition for anyone to prosecute him upon his return to Rome. But when Cicero arrived, it became apparent that Appius Claudius had not taken the same precautions. The province was 'forlorn and permanently ruined', he told Atticus.

The people were unable to pay the taxes imposed, and there were complaints from every community.[49] However, it came as a source of some shock to Cicero that Brutus – a man of whom he was just beginning to grow quite fond – was not entirely without guilt in the matter.[50]

The revelation came as a direct consequence of a memorandum Brutus had given to Cicero before he set out. In this note he listed a number of special concerns he wished Cicero to look into on his behalf. First there was the matter of a large loan he had given to Ariobarzanes, the king of Cappadocia. Cicero was straight on the case but there was a problem: Pompey had also lent money to the unfortunate king, and his demands were more urgent – not least because there was a chance that Pompey might soon appear in person. Cicero did his best but his impression, plainly expressed, was that 'the kingdom is stripped to the bone and the king is a pauper'.[51] Brutus' demands were pressing, however, and eventually Cicero did manage to get Ariobarzanes to pay back 100 of the talents he owed him; in addition, he secured repayments for Pompey too. Neither man got the full amount he was owed, but proportionally, Brutus got the better result.[52] Even if he did not seem particularly grateful to Cicero, the whole affair offers plain evidence of Brutus' ability to impose his will on others.

This episode, however, was nothing compared to what followed. For a second item detailed in Brutus' memorandum for Cicero stated: 'The Salaminians owe money to my friends M. Scaptius and P. Matinius.'[53] Again, upon his arrival in the province, Cicero had sought to look after Brutus' interests and arranged for the debt to be repaid to the latter's 'friends', whom Brutus had warmly recommended to Cicero. But again there was a problem: in the edict he had issued at the start of his governorship, Cicero had officially fixed 12 per cent as the maximum legal interest rate for loans in the province. However Scaptius refused to accept repayment from the Salaminians on these terms: he claimed he was entitled to 48 per cent interest. The difference between the two calculations was vast: if the Salaminians repaid the loan on Cicero's terms they would owe 106 talents, approximately 2.5 million sesterces; if they used the interest rate set out in the original loan agreement with Scaptius, they owed 200 talents, which was nearer to the mark of 5 million.[54]

The reason for this substantial difference in the calculations for repayment rested in the complicated history of the loan, which dated back to 56 BC. For, shortly after Brutus had returned from his mission in Cyprus, the Salaminians sent an envoy to Rome asking to borrow money. Yet under the terms of the Gabinian law (the *lex Gabinia*), the loaning of money to provincial communities was prohibited in the capital, which means that the

Salaminians should not have been allowed to raise it in the first place, and Brutus should certainly not have been allowed to fix a loan agreement. However, he used his influence in the Senate to bypass this legal technicality: Brutus said he had 'friends' who were willing to lend the money, provided they could charge repayments at 48 per cent (four times the usual rate), and the Senate raised a special decree in his favour. Then a second problem arose: there was a clause in the law which invalidated such contracts. And so Brutus arranged for this to be bypassed too, and a second special decree was issued by the Senate, upholding the terms of the first loan-contract between Scaptius and the Salaminians.[55] This was why Scaptius had argued he was entitled to repayment with 48 per cent interest, and it left Cicero in a difficult position when he tried to insist on the lower interest rate.

It was not the first time, however, that Scaptius had tried to get his money back; this is where the story gets particularly scandalous in Cicero's telling of it. Under Cicero's predecessor, Appius Claudius, Scaptius had been appointed to the rank of prefect and allocated cavalry troops. But he had used these troops to intimidate the Salaminians and, on one horrific occasion, Cicero reports, he had besieged the senators of the city in their own Senate house for so long that five of them died of starvation. Cicero was appalled when he heard about the incident from some Cypriot envoys, and he ordered Scaptius' troops to leave the island immediately. Yet Scaptius was not deterred from wanting to get his money back. In fact, he even asked Brutus to write another letter of recommendation to Cicero asking for him (Scaptius) to be given a second prefecture and further troops; unsurprisingly, though, Cicero refused.[56]

However, Brutus' letter did more than ask for help for Scaptius; it seemed to Cicero that he had been misled all along. For it turned out that Brutus was the real creditor of the loan to the Salaminians, not Scaptius; or at least that his money was somehow heavily involved. 'I never once heard him say that the money was his own', Cicero complained bitterly to Atticus, for he now found himself in a bind.[57] The Salaminians were willing to repay the money on Cicero's terms (i.e. with 12 per cent interest), but Scaptius, acting on Brutus' behalf, was still demanding repayment on the agreed rate of 48 per cent. The problem was never fully resolved, as far as we know: Scaptius took Cicero to one side and asked him to leave the matter for another governor to decide upon in the future, and Cicero weakly agreed. Even though the Salaminians requested to deposit 106 talents in a temple and thereby be released from the liability, Cicero denied that too. Scaptius' request was shameless and Cicero knew it. 'I gave this whole matter up as a favour to Brutus', he explained to Atticus.[58] Meanwhile the loan arrangement stayed in place, and the interest on it continued to grow.

What irked Cicero more was that Atticus, a banker himself, was on Brutus' side. Yet Atticus clearly understood that a considerable level of risk was involved, which may have justified the high interest. And it is not impossible, in the specific case of Salamis, that the senators were attempting to hoodwink their creditors and delay repaying their debts: at least, the ease with which they accepted Cicero's terms and surrendered their repayment certainly suggests they had more assets available to them than they had initially let on. Hence, Atticus seems to have appreciated first-hand the problems of lending money to provincials, and he was deeply concerned for Brutus' investment; he even shared Brutus' view that Scaptius should be given another prefecture and requested that Cicero give him more troops.[59] Taking this line of thought further, modern scholars have pointed to comparable cases of loans made at such a rate to support the view that Brutus was not doing anything out of the ordinary for his day and age.[60]

On the other hand, Cicero was clearly not alone in viewing money-lending as an extortionate practice; after all, it involved loaning money to people who might not be able to afford the repayments or the accumulating costs of interest. Ravenous money-lending, wrote the later Roman poet Lucan, was an act of venality.[61] Cato, for one, who used his administration of Cyprus as an example of fair and judicious government, might not have approved of the rate of interest charged on Brutus' loan to the Salaminians.[62] There is also the fact that senatorial legislation had attempted to curb lending above 12 per cent, which is suggestive of a more widespread anxiety. At any rate, Cicero was disappointed because Brutus did not live up to the ideals he expected of him: 'If Brutus is going to think I ought to have imposed forty-eight percent . . . if he is going to be annoyed at my refusing a prefecture to a businessman . . . if he is going to be put out by the withdrawal of the cavalry . . .' Cicero complained to Atticus, 'well, I shall be unhappy that he is angry with me, but even more unhappy that he is not the man I thought he was.'[63]

These are damning words, and Cicero's own disappointment has reverberated through the centuries of scholarship on Brutus. His behaviour in the Salamis episode has been denounced as 'an instance of unrelenting avarice'; his character, famed for its virtuosity, has been found hypocritical. David Stockton, who wrote an influential biography of Cicero, subsequently issued a stark denunciation of Brutus condemning 'his blatant lies to Cicero, his manipulation of his father-in-law's influence, the use of rigged *senatusconsulta* [senatorial decrees] to evade decent and just legislation, his petulance when Cicero would not fall in with his wishes, and the misery of Salamis and the death of its five senators who were victims of his greed and disregard for legality'. Insofar as Stockton was aiming to correct the presentation of Brutus as 'a sincere and consistent champion of legality' in the work of Ronald Syme, he was absolutely correct to remind us of what he calls 'a dirty corner of Rome's imperial cupboard'.[64]

Yet one point we must bear in mind when we read Cicero's exposition of the affair is that our sole evidence comes from the pen of Rome's greatest orator. The 'case' he presents to Atticus – as Cicero himself termed it – is his interpretation of events in a dispute that was far from straightforward. After all, Cicero was engaging in an argument with his closest friend by whom he felt betrayed and unsupported.[65] It was not just the problem of the loan that was troubling Cicero; it was the fact that Brutus was shamefully conducting extortionate affairs under *his* (i.e. Cicero's) watch as a provincial commander, and that he had been forced to turn a blind eye. Cicero's disappointment in Atticus for siding with Brutus must thus be put back into our picture of this narrative.

If the different reactions to Brutus' transactions by Atticus and Cicero tell us one thing, however, it is that the rights and wrongs of lending money in the provinces were a matter of contemporary debate: in the eyes of some, the provinces provided a routine investment opportunity, to others such activities seemed irresponsible and self-interested. In this context, we should neither overplay Brutus' financial transactions as monstrosities nor seek to downgrade them on the grounds that he was only doing what was typical of his times; he was not. The best that can be said for him is that he may not have known about the actions of his agents; yet still he acquiesced in them after the fact, and Scaptius may even be seen among Brutus' close circle of acquaintances in later years, too. Brutus' behaviour was thus representative of the darker side of Roman provincial management, but this attitude was precisely the kind of arrogance that others (including Cato) were trying to quell.

Leader of his Generation

The disappointment in Brutus expressed by Cicero in the letters concerning Salamis is not a unique occurrence in the collection. It was Atticus who instigated the relationship between the two men in the 50s BC, and it is clear that their friendship did not come naturally. Cicero complained more than once about Brutus' rude and conceited nature, and Brutus doubtless felt exasperated at Cicero's righteous handling of the Salaminian affair.[66] To Appius

Claudius, however, Brutus' father-in-law, Cicero found only positive words to describe the young man. And, writing in 50 BC, he professed to hold high hopes for Brutus: 'for a long time now, he has been the leading man among the younger generation', he wrote, 'and will soon, I hope, become so in the state at large'.[67] Despite Cicero's frustration over events at Salamis, he continued to take an interest in Brutus' political career.

Part of the reason, as we shall soon see, was that by the end of the decade Brutus was drawing attention to himself as an orator in the making. But even while he was away from Rome in Cilicia, from where he probably only returned at some point in mid-52 BC, Brutus took care to maintain an active political profile by contributing to topical debates. He had strong opinions that he wanted to share at the beginning of this year, for instance, when Clodius – the populist tribune to whom Brutus was now connected by marriage – was found brutally murdered on the Appian Way. His death sparked a period of intense political violence during which even the Senate house was burned down by Clodius' angry supporters. As Rome descended into chaos, there was mounting pressure for Pompey to be made a dictator to restore peace and order; however, it was a title which stirred chilling memories of the Sullan regime.[68]

In these heated circumstances, Brutus composed a bitter tract *On the Dictatorship of Pompey* (*De Dictatura Pompei*), in which he staunchly opposed the idea of giving Pompey such a position of power. 'It is better to rule no one than to be another man's slave', runs one of the only snippets of this composition to survive today: 'for one can live honourably without power', Brutus explained, 'but to live as a slave is impossible'. In other words, Brutus believed it would be better for the Senate to have no imperial power at all than to have *imperium* and be subject to Pompey's whim.[69]

Scholars have often noted the philosophical colouring of Brutus' words; 'to live an honest life' (*vivere honeste*) was a slogan both in the Old Academy and in Stoicism.[70] But before we conclude that Brutus' oratory was too lofty to meet the practical demands of political debate, we should note that his tract was arguably not meant to represent a real speech. And, besides, other accusations which Brutus appears to have made in the course of his denunciation of Pompey may indicate that its tone elsewhere was slightly different. Thus, according to Seneca, Brutus had raked up old charges against Pompey, whose hands, he said, 'were not just imbued but even infected by civil blood'. He may also have thrown in Pompey's face the occasion when, probably in 59 BC, a deranged and rather outspoken man called Octavius saluted Pompey as king (*rex*) and Caesar as his queen (*regina*). On one reading, the joke rested on the latter's notorious sexual proclivities; at the same time, it made clear that there were some who thought Pompey had regal ambitions.[71]

In short: Brutus' publication of *On the Dictatorship of Pompey* was a considered attack on those who were willing to give in to what Brutus saw as Pompey's power-seeking manoeuvrings – Cato and his circle included. For they were the men responsible for the compromise that was reached when Bibulus proposed to the Senate that Pompey should be appointed sole consul instead of dictator. It was an extraordinary solution, and one which still gave Pompey an unrivalled amount of control. Yet even Cato is reported to have said that 'any government at all is better than no government' – and with this verdict, he sealed the motion.[72] When we compare this expression to the fragment of Brutus' attack from *On the Dictatorship of Pompey* quoted above, we can see just how diametrically opposed Brutus and Cato were on this point.

It is important to stress Brutus' continued opposition to Pompey here because, as Kit Morrell has recently demonstrated, it came at a time when Pompey and Cato were making their first steps towards some sort of political cooperation.[73] Yet further proof of Brutus' stance comes from a second speech he published. For as soon as Pompey entered office as sole consul, he denounced the death of Clodius and the violence that ensued as against the interests of the *res publica*. What is more, under these terms he passed a special law – the Pompeian law on violence (or *lex Pompeia de vi*) – to bring to justice all those who had participated in the recent disturbances. Pompey's prime target was naturally Clodius' murderer: a rival gang leader and high-ranking senator called Titus Annius Milo, with whom Clodius had bitterly wrangled for over five years, and whose guilt was an established fact.

Even though Milo had secured the services of Rome's leading orator to defend him, by the time Cicero took the stand in April 52 BC the odds of an acquittal looked stacked against his client. For, according to Cicero's speech *For Milo* – or the *Pro Milone*, as the published version has come down to us – the prosecution alleged that no man who murdered another should see the light of day; the Senate had decreed that the death of Clodius and the events that followed were against the interests of the *res publica*; furthermore, common opinion had it that even Pompey was trying to secure the condemnation of Milo.[74] Under these circumstances, Cicero put a premium on the only argument left available to him: namely that Milo had killed Clodius in self-defence. But Brutus thought otherwise, and free from the constraints of the legal proceedings, he circulated his own version of a speech *For Titus Annius Milo* (*Pro T. Annio Milone*). The text of this speech is entirely lost to us today; however, writing in the first century AD, the scholar Quintus Asconius Pedianus had access to a copy and from him we gain an impression of its argument.[75]

Asconius tells us that Brutus triumphed over Clodius' death on the grounds he was a bad citizen. Taking no account of the fact that Clodius was the uncle of his wife and the brother of his father-in-law, Brutus argued that Clodius' death was necessary for the *res publica* and that it was therefore a justifiable homicide. Commenting on this speech as if it were a specimen of actual oratory, scholars have often noted Brutus' ideological stance, and the fact that it would certainly have failed to persuade a court of jurors. Others have tried to dismiss the episode as a mere rhetorical exercise without any further comment. Andrea Balbo is much closer to the mark when he suggests Brutus' publication had a political aim 'designed to support the necessity of fighting every public enemy'.[76] But we cannot rule out the possibility that Brutus' pamphlet also continued his anti-Pompeian stance: after all, it makes the very argument that Pompey's law and the senatorial decree had rendered inadmissible in court. Far from being *against* the interests of the *res publica*, in depicting the death of Clodius as a benefit to society, Brutus presented an intellectual challenge to that line of thought – and hence to what he saw as Pompey's abuse of power in 52 BC.

It is important to remember that neither Brutus' speech *On the Dictatorship of Pompey* nor *For T. Annius Milo* was ever delivered; he only published them to make his point clear, a typical procedure for a magistrate who was absent from the city.[77] But already we see in them the determined stand which was to become the hallmark of Brutus' political career: the importance of *libertas* for the *res publica*, and death to anyone who stood in its way. By his varied publications and protestations throughout 52 BC, Brutus thus demonstrated that he was as openly hostile to autocracy when exercised by Pompey as he was later to Caesar's ambitions to be the leading man at Rome.[78] His intense engagement with the internal political struggles of Rome mark him as a man who wanted to play at the highest level of the game. Even though he does not seem to have been attracted by the opportunities of the aedileship, for which he would have been eligible, other appointments made sure that his name was in the public domain.

At some point in the 50s, maybe in either 51 or 50 BC, he was elected to the pontifical college, one of the four major priestly bodies at Rome, responsible for organising Roman public cult.[79] It was a position for life, open only to those who were nominated first by the existing priests in the pontifical college (the *pontifices*) and then elected by the people. On the one hand, then, Brutus gained more experience of standing for election. On the other, as one of only fifteen *pontifices* who served at any given time, Brutus acquired a distinct and prestigious religious identity to complement his growing political profile.

From then on, his duties as a *pontifex* involved him advising the Senate on issues pertaining to the gods, such as the interpretation of prodigies, or disputes over sacred land; it was also the job of the *pontifices* to help supervise the calendar and the correct performance of ceremonies and ritual.[80] In other words, the role of the pontifical college was to help maintain the peaceful relationship with the gods which was crucial for the success of the *res publica*. Brutus' appointment thus propelled him into the centre of Roman religious activity. Yet, at the same time, it brought him into closer working contact with the *pontifex maximus*, then Caesar, whose role as the head of that college must presumably mean he had supported Brutus' nomination and election.[81]

Brutus' networks were evidently expanding in several directions during this period, and he had also started to build something of a reputation as an orator. Although his active profile is difficult to sketch out in full, writing in 46 BC Cicero attests to the fact that he and Brutus had pleaded alongside each other in several cases. It is possible that already in the 50s BC Cicero had in mind what John Dugan has called 'a process of filiation' towards Brutus: that is, an attempt to establish himself as a father-figure to Brutus, with whom he sought an oratorical and political alliance.[82] Whatever the matter, without knowing the details, or what period was being referred to, Cicero's remark nevertheless points to the fact that Brutus was engaging in prominent trials. More certain information regarding Brutus' oratorical activity comes from 50 BC, when Brutus undertook the defence of his father-in-law on two charges following his return from Cilicia: of treason (*maiestas*) and electoral malpractice (*ambitus*).[83]

The stakes were high. If Appius Claudius was found guilty, it would be the end of his political career and he would be forced into exile. As a result, Appius enlisted a stellar defence team which included Pompey and Quintus Hortensius Hortalus, who had been Rome's foremost advocate before the emergence of Cicero. Even personal hostilities were put to one side as Brutus and Pompey cooperated for the first time. Considering the greater influence of his co-speakers, some historians have questioned the extent to which Brutus can be credited for his father-in-law's eventual acquittal.[84] But there is some evidence to suggest a more positive reconstruction. For it seems likely that the division of labour was spread across the trials and that, although Brutus defended Appius at both trials, he cooperated first with Pompey against the charge of treason, and then with Hortensius against the charge of electoral bribery.[85] If this is indeed the case, it means that Brutus' own role in securing this result for Appius was not without significance. And his performance in the two trials would have brought him a vast amount of recognition in the public eye: 'it was a rather illustrious affair', Cicero later remarked.[86] Brutus had made his name in the Forum (Plate 6).

As we saw in the quotation which opened this chapter, by the end of the decade Brutus 'was racing ahead to the applause of all'. So what were the key factors shaping his public profile at Rome? And how did the range and intensity of his activities compare to the efforts of other young *nobiles* at this career stage? From these opening two chapters, we have seen how Brutus used his ancestry and name to forge a political identity, and how his wealth and education enabled him to accumulate both the social and cultural capital needed to succeed in political life. His manifold activities in the 50s BC attest to Brutus' desire to spread his name at Rome – via actions, coins, pamphlets and speeches – all with a consistent political message founded on his version of *libertas*. Thus, he had been implicated in a plot against Pompey's life, when it was thought the latter was accruing too much power; he issued coins bearing reminders of his historical ancestors; and his pamphlets reiterated and amplified the message: Brutus was a champion of liberty and an enemy to tyrants. At the same time, his commitment to his ancestors was notable for the familial piety Brutus displayed, an impression that was further enhanced when he twice defended his father-in-law in court.

Even if the affair at Salamis caused distress to Cicero, there is no evidence that the tale of Brutus' involvement was ever spread outside his innermost circle of friends and alliances. But the trace of it does survive to help us form a more rounded picture of Brutus' activities in this decade. Whereas some young men often attached or indebted themselves to a patron or a military leader at the beginning of their political lives, Brutus' early career seems to be a product entirely of his own making. He certainly had help along the way: his attachment first to Cato, then to Appius provided him with significant career opportunities. But Brutus went on to generate his own income, while the alliances and political decisions that he made demonstrate his independent spirit of mind. Having turned down a close working relationship with Caesar in Gaul, for example, he nevertheless accepted a position in the pontifical college of which Caesar was head. All in all, then, we should see Brutus not just as eloquent, cultured and an outspoken defender of the *res publica*, but as an active manipulator with his own interests, an independent operator who knew what he wanted and how to get it. Only from this beginning should the more familiar picture follow.

Yet there is little to suggest that there were any particularly decisive or significant moments that set Brutus' public career apart from those of the rest of his generation at this stage. As Henriette van der Blom has recently demonstrated in a study of political career-making in republican Rome, the factors that enabled Brutus' rise – his ancestry, wealth, networking and oratory – were all part and parcel of a larger system which placed more emphasis on a man's ability to nurture and sustain a credible and attractive public profile than any other single criterion. At the same time, a man's 'brand' had to be appealing both to the elite and the general populace at Rome.[87] In short: there was still a lot to compete for and the unpredictable nature of politics meant that a man's adaptability to new circumstances might very often prove his best chance of success. Already we have seen Brutus responding to the rise of Pompey, Caesar and Crassus to present himself as the new Liberator for his times. But, as the chariot of war came crashing upon his path, soon the decision was not how to continue the fight against the triumvirs; rather, Brutus needed to decide whom to support as Pompey and Caesar turned their arms against each other.

CHAPTER 3

THE POLITICS OF WAR

Pompey or Caesar?

> Power was divided by the sword, and a mighty people's prosperity, which possessed sea and lands, the entire world over, was not big enough for two ... Caesar could not now bear anyone ahead, nor Pompey any equal.
>
> — Lucan, *Civil War*, 1.109–11; 125–6

During the last years of the 50s BC, while Brutus was busy making a name for himself at Rome, there had been significant shifts in the balance of power between the triumvirs. As had been agreed at Luca in 56 BC, Pompey was still resident in his suburban villa near the capital, governing his Spanish provinces through legates; Caesar was in Gaul where he was expected to remain until 51 or 50 BC, and Crassus had assumed his Syrian command – the whole purpose of which was the war with Parthia. But by the end of the decade this picture looked rather different. Crassus was dead, following a major military defeat in 53 BC: the three men had become two. Worse still for their relationship was the fact that, a year before in 54 BC, Julia – Caesar's only daughter and Pompey's beloved wife – had also died. With both the marriage alliance and the agreement with Crassus dissolved, the only resource left was trust; this, however, was in rapidly depleting supply.

From the start, opponents of the coalition worked to persuade Pompey to rethink his position. Yet the ancient evidence does not point to an immediate breakdown in the Pompey–Caesar coalition following the deaths of Julia and Crassus. Rather, as we shall see, it seems better to accept

Erich Gruen's view that the allies continued to behave towards one another respectfully, albeit rather suspiciously, until the final break occurred around the summer of 50 BC.[1] From that point onwards, however, events spiralled increasingly out of control. There is not space here to chart in detail the origins, means and aims that led to open warfare in 49 BC or to analyse which side (if either) was the more justified in taking the actions it did. But some background to these years is necessary to contextualise the decision facing Brutus over whom to join as Rome headed towards its next major conflict.

On the one hand, there was Pompey. Even though the last three decades of his career had pitched him in opposition to the *nobiles*, Pompey had long hankered for a position of respect within the Senate, and two main factors in the years 53–50 BC had helped him come closer to realising that dream. The first was his new marriage after the death of Julia. Although Caesar had tried to reaffirm their alliance by proposing a fresh engagement, Pompey had declined and instead taken a different bride: in 52 BC, Pompey married Cornelia, the daughter of Quintus Caecilius Metellus Pius Scipio, heir to the legacies of two of Rome's most noble households (the Metelli and the Scipiones).[2] This last point is important because Pompey's marriages tend to reveal something about his political intentions at the time: though he might have claimed to Caesar that he was expanding their network of connections and fortifying their coalition, to any contemporary observer Pompey's marriage marked part of his gradual shift over to the side of the nobility.

The second opportunity for Pompey arose from the extraordinary events that followed the murder of Clodius. As we saw in the last chapter, although men like Brutus and Cicero welcomed Clodius' death and believed he had posed a threat to the *res publica*, as an influential popular politician he had nevertheless accumulated a wide following from a cross-section of the urban populace; such that, in the aftermath of Clodius' death, there were mass riots and violence on the streets of Rome – a crisis which was only averted by the appointment of Pompey as sole consul. For his part, Brutus had protested the amount of power being vested in Pompey's hands, but to the latter's credit he managed to stabilise domestic politics with alarming efficiency. Caesar too had to admit it: 'city affairs had been brought to a more agreeable state by the energy of Pompey'.[3] For as soon as the immediate crisis was over, Pompey made a point of holding elections to appoint a co-consul for the rest of the year; then he held the regular elections so that consuls were in place to succeed him in January 51 BC. By the end of his 'divine third consulship', as Cicero later referred to it, Pompey had restored civil government and shown that he pitched his ambitions within constitutional boundaries, rather than above them.[4] All of this meant that, by the time the civil war began, Pompey could quite consistently claim to represent the cause of the *res publica*.[5]

Caesar, on the other hand, was perceived as a threat to that stability and it left him in a precarious position. What finally turned suspicions between the former allies into open conflict, however, was the debate over Caesar's Gallic command: a political issue which had already dominated senatorial discussions over the course of 51–50 BC. Caesar wanted to come back from Gaul, celebrate a triumph, and enter straight into a second consulship, without laying down his *imperium*. But the law stipulated that electoral hopefuls had to present themselves for candidacy in Rome before the summer elections; which meant Caesar would have to surrender his command and return as a private citizen ahead of his planned departure from Gaul – a circumstance which would have left him vulnerable to legal charges, should his enemies have wished to pursue them.[6] Thus, initially with Pompey's help in 52 BC, Caesar managed to secure legal permission to stand for the office of consul *in absentia*: that is, he did not need to present himself at Rome in the run-up to the election, as the law typically required. However, from March 50 BC onwards, Pompey's position shifted as the debate on this issue raged in the Senate. Pompey wanted to keep his new father-in-law and allies on side; by the same token, there were many senators who wished to drive a wedge between Caesar and Pompey.[7]

At first the focus switched so that the question became the terminal point of Caesar's Gallic command; then it returned to the problem of his candidature *in absentia*. We can follow the twists and turns of the unfolding crisis in the correspondence of Cicero, because the latter was away from Rome, and he had charged his young friend Caelius with the task of keeping him fully informed of developments in the capital – which he did.[8] Unfortunately, however, no mention of Brutus survives in the extant correspondence, so what part, if any, he contributed to all of these debates is unknown – a point to which we shall return shortly, when we analyse his decision. Yet, crucially, Caelius does record the final stance of the two major combatants: 'Pompey has decided not to allow Caesar to be elected consul unless he surrenders his army and provinces; whereas Caesar is persuaded that he cannot be safe if he leaves his army.'[9]

In other words, as the poet Lucan was to put it a century later, the whole empire, not even the world, was big enough for the two men now; a power contest was at last coming to the boil. Pompey had the most support in the Senate: on 1 December 50 BC a proposal that he should give up *his* army was easily defeated, while the proposal that Caesar should do the same was passed. However, a third proposal presented at the same meeting – that Caesar and Pompey should *both* lay down their commands – passed by an overwhelming majority of 370 votes to 22. It offered a glimmer of hope; there was a chance civil war might be averted. Curio, who had put forward the motion, received loud applause when it was announced in the popular assembly; later sources tell us he was showered with garlands and flowers, as if he were a victorious athlete.[10] Yet the compromise was unacceptable to Caesar's enemies. One of the consuls, Gaius Marcellus, a hard-line republican, dismissed the meeting in a rage and shortly afterwards responded by placing a sword in Pompey's hand, urging him to save the *res publica*. In this he was supported by the new consuls for 49 BC, who passed further resolutions to limit Caesar's power until, finally, on 7 January 49 BC, with civil war inevitable, the Senate was persuaded to pass an emergency decree. The result was that, in a matter of days, Caesar had crossed the Rubicon, the small river which separated the frontier of his province from Italy. And from there he marched his army to Rome.[11]

Brutus' Decision

Brutus' silence on the debates over Caesar's command leaves us in a frustrating position when we come to assessing the stance he adopted in these years, and given his outspokenness in previous years it may even require some critical attention. We know that up until 52 BC, Brutus had continued his anti-Pompeian outbursts. But the coalition of senatorial youths who opposed the tyranny of the triumvirs at the beginning of the 50s had long since dissolved. And to go it alone in continued opposition of Pompey thereafter ran the risk of being labelled a Caesarian. Silence, under these circumstances, was preferable to taking sides openly; and Brutus was probably still considered junior enough for his voice in the Senate to perhaps not be expected. It is certainly possible, then, that Brutus positioned himself on the sidelines of the fray – to watch from a distance for as long as he could safely do so.[12] However, as the year 49 BC descended into civil war at dizzying speed, the luxury of avoiding side-taking became an impossible solution – at least for men of Brutus' generation.

In mid-January, as reports reached Rome that Caesar was marching towards the city with his army, Pompey decided to evacuate his supporters from Italy. Meanwhile, many of the Roman senatorial youths were flocking to Caesar. As Caelius had explained to Cicero in the August of 50 BC, although Pompey's cause was the more honourable of the two, 'when it comes to actual fighting a man should reckon the stronger and the safer cause the better'.[13] Although some modern scholars remain divided on the question of how well prepared Pompey really was in the run-up to the civil war – that is, whether Caesar's rapid march to Rome truly caught Pompey by surprise, or whether he had been making preparations for an evacuation long before the January of 49 BC – his contemporaries almost certainly viewed Pompey's side as the weaker militarily.[14]

Caesar was also making overtures to Brutus and others like him by taking up the cause of avenging Pompey's past victims: 'he [Caesar] talks of avenging the deaths of Cn. Carbo and M. Brutus and all those upon whom Sulla inflicted the cruelty in which Pompey participated', Cicero told Atticus.[15] The fact that Caesar had specifically mentioned avenging the death of Marcus Brutus the Elder confirms the proposition that Brutus' support was, or at least appeared to be, for the taking. Nor were Caesar's hopes groundless: he had watched over and supported Brutus' career for several years now;[16] Brutus' sisters were married to prominent Caesarians; and Servilia doubtless encouraged her son to follow the example of his peers and take thought for his future safety under Caesar's protection.[17] We should not forget the influence of the sexagenarian Atticus either. Reading between the lines of his correspondence with Cicero, although he was no advocate of Caesar's, he seemed to hold the opinion that it would be madness to follow Pompey out of Italy.[18]

But still Brutus chose the side of Pompey – the man, as Caesar was reminding him, who had so brutally murdered his father. For, despite Brutus' past enmity towards the 'teenage butcher', the two men had recently cooperated in the defence of their mutual father-in-law, Appius. Whether or not this last act had brought Pompey and Brutus closer together is impossible to know; indeed, Plutarch even claims that Brutus had still never spoken to Pompey, although that is debatable.[19] Either way, what would certainly have influenced Brutus was the fact that many of his closest contacts had joined the 'republican' cause: Appius Claudius, Cato and Bibulus were all there, as well as several other men with whom Brutus was on good terms, including Cassius.[20] Cicero too eventually joined Pompey and his allies, after all attempts at a peaceful mediation had failed. Given the cloak of constitutional correctness the cause donned and its appeal to represent the senatorial side, the final decision of men like Brutus and Cicero was perhaps unsurprising.

Still, Plutarch explains Brutus' move in moral terms – as a clash of private and public duties, over which the common good triumphed[21] – while the poet Lucan fabricates a meeting in which Brutus was persuaded to join the cause by Cato.[22] These representations, however, tell us more about the reception of Brutus and how he was perceived at the time at which these authors were writing, in the first and second centuries AD: as a philosopher, a man of virtue, and a follower of Cato. It is far more likely that a simple combination of personal and political alliances – combined with his natural inclination to champion the senatorial cause – had influenced Brutus' decision. Above all, however, he acted according to an ancient concept of obligation (*necessitudo*), the powerful bond which tied him to his family and friends, especially his father-in-law.[23]

Even so, Brutus did not join Pompey and his forces straight away but, instead, set off once again for Cilicia, where he served as a legate to Publius Sestius in 49 BC. His activities there are nowhere documented, nor do we have a precise timetable for his next major steps. It is possible that his main contribution to the war efforts at this stage was to recruit men to serve on Pompey's fleet, as Walter Stewens has suggested. Or he may have used the journey as a cover to check in on his own financial interests in the province. A more likely explanation, however, is that he engaged in both activities as he prepared for the war and his own long-term security.[24] In any case, he was probably on the move again by the end of 49 BC, and we know for certain that Brutus was fully settled in Pompey's military camp in Dyrrachium by June 48 BC at the latest.[25] That month Cicero sent a letter to Atticus: 'Brutus is my friend; he is zealous in the cause', he wrote. 'But that is as much as I can prudently put on paper.'[26]

This tantalisingly brief mention is the closest we get to a contemporary glimpse of Brutus in action, and it forms an intriguing snapshot of a man firmly committed to the war against Caesar.[27] However, Cicero's comment that he cannot prudently give much away also explains why precise information is nowhere available: it was simply not safe to exchange news of the war's progress. Nor were there many records to be found after the war, if we are to trust the story found in Dio, that Caesar promptly burned any documents and letters he found in Pompey's camp for fear he might be forced to take severe measures by their contents.[28] But the biographical tradition surrounding Brutus does at least sketch in some of the gaps for his role in what happened next, and so Plutarch's *Life of Brutus* must be called in aid. However, even that does not provide us with all the information we might hope to find there.

We do not know for certain that Brutus actually fought in the decisive battle of Pharsalus in the August of 48 BC;[29] or whether he played a role in the smaller battle of Dyrrachium earlier in July, when the Pompeians scored a victory against the Caesarians.[30] Plutarch tells us that, when he was not with Pompey, Brutus immersed himself in literature – even up to the moment of the great battle. Such stories may well have been embellished to help develop Plutarch's portrait of a man devoted to the maintenance of his routine and literary pursuits; or 'a philosopher going about his business', as John Moles has put it.[31] However, one thing that seems sure is that Brutus was not entrusted with a major military command at any point during the campaign.[32]

None of this should be taken to suggest that Brutus was entirely inactive in the camp, or that his presence was only required as a trophy name for the republican side, as some have assumed.[33] As mentioned above, Cicero considered him a zealot to that cause and, at the very least, as we shall see, Caesar *expected* him to make an appearance on the battlefield. Thus, it is by no means impossible that Brutus played his part in the fighting and he was certainly included among Pompey's innermost circle of advisers. Whatever role he took, then, there was no denying that Brutus bore some responsibility for the mass of Roman bloodshed: he was culpable either indirectly as an adviser to Pompey, or directly by fighting on the battlefield – or perhaps both. The question facing him after Pharsalus was whether he wanted more.

The Dictator's Pardon

Despite the numerical superiority of the Pompeian forces at Pharsalus, on 9 August 48 BC they suffered a crushing defeat: thousands of Pompey's men were slain, compared to just a few hundred Caesarians.[34] Consequently, in the words of one modern biographer, Pompey's 'nerve cracked' and he swiftly fled from the battle to review his options.[35] Some of his supporters followed him, first to Mytilene and then to Cilicia, where Pompey held a council of war; others regrouped at Corcyra (Corfu), from where Cato later led them to Libya.[36] But Brutus, independently minded as ever and not as consistent as his uncle, chose a different path for himself: a path which he may have known remained open when *his* nerve cracked in the face of Caesar's almost certain victory. For although Brutus had thrown in his lot with Pompey at the start of the war, Caesar's special concern for Servilia's son had by no means diminished. Indeed, the dictator was quite explicit on this point: should any of his officers come across him in the battle lines, he is reported to have ordered that no one was to kill Brutus.[37] It may come as little surprise, then, that it was to Caesar that Brutus now turned.

According to Plutarch, shortly after Pompey's own flight from battle, Brutus dared a night escape through marshlands to the nearby city of

Larissa, from where he sent a letter to the victorious general.[38] And just as Pompey had greeted the young man with open arms at the onset of the battle, so Caesar welcomed him graciously among his number at Pharsalus' end.[39] It stands as testament to the high regard (*existimatio*, in the Latin) commanded by Brutus that the leaders on both sides of the dispute welcomed his presence in their camps. But the propagandistic value and prestige that derived from high-profile defectors such as Brutus should not be overlooked either. Caesar's own programme of *clementia* in offering mercy to his former opponents was, to be sure, a remarkable departure from the gruesome precedents of earlier generations of fighters; there were no Marian bloodbaths or Sullan proscriptions this time. However, Caesar's pardoning act was also a strategic and carefully calculated move. A tendency to elevate Caesar's generosity and compare it to Brutus' ultimate betrayal has often clouded the picture of what was a mutually beneficial agreement. Brutus had accepted a favour (a *beneficium*) from Caesar and was henceforth obliged to him.

It has been suggested that his first repayment of Caesar's kindness and proof of his loyalty came when Brutus disclosed information about Pompey's whereabouts after Pharsalus.[40] The foundation for this belief rests with Plutarch, who tells us that it was only after Caesar sounded Brutus out on the topic that he focused exclusively on and hastened towards Egypt in pursuit of Pompey. But it is an act which sits uncomfortably in the pages of scholarship on Brutus. Later writers and analysts who accept the story have consequently censured Brutus for his treachery and disloyalty to Pompey; others have tried to dismiss the reliability of Plutarch's account or ignored it altogether.[41] On balance, however, it is likely that something of the sort did happen, but perhaps not entirely in the manner described by Plutarch.[42]

We can fairly imagine that Brutus had assumed an advisory role within the camp of Caesar; this would be in line with his station and experience. But the revelation of Pompey's plans cannot have resulted in the same affirmative action as Plutarch suggests. For a start, Pompey himself had not decided on a firm plan of action when he escaped the field; nor was Brutus present at the council of war, when the decision for Egypt was finally sealed. However, Brutus did have inside knowledge of the options facing Pompey and it is not unreasonable that Caesar asked his opinion. Given the position he now found himself in, and presumably because Caesar was not broadcasting any intention to kill Pompey, there was probably little that Brutus could do but to offer his thoughts on the matter: Pompey's options were Parthia, Africa and Egypt.[43]

It is important to note, however, that Pompey's own first preference as a destination was Parthia, because it reaffirms that Brutus would not have been able to second-guess Pompey's movements with any certainty, as Plutarch himself seems to imply. Caesar, too, says as much in his own first-hand account of the civil war: Pompey's plans were difficult to gauge.[44] And so we may as well also bear in mind Caesar's own reconstruction of events: namely, that he first made his way to Asia where he heard Pompey had been spotted at Cyprus, and only then guessed that Pompey was heading for Egypt. After all, it was only a three-day journey from Cyprus to Egypt, where Caesar also knew Pompey had local connections.[45]

As it happened, the decision to travel to Egypt proved disastrous on Pompey's part. Defeated in war and with a much weakened force, he sent a messenger in advance to announce his arrival and ask for help. But, far from being welcomed, Pompey was stabbed to death and beheaded: the thirteen-year-old Egyptian king Ptolemy had been persuaded to champion the rising star of Caesar, for whom Pompey's severed head was hence preserved as a special gift. By killing his foe, Ptolemy's advisers had sought to win the dictator's favour. However, the story goes that when Caesar arrived in Alexandria he turned away in horror at the sight of the gruesome remains and burst into tears when presented with Pompey's signet ring. His distress may or may not have been feigned; later writers attempting to reconstruct the scene said that the hypocrisy of it was transparent.[46] Either way, if Ptolemy's advisers were disappointed by Caesar's reaction, they were horrified at what happened next, when Caesar stayed and became embroiled in Egypt's own civil war – as well as with Cleopatra, the 21-year-old exiled queen who was fighting her younger brother for the throne.

At this point, Brutus fades out of the picture as our sources instead focus on the famous meeting of Cleopatra and Caesar, as well as their subsequent love affair. Scholars have hence suggested a range of alternatives for Brutus' movements after accepting Caesar's pardon: perhaps he remained in Greece, or maybe he returned to his affairs in Cilicia; after all, his contacts there could have proved useful for the Caesarian cause.[47] It is tempting, however, to imagine that Brutus accompanied Caesar to Egypt as part of his entourage;[48] if so, he would have been there when two of Ptolemy's advisers, Pothinus and Achillas, were killed on Caesar's orders; and he might have witnessed the death of the young Ptolemy himself, in battle early the following year; if he was there, he might even have encountered Theodotus the Sophist, who had been a third adviser instrumental in the decision to kill Pompey. If so, it would lend a nice circularity to the narrative of Pompey's death, because this Theodotus had managed to escape and evade punishment; yet several years later, in 42 BC, it was said that Brutus found Theodotus in Asia and had him put to death with every possible form of torture.[49] He may not have been Pompey's friend, but still Brutus succeeded in avenging the death of a commander of the Roman people.

The truth is, however, that we do not know where Brutus was during the events of 48–47 BC; only that he may have been in Cilicia in the early part of 47 BC, when Caesar visited the capital city of Tarsus, and that he may have accompanied the dictator as he proceeded to Asia Minor, where he intended to engage in battle with the eastern potentate Pharnaces II.[50] Our first real sighting of him in the evidence comes in August 47 BC, at Nicaea, as Caesar journeyed back through the provinces following his swift victory against Pharnaces in Zela – the occasion of his famous boast *veni, vidi, vici* ('I came, I saw, I conquered').

As he concluded his operations in the east, Caesar heard and settled all the disputes there, and among those which came to adjudication were the territorial claims of the Galatian king, Deiotarus. This man had earlier sought Caesar's pardon for having supported Pompey in the civil war, and now Deiotarus begged the dictator to review the terms of that pardon which had limited his territories. But what is most interesting about this episode for our purposes is that representing and speaking in Deiotarus' interests was Brutus, who gave an impassioned plea that both moved and impressed Caesar. Brutus spoke with 'great spirit and freedom', Cicero later commented. And even though his speech did not entirely win the day, for the king was still stripped of many territories, the important part was that Brutus had tried.[51]

This episode, Brutus' first appearance since his escape from Pharsalus, goes some way towards helping us understand his new position and status under Caesar, and it shows that even now Brutus was not afraid to speak his own mind. Caesar himself is said to have commented on this feature of Brutus' personality in an oft-discussed piece of wordplay: *magni refert hic quid velit, sed quicquid vult valde vult*, which means 'it matters greatly what that man wants, but whatever he wants, he wants it very much'.[52] But what exactly did Caesar mean by this?

Biographers of Brutus are wont to use Caesar's expression as evidence for the young man's character or intentions; a contemporary reflection on either Brutus' obstinacy, his peculiar independence of mind, or even his unpredictability.[53] Some have even suggested we should read the future tense *volet* ('he will want') instead of the present tense *vult* ('he wants'), to argue that Caesar could foresee his grim and violent end at the hands of Brutus: 'whatever he will want, he will want strongly'.[54] Interpreted this way,

Caesar's remark becomes a harrowing assessment of the extent to which Brutus would push his ambition. But to read Caesar's dictum as a prediction of his own doom places too much value on hindsight; subjectivity too risks distorting the evidence. Instead, we will find it more constructive to consider the original context that occasioned Caesar's comment. For Cicero's letter makes it clear that, whatever Caesar inferred by the expression in later reiterations of it (he was allegedly proud of the witticism), he had initially been commenting on the quality of Brutus' oratory. We should focus then on the fact that, according to the report Cicero heard, Brutus possessed force (*vis*) and spoke freely (*libere dicere*), as well as the effect this speech had on his audience.

Three points subsequently emerge from the story of Brutus' passionate and forceful appeal. To begin with, these are not features of Brutus' oratory that are often commented upon. And such an assessment challenges the general consensus that Brutus' speech was lacklustre and unemotional.[55] For the force with which he spoke on this particular occasion was apparently remarkable; even Cicero had to admit it. In his dialogue on the history of oratory, Cicero says he had heard that Brutus spoke with the best ornaments (*ornatissime*) and great richness of speech (*copiossime*) – which is high praise indeed, when we reflect that these were the very qualities that gave oratory its edge (the *vis oratoria*) in the ancient rhetorical tradition.[56]

Secondly, Brutus' speech signals the autonomy of his mind. It is entirely possible that Caesar wanted a vigorous presentation of Deiotarus' case to indicate his own commitment to justice and good government. Yet even so, the fact that Brutus was the man to deliver the defence of Deiotarus' interests is consistent with Brutus' own political line; after all, Deiotarus had a long-standing connection with Cato which Brutus seems to have continued.[57] Thus, living under Caesar's dictatorship does not seem, for Brutus, to have meant compromising his political position yet. In turn, Caesar had seen a new side to Brutus' determination: an attitude he seems to have appreciated more than feared.

Yet a third point also arises from the fact that Caesar was not entirely clear what Brutus was passionate about, hence part of the play on words resting on what Brutus wanted: 'it matters greatly what that man wants, but whatever he wants, he wants it very much'. By choice, perhaps, rather than by a lack of ability, Brutus' political statements were vague. When we reflect that Brutus' whole career displays a remarkable knack for political side-switching, this point may be more relevant than at first appears. His oratory was forceful and impressive to onlookers, but like many a political leader, he may have exploited vague expressions as a tactical strategy: in being non-committal, Brutus tried to speak to everyone.[58] If this reconstruction of his abilities is correct, it was a skill that was to serve Brutus well in the anxious times ahead, as he worked with Caesar towards a programme of rehabilitation after a bitterly contested civil war.

Coming to Terms with Caesar

Brutus may have been the first prominent republican to defect to Caesar, but he was not alone in his decision to leave the war after Pharsalus. Throughout 47 BC, Brutus worked hard to secure grants of pardon for other former comrades, and Plutarch tells us that Caesar bestowed mercy upon many ex-Pompeians, including Cassius, at Brutus' request.[59] Cicero too was one of the men who refused to continue the fight after Pompey's defeat; however, unlike those who had travelled to Greece or Asia to receive the dictator's pardon, Cicero made his way back to Italy where he was expecting Caesar to return. But the more Caesar's return was delayed by his wars, the more anxious Cicero became as he was forced to wait at the harbour town of Brundisium. His letters from August 48 to September 47 BC tell a bleak story as he waited to receive Caesar's formal interview: he felt despondent and alone – a cast-off from the republicans, and not fully accepted by the Caesarians either.[60]

What made matters worse was that, at least from the beginning of 47 BC, the republican camp in Africa was regaining its strength: 'Unbearably painful as my circumstances are', Cicero confessed to Atticus, 'the worst part is to find myself in a situation where my only advantage lies in what I would never wish for [i.e. a victory for Caesar].'[61] However, news from Alexandria was in short supply and people began to fear that Caesar's position was weakening. By April of that year, Cicero had heard that several ex-Pompeians were even changing sides again, to rejoin Cato and his troops. As Cicero saw it, some of these men had a loophole and a reasonable chance of making peace with their former comrades: some had been taken prisoner and others had been cut off. And then, Cicero adds, 'there are many who will be welcomed back no matter how they return to the fold'.[62] He was presumably thinking of men like Brutus, who could quite easily gain readmittance to Cato's circle, and it is impossible not to detect a note of bitterness in Cicero's tone.

Yet throughout this period of Cicero's suffering the two men were in touch and Brutus even tried to encourage the senior statesman's hopes. One letter in particular, which Brutus sent from the province of Asia, was a cause of great comfort and it helped restore Cicero to life and literary activity – or so he wrote later in 46 BC, when he composed his dialogue on oratory, *Brutus*, named after its eponymous dedicatee.[63] The letter itself does not survive but it contained prudent advice and friendly consolation; according to Cicero, Brutus reminded the senior statesman of his achievements and the eternal glory they would guarantee him. Such words were sweet to his ears and, although Cicero largely shied away from the public eye during this period, a shared intellectual appreciation did at least develop between Cicero and Brutus.[64] In addition to *Brutus*, a review of the great orators of the last two or three generations, Cicero composed another treatise, *Orator*, which was likewise dedicated to his younger friend. Both these works were composed in the early months of 46 BC, but they are only a fraction of the vast output Cicero achieved. Before the end of 44 BC he had added books on ethical theory, philosophical thought, and topics to do with suffering, death and immortality. There were essays on fate and divination, as well as friendship and old age – to mention but a few.

Brutus, too, was spurred on in his literary activity with philosophical works such as *On Virtue* (*De Virtute*), *On Duties* (*Peri Kathēkontos*) and *On Endurance* (*De Patientia*), all known to have been published by him.[65] Only three words survive of the last – 'they mock these men's tears' (*inridunt horum lacrimas*) – which barely makes an analysis of its content possible. But, according to the Roman philosopher Seneca, by reading Brutus' work *On Duties*, you could find all you ever needed to know about how to behave as a parent, a child or a brother – even if, as Seneca complained, it lacked rigorous philosophical precepts upon which men should base their conduct. As for his work *On Virtue* Seneca had read this too and he provides some clues as to its argument.[66]

Among the 'cast' of Brutus' *On Virtue* we know was featured Marcus Marcellus, a staunch opponent of Caesar's who had taken himself into voluntary exile after Pharsalus and there remained in a state of self-sufficiency. From what we can glean of the work, Brutus recalled visiting Marcellus on the island of Mytilene on his return from Nicaea in 47 BC, and his composition showed Marcellus 'living as happily as it is permitted to man to live, and never keener in his pursuit of literature than at that time'. The reason, in Brutus' words, was that: 'those who go into exile are free to take their own virtues with them'.[67] From these small snippets, it seems that in his philosophical works Brutus had much to say on the necessity of virtue for a happy life and the importance of family obligations. And we should not fail to mention here that these are two key themes in the biographical tradition surrounding Brutus: we have already seen how important Brutus' reputation for virtue was to him; in time, we shall also discover the depth of his familial devotion.

However, the fragments and *testimonia* of his *On Virtue* also provide some useful biographical data which we can use to follow Brutus' movements and feelings as he returned to Italy at the end of 47 BC. From what Seneca tells us it seems that Brutus left the east at the same time as Caesar. Yet, whereas Caesar continued sailing past Mytilene on the journey back, 'because he could not bear to look upon a degraded man', Brutus had stopped at the island to conduct his meeting with Marcellus. It was an encounter which purportedly caused Brutus to reflect on how he, returning to Italy after the war, felt more of an exile in leaving Marcellus than Marcellus was in remaining at Mytilene.[68] Part of Seneca's purpose in quoting Brutus was to reassure his own mother Helvia that he, Seneca, was not personally suffering in exile, and to this end Marcellus' case demonstrated that to the wise man the entire world was his country. Yet his observations on Brutus' state of mind should not be passed over; Brutus 'grieved' to leave Marcellus behind, Seneca tells us, and he wanted his companion back at Rome. We cannot know whether Brutus really felt this way as he made his journey back to Italy, but Quintilian – an ardent student and teacher of rhetoric, writing in the first century AD – found his expressions sincere: 'you know he means what he says', was his considered verdict.[69]

Even then, however, Brutus did not return to Rome immediately but instead journeyed from Mytilene to Samos, where he met another old connection: Servius Sulpicius Rufus, a distinguished and committed republican who had avoided the war altogether by remaining neutral and leaving Italy.[70] About the same age as Cicero, Sulpicius enjoyed a reputation for legal knowledge and Brutus spent some of his time there studying the relationship between pontifical law and civil law – a point that hints at the role Brutus would be resuming as *pontifex* upon his return.[71] But was there another purpose to Brutus' visit besides his studies? For in a telling move, Sulpicius was soon afterwards pardoned by Caesar and even appointed to the prestigious post of governor of Achaea for 46 BC. Was this, then, the real reason for this stop at Samos, as well as for his visit to Marcellus, and even perhaps the sweet words of encouragement to Cicero: in other words, was Brutus on a recruitment drive for Caesar?[72]

That Caesar enlisted former Pompeians to help mediate with others is clear enough from the contemporary evidence: thus, in the words of Cicero, Cassius played the part of 'ambassador' and 'intercessor' in the province of Achaea.[73] And Brutus, it appears, was performing a similar role, negotiating the return and rehabilitation of his former comrades in 47 BC. In this connection, the successful story of Sulpicius' promotion under Caesar might serve us well in reconstructing Brutus' intentions for visiting or writing to men who had either opposed or failed to support the dictator before; and it might further explain why he was particularly aggrieved to leave behind Marcellus, whom he had failed to persuade. But what was in it for him? For it is important to stress that Brutus was not simply furthering Caesar's agenda; there are ostensible reasons why Brutus would have wanted to help in the formation and publicising of Caesar's platform.

Perhaps, we can assume, the return of all these men would have eased Brutus' own conscience at having accepted Caesar's pardon, rather than continuing the fight under his uncle Cato. To this end, the fact that Cicero was already at Rome meant that Brutus only needed to convince the elder statesman that his conduct was consistent with the republican principles for which he had always fought. And we should also not overlook that the *res publica* of former years had always depended on having a body of wise ex-consuls and aristocrats for its success and survival. In working for the restoration of men like Marcellus and Sulpicius Rufus, then, Brutus arguably had in view a return, as far as possible, to the senatorial *status quo* in the days before civil strife. But, as he made his return journey to Rome, now in the service of Caesar, it does not seem to have entered Brutus' mind to question what a *res publica* might look like with Caesar at the helm.

Cato's Last Fight

While Brutus lingered at Mytilene and Samos in the late summer of 47 BC, Caesar pressed on and arrived back in Rome in September of that year; about a month later Brutus too was home. But no sooner had Caesar returned than he was off again, in December 47 BC, to fight the republican forces who were continuing the civil war in Africa under the leadership of Cato and Metellus Scipio (Pompey's former father-in-law). Unsurprisingly, Brutus did not go with him; nor did Cicero or any other ex-Pompeian. The wait for news prompted much anxiety in Cicero: talk of politics brought only troubles and apprehension.[74] For, if the outcome went in Cato's and Scipio's favour, there would be challenging times ahead for the men who had defected from the republican cause, and there would always be the fear of how Caesar's men in Italy would react at either outcome.

Yet things stood rather differently for Brutus. Before Caesar left for Africa he had entrusted him with the governorship of Cisalpine Gaul, a highly esteemed position for two reasons.[75] First, Brutus probably went to the province with the standing of an ex-praetor (as *legatus pro praetore*), which bestowed *imperium* upon the young man and the right to command an army – a significant leap when we remember that he had never held any office higher than the quaestorship before.[76] Second, the strategic position occupied by Cisalpine Gaul implies that Caesar had faith in Brutus; it was the very location from which Caesar had crossed into Italy at the head of an army back at the beginning of the civil war, and not one over which he would grant control lightly. 'There you reap the full reward for your virtue', Cicero remarked in his *Orator*, with evident approval of Brutus' conduct. It may have been little more than a conventional compliment, but he was not the only one to comment on Brutus' alleged success. Thus, Decimus Brutus – a relative of Marcus' and later a governor of the region – reported to Cicero that the Gauls still remembered Brutus kindly three years after he had left the province, while Plutarch tells us that the people erected a bronze statue in his honour.[77] Otherwise, however, we hear next to nothing about Brutus' provincial administration, which lasted through 46 until March 45 BC.[78]

Meanwhile, civil war was raging in Africa, where on 6 April 46 BC Caesar's army routed that of Metellus Scipio at Thapsus. The republicans were all but defeated, though Cato himself had not been with them; he had stayed behind to guard the city of Utica, which lay to the north of Thapsus, and to which Caesar quickly advanced. This was Cato's last stand for the freedom of Rome, a fight Brutus had already given up on, and our sources tell us he played it out in a scene of heroic martyrdom. First, he saw that all the survivors were evacuated and that the fleet was safe. But, then, as the news arrived that Caesar was approaching, Cato decided to take his own life rather than accept the pardon of a dictator, or else engage in further warfare and face the disgrace of defeat.[79]

The details of his death are gruesome and dramatic. Plutarch tells us that Cato took his sword, read Plato's dialogue *On the Soul*, and then stabbed himself below the breast before tearing at the wound to release his bowels.[80] Such, at least, were the stories which circulated after his death; almost immediately, Cato's suicide earned him the status of a legend. Cato had preferred to die rather than look on the face of a tyrant, wrote Cicero in the months after Caesar's death.[81] By the time of Seneca, the name of Cato was synonymous with the principles of both *libertas* and the *res publica*.[82] But how was Cato's end viewed by those living at the time? And how did Brutus react to the fact of his uncle's suicide?

Champion of Cato, Champion of Caesar

News of the death of Cato evidently spread fast, for back in Italy Cicero was already considering writing a eulogy of him just one month later, in May.[83]

But this, Cicero complained to Atticus, was a 'problem for Archimedes': how could he go about praising the man without paying tribute to his greatest feat – the fact that he had foreseen and sought to prevent Caesar's domination, even to the point that he had abandoned his life rather than witness it happen. Such content would certainly be taken as an affront by Caesar and the other Caesarians, with whom he was now associating. Indeed, when he composed his treatise *Orator* in the latter part of the same year, Cicero could not help but reflect on the enormity of the task, his reluctance to undertake it at the time, and his fear that he might be held to blame for its contents. But he was doing it at the request of Brutus, he added, prompting some to think he was hiding behind Brutus' name as if it were a shield.[84]

As we shall soon see, Brutus too eventually went on to write his own version of a *Cato*, but we might still question why he turned to Cicero to make this request in the first instance. After all, as Cato's nephew and his closest adult relative, Brutus might have been expected to write the eulogy; what is more, he had already written and circulated one for his father-in-law Appius, who died just before the battle of Pharsalus.[85] Perhaps Brutus simply saw the request as an extension of the general intellectual exchange between himself and Cicero at the time; he may also have thought that Cicero's authority would make more of an impact than his own. In return, Cicero's own admiration of Cato, coupled with the fact that the older man had long sought to obligate Brutus to himself, might explain why the first work entitled *Cato* came from Cicero. More cynically, however, we might ask whether Brutus wanted to transfer the responsibility of commemorating Cato onto Cicero, so that he need not risk offending Caesar himself – as Maria Dettenhofer has suggested.[86]

The truth, if we can ever hope to know it, probably includes some element of all these suggestions. But I would also argue for a more nuanced explanation, and one which is entirely consistent with Brutus' own policy at the time. For, as we have seen, in the years 48–46 BC, Brutus had worked hard to secure the integration of former Pompeians within Caesar's new *res publica*, while, now, after Thapsus, he could turn his attention to building a bridge between the dictator and the men who had fought under Cato. This hypothesis may help us go some way towards understanding the circumstances that led to the production of the first volumes on Cato, as well as the larger picture behind Brutus' grand strategy. But first we must try to reconstruct something of the form and contents of the eulogies, as well as the verdicts that were pronounced upon them.

Snippets of information preserved in the ancient sources cannot make up for the fact that neither Cicero's nor Brutus' *Cato* has been preserved;

however, they do provide some context. For, although Cicero was personally pleased with the results of his version, which he finished in the summer of 46 BC, Caesar was less enthralled.[87] Politely he commented on its literary quality and showered Cicero with praise for the power of his expression. But he cannot have approved of the content: that Cato was 'in every respect greater in fact than he was famed to be' is one of the only fragments to survive, and it gives us a strong hint of the tone.[88] An even clearer indication might be sourced from the response it prompted: for Caesar felt compelled to write an *Anti-Cato*, in two volumes, containing a whole catalogue of scurrilous charges against Cato, from accusations of incest, drinking and debauchery, to attacks on the way he treated his friends and wife.[89] So that no time should be lost, Caesar also ordered his friend Hirtius to write one too – a preview of which reached Cicero at the beginning of May 45 BC.[90]

Before then, however – and possibly to avert what he perceived as a diplomatic crisis – Brutus had also set to work on his own *Cato*, which he sent to Cicero in March 45 BC. However, this time it was Cicero who was displeased; not so much at the general tenor of the piece but because Brutus had, in Cicero's words, been 'shamefully ignorant' about one point in particular: Cato's role in the Catilinarian conspiracy of 63 BC. In Cicero's eyes, this had been the crowning moment of his own political career: the moment he saved Rome from an attempted coup d'état by relentlessly pursuing and exposing its leader, the patrician Lucius Sergius Catilina (Catiline), and then executing several of Catiline's urban accomplices caught in the act of plotting the takeover.[91] Yet Brutus had given the starring role to Cato, whose argument in support of execution had spectacularly trumped Caesar's proposal that the conspirators should be put under house arrest. Worse still, Brutus had diminished the part Cicero had played: 'he only praises me for bringing the question before the Senate – not for revealing it, or for urging the senators on, or for passing my own verdict before consulting them', he complained to Atticus.[92]

What, then, had Brutus been hoping to achieve by pitching Caesar and Cato as the chief protagonists in the Catilinarian conspiracy at the expense of Cicero? We cannot of course recover his authorial intention, especially not from so few *testimonia*. But it is interesting to set beside this account one other possible indication of the contents of Brutus' *Cato*, preserved for us almost incidentally in a passage of Plutarch, in which Brutus criticises the suicide of Cato at Utica.[93] 'I blamed Cato for making away with himself', Brutus is made to say to Cassius in the *Life of Brutus*, 'because it was impious and unmanly to yield to one's evil genius, not accepting fearlessly whatever befalls, but running away.' In other words, taking a view straight out of the pages of Plato, where Socrates condemns suicide as an act of cowardice and desertion, Brutus was known to have condemned rather than celebrated the death of his uncle.[94] If we can locate the source for this anecdote in Brutus' own published *Cato*, then the form and function of that work at once become more tangible.

The fact that Brutus' *Cato* may have contained narratives of the Catilinarian conspiracy and (possibly) Cato's death suggests it was essentially biographical in nature.[95] And yet, without denying Cato's committed and celebrated career, it also seems to have emphasised and even exaggerated the moments at which his uncle came into head-to-head conflict with Caesar. His aim was not to strike a blow at Caesar, and it may even have highlighted his *clementia*: both in his proposal to avert the execution of the Catilinarian conspirators and in the pardon he would have extended to Cato, had the latter not ended his life. But the point is this: if I am right to suggest that Brutus' strategy in 45 BC was to somehow make himself agreeable to supporters both of Cato and Caesar, then both details from the *Cato* speak to this agenda. As Alexei Zadorojnyi has said of other pro-Catonian writers, the trend was not to gloss over the controversial aspects of his life and personality; rather, Brutus' strategy may have been to assemble a 'realistically idealized' picture of Cato – one which admitted his defects while reinterpreting them 'as shortcomings on the essentially right side of *virtus*'.[96] Thus Brutus' eulogy for Cato seems to have pitched his uncle as ideologically, philosophically and politically at loggerheads with Caesar – the other 'great man' in the narrative. Its great achievement, however, was that it did so in a way that also reflected positively on the dictator.

Working for Caesar

When Brutus sent his *Cato* to Cicero in March 45 BC, he was probably already on his way back to Rome. But the relationship between Cicero and Brutus had seemingly taken a turn for the worse, with the result that Atticus was largely mediating between the two men. To start with, Cicero did not know where Brutus was: on 14 March, he reported that Brutus' replacement as governor was probably on his way; on 23 March, he was predicting that Brutus would return in April, when in fact the young man was back in the city by 25 March.[97] To Atticus at least it seemed that Cicero was to blame for avoiding Brutus; yet Cicero in turn asked Atticus to scold Brutus for not visiting him at Cumae.[98] The cause for their rift, however, was not just the dispute over their respective *Catos* (although that cannot have helped); Cicero, in particular, had personal matters preoccupying his mind.

In February 45 BC Cicero's beloved daughter Tullia had died in childbirth; nor did her baby son survive beyond the end of March.[99] Although his friends, including Brutus, had sent him letters of consolation, nothing worked: 'Brutus' letter was written both sensibly and friendlily', he confided in Atticus, 'but it cost me many tears.' Elsewhere, he added: 'There was much wisdom in it, but nothing that could lighten my spirits.'[100] Cicero was experiencing one of the darkest times of his life, and he was inconsolable. But there is more than one hint in his writings that he felt especially let down by Brutus and Atticus. Some of Cicero's friends were criticising the prolongment of his grief; Atticus had told him that others were talking in 'far sterner' words than he or Brutus had used in their letters. More precisely, Brutus had criticised Cicero for not bearing his grief like a man should; the philosophers after all commended iron self-control in the face of loss.[101] Cicero had himself praised Caesar's reaction to Julia's death in 54 BC on precisely these grounds and, in time, he would urge Brutus to stay focused on business when his wife died.[102] Brutus' advice might appear unfeeling to a modern reader, but it appears to reflect a general attitude of the day. And by the beginning of June 45 BC, he and Cicero were back on more amiable terms.

By that time, however, Brutus' actions were also causing quite a stir in political circles. Shortly after his return from Cisalpine Gaul he divorced Claudia, his wife of almost ten years; a move which prompted speculation that Brutus was dissociating himself from the lost cause of the Pompeians.[103] After all, Appius Claudius, his father-in-law, had died shortly before the battle of Pharsalus, while the husband of Claudia's sister, the young Gnaeus Pompeius, had also recently perished in Caesar's last battle against the republican survivors – the battle of Munda in March 45 BC. Was this another signal that Brutus was siding ever closer with the Caesarians and abandoning his past allies? On the contrary, as insiders already knew, a second bride was waiting in the wings: Porcia – the daughter of Cato and widow of Bibulus, both men enemies to Caesar. Cicero, for one, was keen that the new marriage be conducted as quickly as possible: 'so he might extinguish or dampen down all this tittle-tattle', he remarked.[104] And so it was: at some point towards the end of June 45 BC Brutus and Porcia were married. His commitment to the memory of Cato and the cause for which he had once fought seemed simultaneously proven and fulfilled.

As always, several theories have evolved over Brutus' decision to marry Porcia. Some biographers have sought to explain the seemingly inexplicable move and the speed with which the marriage was conducted by resorting to the idea that it was a genuine love match.[105] Others see in Brutus' marriage firm evidence of his sense of obligation to the dead Cato, and even a move away from Caesar. In support of this hypothesis, we might add the reactions of Servilia and Porcia, who did not take fondly to one another. 'The ladies are hardly behaving considerately in letting their hostilities show', Cicero remarked to Atticus.[106] When we remember that Servilia was the friend and prior lover of Caesar, while Porcia was Cato's daughter, the bad relations between mother and daughter-in-law are not altogether surprising. Looked at from another perspective, however, Brutus had forced two diametrically opposed women each to be bound to him in terms of unfailing loyalty – as mother and as wife.[107] Thus, we cannot exclude the possibility that Brutus' marriage to Porcia was politically motivated after all. In fact, it was perfectly consistent with Brutus' position in 45 BC as the natural heir to Cato's circle and as a champion of Caesar's new *res publica*.

More than anything else, in the years after the civil war, Caesar desired to win the political contest by securing acceptance from everyone who held a stake in the Roman community – both at home, in the provinces and across the empire at large. And, as we have seen throughout this chapter, no one had embraced Caesar's policy of reconciliation more than Brutus. In fact, when Caesar finally returned to Italy, victorious from the battle of Munda, with the final republican wing defeated, Brutus went to meet him.[108] Far from being annoyed at Brutus for making his own reconciliation with Cato's circle, Caesar took great delight in Brutus' company: he complimented his recruit and he was particularly pleased with the way Brutus had conducted affairs in Cisalpine Gaul. As a reward, Brutus was promised the urban praetorship for the following year, 44 BC – purportedly much to the chagrin of Cassius, who had to make do with the less prestigious peregrine praetorship – and it may have been now that he also earmarked Brutus for one of the two consulships of 41 BC.[109]

All of this led Brutus to hold positive hopes for the future of the *res publica* under Caesar. He even tried to persuade Cicero that Caesar had joined the side of the right-minded republicans. 'Halleluiah!' was Cicero's sardonic reply, 'but where is he going to find them unless he hangs himself?' All the men Cicero had once called 'good' (the *boni*) were dead; at the same time, he was beginning to have serious doubts about Brutus' own political inclinations: 'As for *him*, Caesar has his back', he wrote to Atticus. Brutus had forgotten his ancestry – or so Cicero claimed: 'What then of that work of art of yours?' he asked, referring to the family tree Atticus had once created for the young man, displaying his claim to descend from Lucius Brutus and Servilius Ahala. But Cicero did not push his criticisms too far: 'What else is he to do, after all?'[110]

The civil war had cut a deep and irreparable swathe through the ranks of Rome's politicians between 49 and 45 BC. At various times, men had been forced to decide who were their friends and who their enemies, whether to make their peace or continue with the bitter fighting. But now in 45 BC Caesar had emerged as the unambiguous winner. Many men had died, and many survived. Some, like Brutus, had even prospered – thanks to his quick decision to defect to Caesar in 48 BC and his loyal service thereafter. By the late summer of 45 BC, then, when Caesar finally returned to Rome, there was every reason for Brutus to think that he had made the right decision in accepting the dictator's pardon, and he appears to have held – or at least he professed to hold – high hopes for the *res publica* under Caesar's watch.

But, in less than six months' time, Caesar would be lying dead on the Senate floor; as we shall see, much happened in the intervening period to turn Brutus' mind against his friend and benefactor.

CHAPTER 4

THINKING ABOUT TYRANNICIDE

Caesar and the New Order

> Should a man remain in his country under a tyranny? Should he endeavour to depose tyranny by all means possible, even if the existence of the state will be put at risk as a result? Should a man beware of the liberator in case that man is himself elevated? Should he try to help his country under a tyranny by seizing an opportunity and by diplomacy rather than by war? Should a statesman live quietly in retirement while his country is under a tyranny, or should he run every risk in defence of freedom?
>
> — Cicero, *To Atticus*, 9.4.2 = SB 173

Back in 49 BC, when the civil war between Pompey and Caesar looked certain, Cicero had contemplated the outcome and concluded that, whichever side won, a tyranny looked inevitable.[1] What a man should do under such circumstances forms the subject of one his most anguished letters of the period. Written in Greek to his friend Atticus and presented as a set of themes for debate in a manner true to philosophical discourse, Cicero's list of questions reflected on whether a man ought to tolerate or depose a tyranny, retire or risk everything for his country.[2] Then, his decision had been whether to join Pompey's forces; but in the years of Caesar's domination such troubles pressed hard upon him once more: 'I'm ashamed of being a slave', he wrote to Cassius at the time of the war in Spain, 'so I pretend to be occupied by other activities, lest I hear Plato shouting at me.'[3]

By that time Caesar had defeated republican forces at Pharsalus and Thapsus, and he was soon to defeat them at Munda; thereafter, although small pockets of resistance remained, they did not pose an immediate threat, and any former enemies who had survived were bound to Caesar by his grants of mercy. All this meant that by the end of 45 BC Caesar was supreme and unstoppable. Yet unlike Cicero, Brutus had said he was happy with Caesar's programme. So what happened to change his mind? As we shall see in this chapter, the philosophical questioning expressed by Cicero offers us one route into understanding the intellectual mindset towards tyranny in Brutus' day. To understand what finally drove him and his fellow conspirators to assassinate Caesar, however, we must first look at the man they all wanted dead.

Many years of military campaigning and subsequent triumphs had not only made Caesar the wealthiest man at Rome; he had also carved for himself a unique position of power. During the crisis of 49 BC he had resurrected the office of dictator – not used since the dreaded days of Sulla – to give him the authority he needed to manage the city and military campaigns, while the two elected consuls, both opponents of Caesar, had left Italy to join Pompey. From that moment on, he never permanently relinquished the title, and often held other offices alongside it. Thus, he also held the consulship for the years 48 and 46–44 BC, even holding it without a colleague, as Pompey had once done, in 45 BC. Finally, in 44 BC, Caesar was consul again; this time, with Antony as his colleague. And, not to be forgotten, his political powers were supplemented by his priesthoods: Caesar had been *pontifex maximus* at Rome from 63 BC, and from 47 BC onwards he was also on the board of augurs. Now, in addition to his role as the head of the college organising public cult, Caesar's religious capacities had expanded to include the taking of *auspices*: the interpretation of signs from the gods, which had the power to ratify or suspend public business, depending on whether the omens were favourable or not.

We shall return to the question of his dictatorship and other offices shortly. But, first, we should also take note of the bigger and greater honours that were being bestowed upon him. To focus on just a few of the more eccentric ones, Suetonius tells us that statues of Caesar were set up in privileged places; the month of *Quinctilis* was renamed after him (*Julius* – or 'July', as we still call it today); he sat on a golden throne and even had his own priest – the *flamen Caesaris*. The Senate decreed a temple be dedicated in honour of his famed *clementia*; meanwhile, he was given the forename *Imperator*, as well as the prestigious title *Parens Patriae* ('Father of his Country'), usually reserved for one who had saved his country in a time of crisis. All of the ancient sources focus, in differing degrees, on the special privileges that Caesar accrued; as a result, it is sometimes difficult to detangle those he accepted from those that he was merely offered, and perhaps even turned down. Still, the significance of this catalogue in the run-up to the assassination is hard to overlook.[4]

'There were no honours which he did not receive or confer at pleasure', Suetonius continues. And this last point is equally crucial to remember: Caesar was using time-honoured political posts as favours he could hand out to his friends. His abuse of, even disdain for, the ladder of offices became all too clear when he returned to Rome in 45 BC. First, he gave up his own period as sole consul and replaced himself with two senators. But worse was to come when one of these men died on the very last day of the year, for Caesar appointed a new consul in his place, to serve for just one afternoon – Gaius Caninius Rebilus. 'And so, during the consulship of Caninius, you should know that no one had breakfast', joked Cicero, 'not one crime was committed when he was consul.'[5] Although his joke was made in private to Atticus, the appointment was most irregular, and a bitter blow to those who cherished the free *res publica*. 'If you could see it, you would weep', Cicero added. Members of the senatorial elite must have hated themselves for it; for they had allowed, or even in the case of Brutus, supported Caesar's rise to power. In return they began to hate Caesar.

The ancient sources record numerous other instances of behaviour that went against the grain of traditional sensibilities. In public Caesar had been overheard saying that 'the *res publica* was nothing – a mere name without a body or form'. Perhaps worse still, he arrogantly joked that 'Sulla did not know his political ABCs, because he laid down the dictatorship', thereby intimating that he should have kept hold of it.[6] Even though these anecdotes derive from a hostile source, their sentiments seem credible and may reflect the rumours that were circulating about Caesar's ever-increasing arrogance. Closer in time and from a good friend of Caesar's comes surer evidence of how the dictator was perceived; or rather, how he feared he was perceived. 'Can I have any doubt how much I am hated', Caesar is said to have asked, 'when Marcus Cicero is kept waiting and cannot see me at his own convenience?'[7] He was referring to an incident when Cicero – formerly one of the leading men of the state – was left queuing for an appointment to see the dictator. Although the news that Caesar had acknowledged his faux pas was later music to Cicero's ears, we can only imagine how the humiliation of this episode irked him at the time.

But Caesar also managed to offend whole groups of people by his displays of absolute power. On 14 February 44 BC, he insulted the Senate by refusing to stand when a dignified cohort of its order approached him as a body, carrying silver tablets engraved with the latest batch of sycophantic honours. His decision not to stand was all the more intolerable because Caesar himself had recently turned on a tribune of the plebs who had failed to rise for *him* during one of his triumphs. By turning his attacks on the tribunes, Caesar further demonstrated a distinct lack of respect for their accustomed sacrosanctity. Of all the executive positions, the tribune of the plebs was uniquely protected by the majesty of the Roman people; each tribune was inviolable. It was in defence of the tribunes' rights, among other reasons, that Caesar claimed he had been pushed to war in 49 BC.[8] Yet this episode was just one of several blows against the tribunes' rights which now seemed to question the integrity of that claim.

Several weeks earlier, on 26 January, two tribunes, Lucius Caesetius Flavus and Gaius Epidius Marullus, had fallen victim to Caesar's anger and suspicion when he accused them of conspiring to degrade his *dignitas*. Someone had put a laurel crown with a white fillet, a symbol of monarchy, on a statue of Caesar. The two tribunes gave orders for it to be removed, and had the perpetrator dragged off to prison. Later another man hailed Caesar as *rex*, to which Caesar famously replied he was not king, but Caesar.[9] Caesar's response was a joke: 'Rex' was the family name of the Marcii clan to which his grandmother, Marcia, belonged. It was a play on words. Thus, when Caesetius and Marullus stepped in to have the heckler arrested, Caesar thought they had overreacted. The tribunes had acted because they thought Caesar would be annoyed at such trappings of monarchy; in fact, he was annoyed at *them*, and thought they might even have engineered the whole incident to make him look like a tyrant.[10] As a result, Caesetius and Marullus were deposed from their tribunician offices and expelled from the Senate; the whole affair cast a dark shadow over Caesar's image as a man of the people.

Whatever he did, and we should remember that Caesar also made many positive reforms, he could not rid himself of the claim that he was aspiring towards monarchy. On 15 February 44 BC, exactly a month before the assassination, Antony famously put Caesar's kingly ambitions to the test at the festival known as the Lupercalia. Cicero has left us an eyewitness account: Caesar was sitting on a golden chair above the *rostra*, dressed in a purple toga and with a wreath upon his head, when Antony climbed to offer him a crown – not just once, but several times.[11] The whole Forum gasped, Cicero tells us, and people shouted their disapproval. But each time Caesar rejected the crown, the people applauded his decision. It is impossible to know what Caesar was thinking – although, as usual, a number of interpretations have been offered. Either Caesar wanted the crown and was displeased by the reaction of the crowd; or he really did not want the crown, and he used the event to broadcast a definitive statement to that effect. Cicero adds that an entry was made in the official calendar to record that Caesar declined the title of king. Yet still the rumours did not cease.

Ultimately, however, Caesar was not just killed for fear of what he might become. Tales of oracles predicting his kingship and other such stories, which circulated after his assassination, rather exploited a rhetoric of fear – 'it is lucky we killed him when we did' stories, as one scholar has called them.[12] Instead, it is more plausible that Caesar was killed for what he had already become. For shortly before the Lupercalia, the dictator had accepted a status that was far more telling of his intentions than any royal crown, when he took the controversial title of *dictator perpetuo*: 'dictator for life'. Almost immediately coins were minted and circulated to advertise his unique and supreme position within the state. He may not have been a king but there was no doubting that Caesar was the *de facto* master of Rome.[13]

'This was acknowledged tyranny', comments Plutarch, in a clear echo of Platonic thought on political constitutions: Caesar had turned from being a demagogue – a man who courted the people – to a tyrant.[14] As dictator, Caesar already had a power that outranked the consuls, that gave him immunity from any veto and unlimited *imperium*. But now that power was permanent. There had never been a perpetual dictator before; the office was only ever meant to be used in an emergency, for a maximum term of six months. Even Sulla, who was the nearest precedent for holding an extended dictatorship, had set his term of office aside after eighteen months. One problem arises in that the term *perpetuo* is ambiguous in the Latin: it can be translated as 'continuous', in which case Caesar may only ever have intended to hold the dictatorship for an uninterrupted period of undetermined duration; but it could also mean 'for life'. Either way, however, the new title signified a change that cut deep into the heart of republican ideology; one-man rule, the fear of which had so completely permeated the Roman aristocracy since the days of Lucius Brutus, had finally come to pass.

The Beginnings of a Plot

Most historians of the period would probably now agree that the perpetual dictatorship was the step that finally marked Caesar's break from the tradition of the *res publica*, and that it was this act that sealed his fate. But how did the conspiracy against the life of Caesar begin? What motivated Brutus to join or even lead it? One thing that seems sure is that Brutus' hopes for

Caesar had been dashed in the six months separating the dictator's return to Rome and his assassination. For, as we have just seen, in that time Caesar had consolidated his position as the sole ruler of Rome; he had made it clear from his treatment of the two tribunes that he would not tolerate dissidence; and with his departure to Parthia imminent, he had also taken measures to secure and extend his control by appointing magistrates of his choosing for the coming years.

A part of the answer as to what motivated Brutus, then, must simply be that his perception of Caesar had changed. However, reconstructing the rest of the conspiracy must be handled with care. Not only were our extant sources written up long after the fact of its happening; as Victoria Pagán has pointed out in her detailed study of conspiracy narratives, there will always be 'an epistemological gap caused by the secrecy and silence that shroud the event': key facts will always remain in the shadows because the beginnings of such plots are necessarily secret.[15]

It is only because the assassination of Caesar was successful that so many details of the conspiracy were brought to light in the first place; hence attention was quickly fixed on Brutus and Cassius, whose high profile after the assassination confirmed their leading roles in its planning. Yet Cicero cannot tell us much about what the conspirators were thinking, for as we shall see he was not invited into the plot, and besides there are no letters for the period from January 44 BC until after the murder. Friends and contemporaries of the conspirators might have discussed the plans after the event, but the temptation to justify, criticise, or form moral judgments would have by then been hard to resist.

An interesting result of the assassination, for example, is that it also brought to light several conspiracies that had failed to gain momentum against Caesar in the years prior to 44 BC. Attacks on Caesar were hence alleged to go back as early as 47 BC, in the aftermath of Pharsalus,[16] while Cicero even mentions Caesar's 'awful suspicion' of a conspiracy against him in a speech he delivered in September 46 BC.[17] There was a rumour too that Gaius Trebonius had been openly recruiting for a plot of his own in the summer of 45 BC, and that he had tried but failed to enlist the support of Antony.[18] Suetonius tells us that Caesar consequently published edicts and issued warnings against those who criticised him.[19] Yet Plutarch adds that, when two of Caesar's close allies, Antony and Dolabella, were accused of plotting a revolution, Caesar dismissed the report, claiming he did not fear the fat, long-haired men so much as 'the pale and lean ones': that is, men like Cassius and Brutus who spent their days immersed in philosophical studies rather than at Caesar's table.[20]

So Brutus, too, was allegedly suspected of conspiracy-planning before 44 BC. But Plutarch tells us that, although Caesar feared Brutus' way of thinking, the high esteem in which he was held, and his friends, 'he had faith in his character'.[21] After all, having abandoned the cause of Pompey and joined the Caesarians, Brutus had been elevated to unparalleled positions of power for a man who had fought on the opposing side. There was no reason for Brutus to strike Caesar down, or so Caesar thought: 'Do you not think Brutus would wait for this little piece of flesh?' he reportedly asked those who suggested otherwise.[22] The implication would seem to be that Caesar saw Brutus as worthy to follow in his footsteps – either as a successor or, more likely, to a position of high influence at Rome.[23] From Caesar's own mouth, then, Brutus is spared the kind of accusations of jealousy and ambition which were later heaped upon Cassius.

One problem in our evidence is that, by the time Plutarch came to write his *Life of Brutus*, the oral and written tradition had been worked over to create a streamlined, and largely positive, narrative of Brutus' motives. Thus, in the terms of modern literary criticism, Plutarch's account of the plot offers a powerful instance of 'backshadowing': that is, Plutarch builds on his readers' shared knowledge of Brutus' role in the conspiracy to make Caesar's death look inevitable, a 'foregone conclusion'. Hence, we begin to despair at the ignorance of Caesar, who stumbles foolishly towards his death, and we are led to believe that Caesar has underestimated the man of whom, in Plutarch's telling, he had just said: 'it matters greatly what that man wants, but whatever he wants, he wants it very much'.[24] The effect of the 'piece of flesh' anecdote we saw above, then, is that Brutus' motivations are brought sharply into relief. It is not personal power Brutus is after; even Caesar dismisses that suggestion in Plutarch's telling of the episode. Instead, as in other writers (especially Appian and Dio), it was primarily public opinion, pressure from his peers and his own philosophical conviction that awakened in Brutus a sense of duty both to his country and to his family name: an obligation which meant he had to put the public good ahead of any private concerns.

Clearly, as we shall see in more detail below, Plutarch cannot escape the positive tradition of Brutus he found in his sources; it is possible, too, that Plutarch imparted some of his own philosophical ideas upon the character he created.[25] Part of the intrigue surrounding Brutus must consequently be that we can never claim to know definitively his state of mind leading up to and during the formation of the conspiracy. However, what we do have is a set of hypotheses from later writers, which we can test against both the literary traditions to which they belong and the contemporary evidence for the political climate in 44 BC more generally.[26] In what follows, we shall consequently balance the evidence of our literary sources against the experience of political and intellectual life at Rome, to arrive at a fuller analysis of the manifold reasons leading to the assassination of Caesar, as well as Brutus' own part within it.

Public Opinion

In the time that he was dictator, Caesar took a number of important steps towards improving the condition of living at Rome. Examples include his famous calendar reforms, which corrected the misalignments resulting from only having 355 days in the year, and his attempts to solve the interrelated and crushing problems of debt, high rents and unemployment.[27] He was also generous with money, entertainment and official posts. Some people doubtless welcomed the positive steps he had made towards improving living conditions at Rome. And, as we shall see, the anxiety at Rome in the aftermath of his murder would seem to support such a conclusion. But it would be wrong to think that the Roman people shared a unanimous view of the man, his aims and the effect he was having on the electoral process. In fact, all the evidence seems to point to the fact that there were many upon whom his dictatorship weighed heavily, especially among the elite class that had been accustomed to power before.

At the heart of the problem was the time-honoured concept of *libertas*: perhaps the most cherished quality of a Roman citizen's existence under the *res publica*. But freedom meant different things to different people at Rome.[28] After all, at the outbreak of the civil war in 49 BC, Caesar had declared that he was liberating Rome from the tyranny of an oligarchic faction.[29] By this he meant something like: 'equality before the law, equality of all personal rights, and equality of the fundamental political rights'.[30] When we reflect that twenty-two die-hard republicans had overruled and ignored the votes of 370 senators in favour of peace at that time, Caesar may have had a point. But then he established himself as a permanent dictator and the cry of *libertas* was used against him, this time by another faction of would-be oligarchs who resented the fact that elections were not free and open for them anymore.

Consequently, there are two broad ways of looking at the concept of *libertas*: from the general perspective, it meant the freedom to be treated like an equal in the eyes of the law, to be protected from wrongdoing, and to be in possession of those rights that enabled a man to enjoy the life of a free citizen. But for men like Brutus and his peers, *libertas* symbolised the freedom to take a share in the political management of the *res publica*; only thus could they establish their reputations and gain dignity in the eyes of the people and the Senate of Rome. However different these goals might appear at first, though, they nevertheless point to a shared understanding about the importance of *libertas* for the commonwealth as a whole; for central to the fulfilment of each was the need for the *res publica* to be free. In other words: the citizen body, not Caesar, had to be in control of the decision-making processes.

As early as autumn 45 BC rumours were circulating to the effect that Caesar was hated: he was considered a tyrant; men were offended that a statue of Caesar had been placed among those of the kings of Rome; his public appearances were not welcomed anymore. This was the 'city gossip of spiteful men', according to Cicero, who tried to dispel the reports in a speech he delivered before Caesar himself. 'Who complains about a statue?' he asked rhetorically. 'Especially when it is just one among so many.'[31] But in 44 BC, shortly before the assassination, all our major sources report that this same statue was decorated with a diadem.[32] It may just have been 'city gossip' but the anti-Caesarian movement was gaining currency.

Graffiti provided another outlet through which people could channel their frustration; as recent studies into the phenomenon have shown, its source lay in the oral culture of Rome, which had strong social, economic and political undertones.[33] Hence Plutarch, Suetonius, Appian and Dio all unearth stories about the vast array of graffiti that appeared in the last days of Caesar's dictatorship. *Utinam viveres* read one graffito, scrawled beneath the statue of Lucius Brutus: 'If only you were alive'. Another allegedly appeared under the statue of Caesar:

> Brutus, who threw out the kings, was made first consul:
> This man, who threw out the consuls, finally became our king.[34]

Yet more in this vein was said to have appeared on the praetorian tribunal where Marcus Brutus sat to conduct his official business: 'Brutus, are you asleep?', 'You're no Brutus', 'Brutus, have you received a bribe?', 'You're not *his* descendant' – and so on.[35]

As we might naturally suppose, these graffiti do not survive among the urban fabric of the city today; yet the literary traces of this activity remain to support and lend weight to the idea that public opinion was one of the pressures to which Brutus finally succumbed. The message was clear and Brutus, we are led to suppose, felt ashamed that his honour and descent had publicly been called into question. For the location of these graffiti was emotionally charged: the vandalised statue of Lucius Brutus stood in the temple of Concord, along with those of the seven kings of Rome, as well as the newly added statue of Caesar, mentioned by Cicero above. According to Dio, its placement played no small part in inciting Marcus Brutus' wrath against Caesar, for the dictator's statue provocatively trumped the elder Brutus' glorious achievement as *the* Liberator of Rome.[36] But in case Brutus still had not got the message, the people – in the version told by Dio at least – made it abundantly clear for him: 'Brutus, Brutus!' they repeatedly called after him. 'We need a Brutus!'[37]

Whether these slogans really represented the voice of the common people is uncertain. Dio is explicit on this point: in his account, the graffiti and the appeals come from *hoi polloi* – the Greek expression for a collective body of non-elites in the political community. On the other hand, Plutarch has the graffiti engineered by a group of elites with a view to playing on Brutus' conscience. Yet, either way, as Robert Morstein-Marx has recently argued, there is a strong chance that some element of popular opinion had turned hostile towards Caesar by the start of 44 BC.[38] And, if so, perhaps it was this change in circumstance that finally spurred Brutus' decision to take his share in or even lead the plot. After all, Brutus had structured his entire career and reputation around his ancestors' opposition to tyranny: now he had to live up to that name.

Peer Pressure

The occurrence of the graffiti was not the first time the memory of his ancestors had been thrown in Brutus' face since his alliance with Caesar. Approximately two years earlier, Cicero had also found cause to remind the young man of his illustrious descent in his dialogue *Brutus*.[39] One passage in particular, towards the end of this work, has received a lot of scholarly attention. As he rounds up his discussion of the history of famous orators, Cicero turns to the addressee of the work, and – speaking for himself and his friend Atticus, the third character in the dialogue – he mourns that Brutus' career has been cut short by the impact of civil strife:

> This is the grief which touches me, the anxiety which worries me, as well as my friend here, whose love and opinion of you is the same as mine. We cherish you, and long for you to enjoy the fruits of your virtue, our hope for you is a *res publica* in which you can renew and expand the memory of your two most distinguished houses.[40]

As we have seen in earlier chapters, Cicero had held high hopes for Brutus' reputation and career as an orator, the topic that forms the context for this quotation. Are we really to believe that Cicero also saw in Brutus the potential to be a tyrannicide, following in the footsteps of Lucius Brutus and Servilius Ahala?

'Our hope for you is a *res publica* in which you can renew and expand the memory of your two most distinguished houses.' Some scholars have seen this either as an 'unequivocal invitation'[41] or as 'a cryptic message' – one which 'must have been obvious, not least to Brutus himself'.[42] After all, to quote one authority on Roman history: 'How except by murder could Brutus do as well as, or even better than these ancestors of his?'[43]

Others have dismissed any such interpretation on the grounds that Cicero's words can all too easily be tainted by the hindsight of what happened on the Ides of March.[44] Indeed, it is hard to believe that Cicero really was advocating tyrannicide at the time he wrote *Brutus*; as Michael Winterbottom has so masterfully shown in a detailed analysis of Cicero's correspondence and philosophical treatises dating to this period, his hopes in 46 BC were not yet tending in this direction.[45] Rather, it is likely that Cicero was reminding Brutus of his ancestry, not so that he might kill Caesar, but to make the young man reconsider his political alliance with the dictator.[46] For, as we saw in the last chapter, by the beginning of 46 BC Brutus was on his way to his province of Cisalpine Gaul: the esteemed post bestowed upon him by a grateful dictator. To any contemporary observer of his political strategy and actions, Brutus was an out-and-out Caesarian.[47]

'Our hope for you is a *res publica* in which you can renew and expand the memory of your two most distinguished houses.' Whatever Cicero *had* intended by this comment, it was meant to pull Brutus back into line: back onto the '*optimate* path', as he had once called it – the path followed by the 'best men'.[48] Cicero did not hate Caesar (yet); he may even have harboured a slight hope that Caesar would still restore an open, more republican system of government. However, as the year 46 BC drew to its close and certainly by the time Caesar returned from Spain, his feelings of hatred and servitude had grown, and so it is more than likely that Cicero continued to goad Brutus in the years after 46 BC. For, as we shall see, the name of Cicero was one of the first words to spring to Brutus' lips after he had drawn his dagger from Caesar's body. For Antony – and many subsequent scholars – although Cicero was not actively involved in the conspiracy, he was still its intellectual author.[49]

Deep down the thought must have troubled Brutus. But he did not need Cicero to remind him of his failures in life. Every morning he would have had to walk past the busts of his ancestors, the *imagines*, as well as the glorious family tree that Atticus had constructed for him. And he needed only to look upon his wife, Porcia, to be reminded of Cato, her father, Brutus' uncle, and by now the very embodiment of republican ideology – all the ideals Brutus had betrayed. Porcia had, of course, married Brutus following his return from Cisalpine Gaul, when he had already accepted and returned Caesar's favours. But how did she feel about her husband siding ever more closely with the man who had been her father's mortal enemy? *Cherchez la femme*: there is always a woman lurking behind the actions of men – or so historians like to remind us.[50] For Porcia too is alleged to have played a role, and this we need to assess.

More than any other ancient author, Dio attributed a key part in Brutus' final decision to Porcia. According to his version of events, Porcia became worried when Brutus refused to reveal what was troubling him, and so she set out to prove herself a strong and worthy confidante: she placed a knife to her thigh, slashed it deep, and thus demonstrated that she could endure any torture.[51] In so doing Porcia is made to support and spur on her husband's murderous schemes; in Dio's telling of the conspiracy he then becomes the mastermind of the plot – only after his wife's intervention does Brutus deign to broach the topic with Cassius, we are told.

Yet other accounts reverse the order of events and lessen the role Porcia played in its formation. Thus, Plutarch and Valerius Maximus also record the story of her self-wounding, but it appears only after the conspiracy has been hatched and on the eve of the assassination. In Plutarch, Porcia tests her ability to keep a secret under torture; while Valerius – also our earliest evidence for this story – has Porcia test her ability to kill herself in the event that the plan should fail.[52] Either way, however, by placing Brutus' revelation of the plot to Porcia later in the narrative, Plutarch and Valerius both diminish the part Porcia plays: she still supports her husband's decision, but she has no real influence over it.[53]

The reason for her appearance in these sources at all is that a 'Porcia legend' developed in the aftermath of Brutus' death, prompted by the memoirs penned by her own son, Bibulus. As Holt Parker has argued, the inclusion of her story in the later narratives can be explained by the fact that it is a 'tale of loyalty', which in turn suggests that the Porcia we see in these accounts is more of a literary construct. Yet, in such stories, the wife's virtue essentially serves as a mirror of her husband's moral authority: in other words, 'the tale is told equally about him'.[54] Hence we can understand why different versions existed. Whether Porcia spurred Brutus into action or supported his schemes depends on who was interpreting that material: a friendly voice who championed her loyalty to her husband, or a hostile writer who rather depicted Brutus as under her influence. That is not to suggest we should erase Porcia from the picture entirely. We can probably assume that Brutus had confided in his wife to some extent; after all, Porcia's own circumstances and security would have been dramatically compromised had the plan failed. More hypothetically, we might even assume that, as the daughter of Cato and widow of Bibulus, she would have supported any plan to depose Caesar. But, if we 'look for the woman' behind the origins of this conspiracy, we may find ourselves disappointed.

That leaves us to consider Cassius: the man often alleged to be the instigator of the plot. Rumour had it that he had planned to assassinate Caesar before. Back in 47 BC, it was said that he had plotted but failed to kill Caesar at Tarsus almost as soon as he had accepted his pardon. Like so many stories of the time, however, this one is hard to validate and it may rather have been circulated later to legitimate Cassius' reputation as the real mastermind behind the Ides.[55] Since 47 BC, however, he had worked as Caesar's legate and had been appointed to the praetorship in 44 BC. So what reason must Cassius have had to hate Caesar so fervently?

Some thought he was jealous. After all, Cassius was roughly the same age as Brutus, a little older even, and they had made their way up the *cursus honorum* at about the same time. But while Brutus had been profiting from his provincial investments, Cassius had been picking up the pieces after Crassus' devastating defeat in the Parthian War of 53 BC. Cassius had skill and energy; unlike the many that lost their lives in this ill-fated campaign, he led the survivors to safety in Syria, where he remained until 51 BC, defending the province against further Parthian attacks.[56] He had since served as a tribune of the plebs in 49 BC and, although he sided with Pompey in the civil war, he had proved himself once more as an efficient naval commander. Even Caesar had to admit it in his account of those campaigns: Cassius was capable of great speed, surprise tactics and ability.[57]

In ordinary years, Cassius' reputation as a capable and efficient soldier would have been more than enough to earn him great fame and distinction; in this way, he had more in common with Caesar than Brutus. Perhaps it irked him to watch Brutus' career progress so rapidly under Caesar's dictatorship. Plutarch tells the story that Caesar's favouritism of Brutus was openly acknowledged and that it caused Cassius to lose out on the most prestigious of the praetorships: the urban praetorship in charge of the city's judicial affairs.[58] It is not impossible, then – especially when we come to review the political climate in Rome more generally – that Cassius felt aggrieved at the way the new regime was controlling access to honours. It is not out of the question, either, that Cassius felt some resentment towards Brutus; for, although our later sources always show them as a pair it is not clear they had much in common before the Ides united them in a common purpose.[59] But were Cassius' motives really that different from those of Brutus?

Indeed, Cassius' commitment to Epicurean philosophy also demands attention in any reconstruction of his attitude to Caesar. As a philosophical system which advocated withdrawal from political life, in the early years of Caesar's dictatorship it provided some solace to Cassius.[60] Cicero could hence pointedly remark that Cassius devoted his attention more to his cuisine than to the critical issues of Caesar's tyranny, since Epicureanism was often associated with the pursuit of happiness.[61] Cassius phrased it another way: his philosophy taught him that peace of mind (*ataraxia*), a goal which Epicureans identified as the greatest mental pleasure, was obtained through virtue, justice and what was right.[62] It made him prioritise honesty and clemency and shun cruelty. When Cassius wrote this letter in mid-January 45 BC, Pompey's eldest son Gnaeus was still leading the campaign in Hispania, and Cassius would have faced danger in the event of a republican victory. 'I'd rather have an old and clement master [*malo veterem et clementem dominum*]', he explained to Cicero, 'than try a new, cruel one.' But, by the same blow, Cassius was accepting Caesar as his master, his *dominus*.[63]

Was it Brutus then who persuaded Cassius to kill that same master? Or did Cassius have plans that he divulged first to Brutus? To judge from the mixed reports in Dio, Plutarch and Appian: both opinions were evidently current from the start.[64] We have seen how Dio has his Brutus, prompted by Porcia, approach Cassius. But Plutarch and Appian both record that Cassius needed Brutus to lend the cause a cloak of respectability; for their source had it that, when Cassius asked his friends what they thought about an attack on Caesar, they all agreed that they would do so only if Brutus took the lead.[65] What then of Cassius' philosophical adherence to Epicureanism? On the one hand, it could be argued that an Epicurean should not risk his peace of mind for anyone; on the other, as we have just seen, Cassius believed virtue, justice and proper conduct were prerequisites for reaching a state of *ataraxia*. The wise man, it seems, ought to risk his own tranquillity for those in need; and Cassius seems to have believed something like this.[66]

Further evidence, however, also hints at the possibility that Cassius was the main ideologue behind the operation, not Brutus. For the historian Dio had found in his sources that Cassius was one of only a few men to vote *against* a senatorial proposal to offer fresh honours to Caesar at the end of

45 BC; this time the honours included a golden chair, a golden wreath adorned with jewels, a divine image in his likeness, and a pediment for his house – the architectural feature typically only ever found on temples.[67] This was all too much for Cassius, who like Brutus had been born into a family – the Cassii clan – that could not bear to tolerate the domination, or even the influence, of another man.[68] If at the start of the year he had thought he could live under a clement master, now at its end Cassius' wishes for a free *res publica* were coming to the surface. Whether he was the one to approach Brutus or the other way around is impossible to know; we should probably assume that the idea had crossed each man's mind before one of them gave expression to it. But in either case, Brutus may never have dreamed of actually killing Caesar without Cassius' cooperation – and, presumably, vice versa.

Political Ambitions

As we have so far seen, public opinion combined with the grievances of Cicero, Porcia and Cassius may have all helped to steel Brutus' nerve. But these explanations sound more like justifications compiled after the event, and so we also need to consider what was in it for *him*. After all, there can be no doubting that he was the special object of Caesar's attention and trust; Brutus had flourished under Caesar. To kill the dictator, or even just to attempt to kill him, would mean risking everything.

At the same time, however, Brutus had gained his position via extremely un-republican means: appointment by a dictator rather than election by the people. As the name of the famous career path, the *cursus honorum*, suggests, political office was perceived as an honour at Rome. But it was one which had to be bestowed by the *populus Romanus* in recognition of a man's *dignitas*.[69] In other words, a man's 'worth' or 'standing' was only really demonstrated by his prior services to the state and his moral qualities, and that was what was needed to gain public recognition. Brutus had got it wrong. As Cicero not too subtly reminded him in the treatise he dedicated to Brutus: 'Honour is the reward for virtue in the considered opinion of the citizenry.' But the man who gains power (*imperium*) by some other circumstance, or even against the will of the people, he continues, 'has laid his hands only on the title of honour, but it is not real honour'.[70]

Brutus may have secured political office, then, but he had not done so honourably; nor had he acted in a manner that would earn him a reputation for virtue or everlasting fame. In short: if we want to understand what united the men who conspired to kill Caesar, we need to consider the one thing they all shared in common: political ambition, the desire to accrue *dignitas* and win glory – both in their lifetimes and beyond. As Maria Dettenhofer has persuasively argued in her detailed study of the young aristocrats of Brutus' generation, the questions concerning the assassination of Caesar should not just focus on motives and goals; we need to question what conditions and opportunities awaited them.[71] In other words: did Caesar's dictatorship allow other men to succeed in the ways that Romans understood and measured success?

In the case of Brutus, Caesar may already have dangled, if not promised, the reward of the consulship before his eyes; at least several sources report that he was in the pipeline for the consulship of 41 BC. But the consulship no longer brought the glory it used to bestow upon its holders. So what then? He would be entitled to hold another provincial command. But it was what happened next that was more important. For in the past ex-consuls had gone on to hold more prestigious positions in their collective capacity as *consulares*: they became consultants, advisers even, during senatorial debates. Ex-consuls were traditionally men whose opinions needed to be both asked and respected. They were the leading men of the state. However, there was no room for political discussion in Caesar's Senate; Cicero had experienced that.[72] Brutus may have been one of the favoured few, but the sorry fact was that the Senate served merely to rubber stamp the decisions made by Caesar. This was just one of the ways in which Caesar failed to provide others with opportunities to attain fulfilment of their *dignitas*.[73]

Furthermore, Brutus doubtless understood the implications of a career that rested on Caesar's prerogative. In the blink of an eye, the dictator could revoke any concessions he had granted; which meant Brutus was realistically unable to conduct his life according to his own will. Not only that, as he must have experienced in the few months in which he had held the urban praetorship, there was no longer any room for shaping policy, even in the top jobs. Under Caesar's dictatorship (whether 'for life' or merely 'continuous'), the fortunes of Brutus, and many others, would remain at his mercy, under his control. Political success demanded that a man be among Caesar's circle of friends, and that he do his bidding.

'Do you not imagine Brutus would wait for this little piece of flesh?' Caesar had allegedly asked.[74] But, according to the best estimate, at the beginning of 44 BC Brutus had just turned forty. This is certainly not old by modern standards. However, in the context of Roman demography and life expectancy, it means that Brutus was now older than most of the people he would have encountered in a typical day. He was nearly a *senior* according to the life stages sketched out by the Roman writer Varro: not elderly, but certainly advancing in years.[75] Little wonder, then, that Brutus and his peers were taking thought, while still in their prime, for what the future might hold. The answer to Caesar's supposed question, it seems, would have been 'no' – Brutus did not want to wait. The dictator's existence had already cast too long a shadow over the men of the next generation.

Philosophy

It is one thing to hate a man: to hate who he is, what he is doing and what he stands for, as well as to hate the impact he has on your own existence. But it is quite another to kill him. And here we return to the questions that had plagued Cicero as early as 49 BC and with which we opened this chapter. To paraphrase them: what would you do if you thought your country was on the path to tyranny? If you saw one man gaining too much power, would you try to stop him? If so, would you help your country by words or by war? Or is it better to retire somewhere quiet and leave your country under a tyranny? These were the questions that now beset Brutus in 44 BC, too.

It is important to stress that the time-old hatred of kings in the Roman tradition never actually advocated death as a legal punishment. Lucius Junius Brutus had not killed Tarquinius Superbus in 509 BC: he had merely expelled the king from Rome. And when Servilius Ahala challenged Spurius Maelius' aspirations to *regnum* in 439 BC, he was allegedly acting on the orders of the Senate and not as a private citizen. Furthermore, although statues of the famous Athenian tyrannicides stood in the Forum of Rome, and although Cicero's rhetoric to the contrary might cloud our judgement at times, political murder was a relatively new phenomenon at Rome; and it was not an action that was even slightly revered. Consequently, neither Brutus' family *exempla* nor Roman practice could provide him with the answers he needed for dealing with the problem of Caesar. This was a solution for which he needed to turn to Greek thought – and especially Greek ethical philosophy, a subject dear to the hearts of many educated Roman senators.[76]

It is difficult to emphasise just how much influence Greek culture exerted over the Roman elite of the late Republic. As we saw in Chapter 1, by Brutus' day it had become natural for young men to spend some time studying Greek rhetoric and philosophy abroad. If rhetoric provided them with the tools with which to argue and debate their ideas, philosophical studies provided many a man with his very own code of conduct. Roman adherents of Greek philosophy based their entire lives on their chosen schools of thought, and it had also become relatively common for men to keep a resident philosopher on their Roman or Italian estates.[77] Brutus was no exception. As we have seen, he had studied in Athens as a young man and attended lectures in all the major schools of philosophy. Later in life he had even invited the philosopher Aristus into his household at Rome, and he always regarded him as a close friend.[78] Although the precise dates for Aristus' stay with Brutus elude us, he was almost certainly in Rome in 46 BC, and perhaps also later, too.[79]

In particular, the view of the Old Academy promulgated by Aristus' brother Antiochus was that, although virtue was enough to provide for a happy life, it could not in itself bring about a *supremely* happy life. Only when virtue was combined with other conditions – such as health, wealth, and honour – could a man attain the greatest happiness.[80] As we have seen, such concerns were indeed playing on Brutus' mind in 44 BC. But Antiochean Platonists followed the text of Plato's dialogues to the letter on other matters, too. And, as David Sedley has cogently argued in an important article on the ethics of the assassins, there was much in Platonic dogma that had the potential to sway Brutus towards the act of tyrannicide.[81]

It had been Plato who developed the first great theoretical analysis of tyranny, when he set it alongside and ranked it against alternative forms of constitutions. In the Platonic scheme there were three basic types of government: rule by the one (monarchy), the few (aristocracy) and the many (democracy); however, these were further subdivided according to whether they were 'law-abiding' (and therefore 'good') or 'lawless' (i.e. 'bad').[82] The result was a sixfold scheme ranked on a sliding scale of preferability that took into account the relative happiness of its subjects: according to this train of Platonic thinking, tyranny was the worst form of constitution – it was a 'lawless monarchy'. In his *Republic*, Plato went so far as to call it the worst form of enslavement, too.[83]

So how should an Antiochean Platonist live under a tyranny? On the one hand, to protect his own virtue, a man might go into exile or retreat into his studies. On the other, if the happiness of his fellow citizens could also be improved, alongside his own, a man should act to restore justice: this was his responsibility, his moral duty. The guidelines were vague; Plato provided no actual indication of how the tyrant might be removed. However, the Platonic tradition at least offered an example of how the task might be achieved: Chion of Heraclea, a disciple of Plato, had assassinated the tyrant Clearchus in 353/2 BC. It may only have been one example out of many, but his legend had lived on and was celebrated in Brutus' day.[84] It served to encourage the Platonist commitment to promoting constitutional reform, whatever it took.

But less formal methods of deliberation besides reading Plato were also available, such as the school exercises, declamation and the *progymnasmata*, which helped exercise the mind on the dilemma of tyranny. To help us reflect on Brutus' situation in 44 BC, let us return to the questions with which we started. What would you do if you thought your country was on the path to tyranny? If you saw one man gaining too much power, would you try to stop him? Brutus, it seems, put his political thought into action, concluding that something had to be done. Of course, not all Platonists would have landed on tyrannicide as the answer; there were other examples of constitutional reformers who had not resorted to such violent measures. And Plato himself had shown how to endure life under a tyranny (a point which can also be used to explain Brutus' acceptance of Caesar's rule in the early days of his dictatorship). But in the case of Caesar, it is not clear how else, except by murder, he could have been deposed.

It would be impossible to remove a man who had the majority of Rome's army at his disposal. The civil war with Pompey and the republicans had already demonstrated that point. And evidently it had got to the stage where Brutus could not bear to live under a 'lawless monarchy'.[85] We may remember that in 52 BC, when he spoke against a potential dictatorship for Pompey, he had already declared that 'to live as a slave is impossible'. And we may also remember that he had criticised Cato's suicide because it was 'impious and unmanly'. Death, at this stage, was not an option for Brutus. And so, faced with the prospect of life under a tyrant, the only remaining alternative was to kill him.

And what if that tyrant was one of your closest friends and allies? That dilemma was not addressed in Cicero's original list of Greek declamatory questions in 49 BC, but it was certainly a factor for consideration, and it features in his writings after the assassination. Friendship (*amicitia*) at Rome was a formal bond between men; not one that could easily be broken. Since he owed his life to Caesar, Brutus was under the deepest of obligations to his benefactor. He had since become a collaborator in his political regime, and had even sworn an oath to protect the dictator's life. Once again, the ethical principles of the Old Academy may have furnished a solution to this very Roman problem: the need to weigh up the honourable (*to kalon*, in the Greek) versus the most beneficial (*to sumpheron*). As Cicero put it in his ethical work *On Duties*:

> What greater crime can there be than to kill not merely another human being, but even a close friend? Surely then, anyone who kills a tyrant, although he is a close friend, has committed himself to crime? But it

> does not seem so to the Roman people, which deems that deed the fairest of all splendid deeds. Did the beneficial therefore overcome honourableness? No indeed; for honourableness followed upon what benefited.[86]

To be sure, coming in the aftermath of the assassination, Cicero's comments may better be interpreted as an after-the-fact justification for the assassins' actions. And if any such reasoning did cross Brutus' mind, we certainly have no contemporary evidence for it. When pushed for answers, however, the philosophical doctrines of the Old Academy do at least enable us to see how Brutus – a man who cherished and nurtured his reputation for virtue – could potentially see his actions as consistent with the image he had so carefully crafted. If it did not provide the stimulus, Brutus' commitment to his chosen philosophy almost certainly sealed his decision to join the conspiracy.

The Conspiracy

So far we have focused on the reasons that led Brutus and, to some extent, Cassius to form the plot against Caesar. But the conspiracy was much bigger than my discussion has so far suggested. To begin with, there was also Decimus Brutus (henceforth just Decimus), a relative of Marcus Brutus' and, according to some accounts, deserving of a place in the 'top three' of conspirators.[87] As we shall see in the next chapter, his role after the assassination seems to suggest that he left the bigger questions and initiatives to Brutus and Cassius. But he was certainly a major force in the movement, and his betrayal of Caesar was perhaps the greatest of them all. He had served Caesar in Gaul, had been promoted to positions of great responsibility, and was consul-designate for 42 BC. Before then, he was due to take over as governor of Cisalpine Gaul – that strategically advantageous place to which Caesar only ever entrusted his most loyal allies. As a fully fledged Caesarian, and not a late defector to the cause, he had Caesar's full trust and access to the dictator's mind in a way no other conspirator had. Decimus dined with Caesar on the night before the assassination; he called on him on the morning of the Ides and persuaded him to attend the Senate, when Caesar was inclined not to turn up. Had it not been for Decimus, the conspiracy might have failed. Before all that, however, he had a role to play – alongside Brutus and Cassius – in recruiting more men to their cause.

If we are right to set the beginnings of the conspiracy in February 44 BC, there was not much time.[88] Fortunately, however, there were perhaps some men who were obvious candidates: men like Trebonius, who had allegedly hinted at assassination as early as the summer of 45 BC.[89] Others included the Casca brothers (Publius and Gaius), Servius Sulpicius Galba, Lucius Minucius Basilus and Lucius Tillius Cimber. But these are just a handful of the names that survive in the records, which also state that there were more of Caesar's friends in the conspiracy than enemies.[90] In more recent years, Rudolph Storch has analysed the motives of these men and suggested that we should consider the ways in which they felt let down by the man they had served. For what they expected to gain in return for their loyalty and what they received from the dictator were not always the same thing. Worse still, it must have annoyed them to see Caesar rewarding men who had fought against him in preference to them. 'He afforded hope for all', Plutarch says of Caesar's means of distributing privileges.[91] But this was a blow for lifelong Caesarians, some of whom were ultimately left disappointed, and presumably bitter.[92] It is not unlikely that such considerations played a role in convincing at least some of Caesar's former friends to turn against their one-time benefactor, and Decimus would have been just the man to persuade them.

For their part, Brutus and Cassius also went on a headhunting mission, purportedly using philosophical discourse as a means of testing their friends' willingness to participate. Presumably direct questions regarding tyrannicide, such as those we have already discussed, would have been too obvious a give-away of their intentions. But we can piece together a rough version of their deliberations based on the account Plutarch had read in his sources, and which he seemingly relates with some accuracy.[93] What kind of constitution is the best, and which the worst? And how far should a man go to protect the state against dangerous reforms? By probing their friends along lines such as these, Plutarch tells us that Brutus and Cassius managed to rule out two of their friends: Statilius the Epicurean and Favonius, a devoted follower of Cato. The former argued that the wise man should not throw himself into turmoil for the sake of others, while the latter thought that civil war should be avoided at all costs. However, they did manage to gain the ear of a third man called Labeo, so the mission was not a complete failure.

A conspiracy was being set in motion and men, probably no more than twenty in total, were beginning to enlist. But at quite a late date in the final preparations someone mentioned the question of Antony: should he too be invited to join the conspiracy? His personal relations with Caesar were known to be bad; although he later took up the Caesarian banner with some zeal, the two men had not always seen eye to eye. What is more, he was of approximately the same age as Brutus and the rest of the conspirators – the overshadowed generation – and there was evidently sufficient reason to suppose he might be tempted to join. But then, Trebonius, a fourth prominent conspirator, must have spilled the beans on his earlier, failed attempt to lure Antony into a conspiracy; for Plutarch adds that it was only because of Trebonius' intervention that Antony was not consulted.[94] And subsequently the discussion is said to have turned down a much darker path: in that case, should he too be killed? And what about other Caesarians who might either be hostile towards the conspirators afterwards or, worse, aspire to fill Caesar's boots?[95]

It is at this stage that Brutus re-enters the historical narratives as a distinct figure in the conspiracy: according to his considered verdict, under no circumstances should Antony or any others be killed. Plutarch tells us that Brutus insisted the conspiracy follow a just course; he also believed he could transform Antony. Appian puts a speech into Brutus' mouth in which he warns the conspirators to take thought for their everlasting reputation; they would only win glory as tyrannicides, he is said to have argued, if they took the life of the tyrant alone. Whether he was seeking justice, glory, eventual reconciliation with Antony, or all three, we cannot know: Brutus' precise words – uttered in secret among his co-conspirators – are necessarily lost to history. Yet, as we shall see in the next chapter, given the insistence with which Cicero later berated Brutus for not killing Antony, it seems completely reasonable to accept the basic premise that Brutus had been the man who argued against any further bloodshed. And as we know from subsequent events, his opinion won the day.

Other details of the planning can also largely be inferred from what happened next. Hence, once the decision to spare Antony's life had been made, we can imagine that the question of what to do with Caesar's right-hand man must have needed some deliberation. Antony was a strong man and a successful fighter; he would doubtless step in to defend Caesar if the assassination happened in his presence. And so, it must have been agreed that Trebonius would lead him off to one side – to distract Antony from the deed as it was finally taking place. But where and when would be the best opportunity to attack the dictator?

One of our earliest authorities, Nicolaus of Damascus, tells us that the conspirators met in a series of small-scale meetings in private houses in the run-up to the assassination, and he adds that they debated several locations and dates: should they attack Caesar in ambush on the *sacra via* (the main street of Rome which ran through the Forum), at the elections on the Campus Martius, or at a gladiator show?[96] All options were apparently reviewed but the only sure plan we can piece together is the one which came to fruition: Caesar was to be targeted in a meeting of the Senate on the Ides of March. With hindsight, we can say that this decision made excellent sense. To begin with, it would signify that the murder was a political statement. Then there was the fact that the date itself carried some ideological significance: for up until the mid-second century BC it had been the date when newly appointed consuls assumed their positions and took vows before Jupiter on the Capitoline Hill.[97] Most important of all, it happened that there was a meeting already convened for the Ides of March and it was only three days before Caesar went off on his next big adventure: the Parthian campaign.

The Ides of March hence offered the conspirators a prime opportunity to attack: the dictator had dismissed his bodyguard, and would be vulnerable. But how would other senators respond? Our ancient sources offer a range of thoughts that might have crossed the conspirators' minds. Nicolaus presumed that the high number of senators in on the conspiracy would have isolated Caesar from any support, while Appian presumed that senators who were not involved in the plot might even join in.[98] However, both these suggestions are unlikely, because Caesar had increased the size of the Senate and awarded positions to a whole host of men who consequently owed their very seats in the Senate to Caesar. There was no knowing how they would respond, and the number of senators excluded from the conspiracy far outweighed the small band who executed the plot. Dio might be closer to the mark, then, when he suggests that the Senate meeting was chosen because it was the only location that offered a tactical advantage.[99] The conspirators had planned to smuggle their weapons in and then conceal them under their togas, whereas other senators would be unarmed and thus unable to defend Caesar. There would be nothing that anyone could do. And as the event turned out, in this they were correct.

Brutus and Caesar: Final Encounters

We have seen the details of the assassination already in the Introduction: the omens which were ignored, the soothsayer who was spurned, and the note Caesar failed to read – all factors which contributed to the tragedy of Caesar, as recorded in the literature and propaganda following his death. We have also seen how these accounts were embellished with metaphors of trapped wild beasts and the imagery of hunting and sacrifice: images which enhance the sympathy we feel for the victim of this horrific attack, simply by the way they focus our attention upon and help us to visualise Caesar's death so graphically on the Ides of March (Plate 7).

As per the plan agreed by the conspirators, when it came to the meeting of the Senate that day, Antony was detained outside by Trebonius, while Caesar walked into the trap that had been set for him. Almost immediately upon entering the hall, the dictator was surrounded by a mixture of close friends and former enemies whose lives he had spared. Two months before, all of them – Brutus, Cassius, Decimus and perhaps up to seventeen co-conspirators – had sworn an oath to protect him, yet a physician's report recorded twenty-three knife wounds on Caesar's mutilated corpse.[100] Some presumably stabbed him more than once; others may have missed, to judge from the reports of chaos that accompanied the assassination.

Of all our ancient writers, Suetonius captures the moment with an emotional simplicity which owes its origins to Cornelius Balbus, an eyewitness and intimate friend of Caesar's:

> Wherever he turned, he saw that drawn daggers were attacking him, he buried his head in his toga, and at the same time, using his left hand, he drew its fold down to his feet, so that he would fall more honourably, with the lower part of his body covered too. And in this way, he was stabbed twenty-three times. He did not utter a word – just a groan at the first blow. Although some have reported that when Marcus Brutus rushed at him, he said *Kai su, teknon*.[101]

Thus, there were two versions of Caesar's last moments in circulation by the time Suetonius was writing his own account in the early second century AD. In the first and perhaps more reliable account (the one Suetonius presumably got from Balbus), Caesar fell in noble silence; yet in the second he uttered the famous last words *Kai su, teknon* – 'You too, child?' Because this story has significantly influenced the reception history both of Caesar's parting moments and of his relationship with Brutus, it is worth taking a closer look at these variant traditions and their possible implications.

Dramatic death scenes were a staple ingredient in Roman literature generally, and in biographies of famous personages specifically. Pompey's pickled head, Cato's suicide at Utica, and later Cicero's severed neck and hands all bear testament to the importance attached to the way a man exited the world. But, within this bundle of grime and gore, a man's parting words were of particular fascination. Many Romans consequently tended to have famous last words, especially in the case of the emperors, for whom we have more evidence.[102] However, from our own period, samples include: Cato ('Now I am my own master!') and Cicero ('I shall die in the country I have often saved'). In time, Brutus too received a dying epitaph: 'By all means, we must fly! But with our hands, not our feet' – thus signalling his decision to take his own life, rather than run away from battle.[103] Pompey, however, simply drew his toga over his face, and submitted to his killers' blows with only a groan.[104] The pathos of his death scene derives from the nobility of his character and the premature cessation of his life. Versions of Caesar's death which likewise emphasise his silence in the face of his assassins strive after the same effect; they also convey just how suddenly and unexpectedly he died.[105]

On the other hand, the alternative tradition – the one in which Caesar calls upon Brutus with his dying breath – may be seen to divest an added layer of tragedy into Caesar's end, as he acknowledges his special relationship with, and perhaps even paternity of, Brutus. His betrayal was one of the unkindest blows of them all. But how likely is the story that Caesar cried out *Kai su, teknon*? And is there even the slightest possibility that Brutus *was* Caesar's son? The ancient writers who record this second version tend to treat it sceptically: as we have just seen, Suetonius only mentions in passing, as a postscript to his narrative, the possibility that Caesar spoke.[106] But that still means the story existed. And, when compounded with the notorious love affair between Caesar and Servilia, on top of Caesar's clear favouritism towards his younger friend, it is not hard to see why some people arrived at the conclusion that Brutus was also Caesar's son.[107]

On the whole, scholars have rejected the possibility that Brutus was the love-child of Servilia and Caesar on the grounds of chronology.[108] If Brutus was born in 85 BC, Caesar was only fifteen at the time: not biologically impossible, perhaps, but unlikely given that Caesar was already betrothed to a certain Cossutia at the time.[109] Alternatively, if we date Brutus' birth to 79/78 BC, the timings get messier still: Caesar was away from Rome for most of Sulla's *regnum*, and he did not return until after his death in March 78 BC. By then, he was also married to his first wife, Cornelia – a patrician for whom he had abandoned Cossutia.[110] Yet, in any case, the evidence points to a much later date for the love affair between him and Servilia: as Friedrich Münzer convincingly demonstrated, an intimate relationship between the pair probably only started in 59 BC, after Servilia had been widowed for the second time, and when Brutus was already a young man. It is hence unlikely that Caesar was Brutus' father.

So where does this leave us regarding Caesar's supposed last words? And what precisely do they mean? It is possible that they were a later addition to the story on the part of Brutus' enemies, to make his deed seem more hideous still; no simple killer, in this version Brutus becomes a man who has murdered his own father. In a similar vein is the story recorded by Plutarch in his *Life of Caesar* that, when it came to killing Caesar, Brutus was sure to strike him in the groin.[111] But a closer look at the Greek in which Caesar's alleged words are expressed does not support such a conclusion.

To begin with, *teknon* does not necessarily mean 'child' by a biological connection; it is simply used as a form of address by older men to younger. It could be employed affectionately, often when combined with a pronoun ('my child') or adjective ('dear child'); or it could just mean 'child', a word which has more patronising connotations in English when we render it as 'kid'.[112] Of course, we would have to have heard the tone in which Caesar uttered it to know what he meant by the word *teknon*: that is, whether it was a term of affection or a condescending dig. However, a strong clue can be found in the expression *kai su* which prefaces its use, and which nearly always has a strongly negative tone in our other contemporary or near-contemporary evidence.

In an important article that has often been overlooked, even by some of the most recent authors on Caesar and Brutus, James Russell drew attention to the apotropaic function of these words, which are usually transcribed as KAI CY on curse tablets, mosaics and other forms of art (). By definition, this means the expression *kai su* can ward off evil and destroy it with a curse; it can also reflect the evil back onto the recipient.[113] In other words, *Kai su, teknon* was not the emotional parting declaration of a betrayed man to one he had treated like a son – the almost gentle 'Even you, my child', the Shakespearean *Et tu, Brute?* – but a bitter and wilful curse on Brutus, that he should live to suffer the consequences of Caesar's assassination: 'Back atcha, kid!' we might instead put it, or 'See you in hell, punk!' as it has been interpreted by Jeffrey Tatum.

Yet there is still more to it than that. For other scholars have pointed to the fact that the expression *Kai su, teknon* is also the first half of an ancient Greek proverb, which ended something like 'will have a bite of my power'.[114] Perhaps Caesar was cut off mid-sentence, or perhaps the ending could have been easily supplied by someone with Brutus' knowledge of Greek culture and literature. Either way, its purport is that Brutus too would one day suffer a violent death after his own taste of leadership – that his turn would come.

As in the curse interpretation offered by Russell, this reading of Caesar's last words again carries a very bitter threat. However, it also offers us something else besides: our first hint that Brutus' motives were challenged and debated in far more negative terms than Plutarch's *Life of Brutus* suggests. For whereas Plutarch, or Plutarch's sources, had erased any suggestion that

Brutus sought personal power – and had even used Caesar's own 'piece of flesh' dictum as an authority to this end – there was evidently another train of thought in antiquity. Suetonius, for one, did not put much trust in it, which suggests that the story was worked into the account of Brutus' and Caesar's final encounters at a later date. But the insinuation of *Kai su, teknon* should by now be clear: in the anti-Liberator tradition that circulated after the assassination, Brutus was driven by a power-mad ambition, of which the murder of Caesar was just one instance. In short: while the ancient evidence cannot definitively answer for us what drove Brutus to kill Caesar, it does enable us to get closer to a variety of perspectives that were current from the start.

Thus, when Appian came to write his own connected narrative of this period of Roman history about 200 years later, he found a whole array of explanations as to why Brutus may have conspired against Caesar:

> Either Brutus was being ungrateful, or he may have been ignorant, sceptical or ashamed of his mother's transgressions; either he was excessively devoted to liberty and put his country above all else, or being a descendant of that Brutus of old who expelled the kings he was provoked and shamed to this deed mainly by the people.[115]

With this summary, we are reminded of the many possible motives, personal as well as political, that might have spurred Brutus on.[116] And it hence reminds us that we, in the twenty-first century, are hardly qualified to know what Brutus thought, said or did on that fateful day of 44 BC. The best we can do – as I have attempted in this chapter – is to use our knowledge of the contemporary culture and environment in which Brutus lived in order to understand the manifold factors that may have weighed on him. For, as we have seen, public opinion, peer pressure, his own political ambitions as well as a good measure of philosophical thinking may all have combined to turn Brutus' freedom-fighting rhetoric of old into a stark new reality. But one thing is sure: Caesar was assassinated because he chose to put himself above the law, above the constitution, and because he accepted honours that were more appropriate for gods than for men. The Ides of March hence spelled the end of Caesar; yet for Brutus, so long a shadow in his own biography, it was just the beginning.

CHAPTER 5

AFTER THE ASSASSINATION

A Catalogue of Horrors

Earthquakes were frequent. Dockyards and many other places were struck by lightning. By the violence of a tornado a statue, which Cicero had placed before the inner sanctuary of Minerva the day before he went into exile on plebeian order, fell face down and lost its limbs; its shoulders, arms and head were broken – a dire portent to Cicero himself. Bronze tablets from the Temple of Faith were ripped away by the gale. The doors to the Temple of Wealth were broken. Trees were uprooted and many houses overturned. A meteor was seen bearing west in the sky. A conspicuous star blazed for seven days. Three suns shone, and around the lowest sun there flashed a corona resembling a wreath made up of ears of corn, and afterwards, with the sun reduced to one small orb, the light was faint for many months. In the Temple of Castor some of the letters of the names of the consuls Antony and Dolabella were struck out, signifying that they would both be alienated from their country. The howling of dogs was heard at night in front of the house of the Chief Priest; the fact that the largest of the pack was torn apart by the rest portended a shameful dishonour to Lepidus. At Ostia a school of fish was stranded on dry land when the overflowing sea receded. The river Po flooded and as it returned to within its banks it left a huge number of vipers.

— Julius Obsequens, *Book of Prodigies*, 68

When the Roman writer Julius Obsequens compiled his book of prodigies approximately 400 years after the death of Caesar, he managed to find a whole host of miraculous occurrences that were said to have followed on from the Ides of March. Many of the portents he describes can also be found in Dio's account; they are self-evidently fantastic and a reminder, if one were needed, that our sources often contain invention after the fact – tales, presumably passed down through the centuries, which our authors found in their sources.[1] Intriguingly, however, some of our contemporary evidence proves that not all of these stories were entirely fabricated.

Cicero's statue was indeed knocked over, only it happened in a gale the year after.[2] Closer in time to the assassination, in the early months of 44 BC, we hear that Mount Etna in Sicily erupted, which might account for the darkening of the skies in Obsequens' list, since a murky gloom was said to have lingered for the rest of the year.[3] There was a comet too, which appeared in the sky as a 'conspicuous star' – it occurred in July, at the same time as the games held in Caesar's honour.[4] It is also entirely possible that meteorological and atmospheric phenomena, such as we know today, caused the shore to recede at Ostia or the Po to flood. But for Romans living at the time, as well as the writers who recorded them afterwards, such supernatural events were not to be taken lightly: prodigies were perceived as spontaneous signs of divine anger.

The contemporary poet Virgil helps us envisage the feeling on the ground in the aftermath of the assassination: 'Even the sun felt pity for Rome at the destruction of Caesar / when it covered its gleaming head with a dark rusty gloom / and a wicked age feared an eternal night.' 'At no other time have more thunderbolts fallen through / calm skies, nor dire comets blazed so often', he continues.[5] The catalogue of horrors was 'unspeakable', he claims, using the Latin adjective *infandum* which is etymologically linked to the word for 'fate': that is to say, these portents were also interpreted as an expression of divine will and what was to come.[6] It may well be a poetic account of the scene at Rome in the wake of the Ides, yet there is one emotion which Virgil's poetry repeatedly invokes: fear. From the moment Caesar was struck down, it engulfed Rome.

The Fearful Aftermath

No sooner had the assassins withdrawn their bloody daggers from Caesar's body than panic spread like wildfire across the city. If the reports of Appian and Plutarch are correct, Brutus tried to make a speech there and then to the Senate. But he could not be heard above the cries of terror. Not knowing the numbers or the purpose of the conspirators, the senators fled the meeting at once.[7] Nicolaus of Damascus records the names of two men who initially tried to reach the dictator: Calvisius Sabinus and Censorinus.[8] However, this was to no avail. In the rush to get out, not one of Caesar's friends attended to him; not even Antony, now the sole surviving consul. He feared that he might be the assassins' next target, and sought the safety of his house as quickly as possible. The Senate was deserted; everyone had scattered. A glimpse of the horror may be caught through the eyes of Cicero, a witness to the event, who states that Caesar's body had been cut to pieces and left abandoned at the foot of the statue of Pompey – his former ally and son-in-law.[9] According to another near-contemporary account, it was only when silence fell that Caesar's slaves scooped his corpse off the floor, placed it in a litter, and carried it home to his wife. The sight of Caesar's limp limbs and mutilated face was enough to extract tears from the eyes of anyone who saw it; the women wailed when the lifeless body was returned to them.[10]

Meanwhile, Brutus was left to rally the conspirators. Antony later claimed that Brutus raised his blood-spattered dagger high into the air and immediately called upon Cicero.[11] Although the elder orator had not been invited into the conspirators' circle beforehand, presumably Brutus thought that he would be the ideal advocate for their deed afterwards; after all, Cicero had spoken out vigorously against tyranny in his published works, as well as, we can imagine, in his private conversations. But before any speeches were made, with his dagger still in the air, Brutus and his co-assassins led a grisly procession through the streets of Rome that led out of Pompey's complex and up to the Capitoline Hill – the old citadel and temple complex which overlooked the Forum. It not only made for a strategic position for watching over Rome's busy marketplace; it was the centre of religious activity and home to the huge temple dedicated to Jupiter and his divine companions, Juno and Minerva. As a site of great religious and political importance, the Capitoline Hill – or perhaps just the area around the temple – provided the assassins with sanctity; at the same time, their convention was a demonstrable act of piety.

As for what happened next, the precise details are particularly muddled in our sources, which were nearly all written much later;[12] yet fear is, once more, the prevailing emotion. One chance happening that added to the chaos was that, just as the senators were fleeing the scene of the murder, thousands of ordinary folk were spilling out from the nearby theatre, where they had been watching a gladiatorial contest. It was this show that had provided Decimus with the perfect cover for stationing his own gladiators in and around the Senate meeting, gladiators who were now able to escort and shield the assassins. But their presence must have been more alarming than reassuring. Brutus purportedly tried to calm the crowd – but again he was unsuccessful in his endeavour: panic ensued, Dio tells us, as people ran towards their homes shouting 'Run! Lock your doors! Lock your doors!'[13]

In another part of Rome, the news of Caesar's death soon reached Caesar's deputy, Marcus Aemilius Lepidus.[14] As the 'master of the horse' and the dictator's deputy, Lepidus had a power that was both military and political. He oversaw the cavalry in times of war, and because Caesar had been preparing for his Parthian expedition Lepidus had a full legion of soldiers at his disposal. Dio tells us that these soldiers were conveniently stationed on the Tiber Island, just outside the city boundary, and Lepidus quickly advanced there. How quickly he managed to get there we do not know. But some time before the end of the day, and certainly by the next morning, Lepidus' troops had strategically surrounded the Forum.[15]

Suetonius adds that Brutus and Cassius had initially planned to drag Caesar's body to the Tiber, confiscate his property and revoke all his decrees. But their own fear of Antony and Lepidus prevented them from carrying out their plan.[16] If this is true, then their failure to do so is an often overlooked moment that might have changed the course of history. For, as we shall see, it was these factors – Caesar's funeral, the distribution of his property and assets, and the enforcement of the plans he had made for the future – which contributed most to the arousal of anger over the following days and months. Instead, the assassins gradually let any tactical advantage slip to the other side.

At first, as we have seen, the newly self-fashioned 'Liberators' convened on the Capitoline Hill, encircled and protected by Decimus' gladiators, to review their options and decide what to do next. Although the ancient writers largely present their retreat as a defensive flight, had the decision to reconvene at an agreed location been prearranged, it would make excellent sense.[17] As did their next political move: before Lepidus managed to occupy the Forum, Brutus and Cassius came down from their place of safety on the hill complex to address the people in a *contio*. Before they took any further action, the Liberators needed to test out the amount of popular support they might receive for their action.[18] In ordinary times, their authority as praetors as well as their attendant lictors would have been enough to keep order at such a meeting. But this was no ordinary *contio*; as a precaution, some of Decimus' gladiators joined them. This part of the aftermath had been carefully thought through.

Given the importance of this moment in the fight to win the support of the people, it is frustrating that our sources are not better for the speech Brutus made to the people. Plutarch makes no mention of it in his *Life of*

Brutus, while Dio summarises the speech in one sentence. The Liberators had much to say against Caesar, he tells us, and much in support of democracy; they also told the people to have courage and not expect any harm. They had killed Caesar, they declared, not to secure power or any other advantage, but in order that they might be free and independent and be governed rightly.[19] However, Appian paints a rather different picture. According to his version, the assassins said nothing that 'betokened humility'. They simply praised each other, congratulated the city, and thanked Decimus before suggesting that the people imitate their ancestors in recovering their freedom after the expulsion of the kings; further, they recommended the recall of Sextus Pompeius and the tribunes recently deposed by Caesar.[20]

By all accounts, however, Brutus' speech was met with stony silence. Plutarch simply suggests that it was Brutus' authority that caused a lull as the awe-struck crowd awaited his speech, whereas Dio had read that Brutus' speech produced a calming effect which accounted for the silence. Appian maintains the people were intimidated by a band of discharged soldiers and other disreputables bribed by the assassins into supporting them. But Nicolaus provides a more convincing explanation for the people's response. On the one hand, he claims, people respected Brutus for his discretion, nobility and reputation for fairness. On the other – and this is perhaps the crucial point to bear in mind – they were extremely anxious for the future.[21] After all, this was a generation that had already lived through one civil war in recent times; many presumably also remembered the intense violence of the 60s and 50s BC. These were ordinary people who potentially stood to lose their entire livelihoods were a new war to erupt. And now Brutus stood there addressing the people surrounded by a troop of gladiators, having just killed the man who had at least provided some sort of stability.

If there is one thing on which all our sources appear to agree, then, it is that there was little show of public appreciation for the Liberators; instead, it seems, Brutus and Cassius had largely misread the people's opinion of Caesar.[22] As we saw in the last chapter, some people had turned against the dictator in the months leading up to his assassination: hence the graffiti, the heckling of Caesar and other such activity. But the calls for another Brutus had not been a call for assassination. The people had charged Caesar with aspiring towards monarchy, not tyranny; our muddling of this fact is a direct result of the intellectual endeavours of men like Cicero, who grafted Roman attitudes of kingship onto Greek ideas of tyranny.[23] In other words: men who studied Greek philosophy could recognise tyranny – and they might even agree that tyrannicide was the most virtuous of deeds. However, the ordinary people of Rome did not see it that way. For them, the guardian of liberty was not political murder; it was the body of laws which safeguarded all citizens from scourging and summary execution.[24] It is little wonder, then, that the Liberators' claims to have restored freedom after the assassination fell flat.

Other speeches to the people followed throughout the day – all in support of the assassins' actions, but there is nothing to suggest that the people were encouraged by these displays of approval. The praetor Lucius Cornelius Cinna was the first to endorse the deed, even throwing off his praetor's insignia, a gesture to show that he now despised the gift of a tyrant – or so the story later developed.[25] Dolabella also stepped into the fray to come out publicly on the side of the Liberators. He had been due to take over the consulship from Caesar as soon as the dictator departed for Parthia on 18 March. But Dolabella decided not to wait until then. He donned his consular regalia immediately, made a short address to the people and then ascended to the Capitoline Hill, to join Brutus and Cassius where they had since returned.[26]

Other notable sympathisers also flocked to the Capitoline Hill, to advise the Liberators on their next course of action. Cicero, whose name Brutus had called in the bloody mayhem of the assassination, was among them, and he had a specific recommendation to make: Brutus and Cassius should call a meeting of the Senate immediately to garner the support of the body as a whole.[27] But Brutus had another plan. Perhaps trusting too much in the character of Antony, and perhaps also hoping that he could win round Lepidus (who was married to one of his half-sisters),[28] he and Cassius instead decided to send a delegation to the two Caesarians, asking for a meeting to discuss the future state of affairs.

It may have seemed the diplomatic thing to do; Brutus might even have thought that the Liberators and leading Caesarians could form a coalition. But it gave Antony and Lepidus far too much time to think – and to act. The consul and the master of the horse said that they would give their reply the following day. But by then, Lepidus' troops were in place and Antony had gathered weapons of his own: he had obtained from Calpurnia all of Caesar's papers containing his decrees and plans (his *acta*), as well as a large supply of money to keep him going. The day had seen a conspiracy, the assassination of Rome's dictator, panic and flight, and now – to any contemporary observer – it must have looked as if the battle lines were being drawn: the Liberators occupied the Capitoline Hill under the guard of gladiators, while Caesar's troops surrounded the Forum. The citizens and people of Rome were right to be afraid.

The Success of Antony

When Antony fled the scene on the Ides of March, there was no telling what move he might make next. Some evidently shared Brutus' hope that Antony could be persuaded to cooperate for the common good; after all, the original conspirators had already been persuaded to spare his life once before. Others feared Antony's attachment to Caesar's party and saw the urgent need to topple his authority; Cicero, for one, had argued that Antony would promise anything if he was afraid, but that he would return to his 'old self' the minute he felt more confident.[29] The truth, if we can ever hope to recover it, is that each man knew a side to Antony different from that which Cicero's forceful rhetoric has often allowed us to see.[30] Rather, as more recent scholars have argued, it is only when we acknowledge Antony's capabilities as a shrewd political operator, as well as the position in which he, Brutus and Cassius (among others) found themselves after the Ides, that we can begin to understand the tumultuous events that separated the assassination from the commencement of open warfare. Within this course of events, the first five months – from 15 March to Brutus' final departure from Italy shortly after 17 August – are critical.

The details have been pieced together many times before.[31] However, of all the evidence we have for this dramatic period in Roman history, Cicero's correspondence is the only source that allows us to come close to recapturing the feeling and the frustrations on the ground in the Roman world after Caesar.[32] For the year 44 BC alone, we possess 122 letters. Some of these are the letters Cicero exchanged with the main participants in the unfolding drama: Brutus, Cassius and Antony among them. Others are copies of the letters they exchanged among themselves, which the senders or recipients presumably forwarded to Cicero. In the pages that follow, I hence quote from and discuss some of the letters of Cicero for this period of Brutus' life, so that we can view events after the assassination as they happened before a contemporary set of eyes. Primarily my aim is to show how they stand testament to the constantly changing political developments, as well as revealing the challenges to which Brutus had to respond as new and unpredictable circumstances arose.

However, my selection of letters also serves to combat the traditional narrative of Brutus' failings, which have largely been viewed through a Ciceronian lens. They show, for instance, how Cicero's own responses to the assassination developed over time, and often in defence of his own actions. The aim is not to rehabilitate Brutus' reputation or conduct, but to remove the hindsight that has clouded our response to him. It is only by reading between the lines of Cicero's correspondence that we can gain a unique insight into how the assassination was being received and recorded by Brutus' contemporaries. The result may at times have a distorting effect on the chronological structure of the narrative.[33] But this is more than compensated for by the fact that it enables us to bring Cicero's interpretations of events, as well as his objections to Brutus' handling of affairs, into something akin to 'real time'.

16–17 March: Decimus Despairs

Within the first forty-eight hours of the assassination, and probably on 16 March, Decimus wrote a revealing letter to his co-conspirators, Brutus and Cassius: 'Hear how we stand', he begins. For he had received a visit from Aulus Hirtius, one of Caesar's men, who was now acting as Antony's representative. 'He told me what state of mind Antony is in: naturally, a terrible and perfidious one.' Antony was threatening to deprive Decimus of the province he had been allocated by Caesar, that of Cisalpine Gaul. Nor did he think it safe for the conspirators to stay in Rome. So here was the first bind in which the conspirators now found themselves: they had just killed the man to whom they owed their current ranks and future magistracies. What is more, Antony and Lepidus had the support of Caesar's veterans and soldiers. It must have been clear to all, and not just Decimus, that the Caesarians had gained the upper hand.

'No text better illustrates the powerlessness of the conspirators and their failure to think through the consequences of their action', says Andrew Lintott of Decimus' letter. And, indeed, as we re-read Decimus' concerns it seems difficult to conclude otherwise. The Caesarians could potentially muster somewhere in the region of thirty legions, whereas the Liberators' only hope for immediate military aid rested on Sextus Pompeius in Hispania and Caecilius Bassus in Syria. As events would subsequently show, the former had seven legions, the latter only one. But at the time of the assassination, the conspirators had evidently not thought much about the numbers: 'it will be time enough for us to approach them when we know how strong they are', Decimus continues; the plan was only a vague one. Yet this letter arguably says more about Decimus than the rest of the assassins: it reflects his hasty reaction to events and his despondency alone. Although he was one of the ringleaders of the conspiracy, Decimus was not in a steering position; his only offering to the table was a downcast remark: 'we must give in to fortune'.

But the fact that the question of provincial commands was on the minds of Decimus and Antony so soon after the assassination reveals a key point about how the negotiations were going to go. Antony had found the Liberators' weak point and he was going to press home his advantage. If it had not already dawned on the conspirators, they must certainly now have realised the importance of Caesar's provincial arrangements for their long-term security. As Martin Drum has recently demonstrated in an impressive catalogue of the provinces that were at the time governed, or soon to be governed, by men who were friendly to the Liberators' cause, their military arm was not half as weak as it at first appeared to be. In all he identifies four major provinces in the east upon which the Liberators might rely: Macedonia, Asia, Bithynia-Pontus and Syria. When added to Decimus' stronghold of Gaul, our picture of the potential manpower and resources available to the Liberators is dramatically altered.

However, Drum's argument that this was part of a much longer-term strategy on the part of the conspirators, set in motion as early as 45 BC when his killers first lobbied Caesar to allocate them the eastern provinces, is less persuasive. Instead, I would suggest that the possibility of securing the provinces only presented itself as one option after the assassination; after all, there was no guarantee that Brutus and Cassius would receive the support they needed from governors who had not been included in the conspiracy, and there is little evidence to suggest they had thought this far ahead. Now, however, provided that the Liberators could hold onto the magistracies and provinces allocated to them – which in turn meant having Caesar's plans and decrees for the future ratified – they stood a chance of protecting themselves, and possibly even rebuilding a republican front. They may have been powerless in the short term, then, but they were not utterly helpless. In fact, Decimus' letter demonstrates just how quickly the Liberators were able to form strategies and adapt to new circumstances under pressure. To secure the magistracies and provincial arrangements was an effective Plan B.[34]

8 April: The Calm Before the Storm

Plan A, on the other hand, was to help establish peace, a period of calm, and a free system of government. Brutus and Cassius had not planned to stage a coup d'état; their priority from the beginning seems simply to have been to get rid of Caesar and then to work towards reconciliation. And by 8 April, when Cicero wrote one of his first letters to Atticus after the assassination, there seemed to be some positive signs in this direction.

Of particular importance had been a meeting of the Senate on 17 March at the temple of Tellus, just two days after the assassination. Many senators wanted the Liberators honoured for their actions; at the other extreme, others wanted the death of Caesar to be avenged. Another cause for concern was how the veteran soldiers might react, for Caesar had made them promises too – parcels of land in return for their service – and they were keen to get their rewards. In this heated environment, only a compromise would do and so, with Cicero acting as both the spokesman and the brains behind the operation, a compromise deal had been carefully hammered out. There was to be a general amnesty for the assassins; in return, all of Caesar's acts and appointments for the next two years were to have legal force, and the veterans were assured they would get their grants of land. Far from being proclaimed a tyrant, it was agreed that Caesar should have a public funeral. It was hardly the shower of thanks and praise the assassins had expected. But it did at least offer a blanket of forgiveness for the past and a guarantee of safety. Most crucially of all, it also offered hope.

The ratification of Caesar's *acta* meant that Decimus could go to his province of Gaul for the rest of 44 BC, and he could then become consul in 42 BC, just as Caesar had promised him. In that capacity, he could then preside over the elections for 41 BC, when Brutus and Cassius were hoping to be consular candidates. The Liberators might have been outfoxed by the combined forces of Lepidus' troops and Antony's cunning in the short term. However, in the long term, they might have envisaged a day when there would be a free and functioning system of elections again, and this end goal was presumably worth the wait. They might even have felt their security to be assured by the strong military positions and provincial commands, guaranteed under the terms of the amnesty, that they were to hold in the interim. The first forty-eight hours had been turbulent. But on 17 March Brutus and Cassius addressed the people in a *contio* on the Capitoline Hill, and at the end of the third day they were finally able to walk into the Forum again.[35] The people celebrated the reconciliation that had been made. And that night Brutus dined at the house of Lepidus, while Cassius joined Antony.

Although Cicero's letters later complained of wasted time and opportunities in the initial forty-eight hours, affairs at Rome were in fact stabilised relatively quickly. Admittedly, as we shall see, the first few days after the truce were far from plain sailing. But by 7 April, Atticus could at least report some positive signs to Cicero, who had since left Rome to tour his Italian villas. Atticus' own share of his correspondence with Cicero does not survive. But, on 8 April, Cicero sat down to reply to two letters he had received from his friend the day before: 'From your first letter I heard about the theatre and Publilius, good signs of the crowd's approval', he commented. The details are not made explicit but it is clear from the context that

Publilius Syrus, a well-known mime artist, had included in his performance some sort of political expression which had led to a demonstration in support of the Liberators. What had struck Cicero as particularly funny was that the crowd had accidentally broken out in a round of applause for Lucius Cassius, the assassin's brother and a supporter of Caesar, instead of Gaius. But it was a welcome sign of popularity nonetheless.

'The second letter was the one you wrote about "Baldie"', Cicero went on, using a nickname for Gaius Matius, a man who had been a close friend of Caesar's and who was now mourning his death. Cicero had arrived at this man's house the day before and was staying with him briefly. But he found Matius' attitude 'utterly depraved'. Matius had said that 'all was done for'; worse still 'he said it with glee'. For Matius was predicting that the people of Gaul – and especially the legions and veterans stationed there – would be up in arms within a matter of weeks. Matius had not actually spoken to any of Caesar's other friends since the assassination, but he was clearly weighing up the possibilities and his verdict was simple: 'it cannot all go away just like that'. According to this contemporary perspective, at least, the threat awaiting the Liberators did not come from inside Rome, but from an avenging force yet to arrive.[36]

9–11 April: Suspicious Minds

A day later and Cicero's mind was brooding on the dangers threatening Rome. 'Your letter reads like peace', Cicero wrote on 9 April, in reply to another letter from Atticus: 'How I hope it continues.' However, he was far from convinced. To be sure, Brutus and Cassius had taken some important steps to win over the veterans and the people; Cicero could also report that the assassination had met with some approval in the municipalities. But any support for Brutus and Cassius did not yet amount to much: 'they receive commendation and affection, but that's all', Cicero lamented, 'they are prisoners in their own homes'.

Matius was still talking about the threats from Gaul. For his part, Cicero had his own suspicions of Antony; he never did like the man. 'Sniff out Antony's intentions', he advised Atticus, 'although I suspect he is more likely to be planning banquets than devising trouble.' Meanwhile, there were other matters troubling Cicero: 'you see the magistrates', he wrote to Atticus on 11 April, 'you see all the tyrant's satellites in positions with *imperium*, you see his armies, you see the veterans on our flank'. All these spelled clear dangers for Brutus and Cassius. And then there were the rumours about Gaius Octavius (or Octavian, as modern scholars call him), Caesar's great-nephew, whom the dictator had posthumously adopted as his son. 'I should like to know news of Octavius' arrival, whether there is any rallying to him or any suspicion of a revolution. I don't suppose there is, but whatever it is, I want to know.'[37]

The eighteen-year-old had been in Apollonia, waiting to join Caesar on the Parthian expedition, when the news had first reached him of his great-uncle's assassination and, from there, he hurried back at once to Italy. Because Cicero was not present to witness his arrival, and because we do not possess any letter from Atticus to relay the circumstances of his appearance, we have to turn to the later sources, which tell us Octavian first landed at Lupiae near Brundisium. There he learned the news of his adoption and Caesar's troops hailed him as Caesar's son; and then with an entourage of veterans, soldiers and friends he travelled to Rome where he allegedly met with a hostile reception from Antony. In his letter to Atticus, Cicero offers us the only contemporary evidence to suggest that Octavian must have been arriving at Rome on or around 11 April; for Atticus, to whom he was writing, was in the capital, and Cicero was eager for any news. But it is only with hindsight and our knowledge of the significant role Octavian would go on to play that this snippet is of any importance at all. It seemed to mean little to Cicero at the time, and indeed Octavian quickly left again to journey south towards Naples. For the Liberators, however, the arrival of Caesar's popular heir on the scene cannot have seemed a good thing.[38]

12–15 April: Leaving Rome

By early to mid-April, civil unrest at Rome finally forced Brutus out of the capital. But it was not Antony causing the trouble, as even Cicero had to admit: 'Antony's meeting with our heroes is not disagreeable in the birth of new circumstances', he confessed to Atticus on 12 April. For there were others championing the dead dictator's memory and causing disturbances at Rome; the arrival in the city of more of Caesar's veterans created a prime opportunity for any ambitious upstart seeking instant celebrity to jump on the bandwagon of Caesar's popularity – especially since Antony and Lepidus had failed, in the eyes of some, to avenge his assassination. It was not long, then, before there was a resurgence of pro-Caesarian activity among the urban plebs, which was fuelled by a man calling himself 'Marius' (hereafter 'Pseudo-Marius') and claiming to be a distant relative of Caesar through Julia – Caesar's aunt, and wife of the famous general Marius, the seven-time consul.

Cicero had heard rumours of Pseudo-Marius before, but on 15 April he wrote to Atticus again: 'I saw Paulus on the 14th at Caieta', he reported. 'He told me something of "Marius" and the political situation, which is clearly terrible.' Paulus was the brother of Lepidus; Cicero could trust this information as reliable. We are not provided with any further news at this stage, but a later letter reveals that Pseudo-Marius had built an altar on the site where the dictator had been buried and was cultivating Caesar as a god; other rumours had it that he was even planning to trap and kill Brutus and Cassius. In the face of these threats, as well perhaps as the anxiety caused by Octavian's arrival, Brutus had arranged to meet with Antony, and while we cannot be privy to the nature of a private dialogue, it is almost certain that they discussed how to facilitate a leave of absence for Brutus. The presence of Pseudo-Marius at Rome had made the capital a very dangerous place for the Liberators to be.

As the urban praetor, Brutus needed a special exemption to be away from Rome for more than ten days, and Antony made sure that this was arranged: thus, he proposed and carried through a special measure so that Brutus could leave – as we know he did, at some time either on or by 13 April.[39] Cicero was not in touch with Brutus at this time, but he found out everything he could through Atticus or other intermediaries: 'I hear our friend Brutus has been spotted at Lanuvium', he wrote on 15 April. 'But where, I ask, is he going to go? I am longing to know everything on all remaining news, but especially about this.'[40]

19 April: Blame Games

Within a month of the Ides, then, the assassins had all left Rome. Brutus had made his way to the estate he owned in Lanuvium, just 20 miles southeast of Rome, while Cassius presumably left with him. Others, as we shall see, eventually left to assume their provincial commands: Decimus to Cisalpine Gaul, Trebonius to Asia, and Tillius Cimber to Bithynia. The ratification of all their posts under the terms of the amnesty had been a vital part of the negotiations, but those left behind were still living and operating under Caesar's terms: 'Was *this* what my (and your) dear Brutus planned for?' Cicero now asked with evident exasperation in the letter he sent to Atticus on 19 April. 'That he should stay at Lanuvium, that Trebonius should set out for his province using the back roads, that all of Caesar's actions, writings, words, promises, and plans should weigh stronger now than when he was alive?' So what had gone wrong? Cicero's mind was tasked with reliving the past and he cursed the Liberators' lack of proactive intervention in the first forty-eight hours after the assassination.

'Do you recall me shouting, on that very first day on the Capitoline Hill, that the praetors needed to summon the Senate to the Capitol?' Cicero prodded, referring to the first meeting of the conspirators and their allies on the Ides of March. 'Heavens above, what could have been accomplished then, when all the honest men – or even just the moderately honest men – were rejoicing and the bandits were broken.' In a sense, Cicero had a point. Had Brutus and Cassius summoned the Senate before Antony got the chance, they could have pressed forward and consolidated their positions as 'Liberators'. But was the task of restoring peace and liberty as simple as Cicero suggests? After all, as recent events proved, even if the Senate had unanimously supported them, it would only take a few dissenters to stir up the anger of the veterans and plebs. The idea that an earlier intervention by Brutus and Cassius would have dissolved the situation almost certainly represents Cicero's wishful thinking.

Atticus, for one, thought there were other factors to blame. 'You point the finger at Bacchus' day', Cicero piped back – denoting the Senate meeting at the temple of Tellus convened by Antony on 17 March, which was held on the festival of Bacchus. In the absence of Atticus' own letter, we are left to imagine the course of the dialogue between the two correspondents. But it is possible that Atticus was replying to remarks Cicero had been making with increasing impatience since Brutus had left Rome. 'What is more wretched than the fact we are upholding the very things which made us hate Caesar?' he asked on 12 April. 'Are we even to have the consuls and tribunes *he* wanted for the next two years?' Or, as he put it on 17 April: 'the tyranny lives on though the tyrant is dead'. For all Cicero might moan about the amnesty agreement, Atticus could have pointed out that it *had* been Cicero's idea. But Cicero was not about to accept the blame for that: 'By then we were already done for', he defensively reminded his friend. Brutus and the other Liberators, in his opinion, had failed to seize the initiative.

That said, there was one thing on which Cicero and Atticus could both agree: namely, that Caesar should never have been allowed the full funerary rites. This had been Atticus' advice from the very start: 'Do you recall that it was you who shouted out that the cause was lost if he had a funeral?' Cicero reminded him. For there was great pomp and ceremony attached to aristocratic funerary practices: a procession from the deceased man's house made its way to the Forum, and it was followed by a public eulogy, delivered from the *rostra*. The occasion offered great scope for Antony to shape the public memory of Caesar – and in turn, that of his assassins. This was the reason why Atticus had cautioned against a funeral for Caesar, and as the event proved he was right.

Later accounts of the funeral, which had taken place a month earlier on 20 March, seem to confirm the argument presented here, that the funeral was a significant turning point in the people's responses towards the assassins. Appian records histrionic displays as Antony grew increasingly frenzied, lifting his hands to the heavens and calling forth from memory all of Caesar's wars, battles, victories, conquered nations and the spoils he had returned to Rome. As his passions intensified, he is said to have thrown off the garments covering Caesar's body, lifted his robe on a spear and waved it above his head. There, for all to see, was the blood-stained cloth ripped through by the assassins' daggers. Somewhere else in the crowd, a wax effigy of Caesar was reportedly suspended over the bier carrying his corpse, rotating on a mechanical device and offering a graphic image of the stab wounds he had suffered. Pushed beyond all limits of reason, our sources tell us that some of the crowd turned to violence: the Senate house was set on fire and a witch hunt for the conspirators ensued. In the mêlée, the poet Helvius Cinna was torn limb from limb in an unfortunate case of mistaken identity: he had been confused with the praetor Cinna who had spoken in support of the Liberators in a torrent of anti-Caesarian abuse on that first afternoon after the assassination. Fire spread, Caesar's body was half burned and nearby houses were set ablaze.

Such details may owe more to dramatic conventions than reality, as Peter Wiseman has argued in his engaging analysis of the sources: spurious embellishments which may have first been added by the Roman historian Livy, who was more than capable of adding a touch of melodrama to his narratives. And Appian's account is far more elaborate than those of Suetonius and Nicolaus, which are much more subdued, and pay less attention to Antony's own role. In any case, though, in Cicero's first-hand recollections the scene was clearly inflammatory: 'Caesar was even cremated in the Forum and woefully eulogised', Cicero complained in this same letter to Atticus: 'slaves and beggars were even set upon our houses with firebrands'. In his later second *Philippic* oration, he elaborated further: 'It was you [Antony], yes, you, who lit those firebrands.'

There is no denying that the funeral was a carefully orchestrated affair, in which Antony's own funeral speech appears to have played a pivotal role; it was also the first time there had been a large-scale demonstration of popular anger towards the conspirators. As such, it was certainly a turning point in the way the assassination was being received on the ground. Yet still we should resist the temptation to follow Cicero's lead in believing that this was another instance from which the Liberators were entirely unable to recover. For, as we have already seen, even after the funeral Brutus and Cassius maintained some visibility at Rome; the later account of Plutarch is wrong in suggesting they ran away at this point. What is more, as the incident at the theatre in early April suggests, at least some popular opinion was in favour of the assassins.[41] Much had happened since then; but Cicero was so busy living in the past that he failed to recognise the very real dangers facing Brutus in the present.

19–22 April: Trouble Ahead

Buried towards the end of the same letter in which Cicero blamed Brutus and the Liberators for their failures, we find a brief allusion to the previous day's news from Cumae, where Cicero was currently staying: 'Octavius arrived in Naples on 18 April', he writes. Following his brief and profitless stop at Rome, the young man had headed south, where the next day he was met by Balbus, formerly one of Caesar's most trusted advisers. Cicero had met with Balbus too, and he had confirmed what Atticus had already said on the matter: Octavian was going to seek his inheritance and he feared a huge tussle with Antony. But if Octavian did present a source of danger, Cicero could not see it at first. In a letter of 21 April, he reported that Octavian was staying with his stepfather Lucius Philippus at Puteoli, in the house next door to Cicero: 'Octavius has just arrived', he wrote to Atticus: 'he is completely devoted to me'. However, the next day he wrote again, with less certainty:

> His followers were calling him Caesar, but Philippus does not, nor indeed do I. In my view, he cannot possibly be a good citizen. There are too many around him who threaten death to our friends, and deny that things can continue as they are.

To put this comment into context, we should remember that the 'good citizens', or *boni* in Cicero's terminology, were the men who championed the collective authority of the Senate and the *res publica*: the very tradition Caesar had been accused of destroying in his lifetime. By taking Caesar's name, then, a name which both Cicero and Philippus refused to use in addressing the young man, Octavian's behaviour was already giving Cicero reasonable grounds for suspicion. But still Cicero seemed more worried about what the young Caesar's friends were planning than he was about Octavian himself.[42]

22 April: Unfinished Business

As we have seen, Cicero had expressed his dissatisfaction at the way affairs had been managed before now. But, perhaps still smarting at Atticus' suggestion that the amnesty Cicero had negotiated was to blame for Antony's rise to power (and not Brutus and Cassius), he soon found a new axe to grind. For in his letter of 22 April Cicero makes his first mention of a point of view for which he has become famous: Antony should have been killed too.

> My dear Atticus, I fear the Ides of March have given us nothing but joy and the reward for our hatred and suffering. What news I hear from Rome! And the things I see here! 'The deed 'twas fine, but unfinished'.

The conspirators had, of course, discussed this plan. It was only because Brutus objected that Antony had not been murdered along with Caesar. But we may ask what Antony had done to have Cicero bring this argument up now. The problem, as Cicero goes on to reveal, was that he believed Antony was now sneaking through his own measures by pretending they were in Caesar's plans: thus, he posted a law making all Sicilians Roman citizens – 'in return for a massive pay-out', Cicero surmised. The consul also recognised Deiotarus' kingship: a worthy undertaking, 'but not on account of Fulvia', smarted Cicero, for it was rumoured that Antony's wife had accepted a bribe from the eastern potentate. In his defence, Antony might have argued that these were plans that Caesar had intended to pass; the definition of what constituted the dictator's *acta* (his 'mandates') had been a matter of concern from the beginning.[43] However, the clue to understanding Cicero's wrath in this letter lies more in his personal concerns regarding Antony's measures than the future of the *res publica*.

The Sicilians had been Cicero's clients ever since he undertook the prosecution of Gaius Verres, a former corrupt governor of the province, back in 70 BC: *he* was their patron, not Antony. Likewise, he had represented Deiotarus against Caesar, which made the former indebted to Cicero, as well as to Brutus, who had defended his interests at Nicaea in 47 BC. To any sceptical spectator, it would have appeared that Antony was attempting to forge and fortify his own political networks – even winning over those who had formerly been attached to the Liberators and their supporters. However, a final measure was enough to make Cicero wish even Caesar was still alive. This concerned the recall from exile – again under the guise of Caesar's *acta* – of a certain Sextus Cloelius. This man had been an ally of Cicero's personal enemy, Clodius, and was prosecuted for his share of the violence in 52 BC. On 22 April, the same day that Cicero wrote his letter to Atticus remonstrating against Antony's actions, he had received another from the consul revealing his shocking intentions to restore Cloelius: 'how unscrupulously, how shamefully and perniciously' the request had been made, cried Cicero. So there we have it: what first prompted Cicero to wish Antony was dead was the use to which Antony was putting the dead Caesar's alleged decrees, as opposed to the fact of the agreement itself.[44]

From this point on in the correspondence, however, the argument that Antony should have been killed becomes at times fanatical. Writing a year later to Cassius and Trebonius, who he probably knew shared his opinion on this matter, Cicero could complain about Brutus' lack of foresight in a more jocular fashion: 'a pity you didn't invite me to dinner on the Ides of March! For sure there would have been no leftovers then!'[45] In other words: had Cicero been included among the circle of conspirators, he would have ensured the assassins' net had been cast wider. The idea that this was where the plan went wrong has so heavily dominated accounts of the assassination that it is sometimes hard to see the other side: that is, Brutus' side. However, if we leave hindsight to one side and go back in time to review the first few weeks following the assassination, we shall see that there was nothing in Antony's behaviour to suggest Brutus had been wrong. In fact, the decision to spare him may have been the one thing that saved the Liberators' lives.

To begin with, in the first few days after Caesar's death and even long after the funeral, Antony had ostensibly worked in a manner that was respectful towards the assassins. For his part, Lepidus would have preferred immediate vengeance upon his friend's killers, and wanted to move in his soldiers straight away.[46] Yet he agreed to support Antony's plans and later also joined in negotiations with the Liberators. Even Cicero had to admit that Antony had behaved honourably. As he later tried to steer the consul back to the path of moderation on which he had first embarked, Cicero claimed that 'Mark Antony gave an excellent speech on that occasion', referring to the debates in the Senate on Bacchus' Day. 'By his actions, and through his son' – whom Antony had sent to the Capitoline Hill as a hostage to guarantee good faith – 'peace was finally established with our most distinguished civilians.'[47]

'On the first, second, and third days – and all the remaining ones after that in a row – you did not cease to bring the *res publica* a daily gift, as it were', Cicero continued.[48] Antony's benefactions towards the state reached a climax when he even abolished the dictatorship from constitutional practice once and for all: 'a most remarkable gesture', Cicero recalls; it earned Antony a vote of thanks from a grateful Senate.[49] His words in praise of Antony may have received emphatic exaggeration by the time he pronounced them in the first *Philippic*, delivered in September 44 BC, but they were not entirely empty rhetoric. By the end of April, there was nothing yet in Antony's behaviour to suggest that he might turn against his promise to protect the conspirators.

28/29 April: A Turn of Affairs

And yet it is important to remember that Antony had probably never envisaged anything more than an immediate passage of safety for the Liberators, and he certainly would not have wished to see them in positions of power within the state. He was not their friend, nor, despite several points of contact, had he ever been. What is more, with voices of protest crying out across Rome from those who wanted the assassins punished, the pressure was on Antony to improve his own standing among Caesar's veterans and supporters. Under these circumstances, every move he made was closely scrutinised, often with alarm. We have just seen something of Cicero's fears when Antony interpreted the amnesty agreement to include the unpublished acts of Caesar. But worse was to come when he turned the annual Roman festival of the *Parilia* into an occasion to commemorate Caesar's victory at Munda on 21 April the year before. 'You must repeat your story again', he wrote to Atticus about a week later. 'Our Quintus wore a garland at the *Parilia*? On his own?'

Cicero was referring to the antics of his and Atticus' rogue nephew, the younger Quintus Cicero, who was now showing his support for Caesar, and had attached himself to Antony. Yet, light-heartedly as Cicero seems to treat the stories of his behaviour here, there was evidently a darker undercurrent to his correspondence with Atticus this month. For Atticus had written to Cicero on 26 April repeating his arguments from earlier letters: he defended Brutus, Cassius and Decimus from Cicero's criticisms of them; once more he blamed Cicero's handling of affairs on 17 March. 'Let's forget the past', Cicero remarked, before coming to the new point of Atticus' letter: 'you write that on 1 June Antony will bring forward a proposal about the provinces, so that he will have the two Gauls and that tenure will be extended for them both?' He was also disturbed to hear reports that the temple of Ops, where Caesar had deposited vast reserves of treasure, had been plundered.

Whether Atticus had already spelled out the implications of these moves, or whether Cicero's mind was too full of other concerns to engage with them here, the letter hints at a very worrying turn of affairs. Antony was seeking to strengthen his own position by transferring to himself the power over the two Gauls (Cisalpine and Transalpine), while, at the same blow, stripping Decimus of the command he had just assumed. Not only that: he was trying to buy his co-consul Dolabella's favour by proposing for him an extended command in Syria. But, in the same letter, Cicero said that he intended to be at Rome for the meeting in June, and that he was pleased to hear that Brutus and Antony were corresponding: 'It does seem as though things could still get better', he concluded rather optimistically. However, as he admitted, he was rather preoccupied with other matters: 'I must think about where I am going to live, and where to go in the immediate term.'[50]

3 May: Dolabella's Act of Heroism

When Matius made his grim prediction to Cicero that 'it cannot all go away just like that' following the murder of Rome's leading statesman, he had a point. Admittedly, he had been wrong about Gaul; it was 'all full of peace, despite what "Baldie" had said', Cicero happily reported to Atticus on 17 April. But insofar as there were others championing the memory of Caesar, and others who were calling for vengeance upon the Liberators, Matius had understood more about Caesar's supporters than Cicero, Brutus or Cassius did: killing Caesar was never going to be enough to end Caesarism.[51] The dictator's plans, methods, regime and even his cult had become far too deeply ingrained in Roman political life for them to be destroyed at the same time as the man; it had been this fact which had enabled the rise of the man claiming to be Marius, and in turn it had forced the Liberators out of Rome.

Yet the appearance of Pseudo-Marius and the violence of his followers did not just pose a threat to Brutus and Cassius; Antony too must have feared his ability to win the affections of Caesar's supporters. At some point in mid- to late April, then, he took drastic action and ordered the impostor's execution, by an archaic method of capital punishment: Pseudo-Marius was thrown to his death from the high Tarpeian Rock – a steep cliff on the south side of the Capitoline Hill. A few days later, acting on his own accord, Antony's co-consul Dolabella went further still and overturned the altar and a column dedicated to Caesar. 'My magnificent Dolabella', Cicero rejoiced in a letter he sent to Atticus on 1 May – only now claiming as his own his former son-in-law who had neglected and abandoned his daughter Tullia. 'This business is really attracting great attention: over the Tarpeian Rock, onto the cross with them, away with the pillar, get the site paved over!' he remarked, referring to Pseudo-Marius and other Caesarian rioters. Cicero's excitement jumps off the page; it was the first piece of good news he had had since the assassination.

Up until now Cicero had been engulfed by a deep gloom at the failure of Brutus and Cassius to lead a republican revival. But now, in his eyes, Dolabella was stepping in as the champion of that cause. 'Heroic. He seems to have crushed that false display of regret for Caesar, which was creeping up by the day.' Cicero had been afraid at the ground being gained by the cult of Caesar. But this turn of events invigorated his spirit. By this time, Antony had left Rome, on a mission to settle some of Caesar's veterans in Campania and to win their support.[52] Lepidus, too, was on his way to Hispania Citerior ('Nearer Spain') to assume his duties as the governor of the province.[53] This meant that Dolabella was the only consul at Rome – and he had been batting on the side of the Liberators since the Ides of March. Ever one to form coalitions of convenience and to see new possibilities opening, Cicero's mind was buzzing. On 2 May, he wrote again to Atticus: 'It looks to me as though our Brutus can now walk through the Forum wearing a gold crown.' Evidently, he envisaged a safe return for the Liberators, and – with the leading Caesarians all out of the way – the chance to win popular support once and for all.[54]

8–11 May: Contemplating Exile

Brutus, however, had a different plan. By the beginning of May, Brutus and Cicero were communicating directly with one another again, and Cicero had sent Brutus a letter at the same time as he penned others to Atticus, Cassius and Dolabella in the light of the last's 'heroic' activity.[55] However, far from feeling optimistic at the turn of affairs, Brutus now harboured little hope for his immediate future at Rome. On the one hand, we must remember that communications always travelled slower than the daily change in political circumstances, so there was a chance that Brutus had not heard or fully digested the news from Cicero. On the other, even if he had, Brutus probably could not bring himself to entrust his safety to Dolabella; after all, leaving aside all his earlier indiscretions, this was a man who had just recently usurped the consulship and was being proposed by Antony for an extended command in Syria. Dolabella was far from reliable and instead Brutus was reviewing his options.

'He is contemplating exile', remarked Cicero, who thought Brutus' absence from Rome was an act of political suicide. 'If he is not going to come to the Senate on the Kalends of June, I don't know what he will do in public life.'[56] But it seems that Atticus was recommending, at least in jest, that Cicero should do the same: 'You mention Epicurus and dare to say: "Do not get involved in political life"? Is the sombre little face [*vulticulus*] of our Brutus not enough to deter you from that sort of talk?'[57]

It was only a tentative plan. But, to judge from Cicero's comment that Brutus' seriousness was written all over his 'sombre little face', the thought of retiring from public affairs was evidently a decision which weighed upon him heavily. This need not suggest it was an act of desperation on Brutus' part, especially when we consider that he had once written that those in exile could take their virtues with them. That Brutus appeared to be standing in philosophical acceptance of his position, however, tells us much about how he perceived the state of affairs at the time.

Much had happened in the six weeks or so that separated the assassination of Caesar from this moment; and much more was to happen in the next two months before Brutus' final departure from Italy. By focusing on the letters from Cicero to Atticus depicting this tumultuous period, as well as the news they reveal of Brutus' personal situation, we have necessarily omitted many events that occurred beyond these parameters. Yet these letters from one contemporary set of eyes serve to reveal the shifting tides of hope, expectation, fear and anxiety that surrounded events in the first weeks after the Ides of March; at the same time, they demonstrate why it is virtually impossible to present a straightforward answer as to what Brutus could have planned, or what he could have done better to manage his own position in the face of the crisis that engulfed Rome. Not even Cicero and Atticus appear to have been able to agree on that point.

It would become exhausting to continue through Cicero's letters in the same detail; in what follows, it will be better to focus on the major political players and developments that emerge from them, as well as Brutus' own responses to each new turn. In so doing, we can pull together the main threads of Brutus' story, and thus gain a composite picture of his movements and intentions after the Ides up to the end of the summer.

Caesar's Successors

Before Antony left Rome at the end of April 44 BC, he had been forced to contend with Octavian's arrival in the city, as well as the antics of Pseudo-Marius, who had revived and championed Caesar's memory among those who mourned him. Both of these men presented a challenge to Antony's claim to the leadership of the Caesarian faction, and his severity in executing Pseudo-Marius had caused him to suffer a loss of popularity among a portion of the populace at Rome. On other fronts, he must have worried about the amount of military power now vested in Decimus, who had taken up his station in Cisalpine Gaul, as well as harbouring a latent fear of Sextus Pompeius – the only surviving son of Pompey the Great, who had seven legions armed in Hispania.[58] Antony had consequently embarked on a tour around Campania, ostensibly to settle Caesar's veterans, but also to scout for military support. However, his absence allowed for the re-emergence of Octavian, which in turn had devastating consequences for the reputation of Caesar's assassins in the capital.

Octavian had made his second appearance at Rome in early May, just after the execution of Pseudo-Marius and the destruction of Caesar's column by Dolabella; he wanted to accept his name and his inheritance, and to carry out the terms of Caesar's will. First, then, he needed to approach Gaius Antonius, Antony's brother, one of the praetors for 44 BC, who had assumed Brutus' responsibilities as the magistrate in charge of the city's business. Later Octavian asked Antony's other brother, Lucius Antonius – a tribune of the plebs – for permission to address the people in a *contio* so that he could formally announce his intention to accept his status as Caesar's successor. Perhaps, as Ulrich Gotter has suggested, Lucius saw in Octavian a force to check the power of Dolabella, who was still espousing the cause of the Liberators. It is possible, too, that Lucius did not agree with his brother on the need for reconciliation and instead wanted vengeance.[59]

What is significant here, however, is that Octavian was given a platform to address the people – a fact which was giving both Cicero and Atticus cause for concern on Brutus' behalf: 'about Octavius' speech in the *contio*, I feel the same as you', Cicero wrote on 18 May; nor did he like the sound of the forthcoming games, in which Octavian was proposing to display Caesar's throne.[60] Octavian was trying to establish himself as the legitimate successor to Caesar: to gain his name, his wealth, and the support of the soldiers and veterans the dictator had once commanded. The effect was twofold. For the Liberators, it meant that there was a new force to contend with: a son who was calling for revenge, and who was not bound by any of the terms of the amnesty which protected the assassins. For Antony, the arrival of Octavian – a contender for the leadership of the Caesarian faction – changed everything, especially his own attitude towards Brutus, Cassius and their allies. If before Antony had worked to abide by the terms of the amnesty, now he needed to prove himself as a man loyal to the memory of Caesar, and hence distance himself from the dictator's assassins.

Publishing the Past

Under these circumstances, what Brutus needed most was a campaign to improve his public image, but his absence from Rome meant that he had to communicate with the citizenry through edicts and written speeches. In this connection, Atticus was keen that Cicero should help him, but Brutus would be a tricky client and Cicero knew it: 'As it happens, I recently tried to help him in the matter of an edict', Cicero informed Atticus. 'I wrote one for him at your request. I liked mine, he preferred his own.' 'Each man has his own bride', was all that Cicero had to say on the matter; after all, he and Brutus had always disagreed on matters of oratorical style.[61] Yet, for his own part, Brutus had already started the process of composing a published version of the *contio* speech he had given on the Capitoline Hill in the aftermath of the assassination.[62] It was almost two months since he had delivered it, but its publication after the event was a different political move, akin to the pamphleteering we saw Brutus engage in during his earlier career. After all, opinions on how Caesar's rule was to be remembered represented a new battlefield and never had there been more of a need for Brutus to redouble his energies.

When Brutus' speech was ready it would be one of several oratorical endeavours being hurried out for dissemination; for under such charged political circumstances, everyone wanted to have their words broadcast wider and further than the narrow confines of the Forum. On 21 April Cicero reported reading a public speech, presumably by one of the Antonius brothers, which hailed Caesar as 'such a great man' and a 'most distinguished citizen'.[63] On 3 May Cicero had also read the speech Dolabella had given when he took punitive action against the men championing Caesar's memory: 'nothing wiser than that', was his considered verdict. Dolabella knew exactly how to sway a crowd and how to capture the effects in writing.[64] On 11 May he received another speech by Dolabella, as well as one by Lucius Antonius, both of which had been delivered in a recent *contio*: 'Lucius' speech is appalling', he wrote to Atticus, 'Dolabella's is splendid.'[65] As for Brutus' own speech, a written-up copy reached Cicero on 18 May: 'most elegantly written, with words and expressions that cannot be bettered', he admitted, 'but if I had handled the topic, I would have written it far more passionately'.[66]

To be fair, the speech Brutus actually delivered back in March was probably more successful than Cicero acknowledges.[67] Even though he preferred a less flamboyant and more down-to-earth style of speech than Cicero, that does not mean that Brutus was any less dynamic as an orator; as we have already seen, Caesar believed he spoke with great force and freedom of expression, while the expert rhetorician Quintilian later added *gravitas* to the list of Brutus' virtues – that is, he had substance or impressiveness about him. These might have been just the qualities that were needed at the time. However, in the writing-up stage something certainly appears to have been lost; in another passage of his twelve-volume tome on oratory, Quintilian criticised Brutus' published speeches generally because they were not as good as his philosophical works. And, closer in time, Atticus was also concerned for his friend. He hounded Cicero with requests to write another version of the speech. 'How, I ask, could this be appropriate?' Cicero replied. 'Or do you wish me to focus on a tyrant justly and excellently slain?'[68]

Indeed, if we can use the version of this speech which Appian puts into the mouth of Brutus in his *Civil Wars* as evidence for the occasion – as there seems to be some reason to do – then this is precisely the point Brutus had failed to deliver: that Caesar had been a tyrant.[69] Yet, coming so soon after the amnesty agreement and the ratification of Caesar's *acta*, which expressly denied that Caesar had been a tyrant, this was obviously not an argument he could make. Rather, Brutus defended the conspirators against the charge of oath-breaking because, he argued, they had only sworn to protect Caesar's life under duress. In addition, he maintained they had only taken position on the Capitoline Hill because the death of Cinna the poet had alerted them to the dangers of their situation. And finally, he emphasised how Caesar – like Sulla before him – had invaded Rome, killed many of its most prominent citizens and then denied the Romans their liberty by arranging domestic affairs to his own liking. Presumably, the rhetoric of liberty, his measured self-justification, and thoughts of peace-making were something of a comfort to the anxious mob in the immediate aftermath of the assassination.[70] But it seemed to both Cicero and Atticus that his speech was sorely out of kilter with the changed circumstances by the time Brutus published it.[71]

Keeping up Appearances

When Antony returned to Rome around 18 May, he came back a more aggressive man: a bodyguard of loyal veterans accompanied him; several important senators fled from Rome. We only have Cicero's later evidence for it, written up at a time when he was engaging in an intense war of words with Antony, but a hint in one of his letters does provide a flavour of the response to Antony on the ground: 'you write that Marcellus and others are leaving. We will need to sniff things out when we are together and decide whether we can be safe at Rome.'[72] Up until now Cicero had been planning to attend the meeting of the Senate on 1 June, but he had also heard that soldiers were being gathered for the occasion and had personally been warned to stay away.[73]

As we have already seen, the nature of Antony's proposed legislation was causing consternation: he wanted to take command over the two provinces of Cisalpine and Transalpine Gaul for a period of five years. It was a move that looked like a direct attack on Decimus: 'Antony's plan seems set on war, if

Decimus is stripped of his province', Cicero commented. Even though he was technically still abiding by the terms of the amnesty, Antony was sending a clear message of threat to the Liberators: 'You say you don't know what our friends ought to do', Cicero wrote to Atticus, 'but that puzzle has been worrying me for some time.'[74] For the rest of May, Brutus and Cassius remained away from Rome. But, as the cracks in the amnesty agreement began to appear, the pair made an appeal to Antony in writing, which stands unique among the voluminous pages of Cicero's correspondence: in their own words, we hear about the Liberators' intentions from the beginning, their hopes for the future, and the vulnerability of their current position.

The letter begins, appropriately, with a heading that combines formality with a hint of familiarity; they are praetors writing to their consul, but the omission of Brutus' and Cassius' forenames also marks them out as acquaintances:[75]

> From Brutus and Cassius, praetors, to M. Antonius, consul.
>
> If your good faith [*fides*] and friendly disposition [*benevolentia*] had not prevailed upon us, we would not have written this letter to you; but since, in fact, you are well-disposed, you will assuredly take it in the best of part.

Yet the respectful focus on Antony's *fides* and *benevolentia*, the opening words of the Latin text, is undercut by the tone of tension that prevails throughout the rest of the letter. For, immediately afterwards, Brutus and Cassius address their concerns over the number of veterans gathering in Rome; then for their own safety if they were to return to the city, as well as a rumour they had heard that the soldiers wanted to rebuild the altar to Caesar that Dolabella had knocked down. 'It seems unlikely that anyone who wants us to be safe and honourable can approve and wish for that', they remarked. So much for Antony's *fides* and *benevolentia*; the effect of these words serves rather to remind Antony of his earlier goodwill towards the Liberators in a desperate effort to win it back. For, as they go on to argue, their aim was only to establish peace:

> The end result shows that we sought nothing but public tranquillity [*otium*] and the freedom of the community [*libertas*] from the beginning. Nobody can deceive us except you, which would certainly be out of character for a man of your honourability and good faith [*fides*]. Still, nobody but you can deceive us. For you alone we trust and will continue to trust. Our friends are deeply fearful on our behalf: though they have

> confidence in your good faith [*fides*], nevertheless it seems to them that the crowd of veterans can more easily be incited by others, in any direction they please, than held in check by you.

In a sense, this was true: Brutus and Cassius had demonstrated that they were not seeking to seize power for themselves. And *otium* and *libertas* – alongside *pax* ('peace') – appear as their catchwords in enough sources for us to know that they formed a major element of the political message they wanted to spread.[76] The problem was that such words were easily bandied about, and not everyone was convinced that Brutus and Cassius intended to stand by their message. To return to the theme with which we opened this chapter: everyone at Rome was fearful for the future. But now, for the first time, Brutus and Cassius voiced their concerns that Antony might deceive them; although they twice more refer to his *fides* in this passage, there is no escaping the force of the line: 'nobody but you can deceive us. For you alone we trust and will continue to trust.'[77]

A View from the Other Side

However, although this letter appears to be a candid statement of their position, to other observers of the political situation, Brutus' and Cassius' intentions were harder to gauge. That was nothing new, of course: fear of the Liberators' next moves had prevailed from the moment they struck down Caesar; hence Antony's hurried departure from the Senate, his movements to secure his position ever since, and the tensions over the recent months between the consul and the Liberators which we have witnessed. However, a verbal expression of this point of view survives in a letter sent to Cicero by the prominent Caesarian Aulus Hirtius on 2 June. Hirtius was no friend of Antony's but he had been committed to Caesar, and he was also consul-designate for the next year. Cicero had updated him on Brutus' and Cassius' movements, and he was trying to commend the Liberators to his consideration. But Hirtius was afraid:

> You say they were on the point of leaving when they wrote. But where to and why? Hold them back, I beg you, Cicero. Don't let everything go to ruin. So help me, I swear, it will all be overturned from top to bottom in an orgy of loot, arson and massacre.

Like Cicero, Hirtius could see that civil war was on the cards. 'If they are afraid, let them take cautious measures', he further advised, 'but not try for anything more than that.' The longer Brutus and Cassius stayed away from Rome, the more the fear of them increased. But Cicero could not see it: he dismissed Hirtius' worries and assured him that Brutus and Cassius were not up to anything. To Atticus he even laughed off the fears of Hirtius and his friends: 'even now those folk are afraid in case our friends have more spirit than they actually possess'.[78] But, as the month went on, rumours of their activities did not subside, nor concerns over their intentions lessen.

A Blow to their *Dignitas*

One of the reasons for this renewed fear of Brutus and Cassius was that, when the Senate meeting of 1 June finally came around, Antony did not put forward the proposal of his and Dolabella's commands, as expected. Instead, perhaps by design or perhaps because a sufficient quorum had not been present, on the next day (2 June) he took the legislation directly to the assembly and effected the exchange of provinces that way.[79] By this law, he and Dolabella were to have *imperium* and troops in key provinces extending right through until 39 BC; that is, for a period spanning the duration of all the next career stages awaiting Brutus and Cassius.[80] But before then, Antony had another card to play. For the fate of the leading assassins had also to be decided, and Antony was proposing a new ploy to get them out of the way, as well as to prevent them obtaining power – or troops.

That evening, a letter reached Cicero's hands from Balbus to say that there would be a meeting of the Senate on 5 June to charge Brutus and Cassius with the purchasing of grain in Asia and Sicily respectively. 'What a wretched affair!' Cicero lamented. 'First, that they should accept anything from these people, and then something only fit for a legate.' It was a demeaning task: 'what duty in the service of the *res publica* is more sordid?' Cicero later remarked.[81] To be fair to Antony, he had also promised that, as was standard for praetors after their year of service, the pair would be decreed their provinces at the same time. But it was a blow to each man's *dignitas* all the same, and Cicero was running out of advice to give. Not too kindly, Brutus had remarked that Cicero had been bankrupt of advice lately, but that distress had made his mind slower still. Now, however, Brutus changed his tune again. 'What a lovingly written letter I got from Brutus', Cicero wrote to Atticus. It was an invitation for Cicero to attend an emergency meeting at Brutus' house in Antium, some 40 miles from Rome, on 7 June.[82]

On the journey there, Cicero had mulled over the problem of the grain commission and the advice he ought to give. He was not the only person attending: in addition to Brutus and Cassius, there was Brutus' mother and his wife, as well as his half-sister Junia, who was married to Cassius; other than that, we know only of Favonius – the Stoic who had shied away from assassination when Brutus first approached him earlier in the year, but who had been committed to the Liberators' cause thereafter. Timings prevented Atticus' attendance, although he had been invited too, but before the day was concluded Cicero debriefed his friend on how the meeting had gone. Since it is one of the only occasions on which we get to see Brutus interacting with his friends and family, it is worth quoting Cicero's report at length:

> I arrived at Antium before midday; our Brutus was happy at my arrival. Then, in front of quite an audience, including Servilia, Junia and Porcia, he asked me what I thought was the best plan. Favonius too was there. I put forward the proposal I had prepared on the way: that he should accept the Asiatic grain commission; that nothing but his safety concerned us now; on that hung the protection of the *res publica* itself. Such was the speech on which I had embarked when Cassius walked in. I repeated the same ideas, at which point Cassius, with a most determined expression – you might say breathing the spirit of Mars – announced he would not be going to Sicily: 'Should I have accepted as a favour something so offensive?' he asked. 'What are you going to do then?' I asked. He said he would go to Greece. 'What about you, Brutus?' I enquired, to which he replied: 'I'll go to Rome, if you agree.' 'But I don't agree at all, for you will not be safe.' 'Well, supposing I could be safe, would you be pleased then?' 'Of course, and moreover I'd be against you leaving for a province, either now or after your praetorship; but I am not going to advise you to risk your life in the city.'

Cicero had stated all the reasons why Brutus would not be safe in Rome, but he did not need to rehearse these to Atticus. Everyone knew that Brutus could not return. What then should he do? Cassius had stated his intention to head to Greece, and from there, we can suppose, on to Syria – the province which may originally have been intended for him by Caesar.[83] Servilia, for her part, promised to have the grain commission removed from the senatorial decree. Yet it looked to Cicero as if Brutus was intending to set off to Asia directly from Antium – either to accept the position after all, or possibly just to join Trebonius as a member of his staff. As he left Antium and composed his letter to Atticus, however, Cicero had to admit that the whole affair had left a bad impression: 'I found the ship completely falling apart – or rather utterly destroyed. No plan, no thought, no method.'[84]

Brutus' Games

Brutus, however, had his own reasons for wanting to return to Rome. As the urban praetor, it was his responsibility to put on the annual games of Apollo, and it was his last major chance to win the hearts of the people or else gauge their response to him.[85] But there was also more to it than that: in recent years, the *ludi Apollinares* had become increasingly associated with Caesar's person and his victories. As Geoffrey Sumi has succinctly summarised the importance of the games: 'if Brutus hoped to achieve his political objective of being recalled to Rome, he had somehow to reclaim these games for the Republic by removing Caesar's memory'.[86] In other words, Brutus had to win back the games as a venue for staging Roman values and legends, instead of as an arena for celebrating Caesar. And, to that end, he had cunningly chosen an appropriate play to stage: a version of the Roman playwright Accius' *Brutus*, to remind his audience of the moment his famous ancestor had overthrown the monarchy.

However, now that he had agreed that Rome was a dangerous place for him to be, Brutus had to let the games go on under his name without him being there; meanwhile, he prepared himself for the journey ahead. When Cicero next wrote to Atticus, Brutus had subsequently sprung into action: 'He is gathering ships; his mind is on the journey', he reported on 10 June, and by 25 June he was on his way. But from there Brutus made slow progress. His mind was still in fact on the games and he was heavily involved in their preparation: he was meeting actors and procuring large numbers of wild animals for the show and hunts – or so our later sources tell us.[87] In Brutus' absence, Gaius Antonius had been charged to preside over the games on his behalf, and Atticus too was on hand to help with the arrangements. Yet the presence of his friend on the steering committee was still not enough to prevent the Caesarians from outmanoeuvring Brutus once more.

First they changed the dramatic production from Accius' *Brutus* to the same playwright's version of the *Tereus*, a less politically charged theme. Then there was the matter of the date, which was being advertised for the month of *Julius* – as it was now called following the list of honours bestowed upon Caesar before his death. 'How he grieved over the Nones of July', Cicero reported to Atticus after visiting Brutus on the island of Nesis, in the bay of Naples, that month: 'quite astonishingly upset'. After all, the move challenged Brutus' attempt to divorce the games from the memory of Caesar. In response, Brutus decided to send word that the hunt which customarily followed the games should be advertised as taking place on

14 *Quintilis* – as the month used to be called.[88] But it was just quibbling by then; the point had been scored.

Even so, within a couple of days, good news reached Brutus from Atticus in Rome, who said that the games had been a success. There had been great applause and cheers at individual verses which stirred up the memory of the liberation: 'he seemed delighted at the *Tereus*', Cicero reported back to Atticus, 'and no more grateful to Accius than to Antony'. But the news stirred a different reaction in Cicero: 'the more gratifying such events are', he complained, 'the sicker I am to the stomach that the Roman people waste the use of their hands by clapping when they could be defending the *res publica*'.[89] Cicero feared a reaction from Antony and his supporters, and it was only a matter of time before the conflict came to a head. In the meantime, Cicero was going to visit his son Marcus, who was studying in Greece: 'I am leaving behind peace and will probably return to war', he wrote on 17 July from Pompeii. 'Even now Brutus is still at Nesis, Cassius at Naples.'[90]

Brutus' Plans

Throughout June and July, Cicero had kept a keen eye on Brutus' preparations for his departure to Asia in the hope that he might travel with Brutus as far as Athens. Yet, despite the familiarity with which the two men had been conversing, Brutus was not confiding his plans to Cicero in their entirety. All the latter knew was that Brutus was biding his time until the games concluded; occasionally Cicero remarked that Brutus was sluggish, despondent or in a state of despair. He was just taking the journey slowly – or so one of Brutus' friends reassured Cicero, 'in case something turned up'.[91]

But on 10 July, shortly after his visit to Nesis, Cicero wrote to Atticus of his surprise when he found that Brutus was more prepared than he thought: 'He and Domitius both have some excellent double-banked galleys', Cicero reported, referring to Brutus' friend Gnaeus Domitius Ahenobarbus – a descendant of another noble family with links to the lines of Cato and Servilia. Besides these, there were fine vessels belonging to other friends, and Cassius too had a fleet: 'a most agreeable affair', he added.[92] However, Cicero was not the only one who had noticed the Liberators' preparations, and still there were fears over what move Brutus and Cassius might make next.

Back at Rome, however, other crises threatened to engulf domestic politics that month. Mark Antony continued to exercise his full consular authority, assisted by his brothers Gaius and Lucius – one a praetor, the other a tribune. Of all the political contenders on the scene, it was Antony alone who had such access both to the instruments of the Senate and the people of Rome, as well as the veterans and soldiers. For his part, Octavian had taken it upon himself to organise games in honour of Caesar, and so continue the process of establishing himself as Caesar's heir. But every move he made was blocked by his older and more powerful rival. As the struggle between Antony and Octavian escalated in the early part of July, supporters of Brutus and Cassius hoped to win the consul back onto their side. Rumours even circulated to the effect that Antony might make an alliance and facilitate the Liberators' return to Rome, following the recent show of support for Brutus at his games.[93] However, if there were some who wanted to reclaim Antony for Brutus, Cassius and the Senate, a more pressing claim was made by the veterans and supporters of Caesar, who wanted peace among his successors.

Later that month, from 20 to *c.* 28 July, Octavian's games for Caesar went ahead as planned, with remarkable success. Nicolaus tells us that, when he entered the theatre, Octavian was applauded loudly and that rounds of applause followed every performance. A comet, which under normal circumstances would have been regarded as a dire portent, was ingeniously represented by Octavian as proof of Caesar's divinity: a symbol thereafter used in literature, on statues and on coinage as a sign of Caesar's deification.[94] 'From that day', Nicolaus tells us, 'Antony was manifestly still more ill-disposed toward Octavian, who stood in the way of the people's zeal for him.'[95] But he came under increasing pressure from the veterans to come to terms with Caesar's heir. Thus, the conflict was temporarily halted by a public reconciliation staged between Antony and Octavian towards the end of July; however, the damage this inflicted upon the Liberators' cause was irreversible.

All Brutus and Cassius could do was to continue communicating with the people through edicts, which were then read out in the Forum. The Tiberian historian Velleius tells us that, at first in fear of Antony, the Liberators published manifestos promising peace and offering to withdraw into exile; later, he adds, they issued them 'pretending to be afraid so as to increase his unpopularity'.[96] Cicero too attests to a flurry of public exchanges in the form of edicts as well as letters, in which Brutus and Cassius tried once and for all to establish their position vis-à-vis the consul. A copy of one of these edicts survives – sent on 4 August, as Brutus and Cassius prepared to leave Italy – and it provides a fascinating glimpse into the rhetoric surrounding their own actions, as well as the fear Brutus and Cassius were generating in others.

> We have read your letter, which is very like your edict: offensive, threatening, and not worthy of being sent to us by you. We, Antony, have

> inflicted no injury on you, nor did we think you would be surprised if, as praetors and men of a certain standing, we requested something from you as consul by edict. But if you are indignant that we dared to assail it, pardon us to be sorry that you do not even grant this to Brutus and Cassius.[97]

Up until recently, Antony's respect for the nobility and ancestry of Brutus in particular had led him to treat the assassins in a manner befitting a consul to praetors. Brutus and Cassius had, in turn, accorded an appropriate degree of deference towards him. Yet in publishing an edict – perhaps requesting dispensation from the unwelcome duty of the grain commission – the Liberators *had* annoyed Antony; for, whereas communications and arrangements had previously been made face to face in personal meetings, or through private letters, the recent escalation of their grievances into the public sphere must have seemed an affront upon the consul.[98]

As the letter of Brutus and Cassius goes on to reveal, for his part, Antony had stressed his own displays of good will towards the Liberators:

> You say that you have made no complaint concerning our levying of forces and money, our soliciting of armies, or our sending messages overseas. We trust you have done this in an excellent spirit, but still we do not acknowledge any of these accusations; we are also surprised that, having kept quiet on these matters, you should not have been able to restrain your anger from throwing the death of Caesar in our faces.

But in mentioning accusations against the Liberators that had been overlooked so far, this paraphrase of Antony's letter gives away some very real concerns about their suspicious movements since leaving Rome. Naturally, Brutus and Cassius denied the truth of these rumours, yet a closer look at Cicero's letters and other contemporary evidence can provide us with a few examples of the kind of activity Antony might have espied.

To start with the charge of raising forces, there is a clear suggestion that the younger generation were beginning to take sides, at least if Quintus Cicero is anything to go by. As we have already seen, he had openly been championing Caesar's memory at the festival of the *Parilia* when he was spotted wearing a garland, and since then he had announced that he looked to Antony for his future in defiance of his father and uncle.[99] That was in late April to early May. However, in an abrupt volte-face we find him turning to the Liberators in mid-June: 'he cannot bear the present regime', Cicero wrote to Atticus. 'He is fixed on going over to Brutus and Cassius.'[100]

As proof of his new-found dedication to the cause, Quintus had raised 400,000 sesterces which he intended to contribute to the war fund. Whether Brutus and Cassius were openly recruiting young men to their side is not securely evidenced. But, as we shall see in the next chapter, in the months that followed, Brutus had tremendous success reviving republican feeling among this generation. Perhaps Antony was right to be suspicious.

What is more, we know that the Liberators, or someone operating on their behalf, had begun the task of finding donors to the cause. In his biography of Atticus, Cornelius Nepos reports that, in the aftermath of the assassination, it was suggested that members of the equestrian order should set up a private fund for the Liberators. Gaius Flavius, one of Brutus' closest friends, even approached Atticus to solicit his help in taking a lead in the scheme, but he refused: Brutus was welcome to his money, as far as it would stretch, Atticus is said to have replied. And indeed, before Brutus finally left Italy Atticus gave him 100,000 sesterces to help him on his way.[101] But Atticus knew better than to get involved with such a partisan scheme, nor does it seem that the 'Liberator fund' ever came to anything. If Antony had got a whiff of Flavius' antics, however, he most certainly would not have liked them.

In Italy alone, then, there was plenty of suspicious activity seemingly being carried out by the Liberators and their supporters. But what about the charge they were sending messages and soliciting the armies overseas? There was probably some foundation to this accusation too, now that Decimus, Trebonius and Tillius Cimber had assumed their posts in the provinces. Yet Antony presumably had a far greater threat in mind: Sextus Pompeius, whose legions in Hispania had been a major factor in everyone's minds since the Ides. For it was clear by July that some sort of exchange was being conducted between Pompey's son and the Liberators. We know from a letter of Cicero's that Brutus met with Sextus' father-in-law at Nesis that month, and that letters and information had been passed on.[102] There were no promises yet, and certainly there does not seem to have been anything like a plan of action. Still, however, Brutus and Cassius were gauging the level of military support for the republican front, and Antony had presumably got wind of – or guessed – that too. Hence, their denial of the charges cannot have been particularly convincing.

That was not the end of the exchange, however. Rather Brutus and Cassius took Antony to task for recently 'throwing the death of Caesar in our faces', as they put it. What had caused Antony to do this now, they asked, given his silence on the matter hitherto? We can only make informed speculation as to why it was that Antony only started openly criticising the

Liberators for the assassination in July. But one explanation must simply be that the campaign to control public opinion was well and truly under way. Brutus and Cassius took delight in the reputation they conferred upon themselves as 'Liberators', yet the Caesarian party had a different message to convey. Cicero had heard it as early as May: 'their premise and slogan is that a great man has been killed, that the whole state has been thrown into chaos by his death, that everything he did will be of no effect as soon as we stop being afraid, that his clemency was his downfall'.[103] It suited Antony's purposes, then, to present the Liberators' departure as a desperate flight; a direct result of Antony's own punitive measures, especially now that he had Octavian to contend with for the favour of Caesar's supporters. To this end he had stepped up his rhetoric against them.

'But you understand perfectly that we cannot be pushed in any way', Brutus and Cassius retaliated. And, in any case, the conspirators had doubtless predicted from the start that the murder of Caesar might lead to exile or war. Back at the start of the year, Brutus and Cassius had decided that it was their duty to depose the tyrant and they stood by that decision now: 'Make sure you remember not just how long Caesar lived, but for how short he ruled', they shot back to Antony, before closing the letter with a prayer for the future: 'We beg to heaven that your counsels may be salutary to the *res publica*, as well as to you.' And then a polite threat: 'If not, then we pray that – without risking the public safety and honour – they may bring as little harm to you as possible.'

Cicero and the Liberators

Before they left Italy, Brutus and Cassius had one more meeting with Cicero: on 17 August at Velia. The elder statesman had been planning to sail to Greece and visit his son in Athens, but harsh weather had forced Cicero to return; in the event, he was glad he did. Cicero's departure had come under fire for its bad timing: people thought he was deserting Rome, maybe even attending the Olympic Games, at a time of crisis. Atticus too had been unusually damning; even though he had not openly shown his disapproval before, Atticus sent Cicero a long letter containing a whole host of criticisms. 'The most troublesome point comes at the end', Cicero complained upon receiving his friend's indictment of him; for nearing the conclusion Atticus had made the inflammatory remark that 'our Brutus is holding his tongue'.[104]

As Cicero learned when he met with the Liberators, what had annoyed Brutus the most was the orator's absence at a meeting of the Senate on 1 August. This meeting is best remembered for the fact that Lucius

Calpurnius Piso, an ex-consul and father-in-law of the late Caesar, had made the first open attack on Antony in the Senate since the latter's more aggressive return to Rome in May. But evidently, something important and relevant to Brutus and Cassius was on the agenda for discussion: they had wanted as many ex-consuls and ex-praetors to attend as possible and they had dispatched numerous letters to that effect. When combined with the evidence of the edict above, we can imagine that Brutus and Cassius were waiting to hear whether Servilia had lived up to her promise of having the grain commission removed from the senatorial decree of 5 June; it is likely too that they were also waiting to hear which provinces they would be assigned for the next year. As an ex-consul and a supporter, Cicero's presence in the Senate would have been useful for their cause. But when Cicero finally met Brutus again, the latter was 'delighted' at Cicero's turning back and he 'poured out everything he had kept quiet on until now'.

Beyond that, our evidence for what happened in the meeting of the Senate beyond Piso's outburst is almost non-existent, and firm answers concerning the grain commission and the assignment of provinces are consequently in short supply. Yet it seems that Brutus and Cassius were still expected to go to Asia and Sicily, hence their preparation of ships would not have been viewed with suspicion *per se* – even if, as events proved, they had no intention of going.[105] What is more, it is generally agreed that provinces were allocated to them at this meeting: Brutus, it seems, was assigned Crete, which he would be due to take over at the beginning of 43 BC, and Cassius was going to be sent to Cyrene.[106] These were small and insignificant provinces – a further blow to each man's *dignitas*. Yet, although Brutus had been annoyed with Cicero for his failure to attend the meeting on 1 August, there was no point in continuing in his anger now that he had returned to Italy. After all, Cicero could be a great asset to the cause and Brutus now urged him to take the helm of the *res publica* back at Rome.

However, a passing remark in a letter to Atticus betrays the fact that Cicero had no intention of getting involved with politics: 'I am coming now, not to take a part in the *res publica*, as Brutus was recommending. For what can be done? Did anyone support Piso? Did he return the next day? But because they say a man should not be too far from his grave at this age.' Cicero's position here is typical of the stance he had adopted ever since the Ides of March as an interested bystander and critic; he was a supporter of the cause rather than a lead actor. He saw no hope of challenging Antony for as long as the latter remained in Rome as consul. (Little did Cicero know that he was about to become embroiled in his bitterest fight, and that he had less than eighteen months to live.)

Yet, given the intensity with which Cicero later attacked Antony, it is easy to forget just how inactive he had been in the Liberators' cause up until now. When Brutus raised his bloody dagger and called upon Cicero by name, he did not respond; at least, there is no response that we hear of. He had made his support of their deed publicly known, and he had negotiated and addressed the people on the matter of the amnesty agreement. But he had for the most part criticised Brutus' handling of the affair: he blamed the poor planning and believed that Antony should have been killed too. He regretted that Brutus and Cassius had not summoned the Senate immediately and complained that they had allowed Caesar a public burial. He thought that Brutus' oratory was lacklustre and inefficient in winning over the people. At the same time, he pinned the future of the *res publica* on their shoulders alone. 'The deed was carried out with the courage of men and the policy of children', is one of his more damning verdicts.[107]

On nearly all these points, Atticus disagreed with him; a reminder that, however compelling and clear Cicero's voice can be, we should always seek to engage in the debate with him. So what could and should Brutus have done? Caesar's assassination had seemingly failed to restore freedom. Does that mean the dictator should have been left to live out his days and conduct the Parthian campaign on which he was set to embark? Even Cicero blushed to admit it: 'The Ides of March do not please me. He would never have come back; fear would not have compelled us to confirm all his measures . . . *he* was not a master to run away from.'[108]

Yet, here and elsewhere, Cicero has underestimated the extent of the problem; as had Brutus, Cassius, Decimus and the rest of the Liberators. For, as we have seen repeatedly throughout this chapter, Caesar was more than a man and, dominant though he was, there were far more players batting on his side than we sometimes remember, all with far too many vested interests. In other words, his celebrity, popularity with the veterans and plebs, and the movement Caesar spurred in Roman political life were far greater than the force of the assassins' daggers. As the disagreements between Cicero and Atticus reveal, from the differing perspectives of two friends and contemporaries, each with his own view of Brutus, there is no simple answer to the question of why the conspiracy failed. Fear, anger, jealousy and pride have all played their part in this narrative, as indeed they did for a large part of republican history. But one thing appears certain: the real enemy was not Caesar, but Caesarism – and that was proving far more difficult to stamp out.

CHAPTER 6

REVIVING REPUBLICANISM

Leaving Italy

> When Porcia was about to sail back to Rome, at first, she tried to hide the great sorrow she felt. But then, despite the nobility of mind she had maintained up until now, a certain painting gave her away. For its subject was drawn from the Greek world: when Hector was setting off and Andromache was taking their son from his arms, all the while her eyes gazed upon her husband. Upon seeing it – the image of her own suffering – Porcia burst into tears.
>
> — Plutarch, *Brutus*, 23.2

In the middle of August, five months after the assassination of Caesar, Brutus left Italy for the east. Our only sighting of this moment is the story in Plutarch, which he in turn got from the memoirs written by Brutus' stepson Bibulus, in which Porcia bade her husband an emotional farewell at Velia. It was here that she purportedly saw the painting depicting the celebrated scene from the Trojan War, when Hector and Andromache too said their final goodbyes. Read after the fact of Brutus' eventual defeat and demise – and not forgetting Hector's own grisly death at the hands of Achilles – to Plutarch and his readers the story of the couple's parting must have spelled doom for the mission. Yet it also reminds us of another salient fact. Both Brutus and Cassius were praetors of Rome, and they were endowed with *imperium* – the right to lead an army.[1] Like Hector in the sixth book of the *Iliad* (the source of the scene to which this painting alludes), Brutus left Rome as a man prepared to defend his country.[2]

1. Denarius of Brutus, 43–42 BC: (obverse) Head of Brutus, right, bearded; around, BRUT. IMP; around L·PLAET·CEST; border of dots; (reverse) *Pileus* between daggers; below, EID. MAR; border of dots.
The image of Brutus on this coin is the only contemporary evidence for what he looked like, but modern scholars have disagreed as to what his appearance reveals about him: does he look forceful and charismatic or narrow-minded and obstinate? In antiquity attention was rather drawn to the powerful message carried on the reverse, where two daggers flank the *pileus* (the cap of liberty) and the legend spells out the reference to the Ides of March. It was minted either in late 43 or early 42 BC when Brutus was leading his troops in the fight against the triumvirs.

2. *Senatus Populusque Romanus.*
The importance of the 'Senate and the people of Rome' can still be seen on inscriptions today; they can be found anywhere – on street corners, buildings, milestones and even modern drain covers.

3. *Capitoline Brutus*, *c.* 300 BC.
The so-called *Capitoline Brutus* is a bronze bust commonly believed to represent Brutus' famous ancestor, Lucius Junius Brutus, who, legend had it, expelled King Tarquinius Superbus from Rome in 510 BC and initiated the period known today as the Roman Republic. Although we do not know exactly when the statue was made, it was famous in antiquity.

4. Silver denarius of Libertas and Lucius Junius Brutus, 54 BC: (obverse) Head of personified Libertas, right; behind, LIBERTAS downwards; border of dots; (reverse) Lucius Junius Brutus, walking leftward, between two lictors and preceded by an *accensus*; below, BRVTVS; border of dots. Early in his career (*c.* 55–54 BC), Brutus minted coins advertising his connection to Libertas; it was the same appeal he made after the assassination of Caesar when he and his supporters styled themselves as 'Liberators'. The reverse of Brutus' coin displays his name and links back to his legendary ancestor, Lucius Junius Brutus. Here the elder Brutus is shown as a consul accompanied by his attendants. It reflects the importance Brutus attached to the republican constitution in his political messages.

5. Silver denarius of Lucius Junius Brutus and Servilius Ahala, 54 BC: (obverse) Head of L. Iunius Brutus, right; behind, BRVTVS downwards; border of dots; (reverse) Head of C. Servilius Ahala, right; behind, AHALA downwards; border of dots.
Brutus publicised his opposition to one-man rule by issuing coins that bore the images of his two famous ancestors: Lucius Junius Brutus, who expelled the Tarquins from Rome to become Rome's first 'consul' in 509 BC, and Servilius Ahala, the 'master of the horse' (*magister equitum*) who killed Spurius Maelius in 439 BC on the grounds that he was aspiring towards tyranny.

6. The Roman Forum.
The view of the Roman Forum from the Palatine Hill today. Brutus would have watched the great orators deliver speeches in *contiones* or in the law courts in the open space in front of the Senate house (the brick building in the right of this photograph). Later he himself became an orator of note.

7. Jean-Léon Gérôme, *Death of Caesar*, 1859.
Gérôme's canvas beautifully captures an impression of the scene moments after Caesar's assassination. The eye is drawn immediately to the centre, where a group of senators in gleaming white togas jubilantly brandish their daggers. Only then is it that we notice the traces of violence: a golden throne has been knocked over, as have a few wooden chairs, and there is a faint smudge of blood on the mosaic floor. And then, slumped in the bottom left-hand corner, we finally see the corpse of Caesar, still draped in his toga with a wound to the chest. This part of the painting is cast in shadow, but looming above the dead body it is just about possible to make out the statue of Pompey the Great – Caesar's arch-enemy and nemesis. It is probably fair to say that in reality there would have been a lot more blood than Gérôme has captured.

8. *Kai su*?
This mosaic, from the so-called House of the Evil Eye (second century AD), is one of many examples which suggest that the expression *kai su* (shown here as KAI CY) was an apotropaic against the evil eye. In the centre of the mosaic, the eye is pierced by a trident, surrounded by an array of creatures; walking away from it, a horned dwarf with a huge phallus crosses two sticks. The point of the *kai su* here, then, is that it projects the violence enacted on the eye towards the viewer instead: it is a warning that such punishments will be turned back upon those who gaze upon it. This is believed by some to have been the message of Caesar's alleged last words to Brutus (*Kai su, teknon*): as one scholar has suggested, it would have the force of saying 'To hell with you'.

9. Silver denarius of Apollo and Victory, 43/42 BC: (obverse) Laureate head of Apollo, right; around COSTA LEG; border of dots; (reverse) Trophy display of Thracian arms and armour; around BRUTUS IMP; border of dots.
In late 43/early 42 BC, Brutus minted coins to celebrate his victory as commander over Thrace, after which he was hailed as *imperator* (IMP). The connection between Apollo on the obverse and the trophy display of Thracian arms on the reverse is important here, because it projects Brutus' claim to have the support of the gods in his mission to fortify the Greek east in defence of the *res publica* against Antony and Octavian.

10. Philippi today.
(i) (above) The view looking southwest along the line of republican fortifications that linked the camps of Brutus and Cassius.
(ii) (top right) The site of the triumvirs' camp, viewed from the northeast, which shows its vulnerability; the triumvirs were on the plain, while Brutus and Cassius were encamped in the hills.
(iii) (bottom right) The view looking west from Philippi, to the site of the first battle. It was somewhere in the middle distance that Brutus' army overpowered and defeated Octavian's forces.

11. *Augustus of Prima Porta*.
This cuirassed statue of Augustus, from the Villa of Livia at Prima Porta, is a marble copy of a bronze original, which was probably commissioned in 20 BC to celebrate Augustus' Parthian campaigns. The image represents a youthful Augustus dressed in military clothing. The details on his breastplate convey the messages of peace, divine authority and a new world order which also appear in the contemporary poetry of Virgil and Horace.

12. Michelangelo, *Brutus*, 1538.
The rough-hewn state of Michelangelo's idealised portrait of Brutus is plain to see. The Grand Duke Francesco de' Medici had an inscription carved into the base, claiming that Michelangelo had left it unfinished rather than commemorate a murderer.

Bibulus' narrative was presumably contrived to create this effect; as such, we need not take the story too literally.[3] Still, however, Porcia must have felt deeply fearful for her husband's future; the sense of finality at their departure cannot have escaped Brutus and Bibulus either, but the stepson stayed with his stepfather until the end. In surviving to tell the tale, Bibulus could credit his mother with being more than a woman, a trait we saw in her in the run-up to the assassination. As Plutarch continues his retelling of this episode in the *Life of Brutus*, he records how Brutus paid tribute to his wife's courage at this emotional juncture:

> When one of Brutus' friends, Acilius, recited the passage containing Andromache's final words to Hector – 'But Hector, you are to me a father, honoured mother, and brother, as well as my tender husband' – Brutus smiled and said: 'But I would not deign to address Porcia in the words of Hector: 'Ply your loom and give orders to your maids'. For, although her body is by nature unable to perform deeds as heroic as those of men, in her dedication to her country she is as courageous as we.'

Porcia was the daughter of Cato, the republican martyr *par excellence* and, by the time Bibulus composed his memoirs, an exemplary wife to the other great defender of the *res publica*. No inferior being, in Brutus' assessment she was a woman who deserved to be treated on equal terms. Indeed, the rejoinder put into Brutus' mouth – that she was not a wife to be confined to the usual household tasks – lends credibility to Bibulus' embellishment of his mother's virtues. In her own later legend, Porcia became as staunch in her patriotism as the best of men: that is, men like Brutus who now looked forward to achieving deeds as famous in years to come as those of the legendary heroes of the Homeric age.

Brutus and his peers had been nurtured on a diet of Greek literature and culture since their earliest years, as we have already seen, and so it is not surprising that his story should be recast in terms that evoke this literary tradition. But the competitive spirit of Homer's world had another striking resonance with the ethos of the Roman Republic: 'Far to excel, surpassing all the rest', was just one of the mottoes from the *Iliad* which still rang in contemporary ears.[4] Brutus and Cassius had made it clear that they would not tolerate a superior; one of the paradoxical elements inherent in the republican system was that, although in theory it heavily guarded against monarchical ambitions, its leading men strove to outperform each other in the accumulation of wealth, glory and *dignitas*. Now, as they left Italy, these were precisely the sparks of republicanism firing Brutus and Cassius on their way. It perhaps comes as no surprise that Brutus' first major stop was Athens, where the leading young men of the next generation were ambitiously completing the final stages of their own education.

On his arrival, Plutarch tells us, Brutus received an honorific welcome, and official decrees were passed in praise of his actions. Dio supplements this with the information that Brutus and Cassius were honoured in nearly all the major cities of Greece, but especially in Athens, where bronze statues of them were erected in the marketplace next to those of the Greek tyrannicides, Harmodius and Aristogeiton. The juxtaposition and assimilation of Caesar's assassins to these legendary heroes would seem too neat a historical coincidence to be true, were it not for the fact that archaeological evidence supports Dio's account. As Antony Raubitschek has demonstrated in two important articles, the catalogue of finds from the Attic region includes a statue base of Brutus in the sanctuary of Amphiaraus in Oropos, less than 30 miles northeast of Athens, as well as a fragment of the very pedestal on which the statue of Brutus stood in the agora.[5]

Back at Rome, Brutus had been the target of pro-Caesarian activists; he had been humiliated by a Senate which, far from honouring him, had included his name among the recipients of a general amnesty; and, finally, he had left Rome, ostensibly to accept an administrative post he considered beneath him. But it was only now in Greece that Brutus received the recognition he felt his due, and he basked in the acclaim that his famous deed had brought him. Over the following months, the revival of anti-monarchical and anti-tyrannical feeling led to a resurgence of republicanism among the younger generation of Romans in the Greek east which few, if any, might have predicted when Brutus left Italy.

Thinking about War

We may well ask when Brutus first conceived of the plan to go to war but, at this vital moment in his life, he largely slips out of view from our contemporary sources. Cicero had no inkling of Brutus' intentions when he last saw him at Velia. Yet Bibulus' later narrative seems to have hinted at the possibility that he left Italy as a man ready to fight for his country; our later sources, too, nearly all assume that Brutus and Cassius were both planning on war from the very beginning. However, one snippet of information which is hugely valuable in this context is a detail added by Plutarch, who tells us that Brutus attended lectures in philosophy while in Athens. 'He was thought to be wholly given up to literary pursuits', he adds. 'But without any one's suspecting it, he was getting ready for war.'[6] In his book *The Noblest Roman*, Martin Clarke has dismissed Plutarch's account because, he argues, Brutus only later experienced the revival of spirit that spurred him on in the fight for freedom at the end of December 44 BC. But that cannot be right; for Clarke has taken this view directly from Cicero's later version of events, expressed at a time when the orator needed to present Brutus' actions in the best possible light.[7]

A more likely explanation is hence to be found by modifying Plutarch's statement: Brutus probably was immersed in his literary pursuits, but he had not forgotten that he needed to garner support in case Antony failed to stick to his side of the amnesty agreement. After all, the possibility of civil war had been ever-present in his mind from the moment the conspiracy was hatched. If we remember the discussions Brutus had held with his friends in the run-up to the assassination, Favonius the Stoic had been excluded from the conspiracy because he believed that anything – even living under a tyranny – was better than civil war. Further still, when Decimus Brutus wrote his letter of despair almost immediately after the deed had been done, the resort to arms was already looming in the debates over what to do next. In the interests of the amnesty agreement, reconciliation had been the catchword of Brutus' political propaganda throughout April and May 44 BC; he wanted peace (*pax*), tranquillity (*otium*) and later he added *clementia*, in the pursuit of *libertas*. But Cassius, on the other hand, appears to have taken a much harder line towards their opponents.

Already in June, at that infamous meeting at Brutus' house, Cassius was described as 'breathing the spirit of Mars'. Often treated as a throw-away comment, this insight into the mind of Brutus' co-conspirator should cause us to pause and reflect on the policy pursued by Caesar's assassins in leaving Italy. For Cassius had defiantly declared his intention to refuse the grain commission in Sicily; he intended to sail to Greece and from there to Syria – a province he either believed he was entitled to or which he viewed as a more strategic power base.[8] At the time, Brutus' mind had been more fixed on the games and whether it would be safe for him to return to Rome. But when he was talked out of that plan by Cicero, he appeared to be set on heading to Asia to accept the commission. The attitudes and strategies of Brutus and Cassius were evidently at odds. Brutus was far more compliant; he was still trying to cooperate with Antony. Cassius, on the other hand, was more set on war.

It is important to stress the different policies of Brutus and Cassius because it reminds us that these were two individuals who had united in their decision to assassinate Caesar; but they had not always shared a united vision for dealing with the aftermath. As proof of this, we might remember that Cassius had wanted Antony killed too, but Brutus had argued to spare him. Now Cassius was set on heading east and preparing for war; conversely, in the year that followed, Brutus clung to the idea that civil war might be avoidable. For as long as there was a chance of cooperating with Antony, that is the course Brutus favoured. But large cracks had already begun to appear in the fragile foundations of the amnesty agreement when Brutus and Cassius penned their joint edict to the consul in August 44 BC. After all, the last words Brutus and Cassius had sent to Antony had been a thinly veiled threat: 'We beg to heaven that your counsels may be salutary to the *res publica*, as well as to you.' They had already warned him 'to bear in mind not the length of Caesar's life, but the brevity of his reign.'[9]

In other words: Brutus did not decide on war until a much later stage. However, he had to accept that a fight was becoming increasingly unavoidable; under such circumstances, it was necessary to take precautions. The role of philosophy as a tool for reviving republicanism and recruiting for war should consequently not be overlooked in piecing together an overview of Brutus' activities in Athens. For, when we remember the role of philosophical discourse in the fomenting of the plot against Caesar, it seems arbitrary to separate these two spheres of activity in the latter part of 44 BC. Plutarch, it seems, was right to connect Brutus' philosophical studies with his increasingly pragmatic attitude towards civil strife. And there are further clues to be unearthed from his text. Brutus attended lectures of the Academic philosopher Theomnestus and of the Peripatetic Cratippus, he tells us. Unlike the Epicureans, who advocated the need to abstain from politics, or the Stoics, who deemed civil war to be the most injurious circumstance of all, the lecture halls Brutus frequented presumably helped steel his determination for the task ahead; but they also provided the perfect fora from which he could enlist recruits for his cause. Thus, while any reconstruction of Brutus' activities in Athens is necessarily speculative, it is not impossible to imagine him attending lectures, engaging in debates and testing opinions – as he had done earlier that year – on how civil war ranked when measured against the full Platonic spectrum of constitutional arrangements.

Among the men Brutus made an impression on at this time we find the young Marcus Tullius Cicero, as well as a 21-year-old Quintus Horatius Flaccus, better known to the modern world as Horace – one of Rome's most talented writers. As a representative sample of his recruits, the son of an orator and a poet in the making might not sound much of a force to rely on. Yet the young Cicero had commanded a cavalry squadron at Pharsalus at the age of just seventeen, and in time he proved to be an asset; Horace too rose up the ranks to become a military officer.[10] What this means with hindsight is that Brutus' recruitment strategy had been a success. And having gauged the appetite for war in the defence of liberty, it was a short step to lead his new supporters into action when the time came.[11] Even if the precise shape of Brutus' long-term strategy was yet to take form, he did have a plan to secure the provinces and to fortify a power base in the Greek east.

Brutus' Success

Just six months after he had left Italy, in the first half of February 43 BC, a letter from Brutus reached Rome informing the consul and Senate of a remarkable turn in his fortunes. He had taken control of Macedonia and Illyricum, and Greece too was under his watch: 'a great joy and a cause for celebration', as Cicero hailed it in the speech he delivered on this occasion – his *Tenth Philippic*.[12] Up until this point, there had been no word from Brutus or Cassius; no news even of their whereabouts.[13] But, now, for the first time, Brutus revealed that he had not gone to his designated province of Crete. Instead, his letter apparently detailed the number and composition of the forces he had acquired, as well as the steps he had taken to assume control of the eastern provinces. 'How quickly, how carefully, how virtuously Brutus acted', Cicero rejoiced.[14] But, although Brutus' staggering success came as something of a surprise to his peers back at Rome, the operation had been much longer and more involved in the planning.

From his base in Athens, one of the first steps Brutus had taken was to secure the support of the governor of Macedonia, Quintus Hortensius Hortalus – a friend to Brutus and a close connection by marriage. This was an important pre-emptive strike because, back in Rome, on 27 November, Antony had overseen a strategic reallocation of the praetorian provinces for 43 BC. Conventional wisdom has it that Antony's actions were a personal attack on the assassins; they were not. Neither Brutus, nor Cassius nor anyone else was actually deprived of a province he was due to take over.[15] Brutus was probably still expected to go to his insignificant province of Crete. But Antony had strengthened his own hands considerably, as well as those of his supporters. Of particular concern for Brutus was that Antony's brother Gaius was now due to take over control of Macedonia in the coming January.

In a development we shall consider in due course, there were many at Rome who did not accept the validity of Antony's allocation of the provinces and wanted them reversed. From Brutus' perspective, however, it was also crucial that Gaius should be prevented from entering and claiming

Macedonia as his own; he did not want the rich eastern provinces to fall into the hands of Antony's men.[16] Consequently, Brutus had sent an ambassador to negotiate with Hortensius, and the move was a resounding success: Hortensius agreed not to hand over his command to Gaius, and all that remained for Brutus was to gather the forces and finances to help in the fight. It was probably at the end of November or early December then, when news reached him of Gaius' appointment, that Brutus decided to make his move.[17]

As we have already seen, at first Brutus drew his recruits from the young nobles studying at Athens. Later, he marched them north and further swelled his ranks by gathering Pompey's veterans who had stayed in the area around Thessaly after Pharsalus. While there, he also made a journey to Demetrias, where he seized a whole stockpile of arms which had been gathered for Caesar's aborted Parthian campaign. Left behind in what we can imagine was a blind panic at the news of Caesar's assassination, Brutus now used these weapons to equip his own men. Although the conflict between the Liberators and the supporters of Antony had not yet reached a stage of open confrontation, the stage was certainly set for further hostilities. Each side was fully aware of the stigma that would be attached to the aggressor, and so Brutus bided his time. But he was prepared. And by the beginning of 43 BC, he stood at the head of a well-equipped force which was ready to fight under his banner of liberty.[18]

In the letter he sent to the Senate, Brutus singled out Hortensius for particular praise. For having promised to help resist Gaius Antonius, the governor of Macedonia placed his legions at Brutus' disposal when he arrived in the province at the end of 44 BC. However, his act was not simply a matter of personal side-taking or loyalty to Brutus; there was now a legal basis to the move to block Gaius' entry into the province. For, in a move of momentous importance for the rise of tensions, Mark Antony's provincial arrangements in November had been controversially reversed. Many at Rome doubted the legality of the procedure Antony used; there was also more than a hint of suspicion in the way the lot had fallen in favour of Antony's men. In his *Third Philippic*, delivered on 20 December 44 BC, Cicero was hence able to tap into and successfully carry the argument that the allocations had been rigged. The result was that Antony and his men were all stripped of provinces to which they believed they were legally entitled; instead the advantage passed to the Liberators. The stage was set for a struggle.

By the end of 44 BC, then, whatever Brutus had been secretly planning for the past few months had become a matter of public policy: steered by

Cicero's own hostility towards Antony, the Senate decreed that all commanders should stay in their provinces until fresh appointments had been made.[19] At this point in time, Cicero knew nothing of Brutus' endeavours in Greece and Macedonia; yet his proposal played directly in his favour. Now it was official: Hortensius was not to transfer the province of Macedonia to Gaius Antonius, just as Hortensius and Brutus had already arranged.

Thereafter, Brutus' cause gained momentum and his hand was strengthened in other ways. Thus, in late December or early January 43 BC, Marcus Appuleius and Antistius Vetus – returning quaestors of Asia and Syria respectively – transferred to him large amounts of money they were supposed to be transporting to Rome.[20] From Cicero's *Tenth Philippic*, we also hear mention of others whose endeavours Brutus recognised: one of the legions which had formerly served under Mark Antony's lieutenant, Lucius Piso, surrendered to the young Cicero and defected to Brutus' cause; a section of cavalrymen which was making its way to Dolabella in Syria detached itself and joined Brutus in Thessaly, while a second section joined Brutus under the command of Gnaeus Domitius Ahenobarbus.

To these forces were added three further legions which had belonged to Publius Vatinius, the governor of Illyricum – the province which bordered Macedonia.[21] Plutarch tells us that Gaius Antonius had been heading straight for these legions when Brutus was still in Macedonia, and he gives a dramatic account of how Brutus battled terrain, snow and sickness to forestall Gaius' arrival.[22] The heroic patterning might be a literary embellishment but the facts of the case support one thing for sure: Brutus had acted with tremendous speed to gather, train and equip his troops.[23] The result was that, when Gaius Antonius finally landed in Dyrrachium with just one legion, he found himself vastly overpowered by Brutus' superior forces.

There were doubtless many in the Senate who feared Brutus' resurgence at the head of an army; there were also concerns over the reaction of Caesar's veterans. On the day Brutus wrote to the Senate in February 43 BC, Gaius Antonius was holed up within the walls of Apollonia, besieged by Brutus' troops. Cicero hoped that he would soon be captured – 'may the gods grant it!' he prayed. But as yet Brutus had no real legal authority for his actions. True, the Senate had decreed that Antonius was not to be given Macedonia; however, the province was Hortensius' to defend, not Brutus'. Cicero later put a gloss on Brutus' actions, claiming he was acting 'as his own Senate'.[24] However, in reality, he had usurped control of provinces that had not been allocated to him and was now the commander of a sizeable force of men.

By the time Cicero had the chance to speak, however, Quintus Fufius Calenus had already moved that Brutus should give up the armies and provinces under his control. It was Cicero's task to persuade the Senate otherwise. 'Marcus Brutus' every wish', he reassured his listeners, 'his every thought, his whole mind is focused upon the authority of the Senate and the liberty of the Roman people'. As he drew his speech to a close, Cicero switched into a more formal mode, referring to Brutus by his official name and title to make his specific proposal:

> that as proconsul Quintus Caepio Brutus shall protect, defend, guard and keep safe Macedonia, Illyricum and the whole of Greece; that he will command the army which he himself has established and raised; if there be any need of money for military purposes, that he will levy and use whatever public funds can be levied, and that he will borrow money for military purposes from any source he sees fit; he will requisition grain and see to it that, together with his army, he be as close as possible to Italy.[25]

On the basis of this proposal, the Senate decreed that Brutus had acted in the public interest and confirmed the legitimacy of his control over the three regions.[26] It was a major reversal of fortunes for Brutus. Although scholars have debated the precise remit of the power Brutus was eventually granted, the fact remains that it was an extraordinary command; Cicero was in effect proposing *imperium maius*, a foreshadowing of the sort later used in the Augustan principate.[27] It gave Brutus a higher level of authority above that of other governors, and it extended over Greece, Macedonia and Illyricum. Cicero's speech had won the day.[28] However, that a majority of the Senate had voted in favour of an entirely unconstitutional action is not a point to be passed over in silence; nor was the point ignored at the time. The objections of his contemporaries are clear in the lengths Cicero goes to, in his *Eleventh Philippic* which followed, to admit but deflect the accusation that Brutus had seized control of another man's province.[29]

However, it was not just Cicero's persuasive rhetoric that had induced the Senate to support Brutus that day; it was the urgency of an unfolding crisis which had its roots in the arrival at Rome of the young Octavian – Caesar's heir and adopted son. His appearance on the political stage had caused a schism in the Caesarian party and it had prompted Antony to take ever more aggressive measures to shore up his position. Before we can complete the analysis of Brutus' actions in the east, we need to revisit events back in Rome to explain the increased hostility of Antony, the ascendancy of Octavian, and the re-emergence of Cicero at the helm of republican politics.

Cicero's Comeback

As we saw in the last chapter, Cicero had largely remained away from the city after the assassination; first he had toured his villas in Italy and then embarked on an aborted mission to Athens. At their final meeting in Velia in August, upon Cicero's return to Italy, Brutus had urged the elder statesman to take up the republican cause at Rome. But – as he had revealed to Atticus in private – Cicero had no desire to throw himself back into the fray; not at his age.

Yet any plans for retirement from political life were soon thwarted when Cicero became embroiled in a bitter dispute with Antony on his return to Rome at the beginning of September 43 BC.[30] Cicero had failed to attend a meeting of the Senate which was scheduled that day to vote on Antony's proposal to add a fifth day to the Roman games in honour of Caesar. In his defence Cicero pleaded tiredness from the journey, but Antony was furious. He took Cicero's absence as a personal and political affront and delivered a damning attack, which included a violent threat to tear down Cicero's house. All that Cicero could do was to appear in the Senate the next day, on 2 September, to deliver the first of the speeches known today under the title *Philippics*: so-called because they imitated the freedom-fighting rhetoric used by the famous Athenian orator Demosthenes in his fight against King Philip II of Macedon.[31]

This time, Antony was not there, yet Cicero addressed a speech to him and Dolabella, urging the two consuls towards reconciliation and compromise. Compared to the rest of the speeches in the collection, the criticisms of Antony in the *First Philippic* are more cautiously expressed. But still they signal the start of a complete breakdown in the two men's political relationship. To begin with, Cicero praised Antony for his behaviour in the early aftermath of the assassination: the amnesty he had agreed with the Liberators, the abolition of the dictatorship and the suppression of Pseudo-Marius and the cult of Caesar. And at first he presented his speech as a plea for the consul to return to the path of moderation upon which he had started out. But he went on to vehemently criticise Antony's conduct in the months since May. As a result, scholars are often divided in their responses to the speech: some see it as conciliatory, while others view it as provocative. However, one thing is certain: Antony took the speech as a direct challenge to his leadership, and two weeks later, on 19 September, he attacked Cicero bitterly in a wide-ranging denunciation of his character and political career; among the charges, he even accused Cicero of initiating the whole plot to kill Caesar.[32]

In the latter part of 44 BC, Antony's actions had also become noticeably more hostile towards the Liberators. In early October, for example, he had the base of a statue of Caesar inscribed with the words 'To Father and Benefactor', thus implicating the assassins as parricides; he spoke of their act as if they were traitors to their country; and declared that there was no room for Caesar's killers in the *res publica* so long as he was a part of it.[33] The problem was that Cicero knew he could not fight Antony or defend the Liberators' interests with words alone.[34] 'What can be done against violence except by violence?' Cicero wrote to Cassius.[35] But even Cassius had already left Italy by this time, and Cicero could only hope he was planning something worthy of his glory.[36] As matters stood, however, Cicero felt despondent: there was no one to lead the republicans at Rome.[37]

But what had happened to cause Antony's hostility to spike now? This time, it was not the reconciliation with Octavian prompting it; far from it. The autumn of 44 BC had been marked by the failure of Caesar's successors to cooperate, as well as the intensification of their fight to win the loyalty of Caesar's supporters. Under these circumstances, Antony had increased his efforts to champion Caesar's memory; hence the dedication of the statue to the *parens patriae*, mentioned above, as well as the proposal of new honours for Caesar. Yet at every move he found himself outflanked by Octavian's play for the support of the veterans and the urban populace. At the same time, some Caesarians in the Senate had also turned against the consul; the attack of Calpurnius Piso back in August had just been the beginning of a larger turning against Antony, and Cicero's own *First Philippic* cannot have helped.

One advantage of Octavian's arrival, then, was that the presence of the new 'Caesar' played into the hands of those who wanted to check Antony's ambitions. Despite Cicero's private concerns about Octavian, now that the Liberators were all out of Rome he arguably represented the best opportunity to divide the Caesarian faction. For the reconciliation between Octavian and Antony, the two would-be leaders, had failed. In October, there was a rumour Octavian was plotting to have Antony killed: 'Many think that Antony has made up this charge of a conspiracy, to lay siege to the young man's money', remarked Cicero to Atticus. 'But intelligent and likewise good men believe in the deed and even approve it.'[38] In short: it was just a rumour, but – true or not – Cicero could not dispute the likelihood of Octavian's hostile intentions. Throughout the summer, he had been recruiting veterans and soldiers by offering substantial payouts; by November it seemed to Cicero that Octavian was set on war.[39]

Meanwhile, as Octavian made his preparations to go head to head against Antony, the young man needed Cicero's help more than ever. 'Two letters have reached me from Octavian in one day, asking that I come to Rome at once', Cicero explained to Atticus. 'He says he wants to work through the Senate.' Octavian was after Cicero's advice and he needed him to act as his spokesman; at just nineteen, he was still far too young to be a senator. 'He is insistent but I am being cautious', Cicero added. 'I don't trust his age and I don't know what he has in mind.'[40]

But the truth was that Cicero needed Octavian's help, too. At the end of November Antony had left Rome to take control of Cisalpine Gaul away from Decimus. War had become inevitable, and any trace of the amnesty was rapidly disintegrating. Before he left Italy, Cassius had urged Cicero to use his eloquence and authority to help the campaign for liberty at Rome, just as Brutus had urged him to do in their last meeting at Velia.[41] It was consequently vital to the Liberators' cause that Cicero should do his utmost to reverse Antony's policies.

Octavian's political popularity, together with the army he had managed to gather, would be useful weapons in that battle. It was a high-risk strategy – and not one of which Brutus approved, as we shall see. After all, Octavian was urging for the assassins to be punished, and he had publicly declared his aspiration 'to attain to the honours of his father'.[42] But at the end of 44 BC this was the plan Cicero embarked upon in Italy: to have Antony pronounced a public enemy and to use Octavian's troops to help in the fight against him. When Cicero returned to Rome on 9 December he still seemed reluctant to enter the fray. Yet any doubts he had about his future role did not hold him back for long.

On 20 December Cicero delivered his *Third Philippic* – a speech outlining his strategy for preserving the *res publica*. As chance would have it, a dispatch from Decimus arrived from Cisalpine Gaul that same morning, stating his refusal to hand over his province to Mark Antony – just as Cicero had been urging him to do.[43] The timely concurrence of the letter's arrival and the senatorial meeting offered a welcome opportunity for Cicero to launch his attack on Antony – and it was one he fully seized.[44]

As was to become characteristic of Cicero's oratory of this period, his *Third Philippic* vilifies Antony and presents him as a national enemy while lavishly praising the efforts of those who resisted him, in this case Octavian and Decimus. At the end of the speech, Cicero made his proposal: that Decimus be commended for his actions and confirmed in his post as the governor of Cisalpine Gaul. In addition, he asked for Octavian, along with the veterans and legions he had gathered, to be publicly thanked and honoured for their opposition to Antony.[45] It was this same speech which had also proposed the reversal of Antony's provincial allotments.

Cicero's motion was passed with almost unanimous approval.[46] But what is particularly telling is that, in the spirit of their new alliance, Cicero finally committed himself to calling Octavian by the name he wanted to be known: 'Gaius Caesar'.[47] And, speaking to an audience largely composed of the former dictator's supporters, he urged them to join a new coalition composed of republicans, the younger Caesar, the veterans and his troops. As he was later to claim, Cicero managed to draw over to his side all the more moderate Caesarians, which crucially included the consuls-elect for 43 BC: Hirtius and Pansa. And, for all his private reservations, from this point onwards Cicero championed Gaius Caesar's name and achievements; at the same time, the elder statesman had re-emerged as the voice of the *res publica* at Rome.

The View from the East

In his *Tenth Philippic* – the speech he delivered when news of Brutus' success reached Rome – Cicero claimed that Brutus' revival in the east had been a direct result of the Senate's decree on 20 December: 'After he perceived you were ready to fight for freedom, he prepared to defend your freedom', he insisted.[48] But, as hinted at earlier, we should be careful not to take Cicero's words entirely at face value. To be sure, as later events would prove, Brutus was fastidiously concerned to act with senatorial approval; to this end, the decree legitimised and no doubt galvanised his plan to prevent Gaius Antonius from entering Macedonia. However, as we have already seen, Brutus must have been negotiating with Hortensius and collecting forces well ahead of that date; for Brutus was already stationed in the province at the end of December, before any news of the senatorial debate could have reached him. In presenting Brutus' actions as a result of the Senate's decree, Cicero rather aims to paint Brutus' actions in a more positive light: to deflect attention away from the fact that he had been acting upon his own (technically illegal) initiative. The truth was that, up until news of Brutus' success reached the Senate in February, there had been no shared strategy between the Liberators in the east and Cicero in the Senate at Rome.[49]

With this point in mind, we might ask how Brutus perceived the situation in the early months of 43 BC. Fortunately we do not need to search far for an answer. For the period stretching from the beginning of April to the end of July 43 BC, there are seven letters written in Brutus' own hand contained within the collection of Cicero's *Letters to Brutus*, and an additional seventeen written from the elder statesman in reply: a total of twenty-four genuine letters, with a further two letters, in all likelihood forgeries, which were later included in the collection. Although there were many more volumes of correspondence between Cicero and Brutus available to readers in antiquity – a reminder that we are dealing with evidence for only a fraction, and the climax, of their long relationship – the letters we have nevertheless provide the clearest insight we possess into Brutus' mind.[50] At this critical moment in time, it is perhaps not surprising to find that there were numerous differences of opinion between the major actors.

Resources and Priorities

To begin with there was the problem of resources. Brutus was desperately in need of money and men, or so he wrote to Cicero on 1 April 43 BC. In particular, he hoped that Cicero could send troops to Macedonia either by passing a motion in the Senate or, otherwise, by making a secret pact with the consul Pansa. But Cicero was powerless to help: 'any plan is difficult', he replied.[51] For, although the Senate had decreed Decimus should not hand over Cisalpine Gaul, Mark Antony had made his way there anyway. And now he was besieging his old foe in the town of Mutina, in Gaul. A civil war was impending in Italy and all the resources and troops were needed for the fight taking place on home soil. So why did Brutus ask?

In his 1970 study of Brutus, Hermann Bengtson rightly points out the futility of Brutus' requests for help. Brutus, he argues, must have held a gravely mistaken perception of the political conditions; he should have been able to guess that resources would not be forthcoming. To be sure, Pansa was already unhappy about the number of volunteers leaving Italy to join Brutus.[52] As for money, the Senate had already decreed that Brutus could borrow the money he needed from the Greek cities; he could request funds from them, as Cicero swiftly reminded him in his reply. But Brutus' tunnel vision and narrow focus on his own agenda had arguably led him to underestimate the scale of the crisis in Italy.[53] As we shall see repeatedly throughout the rest of the letters, Brutus' priority was now firmly focused on the Greek east (Syria, Asia Minor and Greece, along with its adjacent countries, especially Macedonia and Thrace). It was this point that leads Bengtson to dismiss Brutus' requests as politically out of touch.

Yet there was also more to it than that: for, although Cicero and Brutus were united in their belief that the *res publica* required defending, their attitudes to the prospect of civil war with Antony had been vastly different from the start. For his part, Cicero had advocated the need for war as early as 10 April 44 BC. Less than a month after the assassination, he had written to Atticus saying: 'Our heroes have achieved all they could achieve for themselves most gloriously and magnificently. But for what remains', he continues, 'we need money and men.'[54] A year later, in April 43 BC, Cicero could praise Brutus for the sterner guise with which he had reappeared at the head of an army. But he was still sorely disappointed in the young man's lack of fighting spirit: 'In the period we have just gone through, your whole policy has aimed at peace, an object that cannot be accomplished by diplomacy; on the other hand, my aim is liberty, without which peace is nothing.'

As the letter goes on, however, the second major difference in their policies emerges: for Cicero, the ultimate enemy was Mark Antony and the 'Caesarian party', as they still called themselves.[55] Thus he had decided that Octavian was the lesser of two evils. Conversely, as we shall see, Brutus feared Octavian and he still hoped that a peace with Antony might be achieved; he presumably knew that Lepidus had even written to the Senate late in March insisting upon one.[56] Cicero tried to persuade him otherwise: 'There is only one thing to be decided by this war', he told Brutus: 'whether or not we survive'. His letter attempts, by its highly rhetorical nature, to impress upon Brutus the urgency of the situation. However, it was to no avail. Showing a more cautious and arguably shrewder approach, Brutus could not fully bring himself to share Cicero's appetite for war against Antony. Instead, his plan was to make the republican cause the strongest, the richest and the most fearsome force to put a check on the ambitions of men like Octavian and Antony, who – like Caesar and Pompey before them – aimed to win power through their armies. Brutus and Cicero, it seems, had very different ideas.

Brutus and Gaius Antonius

A related problem was the question of what to do with Gaius Antonius, Mark Antony's brother. When Brutus sent the dispatch containing news of his success to the Senate in February, Gaius was still in the city of Apollonia, besieged by Brutus' troops. However, by the time Brutus sent his first letter to Cicero on 1 April 43 BC, he had defeated his opponent and taken him captive. 'Antonius is still with me', Brutus wrote from Dyrrachium. 'But I swear by the gods: I am both moved by the man's pleas and afraid lest the fury of others might lead him astray. I am really troubled', he confided in Cicero.[57] The fate of his hostage forms one of the most pervasive themes of Brutus' correspondence with Cicero.[58]

Throughout the collection, Brutus makes it clear that he is inclined to treat Gaius leniently. And to begin with Cicero agreed. For as long as

Decimus was still being besieged by Mark Antony at Mutina, Cicero thought it best for Gaius to be detained in custody.[59] However, his attitude soon hardened when two letters reached the Senate on the Ides of April: one was from Brutus, the second from Gaius. The latter had styled himself 'Antonius, proconsul' in his address to the Senate, a fact which caused much astonishment since, by the reversal of Mark Antony's provincial arrangements, Gaius was no longer the recognised commander of Macedonia. However, what caused an even greater commotion was the perceived leniency of Brutus' letter. 'Your letter was read aloud', Cicero wrote to Brutus soon after the meeting, 'but it was short, and rather too gentle towards Antonius.'

Cicero was, by his own account, in a quandary. To argue that the letter was a forgery might prove hazardous if its authorship was later proven genuine; to argue it was genuine would almost certainly damage Brutus' prestige, since he was undermining his own authority by allowing Gaius the title 'proconsul'.[60] Any decision on the matter was postponed until the next day. But by then another of Brutus' friends had pointed out that Brutus' seal was not on the letter, and that it was not dated; nor had any word been sent by Brutus to his own people – all facts which led the Senate to conclude the letter was counterfeit. Whatever the verdict of the Senate, however, Cicero's own view of its authorship is barely concealed. In his eyes, the letter was a genuine example of how Brutus was failing to deal with the crisis appropriately.[61]

By this time, shocking reports had reached Rome from Asia that Trebonius had been brutally executed by Dolabella.[62] He was the first of the assassins to lose his life, and even Antony's supporters in Rome reacted with horror at the news of his death. Calenus, who was otherwise calling for reconciliation between the Senate and Antony, moved that Dolabella should be pronounced a public enemy (*hostis*). Cicero went further still: to push his point on Brutus, he took full advantage of the declaration on Dolabella to argue that Mark Antony – and by extension Gaius – was guilty by association. 'For, what difference is there between Dolabella and any of the three Antonius brothers?' he continues in his letter to Brutus. 'If we spare any of them, we have been too hard on Dolabella.'[63] In the older orator's eyes, Gaius Antonius, as well as Lucius Antonius, who had joined Antony on the march to Gaul, should now also be regarded *hostes* and punished accordingly: Gaius should be put to death, he argued. But this was neither Cicero's nor Brutus' call to make.

For the rest of 43 BC, they continued to quibble. In a letter since lost to us, Brutus defended his decision to hold Gaius hostage. There were doubtless multiple reasons for his reluctance to kill the man; perhaps he felt a sense of duty stemming from the games Gaius had successfully hosted for him back in Rome; we cannot discount that Brutus' own temperament was not inclined in that direction.[64] But as he explained it to Cicero, above all Brutus saw Gaius as a bargaining tool with which to hold Mark Antony to the amnesty. To this end, he had embarked on a policy of *clementia*. 'You say we should be keener to prevent civil wars than to exercise our anger upon the proud', Cicero barked back at him. 'I vehemently disagree with you.'[65] Clemency was a pointless exercise in Cicero's view: 'if you want to be *clement*, we shall never be without civil wars'. His verdict seems brutal, and it is. However, Cicero's words arguably reflect his longer, often bitter experience of republican politics: 'Believe me, Brutus', he continued, 'you will all be overpowered unless you take care.'

But Brutus never was convinced by Cicero's argument that Gaius was in the same camp as his brothers. Nor did he believe it right to punish Gaius until the Senate had formally and specifically declared him a public enemy.[66] Despite Cicero's efforts to convince Brutus that the sentiment of the Senate was against Gaius, even if it had made no official pronouncement, Brutus stood his ground. His reply is worth quoting at length; in it we can see the force, determination and conviction in his own rightness for which Brutus has become famous:

> When you write to me that the three Antonii are embroiled in one and the same campaign, and that the verdict I pronounce is a matter of my own judgment, I declare only this: it is for the Senate or the people of Rome to pass judgment on those citizens who have not died fighting. You will say: 'The fact that you call men hostile to the state "citizens" is an impropriety in itself.' Actually, it is most lawful. For what the Senate has not yet decreed, nor the Roman people ordered, I do not confer upon myself to prejudge; and nor do I make myself an arbiter.

The passage offers a powerful insight into the quality of Brutus' rhetoric.[67] It is packed full with terminology drawn from the spheres of the law courts and senatorial debates: judgment (*iudicium*), to pronounce a considered opinion (*sentire*), to pass as law (*statuere*), to hasten to arbitrament (*ad arbitrium*). Not only that: by upholding the rights and the life of a citizen, Brutus' course of action is presented as the most just (*iustissime*). He could not entertain Cicero's notions of extraordinary times and extraordinary measures. Although admirable, this may have been a weakness in Brutus; as we shall see in the next chapter, Gaius Antonius had some measure of success stirring up mutinies within Brutus' legions before Brutus finally took decisive action.[68] However, the letter captures for us a view of Brutus' political ideology which is not commonly found elsewhere.

The defence of a citizen's right to trial and his immunity from arbitrary punishment, both of which Brutus upholds in this letter, lay at the heart of the kind of *popularis* politics Caesar had championed in his lifetime. And here Brutus was in strict disagreement with Cicero. The arguments drawn from law and justice may sound priggish to some ears, not least because Brutus expresses his ideas in an elevated style of language; but they were part of a carefully orchestrated argument in which he delicately reminded his correspondent of the need to abide by basic civil principles. After all, he was speaking to a man (Cicero) who had once before been exiled for putting citizens to death without trial; an act, it should be pointed out, that Caesar had opposed.[69] It is here that we see most clearly the second fundamental clash of principles operating behind Brutus' and Cicero's dispute throughout the summer of 43 BC. Brutus had not just reconciled himself with Caesar after Pharsalus; he had become committed to Caesarian ideology, much of which he still advocated. It was a mode of political operation which Cicero had never fully shared.

Cicero's Strategy

While Brutus kept an eye on his hostage in Macedonia, back at Rome everything depended on the success of Cicero's strategy. His gamble to use the forces of Octavian to help relieve Decimus had turned into a long struggle on Cicero's part. But by the end of April, Antony's troops were eventually crushed during two battles at Mutina; Antony himself was forced to retreat into Gaul – he was not dead yet, but certainly defeated. And to all contemporary observers, including the orator himself, Cicero's first throw of the die looked successful.

Decimus had been saved; Antony was declared a public enemy. With the war in the west looking all but sealed, and while Cicero was at the top of his game, on 27 April the orator made one last push for the defence of the *res publica* from his seat at Rome. Cassius was finally given command over the war in Syria, a post which came with the responsibility of dealing with Dolabella, who was still wreaking havoc for the republican cause in the east. In addition to his current *imperium* over the Balkan provinces, the Senate granted Brutus more extensive powers, so that he too could undertake military action against Dolabella should he see fit. Taken together, this meant that Brutus and Cassius had pretty much full control over all the Roman territories from the Adriatic to Egypt, while back in the western regions, Sextus Pompeius was made commander of the fleet – a position which gave him Mediterranean-wide *imperium*.[70]

The ratification of all these posts, as Antony Woodman has suggested, is indicative of the high level of 'pro-republican feeling' after Mutina.[71] It seemed just about possible that a final victory might be sealed. And for a while, Cicero shared Brutus' strategic plan of increasing his stronghold overseas. 'If Dolabella has a following, or a camp, or anywhere to make a stand, your loyalty and prestige call you to follow him',[72] Cicero wrote to Brutus on 5 May, when decisive action against Dolabella seemed more critical than events in Italy. For, although Cassius too wrote to Cicero on 7 May, to inform him that he was in pursuit of Dolabella, the slowness of communications meant that Cicero did not receive this news in time. In fact, no one at Rome seemed sure of Cassius' whereabouts at all.[73] Consequently, when Brutus responded by marching his army towards the Chersonese later that same month – hot on the trail of five cohorts Dolabella had allegedly dispatched there – Cicero approved of his decision.[74] Little did Cicero know that his own strategy in Italy was on the verge of collapse.

For despite the victories at Mutina, the fighting came at a huge cost to Cicero's coalition, when, by the end of April, it emerged that both consuls were dead: Hirtius had been killed in the fray, while Pansa died later from wounds sustained in the fight.[75] Their deaths left a large gap at the top of Rome's power structure, as well as an even larger question mark over Octavian's next move. Would he continue the fight against Antony, as the Senate expected, operating alongside Decimus – possibly the greatest traitor to Julius Caesar of them all? Or would he finally be swayed by Antony to join the Caesarian campaign and take revenge for his father's murder? As Cicero was painfully aware, for several months Antony had been urging the young man to join him in crushing the 'Pompeians', as he called the group which had resurfaced under Cicero's leadership.[76] It meant that Octavian's chosen path of action was to play a key role in the outcome of the struggle, and the success or otherwise of Cicero's all-or-nothing gamble was about to be tested.

Throughout the months of December and April, Cicero had openly championed the young Caesar: a boy of 'divine wisdom and courage'.[77] To keep him on the side of the republicans, the Senate had awarded Octavian exceptional honours: the nineteen-year-old was made a senator, given the powers and status (though not the title) of a praetor, and his soldiers were to be paid out of the public treasury. But already in April, when news of Antony's defeat at Mutina first reached Rome, Cicero betrayed his anxieties to Brutus: 'I only hope that we can guide and hold him in the richness of honours and favours as easily as we have done up until now', he wrote.[78]

What Brutus initially thought of Cicero's strategy is muddled in our sources. According to a passage from Dio, at first Brutus supported Cicero's plan to court Octavian, and even attempted to enter into an alliance with the young man himself.[79] At the other extreme, by the time Plutarch was writing, there were copies of Brutus' letters in circulation which seemed to suggest Brutus had openly condemned Cicero's strategy from the beginning.[80] Indeed, two letters survive in the Ciceronian correspondence – one written by Brutus to Cicero, the other to Atticus – both of which appear to confirm his disdain for Cicero's policy. However, the letters are probably forgeries and the result of a hostile tradition which developed in the early history of Brutus' legend.[81] In any case, to determine whether Brutus acquiesced in or condemned Cicero's policy towards Octavian, we are better served by focusing on the correspondence we know to be genuine.

What is particularly interesting to note here is that it was only *after* Cicero admitted his own anxieties regarding Octavian that Brutus too raised the matter. On 7 May, Brutus replied to Cicero's letter of 21 April. He expressed his delight at the news of Decimus' victory, repeated his own determination to await a firm declaration of Gaius Antonius' status before taking punitive action, and then defended himself against Cicero's criticisms:

> It is much more honourable, in my opinion, and can be more conducive to the *res publica*, to not bear hard upon the unfortunate, rather than to make endless concessions to the powerful, which might inflame their ambition and arrogance. On that topic, Cicero, my excellent and gallant man, for whom I care so deeply both on my own account and for the *res publica*, you appear to be trusting too much in your hopes. The moment that someone does right by you, you give and permit him everything, as if it were impossible for a mind corrupted by largesse to be led down evil paths. You are so even-tempered that you will take a warning in good spirit, especially as it concerns the safety of the *res publica*. But you will do what seems best to you.[82]

It was a polite and complimentary refrain: one which pitched his concerns within a tone of amicable respect for the elder statesman. But on 15 May Brutus wrote to Cicero again with more urgency and in more critical terms: 'now, Cicero, now is the time to act', opens the extant portion of the letter, 'lest we turn out to have celebrated in vain at the defeat of Antony, and so that care to excise one evil does not result in the birth of another, worse one'.

In this second letter on the topic of Octavian, Brutus comments on the extent of Cicero's authority in the Senate, reminds him of the need for wisdom and threatens to hold him responsible if anything goes wrong: 'we shall all be to blame', he admits, 'but you more than any'.[83] As he continues, Brutus urges Cicero to follow the paths of law and wisdom in exercising his authority, criticises his generosity in granting Octavian honours, and worries about the latter's rumoured ambitions for one of the consulships made vacant by the deaths of Hirtius and Pansa:

> Because if Antony made use of the machinery of monarchy left behind by another as a means of seizing power for himself, what do you think will be the mentality of one who thinks it possible to covet any kinds of office with the backing, not of a slaughtered tyrant, but of the Senate itself? And so I will applaud your good fortune and foresight only when I start seeing proof that Caesar will be content with the extraordinary honours he has already accepted. 'Will you suborn me as the guilty party for someone else's fault, then?' you will ask. Absolutely, if its occurrence could have been foreseen and prevented. How I wish you could look into my heart and see how much I fear him![84]

When we read these later criticisms of Cicero's policy towards Octavian, it is hard to imagine that Brutus only voiced his opinion for the first time in May 43 BC. On the other hand, we might remember that Brutus had once before held his tongue when he disapproved of Cicero's plans: back in the summer of 44 BC when Cicero had set sail for Greece.

Indeed, in early 43 BC, Cicero had even been sending Brutus copies of the *Philippics* he had delivered in the Senate. From the comments he makes, we can tell Brutus had certainly read Cicero's *Fifth* and *Tenth Philippics*, if not more.[85] 'I don't know whether the greater part of the praise for these works should be confined to your spirit or genius', Brutus had complimented Cicero back at the start of April. To cap it all, he even admitted Cicero's self-styled *Philippic* orations deserved to be compared to the works of Demosthenes. When we consider the disputes the two men had conducted over the styles of oratory in the past, this was high praise from Cicero's younger critic.[86] Regardless of how he felt about Cicero's strategy, Brutus had politely kept quiet until now. The fact that Brutus prefaced his criticism to Cicero on 7 May with a friendly refrain – 'You are so even-tempered that you will take a warning in good spirit' – certainly suggests it was the first time he had broached the topic of Octavian in this way. In the meantime, he could only hope that Cicero would make his plan work – and be ready to act if not.

Increasing Tensions

As tensions rose between Brutus and Cicero throughout May over the matter of Octavian, the two men nevertheless tried to maintain the obligations of friendship. Thus Cicero had written to Brutus commending many friends to him.[87] In return, Brutus wrote a letter of reference for Pansa's former physician, who was under suspicion in connection with the consul's death; he requested for Cicero to support a mutual friend called Flavius in the matter of an inheritance dispute; and he asked Cicero to nominate his stepson Bibulus for the position of augur – a vacancy that arose as a result of Pansa's death.[88] As several scholars have noted, that friendship should form such a dominant motif in the mere handful of letters to have survived from Brutus is no accident; his family, friends and networks were a matter of great importance to him.[89] Back in Italy he had a dutiful mother, a loving wife and sisters – with all of whom Brutus had kept in regular contact. But from June 43 BC onward, as the political world of Rome turned upside down, it was they who fell into danger; not Brutus in the east.

To begin with, Brutus' brother-in-law Lepidus made a decision which had a devastating impact both on the course of the war and on his family's life: he decided to throw in his lot with Antony. His army had forced him into it, Lepidus wrote to the Senate on 30 May 43 BC.[90] But it was an act of 'criminal treachery' that Cicero could not forgive. As the governor of both Hispania Citerior and Narbonese Gaul, Lepidus' support was a matter of critical importance for the republican cause. To bind him to the Senate, whatever his real opinion, Cicero had publicly praised Lepidus for his hatred of servitude, as well as his own moderation, wisdom, compassion, humanity and clemency. He had even passed a motion to erect a golden statue of Lepidus in honour of his services to the state.[91] Now however, Cicero could let other feelings show. He complained to Brutus that Lepidus was 'an enemy of the *res publica*', 'fickle' and 'untrustworthy'.[92] The implications of Lepidus' actions and the language Cicero was using to describe them spelled the situation out in no uncertain terms: he was a traitor to his country.

Yet Brutus was also the uncle of Lepidus' children, and on 1 July he sent a letter to Cicero asking for his help in protecting them. 'I beg and implore you, Cicero, in the name of our friendship and the goodwill you have always shown me, do not forget that Lepidus' sons are the children of my sister.' For the children of an outlawed man might be used as hostages in any future negotiations; they would be deprived of their property, inheritance and status. 'Bear in mind that I will take his place as their father', Brutus added.

'Nothing I can do for my sister's children can satisfy my personal wishes or sense of duty.' More than in any other letter we see here the depths of emotion to which Brutus could allow himself to fall. As he penned this letter, he admitted to Cicero, Brutus was feeling 'anxious' and 'sick to the stomach'.[93] Little did he know that the day before, on 30 June 43 BC, Lepidus had been declared a public enemy.

'Nothing weighs upon me more heavily than my inability to yield to your mother's and your sister's entreaties', Cicero wrote back to Brutus. For Servilia and Junia, as well as Brutus, had all begged Cicero to help protect Lepidus' children. And yet Cicero had supported the motion. 'The harshness of making children suffer the penalty for the crimes of their parents does not escape me', he explained. However, he believed the laws were designed to make better citizens of men who might take unpatriotic action otherwise: 'It is Lepidus who is cruel to his children, not the man who declares Lepidus a public enemy', was his final justification.[94] Brutus' reply does not survive.

The treachery of Lepidus, however, was not the only family matter preying on Brutus' mind at this time. For at some point in June, his wife Porcia had died. We do not know the details (in her later legend her death was turned into an act of martyrdom after the defeat of Brutus at Philippi), but Cicero was not sympathetic to this news either.[95] 'You have indeed suffered a blow', Cicero conceded, 'the like of your loss was nowhere on earth.' But the rest of his letter recalls Cicero's own bereavement two years earlier when his daughter Tullia died, as well as the disappointment he felt then, when Brutus had urged him to put aside his excessive and unmanly grief. 'I should perform the same duty as you performed when I was mourning and write a letter of consolation', it begins. And later continues: 'I hope you find the healing process easier in your own case than you found it in mine.' An old grudge had evidently resurfaced. However, now, in 43 BC, it was Cicero urging Brutus to focus on the task ahead of him: 'When not just your army, but all citizens and – one might say – all nations have their eyes on you, it would be unseemly for the very man who makes the rest of us stronger to appear broken in spirit.'[96]

We do not know how Brutus received Cicero's letter; whether he interpreted it as a cold and unfeeling call to pull himself together or as a philosophical reflection on his general position. But, if we order the letters in the collection of Cicero by the dates on which their recipient would have most likely received them, we gain a slightly different reading experience from that imposed by the standard sequence: in other words, we read the letters from the perspective of Brutus in the order he sent and received letters from Cicero.

For Brutus was still writing to Cicero on amiable terms when he asked for support for Bibulus in late May to early June (Letter 19, in Shackleton Bailey's numbering). Porcia probably died in mid- to late June. On 1 July Brutus, still grieving his wife's death, wrote to Cicero asking him to protect his sister's children (Letter 20). Cicero's letter of 'condolence' (Letter 18), written towards the end of June, would then only have reached Brutus in mid-July. It would have been swiftly followed by Letter 21, in which Cicero refused to comply in the matter of Lepidus and Junia's children.

In Letter 22, written on 14 July, Cicero complained bitterly at the brevity of a letter (lost to us) which Brutus had sent to inform him of Marcus Cicero the younger's whereabouts: 'Does Brutus send me only three short lines these times?' he asked, infuriated by Brutus' lack of protocol, especially at a time of national crisis. The war had been rekindled thanks to Lepidus' defection, and Cicero's mind could only focus on matters closer to Rome; he also believed it vital to the cause for Brutus to return from Macedonia with his legions.[97]

As for Brutus, we can only speculate on his state of mind, but his silence gives us a clue. We have seen him holding his tongue in the face of anger and disappointment before; and given Cicero's lack of feeling and support in the face of Brutus' family struggles, it is not unlikely that he was feeling severely let down by Cicero once again in the summer of 43. For a politician away from Rome, contact with the hub of political activity was vital under any circumstances; but even more so under the volatile conditions of a civil war.[98] Besides the fact that dangers could come upon a man's loved ones quickly and unexpectedly, communications were even more unreliable than usual, and he might expect a friend to intervene to protect his family on his behalf. More than anything, then, Brutus had needed Cicero's help to protect Servilia and Porcia, as well as his sisters and their families.

It is only in his last two letters of the collection, written in the latter half of May, that Cicero finally understood that this was what mattered most to Brutus: 'How diligently I am working for your sister's children I hope you will hear from your mother's and sister's letters', he wrote, in an evident change of heart. 'In so doing I am taking greater stock of your wishes, which mean a great deal to me, than I am – as some see it – of my own consistency.'[99] But, by then, the ever-fragile relationship between Cicero and Brutus had suffered a severe, perhaps irreparable blow.

Home or Away

On 27 July, Cicero wrote his final letter to Brutus in the collection; for all we know, it may have been their last communication ever. Two days before,

Cicero had attended another meeting at Servilia's house, this time to discuss the question of whether or not Brutus should return with his troops to Italy. Although we are nowhere told the final verdict of this select committee, Cicero expressed his call for Brutus to return: his reputation and standing depended on it, he argued. Admittedly, he had hinted at this idea from as early as April, but in May – in the euphoric first moments following Antony's defeat – Cicero had supported the decision for Brutus to head further east in pursuit of Dolabella. It was only after Lepidus' union with Antony at the end of May that Cicero shifted his stance again, and from mid-June onwards he made his appeals with a greater insistency.[100]

'Hurry, I beg you'; 'urge Cassius to do the same': Brutus was needed to bring aid to what Cicero now called 'the tottering and almost collapsing *res publica*'.[101] Cicero's letters on this point become increasingly frantic. Yet there is no extant letter in which Brutus issues a response to Cicero's desperate calls for help; nor did he ever make it back to Italy. There are many reasons why this might be so: perhaps Brutus wanted to avoid association with the historical examples of men like Sulla and Caesar, who had marched their armies into Italy before him; it is also reasonable to suppose that he wanted to avoid a fight on native land. More pressingly, however, the campaign against Dolabella was gaining ground, and reports on his whereabouts and intentions were mixed.

And so Brutus was marching east instead of west, against a man he feared was still dangerous – rather than Antony, whom he considered defeated. It is easy to find fault with Brutus' decision not to return to Italy; it must have been obvious even to contemporaries that, should Antony resurface, his enemies in the west would suffer before those in the east. But not only did Brutus and his comrades have a different perspective on the troubles in store; information exchanged between the various arenas in which the war was being conducted always travelled too slowly, and arrived too late.

Much had happened since the defeat of Antony at Mutina and, as he sat helpless back in Rome, Cicero freely distributed the blame: Decimus had failed to pursue Antony into Gaul when the latter was at his weakest. Lepidus had since joined Antony in his so-called 'Caesarian party' and strengthened their cause significantly; between them, Antony and Lepidus had eleven legions, while Decimus only had ten. Octavian, with eleven legions of his own, was left as the key player. But on 14 July, in the same letter in which he cursed Brutus for the curtness of his correspondence, Cicero finally had to admit it: 'Caesar's army, which used to be excellent, is not only of no help; it even forces us to ask repeatedly for your army.'[102]

In other words, Cicero had to take his own share of the responsibility, too: he had failed to deliver on his personal promise to control Octavian. Encouraged by the honours he had been granted, the popularity he held with the army, and his own ambition – not to mention the 'rascally letters, fallacious go-betweens and messages' urging him on – the nineteen-year-old was edging closer to his dream of becoming a consul.[103] Although Cicero professes hope that he might still exert some influence over Octavian, the elder statesman's urgent appeal to Brutus was his very last throw of the die for the campaign in the west. When Servilia held court at her house on the 25 July it was presumably clear to all that Cicero's gamble had come to nothing. But the extent of the damage was not yet easy to assess.

All the while, the eyes of those in the east had remained fixed on the threat of Dolabella. To begin with, there were rumours that Dolabella had his sights on winning Syria for Antony; if it should happen, a strategic blow to the Liberators. But, should he fail, there were further reports that Dolabella had ships waiting at Lycia, ready to set sail for Italy to join the Caesarians on home ground: a sure danger to those fighting for the *res publica* at Rome.[104] Our source for this information is a pair of letters sent by Publius Cornelius Lentulus Spinther, who had formerly served as Trebonius' quaestor in Asia but had since attached himself to Brutus. The first was sent to Cicero on 29 May, while a second letter addressed to the Senate followed shortly on 2 June; they survive today to give us a contemporary take at a time when the final showdown with Dolabella looked imminent.

By this time, Dolabella had arrived in Syria, in the coastal town of Laodicea, from where he was not expected to escape. Brutus' own crossing into Asia had been delayed (for reasons Spinther does not provide), but the good news was that Cassius and his entire force were believed to be only four days' march away: 'That nefarious bandit [Dolabella] will pay the penalty sooner than we thought', Spinther confidently concluded.[105] And, indeed, further positive reports soon followed, ten days later, when Cassius Parmensis sent word to Cicero of Cassius' successful efforts in raising resources. The Liberator had 10 legions, 20 auxiliary cohorts and 4,000 cavalry stationed near Dolabella's camp at Laodicea; on the sea, he had a sizeable fleet to prevent supplies from reaching his opponent. Adding to the information provided by Lentulus Spinther, Parmensis tells us that Cassius was aiming at a 'bloodless strategy'– i.e. that he was planning for Dolabella to die by starvation. Even though Parmensis hints that Dolabella had amassed some powerful support of his own, he too was confident of a swift victory. 'You can have high hopes for the *res publica*', he cheerfully predicted: 'just as you have freed it in Italy, so you can trust we shall quickly succeed at our end, too.'[106]

Evidently there was little understanding in the east of the effect of Lepidus' defection and the potential crisis awaiting Rome; likewise, in the west, the problem of Dolabella was remote and incomprehensible.

The Culmination of a Plan

Throughout July and August, the battle continued on both sides of the Mediterranean. While Cicero nervously watched Octavian's every move, Cassius successfully besieged Laodicea, until finally Dolabella ended the fight by killing himself.[107] In the event, Brutus had not been needed to help take Dolabella down; but he had stayed close at hand, pressing the local communities for more men, more money and more resources to help in the fight. Dio tells us that twice that summer Brutus led his men across the Hellespont – the narrow strait which separated Europe from Asia.[108] In the intervening period, he had also had to contend with the death of his wife, the loss of his sister's status at Rome, and several attempts by Gaius Antonius to interfere with the loyalty of his men. We shall return to this period of Brutus' life in the next chapter, because it belongs to a spell of increased military activity which needs to be examined through a different lens. Before then, the dramatic arc of the *Letters to Brutus* requires that we follow events in Italy from July through to the end of 43 BC.

So far we have focused on how two pairs of eyes – those of Brutus and Cicero – each perceived the situation in the period from August 44 to July 43 BC. In so doing, we need to remember that the history and relationship between these two eyewitnesses had never been straightforward. But Cicero's penultimate letter in the collection as it stands today is worth revisiting in this context, because it is largely a manifesto of Cicero's own actions at a time when he was already considering making some of his letters public. One cannot but read it as a defence of his entire policy from the moment Caesar was killed; it was, in fact, a response to Brutus' criticism of the exceptional honours Cicero had proposed for Octavian, as well as the severity he had shown towards Lepidus' children. For this important task even a letter was not enough; to plead his case in person and further expound on the current situation Cicero sent a trusty and eloquent friend: a budding orator and statesman, Marcus Valerius Messalla Corvinus (known better as the writer Messalla), who will in turn become an important source of information in the next chapter.[109]

The letter begins with a lengthy section extolling the virtues of his messenger, before Cicero finally comes to the point: a state depends on two things, he argues (using a quotation from Solon not otherwise attested) –

reward and punishment. 'Of course, moderation is required in both', he admits, 'a sort of balance in each of the two categories.' But the hypothesis was a useful tool for justifying to Brutus the varying positions he had taken in the war, and for illuminating how they were all grounded in one guiding principle. At the core of his argument, however, Cicero wanted to explain why his intervention had been necessary at all: the 'apparatus of monarchy', as he put it (*instrumentum regni*), had passed to Lepidus and Antonius. 'The former is more of a weathercock, the latter is pure evil, but both men are fearful of peace [*pax*] and hostile to stability [*otium*].' And, thus, using the catchwords of Brutus' own political propaganda – *pax et otium* – Cicero revealed the real reason why Brutus' plan had been flawed from the start: simply put, he had placed his trust in men who were not to be trusted.

There was more: the Liberators had appeared too bold and Antony had managed to take control of the city. Forestalling any criticism of his own conduct (or lack thereof) in the period from April to December 44 BC, Cicero races through a whole series of events – including his own departure and return to Rome, his clash with Antony in September, his immediate retreat from Rome and withdrawal from politics throughout October and November – to focus solely on his return at the helm of the Senate on 20 December, when he delivered the *Third Philippic*. 'And when I had stirred up Antony against me', he adds, 'I embarked on a truly Brutine policy to liberate the *res publica*.' And so he defends his policy of honouring Octavian: 'thanks to whom we are still alive', 'our only protection'; 'nothing seemed too much at the time'. Recently Cicero had even proposed that Octavian should be awarded an ovation: 'I suspect *that* will not be to your liking – your friends, excellent men that they are, however inexperienced in politics, did not approve either. But *I* think it is the wisest move I have made so far in this war.' Even after his recent experience with Lepidus, Cicero was still thinking that he could buy the young Caesar's loyalty with honours.[110]

Not for the first time in his life, Cicero was wrong. In early August the young Caesar marched his army towards Rome and had himself and his relative Quintus Pedius elected consuls. On 19 August they entered office and almost immediately they set to the task of serving revenge upon Caesar's assassins. First they passed a law, the *lex Pedia*, which made the murder of the dictator a criminal act; then they appointed prosecutors. Brutus and Cassius were tried in their absence and convicted; distance from Rome kept them safe for now. But Decimus was an immediate victim. He was killed at some point in October as a direct consequence of the verdict against him.

As for Cicero, the young Caesar at first allowed him to leave Rome and thus kept him safe in the short term; after all, however much he had rejoiced at the death of the dictator, Cicero had never been actively involved in the plot to kill him. So this was the culmination of Cicero's plans: silenced and cowed, he was forced out of Rome; he had lost the cause in the west. In one of the last fragments of his voice to survive, Cicero wrote to the young Caesar and thanked him for this special permission: 'I rejoice at your provision of leave for two reasons', he writes, 'because you both forgive what has passed and offer protection for the future.' Yet even in these last words, Cicero was being too optimistic in his assessment of the young consul.

Terror at Rome

For the remaining months of Cicero's life, we must make do without any speeches or letters from his hands. It makes little difference; by then Cicero had lost all influence over events at Rome. For no sooner had the consuls Caesar and Pedius entered office than they revoked the *hostis* decrees against Mark Antony and Lepidus, thus opening the way for a reconciliation and union of Caesarians. And, when it happened, the result was as bad as Cicero had predicted when, back in April 43, he had asked Brutus: 'Are we taking thought for men who, if they are the victors, will wipe us out without a trace?'[111] For that was indeed their plan. On 27 November, Mark Antony, Octavian and Lepidus made their move. They formalised their alliance with a law – the *lex Titia* – which granted each man the *imperium* of a consul for five years. Henceforth they were triumvirs in a union of power: three dictators instead of one. But their expressed purpose 'to restore the *res publica*' was, in reality, a thinly veiled ploy to wreak further revenge on Caesar's assassins. And just like that, the amnesty hammered out in the days following the Ides of March was broken.

What is more, unlike Octavian's *lex Pedia*, which while legally condemning the assassins confined its remit only to them, under the *lex Titia* the punishment was extended to include anyone who had shown support for them in the aftermath of Caesar's assassination. And this time, the procedure was not judicial. The three men drew up a proscription list of all their enemies and offered rewards for their heads; in all, some 300 senators and 2,000 equestrians were said to have been named. But many more than that suffered as the triumvirs went on their quest for revenge. No one – not even their own family and friends – was safe in their person, possessions or loved ones, as the three men aimed to enrich their reserves and instil terror across Rome.[112] The effect this had on Brutus and Cassius in the east was momentous, as we shall soon see. Meanwhile, back in Rome, carnage ensued, and the world reacted with horror.

Tales of the terrors of the proscriptions survive vividly in our later historians: a testament to the instinct of survivors to record their traumas and losses for future generations.[113] Appian devotes an unparalleled amount of space to the sufferings of the men, women and children, the slaves and freedmen caught up in these extraordinary times – just a small sample of the tales of danger and survival he found among his sources. Chief among them is the death of Cicero – one of the first to be hunted down and killed in December 43 BC; Antony saw to that. Resolved at first to flee, and then to die on home soil, Cicero finally faced death head on.

The story goes that, as he was being carried on a litter through the woodland leading from his villa to the coast, Cicero heard his assassins approaching and ordered his slaves to stop. The murderers were led by two men, the centurion Herennius and a military officer called Popillius, both of whom wanted the bounty placed on Cicero's head. Yet, allegedly, even these warlike men hesitated and trembled as Cicero held still for their strike, baring his neck as defeated gladiators were accustomed to do. Appian adds that it took three blows and some sawing to sever Cicero's head from his body. But in the event, the deed was done, and on Antony's orders a gruesome parcel of Cicero's head and hands was sent back to Rome, where they were nailed to the *rostra* for all to see. Not even Octavian, it seems, had put any real effort into saving the life of a man he had once tried so hard to win as a friend.[114]

However, we should not let our feelings over Cicero's death blind us to the fact that he was just as willing to kill as to be killed for his republican ideals. In later years, the Roman historian Livy was to point out that Cicero 'suffered no more cruelly at the hands of his victorious enemy than he himself would have acted if he had had the same good fortune'.[115] And it is true. For, in his blind hatred of Antony, Cicero had determined upon the latter's destruction: 'a narrow purpose he recklessly identified with the salvation of the republic', as Jeffrey Tatum has put it.[116] Even Brutus' own alleged reaction to the news betrays something of the ambivalence he felt towards Cicero by the time of his death. 'He felt more shame at the cause of Cicero's death than grief at the event itself', Plutarch explains, in words which have prompted mixed reactions from those who have studied them in any depth.[117]

Did Brutus fail to express his grief properly? Or did he feel ashamed at his own reluctance to return to Italy with his troops? The answer is probably neither. If we want to come close to understanding how Brutus was feeling, we might say that his words on the subject of Cicero's death (if genuine) reflect their fraught friendship and the strains placed upon it in recent months. His shame must have had its foundation in the failure of Cicero's gamble in waging a war against Antony. 'Cicero's policies led straight to the Triumvirate and the proscriptions', as Peter Wiseman has more bluntly expressed it.[118] His assessment is harsh but not entirely unfair. After all, Cicero had backed Antony into a corner – a position from which the latter always emerged stronger and more dangerous. And he had simultaneously provided a platform from which the young Caesar could develop and legitimise his – already advanced – ambitions.

But we should not rest the blame on one person alone. For the tragedy of the proscriptions in late 43 BC was also a result of the general anxieties and political manoeuvring of 44 BC, which had all led Antony to stray increasingly from his side of the amnesty agreement. The young Caesar's arrival at Rome had surely contributed much to these tensions, yet so had the decisions of Brutus and Cassius, who had declined to accept the grain commissions or the smaller provinces of Crete and Cyrene. Decimus, too, had refused to hand over Cisalpine Gaul to Antony, while Antony's own response of leading armed forces against him was a political disaster. And yet, in all of this, there is something else: in the months leading up to the proscriptions, we witness the re-emergence of old habits and ideals, long dead in the days of Caesar.[119] Men were looking ahead and arguing over vacant consulships. The younger generation was being stirred to arms in defence of *libertas*. Among the older generation, each man's *dignitas* continued to be a matter of concern to him. What is more, the audibility of the citizens' voices re-emerges as a defining marker of the system: in the end, Antony had used a popular assembly to confer military honour upon himself, just as others had abused the system in the days before Caesar.

'The *res publica* depends on Brutus', Cicero had written to Atticus in May 44 BC – a point he reiterated to the young man in the year that followed.[120] But what kind of *res publica* did Cicero have in mind: the theoretical and cherished model of government, which had arguably never really existed even in his own lifetime, or the mess of a system he once referred to as 'the gutters of Rome'?[121] It is perhaps not necessary to push the point too far; in either case, the *res publica* for which they were fighting was but a distant dream. The real fight was for supremacy at Rome – a city whose borders had expanded to include most of the eastern Mediterranean, where the fight was now set to take place: between Antony and Octavian against Brutus and Cassius, along with the men whose republican spirit, whose yearning for political freedom, the Liberators had managed to revive.

CHAPTER 7

BRUTUS' LAST FIGHT

Philippi

But the time will come, when in these lands
a farmer, toiling the land with his curved plough,
will find our spears consumed by corroding rust,
or strike our hollowed helmets with weighty hoe
and gape at mighty bones upturned from their tombs.
Gods of my country, heroes, Romulus and Mother Vesta,
you who guard Tuscan Tiber and Rome's Palatine,
don't stop this young champion from rescuing
a generation turned upside down.

— Virgil, *Georgics*, 1. 493–501

Less than eight months after the formation of the Second Triumvirate, in July 42 BC, Brutus and Cassius met on the western coast of Asia Minor to begin their march to Philippi – the hilltop city once fortified by Philip II of Macedon (the father of Alexander the Great). Appian tells us that they had somewhere in the region of nineteen legions (approximately 80,000 men), 13,000 cavalry troops, 4,000 mounted archers and an excellent navy at sea.[1] Money and men were no longer in short supply; nor was food or any other resource. It was only two years since the Liberators had been forced to leave Rome after the assassination of Caesar. But now a battle roughly twice the size of that at Pharsalus was about to begin.

What finally induced Brutus to accept the inevitability of war and to lead his troops against fellow Romans? What were his first moves? And how did the Liberators manage to reverse their fortunes so successfully? Before addressing such questions, we need to pause and reflect on the scale and importance of the war, because the trauma of the fighting, as well as the memory of the confrontation, significantly impacted the way it has been recorded in history. As we can see from the lines of Virgil quoted above, Philippi was remembered for the turmoil, the bloodshed and the shame of Romans fighting Romans as the armies of the triumvirs and the Liberators engaged in two mighty battles, three weeks apart, in October 42 BC. At the end of it, both Brutus and Cassius were dead, along with up to 50,000 others.[2]

From Virgil's expression of bewilderment that the gods would allow such a thing to happen, to his desperate plea that the 'young champion' Octavian (soon to become Rome's first emperor, Augustus) might be able to end the cycles of self-destruction, in his poetry we find a man caught up in the moment. That moment is the disastrous state of Rome in 29 BC, after Antony and Octavian had first continued their fights against the surviving republicans (42–35 BC) before turning against each other (34–31 BC). By the time Virgil's *Georgics* were published, Antony had been defeated in the battle of Actium in western Greece in 31 BC, and within a year had taken his own life. Octavian had emerged as the sole winner and was claiming to restore the *res publica*, to bring peace and stability to 'a generation turned upside down'. Yet it is important to start our investigation of Philippi at the end, so to speak, because the post-war shock expressed in Virgil's poem provides a vital context for understanding the bafflement felt both at the time and in the generations that followed.

As men returned home from this war, either as victors or pardoned survivors, there was an intense desire to make sense of it all. And much of this was done in writing: in memoirs, biographies, tales of the proscriptions and so on – all of it on papyrus or parchment, almost all of it lost to us.[3] The poet Horace was one of those who took to writing after the war, and in his works we occasionally encounter others like him who had fought at Philippi: Messalla, who had served under Cassius but went on to hold a joint consulship with Octavian in 31 BC; Brutus' stepson Bibulus, who was praetor in 35 BC and then governed Syria until his death in 32 BC; Lucius Sextius, who became a suffect consul in 23 BC having formerly been a commander loyal to Brutus; and Quintus Dellius, who seems to have occupied a place within what became Augustus' inner circle.[4] The last wrote about his campaigns with Antony, while Messalla recalled his years with Brutus and especially Cassius. Both these works are lost to us today, but they evidently influenced the tradition considerably, as did the works of the Roman historian Livy, whose books covering this period are known to us only through the eyes of a later summariser.

As Octavian tried to bury his past and carve a glorious new role for himself under the name of Augustus, it doubtless irked him to be presented with reminders of Brutus and Philippi; but in the spirit of liberty and the revival of the *res publica*, the semblance of which he was proclaiming to uphold, he was bound to tolerate them.[5] For his part, Octavian/Augustus too attempted to shape the memory of these hideous years. In his *Res Gestae* – the huge autobiographical statement he wrote and asked to be inscribed on two bronze pillars attached to his tomb – he simply described Philippi as the war in which he exacted vengeance upon 'the men who killed my father', and whom he personally claimed to have defeated 'twice in battle'.[6] In so doing he carefully omitted the names of Brutus and Cassius, famed for their reputations as 'republicans', as well as that of his foe-turned-friend-turned-foe, Antony. But the language of retribution reminds us of the second historiographical tradition, which remembered Brutus and Cassius in far less positive terms than the ones in which they presented their actions. From this different partisan perspective, they were variously called 'cut-throats', 'murderers', 'the guilty ones' and 'man-slayers' – all words which have worked their way into the surviving texts of the Greek historians.[7]

With the death of Cicero, with which we ended our last chapter, we lose our only contemporary check on the historical tradition. Our evidence from this point on is often conflicting, difficult to make sense of, and frustrating. But to ignore the problems and seek to streamline the narrative is to miss a fundamental point, one of far greater interest. After Brutus' death, control over his memory, which was already starting to take shape during his lifetime, was up for grabs; the inconsistencies in our later narratives derive directly from the early efforts of writers to leave their own marks on history. As we retrace the steps which led from Brutus' discovery of the triumviral alliance in November 43 BC to his final defeat and death at Philippi in October 42 BC, then, we need to be mindful of this point: the lens through which we look at this period is backward-facing. For opinions on his character and conduct – who he was, what he did, or what he failed to achieve – had already entered and thus shaped the legend of Brutus by the time our sources were writing about him. In this chapter, we shall aim not just to reconstruct the history of what Brutus did next; we shall begin our examination of how that story was being remembered, rewritten and interpreted in the years after Philippi.

First Response

When we last saw Brutus, he was in pursuit of Dolabella in the early summer of 43 BC; even though he had not eventually been needed to help subdue the threat, he had remained in the eastern provinces and had focused his energies in particular on the communities of Asia Minor and Bithynia. Up until now, it seems his mind had been on gathering resources, as well as undertaking provincial responsibilities such as visiting cities, holding tribunals and negotiating with local rulers. Yet the news of the proscriptions appears to have had an electrifying effect on the republican cause; their champion at Rome had been murdered, as had their major military player. Even if the republican strategy had been disjointed and waged by independent players with independent goals, for as long as Cicero and Decimus were alive, at least they had forces in Italy – and at least they had hope. But now that Antony had turned, all that was gone. By the end of 43 BC there was a new tyranny and a new terror to contend against. Brutus and Cassius would need to do some strategic thinking to devise their next course of action. First, however, Brutus had another problem to deal with: that of Gaius Antonius.

The question of what to do with Gaius had been a problem from the start. Brutus, as he had explained to Cicero at the time, had not wanted to kill a Roman citizen without the authority of the Senate. What is more, he had not wanted to do so while peace negotiations with Antony were still imaginable. And so the problem had rumbled on throughout the summer of 43 BC. Several times Gaius had tried to interfere with the loyalty of Brutus' men; without the help of a contemporary account, untangling the stories of these mutinies and their chronology presents something of a problem.[8] However, each time, Brutus showed himself capable of rising to the challenge.

From his correspondence with Cicero, all we know is that Brutus had easily suppressed one potential mutiny back in late April–early May, when Gaius held secret meetings with Brutus' officers with the aim of inciting a revolt. Yet Plutarch and Dio each record a later, more elaborate plan to rescue Gaius, who had since been put under the watchful eye of a guard in Apollonia when Brutus and his army headed east. Thus, in the early part of the summer, a band of mutinous soldiers was said to have attempted to rescue Gaius; yet, having caught wind of their plans beforehand, Brutus gave orders for his hostage to be smuggled out in disguise in a litter, and then had the soldiers punished severely. According to Dio's version at least, first he executed their ringleaders and then forced the rest of the mutineers to turn on each other, before coming to an understanding with the survivors.

If this reconstruction is right, it shows that Brutus had the ability to act as a forceful and consistent military general when pushed by the circumstances to do so. Even then, however, Brutus was still being too lenient in his treatment of Gaius Antonius: the attempts to rescue him only grew more intense as events developed apace back at Rome. Dio thus tells us that a certain Gellius Publicola hatched a plot against Brutus; meanwhile, Mark Antony sent yet others to rescue his brother. After all, Octavian's passing of the *lex Pedia* back at Rome meant that Brutus and Cassius were now marked men. And it seems highly likely that the *lex Titia* proscribing the assassins and offering rewards for their heads had already been passed, too. This last fact would have incentivised men to turn against the assassins, and it may explain the multiple conspiracies formed against them. For his part, however, Gellius Publicola was spared, thanks largely to the fact that his half-brother was Messalla, who was a friend of Cassius';[9] but it was now that Gaius Antonius' luck ran out.

In his account of this period, Appian attributes Gaius' execution to the sole fact that he had pushed his luck too far: 'after several attempts to tamper with the men's loyalty', he explains, 'he was found out and put to death'. Yet Dio and Plutarch are in agreement that the death of Decimus Brutus back in Italy was an additional motivating factor: 'having taken thought for Gaius' safety at first, he thought nothing of it after learning of Decimus' death', Dio adds. Plutarch, however, is surely correct to add the death of Cicero and the proscriptions to the list of reasons why Gaius was finally killed. After all, the *lex Pedia* was Octavian's doing, not Antony's. So it was the *lex Titia* and the mass slaughter of citizens in Italy – the masterstroke of Antony – that sealed Gaius' fate. And just like that, the first hostile act of war was committed on Brutus' side: either acting on his own initiative, or (more probably) on Brutus' orders, Gaius' guard swiftly executed his hostage. Any doubts Brutus had once harboured about leading his troops into Rome's next civil war were evidently dispelled.[10]

The Republican Assault

According to Dio, Brutus' first move on hearing confirmation of Gaius Antonius' death was to hurry back into Macedonia to prevent an insurrection.[11] Energised by the certainty of war, a new speed of action characterises his every movement; as he passed through Thrace he took cities and invaded the lands of native tribes. His soldiers hailed him as *imperator*: a mark of distinction in war, this also gave him a more official authority, now that, as a proscribed man, his title and command as proconsul – not to mention his status and security – had been stripped from him. By a stroke of luck, Appian tells us that, either now or on his return journey through Thrace, the widow of a local ruler entrusted the care of her son to Brutus, along with all her deceased husband's treasures.[12] The son he sent to Asia Minor, to be protected until a time when he might safely be restored to his kingdom; the treasure was a windfall. A month or two later, using the silver and gold he accumulated from this and other encounters, Brutus issued a whole array of propagandistic coins.

We have already seen the famous coin bearing his portrait, title of *imperator*, the daggers and the Ides (Plate 1); others carried the familiar message of freedom, with images of female deities representing either the goddess Libertas herself or Ceres, her patroness. But as Raphaëlle Laignoux has observed in a full study of the Liberators' coinage, these issues also follow another common pattern, for there is a strong emphasis on sacerdotal instruments and divine figures on their currency of these years.[13] Both men still carried the prestige and authority of belonging to religious colleges (Brutus as a *pontifex* and Cassius as a *quindecemvir* – one of fifteen priests charged with the responsibility of guarding and interpreting the revelations contained in the *Sibylline Books*). Furthermore, Brutus could even trace the connection with Apollo back to his legendary ancestor, who had received and correctly interpreted an oracle from the god telling him to expel the Tarquinii.[14]

The Liberators thus legitimated and grounded their campaign by claiming it had divine sanction, and this message is especially clear in a denarius struck for Brutus in either late 43 or early 42 BC (Plate 9): on the obverse, it features the laureate head of Apollo, while the reverse depicts a trophy display of Thracian arms to symbolise Brutus' victory. To any contemporary, the significance of these images needed little explanation: they advertised that Brutus was supported by the god Apollo, who had guaranteed the former's success in both the past and forthcoming battles. If before we noticed an unnerving contradiction in the fact that Brutus was one of the first men after Caesar to put his own image on a coin, now we might start to modify that observation. In fact, Brutus' coins seem to capture an otherwise unattested example of his ability to communicate with and inspire his troops. According to his representation of it at least, he had the face, the name, the divine authority and the ability to free Rome of tyranny.

Enriched by his raids and buoyed by his army's respect, Brutus rapidly established control over Macedonia, before returning just as quickly to Asia Minor, where he summoned Cassius to an emergency meeting at the port city of Smyrna. It was here, probably in the early part of January 42 BC, that the two men saw each other again, perhaps for the first time since leaving Italy back in 44 BC. How did they react at this critical juncture? What plans did they make? Cassius had been on a mission against Cleopatra when

Brutus called him back, and it is possible, as Plutarch claims, that Brutus rebuked his friend for harbouring self-interested motives; after all, Egypt was notoriously rich. But when they met, Plutarch tells us that they derived great pleasure and courage from the forces they had each gathered. Dio, too, takes pains to stress their comradeship and coming together.[15]

This feature in the ancient narratives might point to the original tendency of the Liberators and their supporters to see themselves as a band of friends, above all else. Yet even if some idealising has coloured our sources, the idea that they put their differences to one side to focus on their united strategy seems plausible. In fact, the meeting at Smyrna gives us the first tangible evidence of a coordinated, Mediterranean-wide approach to the threat of the triumvirs: that is, a united republican response, which included consideration of Sextus Pompeius and other military commanders.

Although, as we saw, the name of Sextus Pompeius had loomed large in the discussions after the Ides, his actual role in the political crisis of 44 BC was forestalled by the agreement Lepidus negotiated with the great Pompey's son in the late summer or autumn of that year. Since then, however, he had re-emerged and declared his readiness to fight for the *res publica*, and by the end of April he had been appointed as a commander of the republican fleet. As Kathryn Welch has persuasively argued, to any contemporary observer there were now three defenders of the *res publica*: Brutus, Cassius and Sextus Pompeius. Hence it was no surprise when his name too appeared on the proscription list, and it must have seemed inevitable that Sextus would now lend his support to the Liberators.[16]

Thus, when Brutus suggested that he and Cassius should head straight to Macedonia and prepare either to intercept or forestall the arrival of the triumviral army, Cassius had another idea. Had Brutus not summoned him to Smyrna, Cassius' expedition to Egypt would have punished Cleopatra for supporting Dolabella, massively enriched the republican war chest, and, most important of all, debilitated her fleets. Now, with these same objectives still in mind, Cassius turned his attention to another power base and suggested that he and Brutus should eliminate the Rhodians and the Lycians, who had helped their enemies in the past. It was a tactical plan. He knew they could leave the western regions to Sextus Pompeius, who was patrolling the seas around Sicily, rescuing victims of the proscriptions, and generally making life difficult for the triumvirs.[17] Macedonia could wait for another day, Cassius is said to have argued, and Brutus agreed. For the next few months Cassius launched his attack on Rhodes, while Brutus terrorised the cities of Lycia.

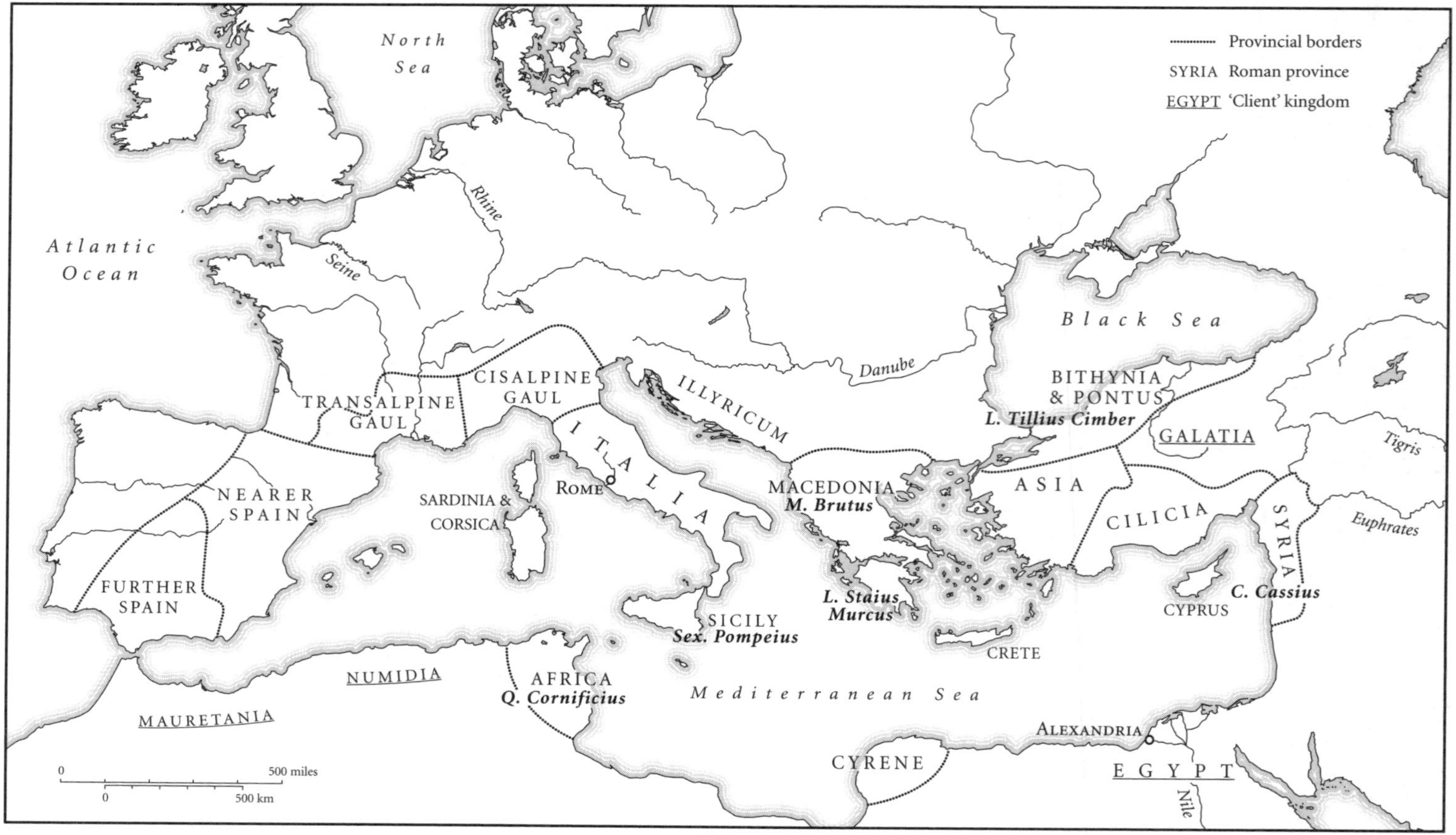

5. Commanders in the Mediterranean in 43–42 BC

In his introduction to this new stage of the campaign, Appian makes the point that 'all the overseas territories were convulsed by the military conflicts caused by this civil war'. He mentions previous efforts around Sicily (Sextus Pompeius), Africa (Quintus Cornificius) and Syria (Cassius), and rightly connects these to the wider movement that had been gaining currency across the Mediterranean. To this list might be added the names of those operating around the Peloponnese (Lucius Staius Murcus) and Bithynia (Lucius Tillius Cimber), who came to the aid of Brutus and Cassius at various stages in their struggles.[18] But the zeal of the republican commanders came at a great cost to the people of the empire, Appian points out: 'Cities endured many horrors when they were taken by force.'

And yet it is of particular significance that, of the territories afflicted, Appian lists Laodicea, Tarsus, Rhodes, Patara and Xanthus as the most infamous examples of them all. These were the cities targeted exclusively by Brutus and Cassius as they first hounded Dolabella and later made their preparations for war against the triumvirs. In what follows, we shall mainly focus on Xanthus and Patara, where Brutus made his presence particularly felt.[19] However, that these episodes follow immediately after the tales of the proscriptions in Appian's narrative tells us something about how Brutus' and Cassius' actions were perceived: the Liberators abroad were little better than the triumvirs back at Rome. Their 'defence' of the Republic was remembered as a shocking and aggressive assault on the Greek east.[20]

The Siege of Xanthus

From Appian's account, we can see that the people of Lycia were as prepared as they could be. Years of Roman misrule in Asia Minor meant that they also knew what to expect: the taxes which plunged cities, individuals and even kings into overwhelming debt; the terrifying conditions which led to men, women and children being enslaved and sold to Roman masters. Defeat or surrender meant loss of personal possessions; it involved a city's most valuable and sacred items being taken away; it was about losing family, life and liberty. Those who wanted to resist Brutus convened at the Lycian city of Xanthus, where, Appian tells us, they first destroyed the suburbs and then withdrew into their heavily fortified city to ward off the Roman incursion. It meant that lodgings and supplies were not at hand for the marauding army to use; and, where the suburban dwellings had once stood, a huge ditch now hindered access to the city walls.

As always, the details and emphases of the accounts vary (see Appendix 2.4a), but the siege of Xanthus forms one of the most dramatic and memorable stories in the biographical tradition surrounding Brutus. The constant feature within each narrative is the Xanthians' bold defence of their city, followed by their mass suicide as a Roman victory became inevitable; they killed themselves rather than be enslaved. Told from a hostile perspective, it is not hard to see how the story might reflect badly on Brutus: for a man who placed so much value on his own idea of liberty, he did not place a value on the freedom of non-Romans. But by the time the story reached our main sources, it had been polished to reflect well on him. Plutarch's focus consequently narrows in on the grief the event caused Brutus, and he largely speeds up the narrative of the Xanthians' own sufferings to get to that point. Dio offers only a short description of the incident, which does not contain anything different, but misses much featured in Appian's longer treatment, to which we shall first turn.[21]

To begin with, Appian sets the scene for the narrative. Brutus 'divided his army into day and night watches'; 'he ran and cheered with his men as though it were a competition, sparing no effort'; 'a task which in the face of enemy opposition was expected either not to be completed at all, or only with difficulty after several months, was finished in a few days'. What Appian conveys in these lines is a picture of Brutus as an effective and energetic leader who incites his men to achieve remarkable results with devastating effect. In no time at all they filled in the ditch surrounding the city and drew up their siege engines against the walls of Xanthus.

Then follow details of the campaign, in which Appian highlights Brutus' relentless determination. He ordered his men to stage a mock withdrawal from the walls in order to flush the Xanthians out from the city, and when they emerged Brutus and his men were prepared. For, believing the Romans to have retreated, the Xanthians made their first counter-attack and set fire to some of Brutus' siege engines; lying in wait, however, Brutus' troops made their move. In the heat of the moment, the Xanthian guards watching the walls shut the gates to save the city; but in so doing they sacrificed a huge number of their own comrades. The result was nothing short of carnage.

But the story goes on: when the besieged Xanthians tried to make a second attack on Brutus' engines, learning from their past mistakes, the guards left the gates open. On the one hand this prevented the loss of Xanthian life witnessed in the first disaster; on the other, it meant that about 2,000 Romans were finally able to burst into the city. 'Still others were pushing through the entrance', Appian continues, 'when the gates suddenly fell upon them, either because the ropes simply broke or because they had been cut by one of the Xanthians'. Some Romans were trapped; others were killed outright. But Brutus took control of the situation; he rallied his anxious men and, with the help of some local allies, they eventually managed to storm the city. Whatever Appian's own opinion of Brutus, we can see that his source has put a favourable gloss on Brutus' leadership of his men, whose safety was severely jeopardised. This apologetic tone extends into the final tragedy as Appian relates the Xanthians' decision to commit mass suicide rather than surrender:

> Now that the town was taken, the Xanthians ran home and put their loved ones to death, a fate they willingly endured. Cries of anguish arose, and Brutus, thinking that it was pillage, had heralds order the army to stop. When he found out what was happening, he took pity on the freedom-loving [*phileutheros*] spirit of the Xanthians and offered a truce, but they hurled missiles at the messengers. They took all their possessions, piled them on pyres which had previously been heaped up inside their houses, and after setting light to the pyres committed suicide on top of them. Brutus saved what he could of the sacred property, but the only prisoners he took from Xanthus were slaves and, of the free population, a few men and not as many as 150 in all.

As the narrative closes, all of Brutus' commanding shots fade into the background as our attention is drawn to the fact of the matter: that, for all the loss of life – Roman as well as Xanthian – Brutus' campaign resulted in poor returns. Still, Brutus' empathy for his victims, his attempt to negotiate, as well as his efforts to save the temples, all point to the apologetic nature of the source material Appian was using. In this connection, it is significant that Appian describes the Xanthians as possessing a 'freedom-loving' spirit (*phileutheros* in the Greek), for this is the exact same epithet he has elsewhere attributed to Brutus. And when Brutus recognises this quality in his victims, his philosophic reflection that they are not unlike him marks him out as a different sort of military commander from his peers.[22]

At this point, however, it is instructive to compare Appian's account to that of Plutarch, which differs in a number of key respects. He only describes one sally by the Xanthians, not two. The Xanthians are 'possessed by a dreadful and indescribable impulse to madness' – a detail which throws the humanity of Brutus into relief, and exonerates him from his share of the blame. He omits mention of the 'freedom-loving' spirit of the Xanthians, which might otherwise reflect badly on his hero. And, crucially, Plutarch has Brutus cry in anguish at the sufferings of his victims. A woman was discovered hanging, he reports, her dead child fastened to her neck; she was still holding a blazing torch with which she had intended to burn her home.

'So tragic was the spectacle', writes Plutarch, 'that Brutus could not bear to see it, and burst into tears on hearing of it.' In Plutarch's hands, Brutus' siege of Xanthus combines both apology and tragedy.[23]

These changes to the narrative structure are not in themselves difficult to explain. To begin with, the passage should be read alongside similar episodes in other works of Greek and Latin literature, where the tragedy of the captured and fallen city was something of a literary set piece; Herodotus, for one, had already told a parallel account of an episode in Xanthus' earlier history, in which the city's inhabitants had killed themselves rather than be conquered by the Persians – a story to which Appian also alludes.[24] The Greek historian Diodorus Siculus relates two examples of mass suicide in his monumental *Library of History* (*Bibliotheca Historica*): in one, the inhabitants of a Lycian rock fortress besieged by Alexander the Great decided to burn themselves alive on pyres rather than lose their freedom; in the second, the Isaurians burned themselves in their homes rather than fall to Perdiccas and his Macedonian troops.[25] These examples do not cast doubt on the core historicity of any of the events described; it seems self-destruction by fire was a last resort in times of extreme crisis by the Lycians and their neighbours. But they do reveal an interest on the part of writers to record – and maybe even to embellish – tragic historical events along these lines. In so doing, Brutus' earliest biographers had placed Brutus in a tradition of legendary commanders stretching from the world of Homer, the mighty Persian Empire and Alexander the Great down through his successors.

But we can go further: what made accounts of military conflict so popular among the literate Roman elite was that the stresses of war had the potential to reveal a man's true character. In this connection, whoever first added the detail of Brutus' tears to the narrative had a point to make; for crying was the appropriate response in this situation. In particular, the tears of Brutus in Plutarch's version seem to nod towards the famous story of Scipio Aemilianus' tears as Carthage fell. This story had featured in one of our lost fragments of Polybius' *Histories*, a work which Brutus had himself summarised and translated into Latin. It tells of the moment the exemplary commander cried when he reflected on the rise and fall of great empires, and pondered the future of his own Rome. The context is different but the sense of humanity remains and is even enhanced by Brutus' compassion for his enemies. As Lisa Hau has explained, the 'crying victor' became a way for writers of history to turn an otherwise condemnable action, such as burning a city, into something that could be praised and even used as a positive moral example. That is not to say Brutus consciously mimicked Scipio, or even that Plutarch made it up; however, Brutus' earliest biographers certainly saw the mileage in drawing attention to the moment of his reaction.[26]

'Good' Brutus

We may well wonder at this point how far the ancient sources can take us towards an understanding of the 'real' Brutus. But the answer must simply be that in some way they all contribute to that quest: thus, we can see Brutus as he himself wanted to be seen and remembered, as he was by his friends in their later memoirs and writings; we shall soon see the way he was hated by his enemies and victims; and we also see the later writers using their sources to form an opinion on the strengths and weaknesses of the Brutus they were writing about. This 360-degree perspective has a blurring and dizzying effect when we try to view Brutus for the man he was. Yet it is worth pausing to take in some of these variant versions and examine why we have these different takes on his character and conduct; this period of his life, coupled with his assault on the Greek cities of Asia Minor, provides a fascinating case study for the development of Brutus' historical reputation.

As Elizabeth Rawson demonstrated some years ago in an influential chapter on the memory of the Liberators in later literature, the portraits of Brutus and Cassius we possess are coloured by the comparisons and contrasts drawn between them, as well as the relative judgments that have been passed on their actions. The general verdict, she argues, was 'favourable in varying degrees'. But Brutus, she goes on to demonstrate, almost always fares better than Cassius: not only do his philosophic interests and blood-ties to Cato work in his favour; his own literary output kept his memory alive in successive generations. Even when it is clear that both Brutus and Cassius suffered at the hands of their detractors, the mud only seems to have stuck to Cassius. For his part, Appian tried to even out the picture, but still Cassius left behind him a reputation for cruelty, anger and personal ambition. 'If one would prefer Brutus as a friend', wrote Velleius Paterculus in the first century AD, 'one would fear the more energetic Cassius more.'[27]

It comes as no surprise, then, that Plutarch tried to shield his hero from any negative press by association. If we take our cue from the narrative of Xanthus, we can see this strategy at play. By his tears and offers of a truce deal, Plutarch places Brutus within the best possible tradition of 'Romans who conquer but spare their foe' – a mission famously articulated in Virgil's epic *Aeneid* as: 'to combine peace with morality, to spare the conquered and to subdue the proud'.[28] In this context, it becomes a point in Brutus' favour that at Lycia he took fewer captives and extracted less cash than (as we shall see) Cassius did in his corresponding campaign at Rhodes. For, if we take the analogy with Virgil's epic characters further, we soon discover that the counterpart to this heroic ideal is the man characterised by his violent passions and his striving for personal glory, the foundation for which lay in the spoils he took from war. That is not to suggest that Plutarch was forming his own characters based on the Virgilian pattern; indeed, Plutarch saw Brutus and Cassius as struggling against the tide of history, whereas Virgil's Aeneas was rather riding on its crest in his mission to found Rome. Still, however, Virgil does represent the contemporary dialogue in which men like Brutus and Cassius were being assessed in the period after the civil wars.[29]

To sum up: if Brutus was seen as the best type of hero, then the rapacious, self-interested and cruel kind was represented, by Plutarch at least, in the figure of Cassius. Between them they represent the two different faces of the republican campaign in the east: the noble versus the discreditable. Nor does Plutarch leave the contrast implicit. In fact, he makes great play of the differences in their characters throughout his *Life of Brutus*.[30] All that was bad about the assassination of Caesar and its aftermath was thus heaped onto Cassius to make Plutarch's hero shine brighter. But was Plutarch trying to edit out a tradition that was hostile to Brutus? And did Brutus deserve to be lumped together with or held separate from Cassius? That debate was probably already starting in their own times.

'Bad' Brutus

Intriguing clues in the ancient texts are all that remain of the stories that once circulated orally about Brutus. But the efforts to label him 'as bad as Cassius' were in part the doing of Antony, who reached out to the communities destroyed by the republicans shortly after the victory at Philippi. In particular, the Jewish historian Josephus documents a letter sent by Antony to the high priest Hyrcanus, who had requested the release of the Jews taken captive by Cassius in Syria. Antony thought the request fair and granted the freedom of anyone sold into slavery. His letter to Hyrcanus is too long to quote in full here, but it is worth including a couple of extracts to give a sense of the rhetoric Antony used to describe the republicans after their defeat:

> Your actions and your words have persuaded me that you are most well-disposed to us; I also see that your nature is steadfast and pious: so I

> count your interests as my own. For when our adversaries and those of the Roman people overran the whole of Asia, sparing neither cities nor temples, and they disregarded the oath they had made [to guard Caesar's life], it was not only our own battle we fought, but that of all mankind in common, and we avenged ourselves on those who were guilty both of lawless deeds against men and of unlawful acts against the gods. Even the sun turned away, so we believe, as if it too were loath to look upon the defilement [*musos*] of Caesar. But their attacks were attacks on the gods, and Macedonia felt the brunt of them as if its climate were peculiarly suited to their unholy and audacious designs.

This is strong language. Antony establishes himself as a man who approves of piety; Brutus and Cassius, on the other hand, flouted the laws of gods, men and even nature. The murder of Caesar was a 'foul deed'. But the word Greek word *musos* is more specific on this point: this was a pollution that needed to be absolved.[31] The battle against the Liberators was a universal struggle of right versus might; we see here vividly the behaviours which Plutarch later tried either to suppress or to explain away – the destruction of cities and sacred spaces. As Antony continues, we can also see how his rhetoric influenced the idea that Brutus' and Cassius' downfall was divinely sanctioned:

> This victory we gained because the gods condemned their unjust endeavours. And Brutus, who fled to Philippi and was there shut in by us, shared the ruin with Cassius. Now that these men have received their punishment, we hope that we may enjoy peace for the time to come and that Asia may be at rest from war.[32]

Syria and Asia had been brutally plundered by the assassins; Appian too formed that opinion. But Cassius' behaviour had been particularly abhorrent. As Josephus has already informed his readers by this stage in his narrative, Cassius had savagely oppressed the Judaeans, from whom he demanded the impossible sum of 700 talents, and had then enslaved four cities when they could not pay it.[33] When Antony wrote this letter, the communities were still trying to heal their wounds. Here we get a unique perspective of Roman militarism from the east; Josephus' source was Nicolaus of Damascus, a native of the area who was composing his biography of Augustus just a few years later.[34] Largely lost to us now, his work presumably preserved vivid memories of how the preparations for Philippi affected those living at the very edge of Rome's empire. Whether Brutus deserved to be paired with Cassius for his crimes is another question. From Antony's point of view, however, they came as a duo. And he did not just want to make the point that Brutus shared in Cassius' punishment; he wanted to ensure he received his share of the blame, too.

After Xanthus

And yet Brutus, who cultivated a reputation for leniency and clemency towards his Roman enemies, almost certainly deserved his share of the blame; not necessarily for Syria, but for his own treatment of the cities of Lycia. As we have already seen in the accounts of the siege of Xanthus, Brutus' apologists had been at work, glossing and shaping the narrative long before it reached our authors; this positive presentation in our sources was then further polished by Plutarch, who saw in Brutus a philosopher in action. Yet this fact of our source tradition becomes even more evident in the stories of what happened after Xanthus (Appendix 2.4b), which represents another important stage of Brutus' preparations for war.[35]

At first, he went to Patara, on the southwest coast of Lycia, where the inhabitants refused to make an alliance with him. Plutarch tells us Brutus feared a second bout of the 'same madness' which had afflicted the Xanthians and was hesitant to attack. In Appian, Brutus taunts the Patarans with the fate of their neighbours by parading captive Xanthians before their eyes. Dio goes further still: Brutus, he claims, staged an auction of prominent hostages, but then released most of the captives anyway when they continued to refuse his demands. According to Dio, it was this last act which appeased the Patarans, who saw Brutus as a man characterised by virtue (*arete* in the Greek). In Plutarch, Brutus' released prisoners praised their captor as 'a man of the greatest moderation and justice' (*sophronestatos* and *dikaiotatos*). And so the Patarans surrendered and got away with a fine of just 150 talents, a result which, as Plutarch is quick to point out, was nothing compared to Cassius' exactions in Rhodes.

Appian begs to differ: in his version, Brutus surrounded the city and ordered the Patarans to obey him in everything; he gave them time to think but then returned the next day with a show of arms. When they finally surrendered, Brutus ordered that all the city's gold and silver be delivered to him – along with each citizen's private stash. There is no suggestion here that Brutus was more lenient than Cassius in his treatment of the cities; in fact, Appian tells us, Brutus went so far as to offer rewards for information 'just as Cassius had announced at Rhodes'.[36] To illustrate the point, however, Appian adds an intriguing twist to the story which is unparalleled in our other accounts. For, whereas Plutarch and Dio both end their narratives of this period with the rest of the Lycian communities surrendering peacefully to Brutus' demands, Appian goes on.

The tale is a curious one. There was a slave, Appian tells us, who, when Brutus' men arrived, turned on his young master, revealing to them a cache of gold. But when he pointed out the hidden treasure to the centurion in charge of the collection, the master's mother intervened. To save her son's life, the woman claimed that she had hidden it, a claim the slave revealed to be false. At this point the whole murky affair was referred to Brutus. Far from punishing the man and his mother, however, it is alleged he had the slave executed for showing excessive zeal in accusing his superiors. Meanwhile, Brutus is said to have approved of the young man's silence and, empathising with his mother's plight, let the pair keep their hoard. It is difficult to know how much we can base on the anecdote; even if it was grounded in a true event, it may have been much altered in the retelling. Still, this episode of one man's dealings with Brutus points to a far richer tradition surrounding his activities in Lycia – and a largely positive one at that. For in his show of severity to the slave and compassion towards the master, Brutus was presumably made to win his ancient reader's approval.

So what are we to make of all this? One thing appears certain from all accounts: Brutus evidently preferred not to attack and fire cities and he probably did want to avoid a repeat of Xanthus; to this end he was successful. However, the difference is this: what we ultimately see in both Plutarch and Dio is the formation of a precise characterisation of Brutus – the 'good' Brutus again – based on his moderation, justice and honour: all key virtues in contemporary discourses on good leadership.[37] It is likely that they are drawing on the same or similar sources, written by friendly hands. However, Plutarch's account has been simplified and 'suitably touched up' even further to reflect well on its hero;[38] it is also clear that Plutarch was drawing on and perpetuating a tradition that was hostile to Cassius' activities.

Appian's version, on the other hand, presents an image of Brutus which, while not 'bad', is both more forceful and demanding: more like Cassius. In so doing, Appian either offers or reflects a 'corrective' to the idealised accounts that had emerged by his time.[39] Yet what is particularly interesting to note is that even the bent of this narrative is largely favourable to the assassins; Cassius emerges as the most remarkable of the pair, but Brutus too is presented as a tough and effective military commander. In his introduction to this period of Brutus' life, Appian had commented on the 'horrors' suffered by cities during his conquest of the east, and he had specifically identified Xanthus and Patara as the most famous examples. By the time he came to write about it, however, the voices of those victims had long been suppressed by his sources.

What might the story of Brutus' exactions have looked like from a provincial perspective? How was he remembered and recorded by the generations of Asiatic Greeks who lived subsequent to these events? And what light, if any, can other sources shed on Brutus' activities in the east? The only way to approach these questions is to focus on the tradition which concentrated on Brutus' Lycian campaign to the exclusion of everything else. We are remarkably fortunate here to possess a collection of letters, written in Greek, which ancient readers believed to have come from the hand of Brutus. Today, the letters are almost universally regarded as forgeries, probably composed at some date in the early to mid-first century AD. As such, they are the product of the rhetorical schools in which boys were trained, among other things, in the art of writing letters by imitating great figures from history.[40] But it is not impossible that whoever wrote them used important historical evidence or that the letters reflect how Brutus was remembered in the Greek east in the period after Philippi.[41]

In this context, it is relevant – and perhaps much closer to the mark than our more apologetic accounts – that the capture of Xanthus was part of a much more ruthless campaign. 'The Xanthians ignored my kindness', begins one letter, 'and so now they have their fatherland as a tomb for their madness.' Far from the remorseful presentation of Brutus' reaction in Plutarch and Appian, the tragedy of the Xanthians is used as a tool with which to inspire fear. In another letter, Brutus positively boasts of his cruelty: 'I slaughtered the Xanthians who rebelled against us, from the youngest upwards, and we burned down their city.'[42] The Brutus presented here punished the Xanthians harshly; he rejects their pleas for mercy; he has burned their town to the ground, killed its young men, and now uses its refugees to present a harsh lesson to others.[43] These letters do not prove that Brutus purposefully razed Xanthus to the ground; it seems entirely likely that the Xanthians had started the fire themselves, as our narratives report. But the fact that Brutus could use the fate of Xanthus and its refugees as a goad with which to threaten the other communities lends weight to the narratives of Dio and Appian which emphasise this feature in his negotiations with Patara.

On the other hand, that the eventual surrender of Patara was used to incentivise the rest of the communities to submit also becomes apparent. In fact, the authorial 'Brutus' of these letters makes great play of the contrasting fates of the two cities: 'The Patarans entrusted themselves to me and they are no less competent at administering each and every aspect of their freedom', he writes, making much of the 'freedom-loving' spirit of the Lycians we saw earlier. In so doing the letters present the essence of Brutus' demands: he was only interested in the money and resources of the Lycian cities, not their lives and liberty. But if they would not give in to him, he would destroy them. 'It is therefore possible for you to choose either the judgment of the Patarans or the fate of the Xanthians', comes the final blow.[44]

These are violent threats but the letters were not written to discredit Brutus; Plutarch and later writers – all of whom believed these could be the real letters of Brutus – expressed nothing but admiration for his laconic brevity and forcefulness of expression. A later editor of Brutus' letters went further still and complimented them for possessing 'the stamp of a leader's genius'.[45] What this means is that we see in these letters a potentially more realistic and plausible picture of how the provinces of Rome suffered in the crossfire of civil war. After Xanthus, it is hard to believe that the communities came willingly to Brutus' side to receive his kindness; it is hence far more likely that they needed compelling. Written from the perspective of these communities, at the very least these letters enable us to recover a hypothetical reconstruction of the experience of Brutus' victims. This point becomes more significant still when we consider how brutally the Romans had treated the Greek east generally in the decades before Brutus' time in Lycia; that his name should survive as a threatening example of Roman misconduct is an observation that should not be passed over in silence.

Quarrel and Reconciliation

Brutus' assaults on the Lycian cities and Cassius' exaction in Rhodes had, however, made them tremendously rich. When the pair finally reconvened after their separate expeditions, they met at the ancient Lydian city of Sardis. Their joined armies, as we saw at the opening of this chapter, must have made an impressive sight; their forces hailed each man as *imperator* for the second time. The plan was to march from there into Europe. But before then they had a few quarrels to put to rest. 'As it often happens in great undertakings where there are many friends and generals', Plutarch explains, 'mutual charges and slanderous accusations had passed between them.'[46] The republican front may have looked united, but some grievances had been bubbling away beneath the surface since the commanders last met. Of all our surviving sources, only Plutarch goes into any detail.

To begin with, Plutarch tells us that the pair withdrew into a private space away from all their friends; 'they exchanged in recriminations, then rebukes and denunciations, too'. There were 'tears and emotional appeals' – the flames of which were only quenched when Marcus Favonius, the Stoic friend of Cato's who had refused to join in the conspiracy, flamboyantly burst into the room and quoted Homer to them. 'But you must listen to me: since both of you are younger men than I', he interjected – a histrionic impersonation of the wise adviser Nestor who intervenes in the famous quarrel between Achilles and Agamemnon in the opening book of the *Iliad*.[47] The impromptu interruption was enough to make Cassius laugh, but Brutus was not amused; he drove Favonius out of the room, making jibes at him.[48] Worse still, when Favonius arrived uninvited to dinner later that evening, Brutus, who evidently held a grudge, tried to have him seated at the furthest end of the couch.

One point of interest arising from this episode is that, although it does not initially appear to tell us much about the quarrel at Sardis, it nevertheless sheds a potentially revealing light on the personalities of the men involved.[49] Favonius is believable and consistent when compared to other sources in which he appears. The warmth of Cassius' humour is attractive, while Brutus comes across as the more petulant and unforgiving of the pair. The portrait that emerges of him is similar to the Brutus that Cicero knew: a man he failed to warm to, whom he found distant, but still a man who knew his own mind and whom he respected. What this means is that Plutarch seems to be working with good, and probably contemporary, material for this information, a source which seems to favour Cassius as much as, and maybe even more than, Brutus. As for the argument itself, while Plutarch's reader is as much barred from it as the men outside the room, in the passage which follows we are presented with suggestive clues for piecing together the gist of their disagreement.

For, the next day, Brutus and Cassius are said to have had a second argument – and this time they aired their grievances in public. Cassius had rebuked Brutus for his harsh treatment of a fellow citizen denounced by the people of Sardis as an embezzler of public funds. He was a friend and former praetor, yet Brutus had him condemned and disgraced.[50] Cassius was appalled; now was the time for kindness (*philanthropia*), he argued, not of dogged devotion to justice (*to dikaion*, in the Greek). What made matters worse was that, just a few days before, Cassius had acquitted and since continued to employ two men accused of the exact same crime. Brutus' harsh response to his friend consequently undermined and contradicted the more lenient treatment Cassius had meted out to his companions.

If we want to use the criticisms expressed here to understand more about the larger picture of their quarrel, we might assume that Brutus disapproved of the crudity of Cassius' conduct in Syria, Rhodes and now in Sardis; conversely, Cassius may have thought Brutus too observant of law and justice. Plutarch does not blame either man specifically for the quarrel at Sardis, and indeed a case could be made in favour of Cassius' position, but his final verdict leaves no doubt as to where the biographer's sympathies lie: 'such were the principles of Brutus', his story concludes.

But the language of this passage and Brutus' concern for *to dikaion* also takes us towards a much more significant conclusion when we read it through to the end. 'Remember March, the Ides of March remember', Brutus reminds Cassius in Shakespeare's re-enactment of the scene, in which the Bard saw great dramatic potential: 'Did not the great Julius bleed for justice' sake?'[51] And this is the essence of Brutus' reply in Plutarch, too: namely, that the conspirators had killed Caesar because the dictator's power had enabled others to commit acts of plunder. Brutus was hence concerned that he and Cassius should practise self-control and not turn a similar blind eye to their own friends' misconduct.

To be sure, concern for justice appears to be a new addition to the list of motives we saw for the assassination in Chapter 4, but it was not an entirely new line of thinking on the causes of the dictator's downfall: more than once in the sources we find expression of the idea that Caesar's companions' behaviour was the cause of his unpopularity.[52] When we consider Brutus' own dubious financial transactions and his treatment of the cities of Lycia, his alleged 'lecture' to Cassius may, of course, appear hypocritical. But the point is this: whatever source Plutarch was using seems to have been reacting to and correcting the versions that marked Brutus and Cassius down as the unscrupulous plunderers of the east. Brutus is even made to admit as much in a line of direct speech given to him by Plutarch, in which he laments: 'but now, added to our toils and perils, we are deemed unjust'.[53] We do not know how Cassius responded. Plutarch simply picks up where he had left off, with Brutus and Cassius, evidently reconciled, on the northward march towards the Hellespont, which they crossed in August. Crucially, however, in his version their reputations were still intact, their cause still just.

Of Gods and Men

Long before they made it to Philippi, however, the legends tell of the extraordinary signs Brutus and Cassius received (see Appendix 2.4c). An apparition appeared before Brutus in the night, 'a monstrous and fearful sight', Plutarch adds. 'What of gods and men are you?' Brutus plucked up the courage to ask, to which the phantom replied: 'I am your evil genius, Brutus, and you will see me at Philippi.' Unshaken, Brutus simply responded: 'I shall see you' – as indeed he did, or so it was said. For Plutarch later tells us that the ghost appeared to Brutus again, on the eve of the second battle of Philippi; this time, however, it simply disappeared without saying a word.[54]

Before then, further portents of doom were recorded. As Brutus and Cassius made their march into Macedonia, two eagles allegedly perched on the foremost standards of the army, only to desert them the day before they finally engaged Antony and the young Caesar in battle. Once encamped, a swarm of bees was said to have clustered on a part of Cassius' fortification, causing the area to be shut off from view lest it send shocks of alarm through the suspicious militia. But then, during the lustration ceremony – a ritual purification of the army before battle – someone presented Cassius with an upside-down wreath; a boy fell down while carrying a sign of victory; vultures and other carrion birds which feed off the decaying bodies of deceased men circled above the republicans' heads. Back at Rome, the sun changed its size; there was thunder, meteors, and the noise of clashing arms; a dog dragged the body of another dog to the temple of Ceres and buried it there; a deformed child was born; a mule gave birth to a hybrid creature; the chariot of Minerva, while returning from the races in the Circus Maximus, was dashed to pieces; and the statue of Jupiter bled from its right hand. These occurrences and more signalled the gods' displeasure at the assassination of Caesar, and they foreshadowed the demise and destruction of the republican side. At least, that is how later writers interpreted them.[55]

As we saw in the stories of the omens both before the assassination of Caesar and in the aftermath of the Ides, for both the Romans of Brutus' day and the writers who relayed these accounts, it was the common belief that the gods manifested their will through natural phenomena. Just as signs, portents and prophecies were often taken to convey political messages in times of uncertainty and fear, so the interpretation of dreams was a popular subject, as was daimonology – the study of spirits, such as the apparition which showed itself to Brutus.

Antony's own rhetoric had peddled the view that divine forces were at work against the assassins. We might also imagine that some of the more fantastic descriptions are venom invented after the fact, not least because the stories of these portents nourished Augustus' own self-advertisement as the divinely sanctioned winner of Philippi. The story of the apparition almost certainly fits into that context: 'part of the general *post eventum* mythology', as John Moles has put it.[56] And yet an eyewitness account did record some strange stirrings – including more bees and eagles – this time, on the eve of the second battle of Philippi. Plutarch had access to the writings of the philosopher Volumnius, who did not leave Brutus' side during the campaign. And Plutarch preserves largely verbatim what he had to say on the topic: 'the leading standard [of the army] became enveloped in bees'; 'The arm of one of the officers spontaneously sweated oil of roses'; and 'before the battle, two eagles fell on each other and fought between the two armies'. As everyone watched, gripped in an incredulous silence, he adds: 'the eagle on Brutus' side gave way and fled'.[57]

While the stories doubtless grew in the telling, the appearance of bees and birds on the battlefield is at least not impossible. And as always, their significance was open to interpretation. On the one hand, bees might have provided portents of military victory for individuals; perhaps the fact they landed on one standard indicated some measure of success to Brutus, Volumnius and other onlookers. But more often than not they spelled doom; among other things, bees signified confusion, wounds, sickness and death.[58] As for the eagles, perhaps the loser represented the submission to one-man rule. What is significant again is that all these accumulating omens, prophecies, portents and extraordinary natural phenomena were coalescing around the time of Octavian's rise to power, and were being written down in the Augustan age. By the time they reached our later writers, the list of 'signs' had become firmly embedded in the legend of Brutus.

In Plutarch and Dio they form a bewitching digression in the narrative of events to build up and intensify the suspense before the final climax of Philippi. In Appian, the list of omens and prodigies appears as an epilogue, providing the means by which he can look back and reflect on the significance of their appearance.[59] The result for the reader of any of these accounts, however, is the same. By the time our sources have described the various signs that preceded and accompanied the two battles, the eventual defeat of the Liberators seems inevitable. But it was not; there was nothing predictable about what happened next.

Battle Plans

As Brutus and Cassius marched their troops into Thrace, having crossed the Hellespont, a preliminary challenge apparently came when they heard that their enemies, the recently allied triumvirs Antony and Octavian, were sending an advance force – eight legions led by Gaius Norbanus and Decidius Saxa – to block their way into Macedonia. In the event, with the help of a local ally, the Liberators managed to bypass their opponents

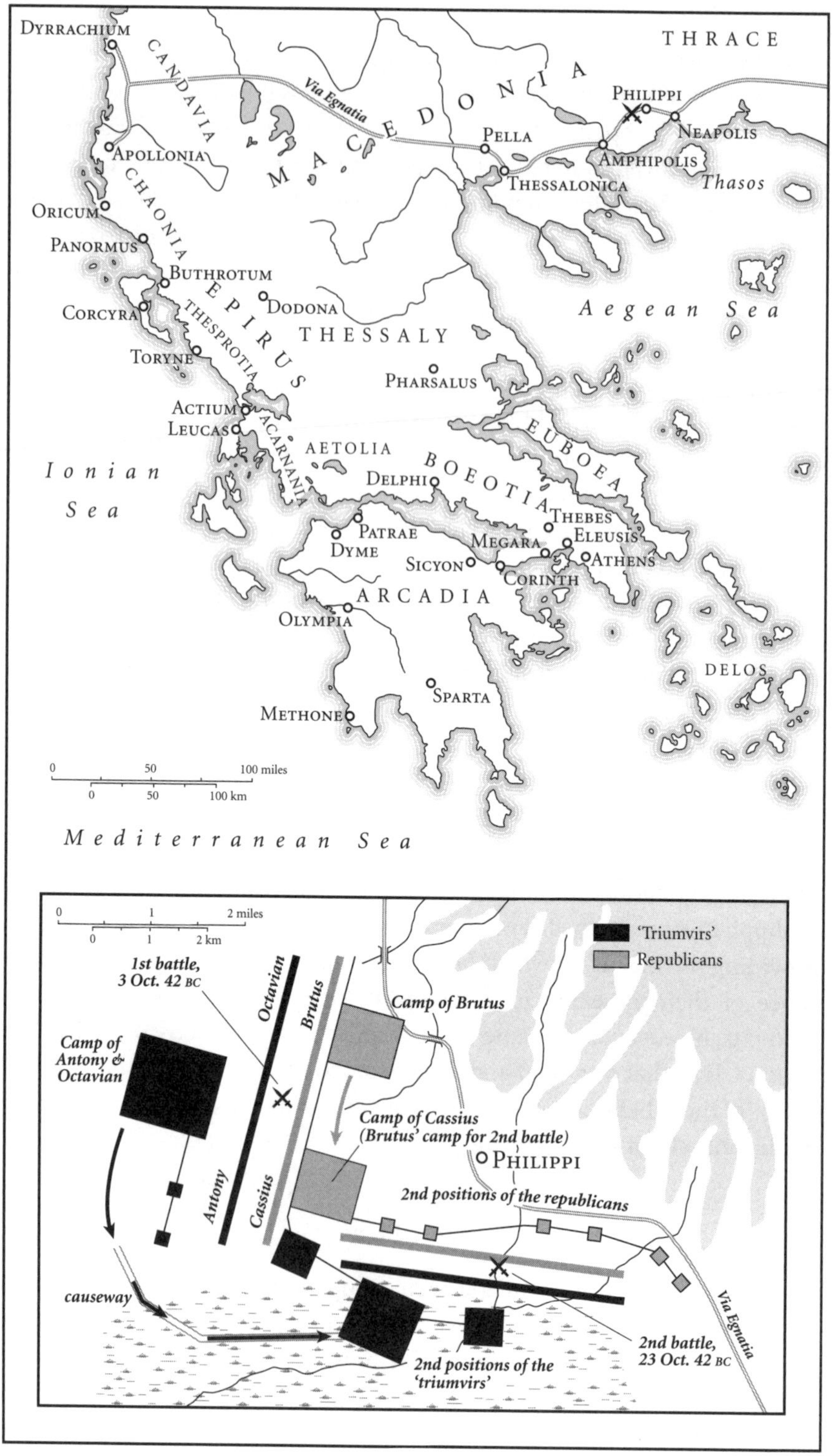

6. Greece and Macedonia, and the Battles of Philippi

completely by taking a longer and more difficult route through the mountains. It meant that, when they emerged, they were just one day's march from Philippi, while Norbanus, Saxa and their legions were forced to withdraw to Amphipolis on the coast. Without any further opposition, the Liberators were free to push ahead and secure strong positions in the hills surrounding Philippi, where they utilised every advantage of the local region. And as they waited for their enemies to arrive, Brutus and Cassius focused on fortifying their camps and devising their strategy (Plate 10).

To begin with, Brutus and Cassius divided their army and encamped on top of one hill each, a mile apart, on either side of the Via Egnatia – the long Roman road which led from Dyrrachium and Apollonia on the Adriatic coast to as far as Thessalonica in the east. A series of fortifications linked their camps so that they could derive safety from numbers, but it also meant that they had effectively cut the main route into the rich eastern provinces and hence had a monopoly over them. What is more, on their respective southern and northern sides, Cassius was flanked by ditches and marshes, while Brutus was protected by barren and trackless hills. The whole area seemed virtually impenetrable by land, yet Brutus' and Cassius' control also extended over the sea. Thus, not only did the area benefit from a lot of natural protection, it also afforded them access to their fleet, which they based at Neapolis, as well as the reserves they heaped at Thasos.

With all the advantages of supplies, resources and position, the strategy appears to have been one of attrition; Brutus and Cassius could easily afford to sit out the winter and let nature take its toll on their opponents. For as long as Sextus Pompeius was patrolling the seas around the western coast of Italy, and while Lucius Staius Murcus and Gnaeus Domitius Ahenobarbus were protecting the Adriatic, Brutus and Cassius could rely on them to intercept and prevent any arriving supplies from reaching the triumvirs. And if the triumvirs ran out of resources, the starving soldiers might force their commanders to turn back or negotiate, or else they might defect. If the plan worked, it meant the Liberators would not have to face their opponents in hand-to-hand combat, or at least not when they were at full strength.[60]

However, Antony was not prepared to wait and play their games. When the triumvirs landed in Greece in the later summer of 42 BC, he rushed ahead to Philippi, leaving Octavian back in Dyrrachium where he was recovering from illness. And then, Appian tells us, when he reached Philippi, Antony embarked upon a bold plan that dramatically altered the course of the war: he set up his camp on the plain just a mile away from his opponents, and from there he secretly worked to reach Cassius' camp at the rear. His plan was to cut the Liberators off from the harbour which supplied them, and thus force them into combat. To divert their attention, every day Antony offered battle, while his men laboured unnoticed on creating a passage through the marshes that protected Cassius' camp on the southern side. In the meantime, Octavian, growing increasingly anxious that the battle might happen without him, rejoined his troops and pitched his camp opposite to that of Brutus. The stage was set for the fight to begin, but still nothing happened bar a few preliminary skirmishes.

To begin with, some raw data: although our figures are only approximations, it is nevertheless clear that both sides had a vast number of men fighting for them. The triumvirs had somewhere in the region of 95,000 legionaries compared with the Liberators' 85,000, while Brutus and Cassius had the advantage of 20,000 cavalry men over the triumvirs' 13,000.[61] Otherwise, to any contemporary observer, Brutus and Cassius easily had the upper hand. As we have seen, their raids of the eastern provinces had made them considerably richer and, unlike Antony and Octavian who could only make wild promises, Brutus and Cassius could afford to pay their soldiers in advance. Every legionary got 1,500 denarii, every centurion 7,500, and military tribunes 15,000 apiece.[62] Although it was not always a common practice to pay troops before a battle, buying the trust and loyalty of their men was a clever move for Brutus and Cassius, not least because some of their soldiers had fought for Caesar in earlier days – and they could always point out that a victory would bring further remuneration.

For their part, then, the Liberators engaged in psychological warfare. It was a typical move for an army to try to dazzle their opponents, and so at first Brutus allowed his officers to wear armour covered with silver and gold. Then, during the lustration of the camps on both sides, Brutus and Cassius distributed their soldiers' pay and great numbers of cattle for sacrifice in full view, while the triumvirs could offer only a little meal and a handful of cash.[63] We have two versions as to what happened next. Appian, whose account we have largely relied on so far and to which we shall return, tells us that the Liberators were forced into battle against their will, while Plutarch tells an elaborate story of battle plans, a last supper, and a suicide pact. We shall shortly see how the two versions can be quite easily reconciled to provide a fuller perspective, rather than relying on just the one to the exclusion of the other. Before then, however, Plutarch's telling is worth dwelling on in some detail.

In his version, on the day before battle, Brutus and Cassius called a council of war to discuss their options with a close circle of friends. Cassius reiterated his preference to delay the fight, but Brutus disagreed. Buoyed by the successes of his cavalry in the preliminary skirmishes, he wanted to minimise the costs of war and restore freedom at the first opportunity; there may also have been rumours of desertions in the ranks. One by one they asked for opinions until finally it was decided to give battle the next day, just as Brutus had been wanting. Plutarch consequently tells us that Brutus was full of hope that evening, but Cassius less so. 'I call you to witness', he told his friend Messalla, with whom he spoke freely and intimately over dinner, 'how I am in the same plight as Pompey the Great, in that I am forced to cast the die of our country's fate on a single battle.'[64] It is a compelling story and Plutarch cites no other than Messalla as his authority, but it goes on.

What if they should lose? 'What is your view on flight or death?' Cassius purportedly asked of Brutus the next morning. To which came Brutus' reply:

> As a young man, Cassius, and when I was inexperienced in such things, I uttered something inconceivable from a man devoted to philosophy. I blamed Cato for killing himself, on the grounds that it was not right or manly to give in to one's demon; not accepting what befalls us fearlessly, but running away. However, now, in these circumstances, I am becoming of a different mind: if a god does not decide the current dispute in our favour, I am not inclined to make trial once more of fresh hopes and preparations. I shall seek deliverance with words of praise for Fortune. On the Ides of March I gave my life for my country, and since then I have lived another life of liberty and glory.[65]

Cassius purportedly smiled and embraced Brutus at this response, their suicide pact sealed with a kiss. 'While we have such thoughts', Cassius is said to have replied, 'let us go against our enemies. For either we shall have victory, or we shall have no fear of the victors.'[66]

The scene is something of a literary set-piece (we have seen Plutarch doing something similar before), in which Cassius gets a last supper and final words, and thus earns a place in the tradition of martyrs.[67] However, Plutarch or his source is doing something very subtle here. As we shall see, Brutus' command of his troops on the day was weak and their entry into battle was confused. It is not impossible, and in fact on the basis of Messalla's testimony it is even likely, that discussions of the sort Plutarch describes had taken place. However, what may have been little more than hypothetical reasoning and a contingency plan – an agreement on what to do if Antony should force them into battle – has become in Plutarch a firm decision to engage in war the next day.[68]

What this means for us is that, although the verdicts on Brutus continue to be mixed in our sources, still the events of the battles can largely be pieced together: in other words, the accounts of Plutarch and Appian are different, but they are not incompatible (see Appendix 2.4c). This is all the more important when we remember that Plutarch was using information from inside the Liberators' camp (Messalla), whereas Appian's source (often believed to have been the Caesarian Gaius Asinius Pollio) seems to have told the story from the view of their opponents – encamped at the bottom of the hill, where they had no real knowledge of what had been happening in the rival camp. From that starting point, then, let us retrace our steps and picture the scene at Philippi as fully as possible from the beginning.[69]

The First Battle of Philippi

As we have already seen, delay was to the advantage of Brutus and Cassius.[70] Yet Antony wanted war – and fast. To that end, unknown to Brutus and Cassius, Antony's men had started work on building a causeway through the marshes to threaten the Liberators' flank and force them to the battlefield. For the first ten days, obscured from view by the tall reeds, they had managed to do just this, with the result that Antony had been able to send a detachment of men to occupy fortified positions under the cover of darkness before Cassius even noticed. So what did Cassius do when he finally discovered Antony's plan? It is not unreasonable to suppose that he called an emergency council of war to decide on the Liberators' next course of action.

If Plutarch is right to insist that some planning had taken place, now would be a suitable context for those discussions: Cassius' eleventh-hour discovery of Antony's activity would certainly have made a contingency plan necessary; should Antony be successful there would be no option but to engage in battle. Cassius would command the left wing which was already facing Antony, while Brutus, commanding the right, was to go head to head against Octavian and his troops. Cassius was never going to be happy with this decision; he was firmly committed to his strategy of attrition, in which he saw their best chances for victory. But, in the meantime, he set to work building a transverse wall to cut through Antony's causeway at a right angle; thus, he saw a way to cut Antony off from his men and protect his own camp. If he was successful, Cassius might have stalled or even prevented conflict for longer yet. Yet it was this act that finally caused battle to erupt.

At midday on or around 3 October, when Antony noticed what Cassius was up to, he was furious.[71] He led his army (about nine legions) against

Cassius' wall, desperate now to storm his camp, too. Meanwhile, watching from their camp up above, Brutus and his officers decided it was time to enact their contingency plan. When his men saw Antony's troops attempting to break Cassius' cross-fortification, their spirit for war was fuelled and Brutus seized the moment. Plutarch tells us that Brutus spurred his men on and that he issued the watchword of 'freedom'. In the high passions that accompany battle, however, only a few caught hold of it as it was passed along the ranks, while the rest 'in one rapid motion and with one war-cry charged upon the enemy'. Some charged the exposed flank of Antony's army; others made for Octavian's troops. But it was at this point that the confusion set in. The disorder had thrown the legions out of line, so that several units – including the men led by Messalla – went charging right past Octavian's troops and only slaughtered a few men. Having outflanked the enemy in this way, Brutus' men found themselves storming Octavian's camp instead.[72]

Scholars have often worried about what seems an irreconcilable difference: namely that in Appian it is Antony who starts the battle, whereas in Plutarch it looks as though the Liberators are equally responsible.[73] But even in Appian there is a hint that the onus fell more upon Brutus' army: Antony, he claims, was 'pleased to have forced it'. The battle had only begun because Brutus' troops finally responded and charged against their opponents. In so doing, it is very possible that Brutus was following a predetermined plan to attack Octavian's less experienced forces in the event that Antony's men were successful in reaching Cassius' camp.[74] And it is as certain as these things can be that there was a good deal of confusion in the chaotic scenes that followed. But what looked like a spontaneous and entirely unbidden charge to those watching from the triumvirs' camp was actually an aggressive assault led by Brutus – and it was very nearly successful.

According to Plutarch, Octavian's men were not expecting battle that day and were surprised by the sudden force of their opponents' charge; Appian too stresses their passivity insofar as Octavian's troops were swiftly 'routed' and 'pursued'.[75] Thousands upon thousands were killed as the troops of Brutus on the plain hacked their way through at least three of their enemy's legions in close combat. Their success was phenomenal. But, back in Octavian's captured camp, the soldiers of Brutus who had initially outflanked the battle lines went on a spree of loot and plunder. While the others fought, they grabbed supplies, equipment, personal possessions and as many prisoners of war as they could. It might be argued that these were precious resources for continuing the war. However, the reverse point of view was also true. Had they returned to the field of battle, many more of the enemy might have been slain.[76]

For as they wasted time plundering, Antony's troops stormed the cross-fortification which Cassius' men had been building and successfully pushed through to break into his camp. His legions were put to flight and it was not safe for him to return. All that Cassius could do at this point was head to a hill, from where he tried to make sense of the battle. At first the dust prevented him from seeing the outcome; then he sent for news. There are two versions as to what happened next to cause Cassius to commit suicide. Appian had read a version of his death in which Cassius first learned of Brutus' victory, and then killed himself out of shame. But otherwise our sources preserve a largely unanimous account of how Cassius' friend and messenger, a centurion called Titinius, failed to relay the news of Brutus' victory in time. As a result, Cassius believed that Brutus had been defeated and that Titinius had been captured by the enemy. And so Cassius offered his neck to his companion Pindarus; in so doing, he prematurely enacted the suicide pact he had purportedly agreed with Brutus.[77]

At the end of the first battle, Cassius' side had lost around 8,000 men; but Octavian had lost perhaps twice that many.[78] It had been a mixture of victory and defeat on both sides, but there is no doubt that it would have been an overall success for the Liberators had it not been for Cassius' death: his suicide was the largest and most significant factor in the eventual demise of their cause.[79] The result, as we shall see, was a disaster. For, although Octavian's camp had been stormed, the young Caesar had escaped unharmed. The story goes that his physician had been forewarned by a vision of the goddess Minerva, and had led the young man (still ill) out of the camp before battle commenced; this, at least, was the official Augustan line, which reinforced the idea that the gods were on his side. But Pliny the Elder, who had as his authority the words of Agrippa and Maecenas, two of Octavian's right-hand men, reports a different version: Octavian fled, he claims, and spent the next three days hiding in a marsh.[80]

Between Battles

Riding back towards camp, it is said that Brutus was amazed not to see the tent of Cassius still towering above the others.[81] At first unaware of Cassius' death, Brutus' heart sank when he learned of the full catastrophe. He mourned over his friend's body and called Cassius 'the last of the Romans'. Next, as quickly as he could, Brutus set to work to protect and rebuild the morale of Cassius' defeated soldiers. First he sent Cassius' body to Thasos for burial; next he promised Cassius' soldiers cash rewards. It was not a given that they would continue to serve under Brutus just because he was Cassius' friend and co-commander; their loyalty had to be won afresh, and Brutus worked hard to get it. His efforts paid off.

Plutarch tells us that the troops sent Brutus on his way with cheers; they celebrated the fact that he alone of the four commanders had not been defeated (Antony, after all, had technically been on the losing side). Appian adds, and Dio concurs, that by the next morning Brutus had put Cassius' camp back into order and even transferred his own troops to what had been Cassius' quarters. For this part of the campaign up to and including the second battle, the sources occasionally differ in the details, but they present a largely coherent chain of events. Brutus had evidently not lost faith in the fight or in his chances.

On the other side of the plain, however, the news of Cassius' death emboldened the men in the triumvirs' camp. One of Antony's men had brought him the robes and the sword he had taken after discovering Cassius' body; suddenly a new burst of energy was injected into those who wanted revenge for Caesar's murder. One of the assassins was dead; not only that, Cassius had been the more experienced military commander of the two. The soldiers were given fresh hope and fresh incentives to continue the battle; as before, it was vital that they should bring it on as quickly as possible. And so, the next day Antony kept up an outward display of confidence and offered battle again. Perhaps learning from past mistakes, however, Brutus now decided that his best chances lay in postponing the fight.

In the speech given to him by Appian, Brutus largely repeats the strategy that Cassius had once before put to the troops: that the sea was shut to their enemy, and supplies were hard for them to come by. 'And so, when you see them pressing their hardest for a fight', Appian has Brutus say, 'hold in mind that hunger is driving them to choose death in battle.'[82] The best line of attack Brutus' men could take at this point, then, was to make their opponents weaker and more exhausted first. The winter was approaching and conditions were lowering the morale in the triumvirs' camp where food and money were both in short supply. According to Dio, as part of this strategy, Brutus' men attacked the enemy in a series of night raids and even had some measure of success in diverting a river into their camp to cause further destruction.[83] Brutus, by all accounts, was working with great energy to secure a victory for his side.

There is, of course, a darker and grimmer side to the narrative; this after all was war, and the effect it has on a man's personality was one of the enduring fascinations of classical literature. To begin with, Brutus made an offer beyond the money he had already dangled before his soldiers' eyes: he promised to lead them to the cities of Thessalonica and Sparta which they could loot at their pleasure. The former was supplying the triumvirs with their only resources, while the latter had sent troops to support them in the war. But still Plutarch recoils in horror at the thought: 'this', he claims, 'is the only accusation in the life of Brutus which is inexcusable'. Not only was Brutus abandoning his principles; he was giving up on something he cherished to please the soldiers. As a city, Sparta was second only to Athens; Brutus even had an estate at Lanuvium back in Italy which included a Persike Stoa and a Eurotas, named respectively for Sparta's famous portico and its principal river.[84] Brutus, it seems, prioritised his duties as a general over any other consideration.

There was also the question of what to do with the huge number of prisoners of war brought into Brutus' camp following Octavian's defeat. Many of them were slaves and Brutus was suspicious that a large number of them seemed to be moving among the militia. Without hesitation, then, he had them killed.[85] And then he turned his sights on the rest of the prisoners: the freemen and citizens. According to Plutarch, he helped many of these men to escape and thus saved their lives. However, the story of two prisoners, the actor Volumnius and the jester Saculio, survives to reveal a more disturbing picture of the regime inside Brutus' camp. These men, it was said, had not held back from making mocking and insolent speeches. As a result, Messalla suggested they should be publicly flogged and sent back naked to the triumvirs' camp from which they had been taken; but Casca, the first assassin to have struck Caesar, disagreed. It was inappropriate to be making jests while Cassius' last rites were being performed, he argued, and he warned Brutus that how he dealt with this incident would reflect the value he placed on the memory of his friend.

Some have detected in this story a foreshadowing of Brutus' inability to stand up to his subordinates; others have read it as revealing an increasingly tyrannical aspect to Brutus' own character. For at the beginning of the episode he is indifferent: 'Brutus had his mind on other matters', Plutarch tells us; then he loses his temper: 'Why do you bother asking my opinion, Casca', he asked, 'instead of doing what seems best to you?' In so doing, he leaves it to his men to divine his intentions without describing the horrible deed he wants them to perform; nor was there any further discussion. The men were led off and killed. Plutarch does not pass his opinion on the matter, but given the context in which the passage occurs, it is not hard to read between the lines. As John Moles has suggested in his analysis of this passage of Plutarch, the personality of Brutus was apparently deteriorating under the stresses of war.[86] By the time our later sources were writing, and perhaps even at the time, there was a clear sense that Brutus was becoming as much a tyrant as the man he had killed.

All the while war rumbled on in the background: the plight of Antony and Octavian was worsening. Unknown to the men in Brutus' camp, a force of ships sailing to the triumvirs with more provisions had been destroyed by Staius Murcus. Why this news did not reach Brutus in time is a mystery, but if it had, he might have been able to persuade his troops to continue with their strategy. As it was, his army and officers were now spoiling for a fight. Dio tells us that Antony and Octavian had been throwing pamphlets into Brutus' camp urging his men either to defect or to join battle. Brutus continued to disagree, Appian tells us, but he was under pressure. What is more, since the position of Brutus' camp had changed, he now also found his supply lines were threatened. In a suspicious echo of the words Cassius had already used to describe his predicament in the war, Brutus is made to say: 'I seem to be conducting my campaign like Pompeius Magnus, no longer giving the orders, but receiving them.'[87] However, all our sources appear to agree that it was the defections of his troops, either real or only feared, that finally stirred Brutus to act. He at last committed to another battle.

We have already seen that his phantom appeared again to Brutus on the eve of the second battle, as well as the omen of the bees and the two eagles. But as the gate of the camp was thrown open on the morning of battle one final menacing sign was said to have greeted them – an Ethiopian man, who, because of his colour, was allegedly cut to pieces by Brutus' men.[88] Black was associated with death, evil and the underworld; his appearance must have spelled doom and, if true, it must have instilled in Brutus' men a level of superstitious fear from which they did not recover. He led his men out in battle array and stationed them opposite the enemy; for a long time he scanned their faces, unsure whether or not he could trust them. However, Brutus had little choice by this point; the fate of Rome was hanging in the balance.

The Second Battle of Philippi

On 23 October 42 BC, twenty days after the first engagement, Brutus faced the joint forces of Antony and Octavian. There had been much manoeuvring in the lead-up to the second battle: Octavian and his men had seized a hill close to Brutus' camp; at the same time, the triumvirs continued with their plan of trying to cut Brutus off from his supplies.[89] And yet, at each turn Brutus had countered them by throwing up more fortifications until his camp now sat perpendicular to its position during the first battle.

Based on the death toll of the last encounter, his forces must have been numerically superior, and he still occupied the marginally better position. This time, however, he did not have Cassius fighting beside him.

All our sources appear to agree that Brutus was still reluctant to engage in battle at this stage (see Appendix 2.4d); Plutarch is explicit on this point, and Appian confirms it. Brutus formed his troops in their ranks, Appian tells us, and urged his troops to fight cautiously. At some point in these proceedings, in full view, one of Brutus' soldiers – a man named Camulatus who had earlier been honoured for his bravery – rode out of the ranks and joined the enemy. It was now quite late in the afternoon, around three o'clock, Plutarch tells us, but partly motivated by anger, and partly by fear, Brutus finally reconciled himself to the fight. He offered war, and the triumvirs readily accepted the challenge.

Our sources do not record any subtle tactical moves; Appian states that they simply came into combat with drawn swords, inflicting and receiving as many blows as they could: 'Much was the slaughter and mighty the groaning.' Dio too gives the impression of a long, drawn-out struggle, but does not add any further details. Plutarch says that the wing under Brutus' command was victorious, but that the other wing was too far stretched and gave flight. Antony rampaged 'with magnificent energy', Appian tells us; Plutarch adds that Brutus displayed all the valour of a commander and soldier. But, by then, the triumviral army had enveloped his wing, and what follow are the stories of individual prowess and self-sacrifice; a final roll call of noble men who died fighting on Brutus' side.[90]

'No other war was more steeped in the blood of such illustrious men', wrote Velleius Paterculus almost a century later. According to Plutarch, Marcus Cato, the son of Cato the Younger, 'fell dead upon the many corpses of the enemy he had slain'. Velleius goes further still: 'the same fate carried off Lucullus and Hortensius, the sons of very eminent citizens', he tells us, before adding the names of other eminent republican households.[91] This time we are not given a death toll, but its scale lived on in contemporary and later reflections. For the Roman poet Propertius, Philippi was 'the citizen's graveyard' – a theme of epic importance he refused to write about.[92]

'But the time will come', wrote Virgil in the quotation which opened this chapter, 'when in these lands / a farmer, toiling the land with his curved plough, will find our spears consumed by corroding rust, / or strike our hollowed helmets with weighty hoe / and gape at mighty bones upturned from their tombs.' As he projects his poetic imagination into the future, far away from the bitter realities of his day, Virgil captures the baffled expression of a simple farmer finding the bones of men larger than any known to mankind. These bones can only be the relics of a bygone age; the bones of heroes. Already in the first century BC, the exploits of those who had died at Philippi were becoming the stuff of legend. However, the death of Brutus, his heroism and the ideals for which he had stood and fought, inspired the most reminiscence of them all (see Appendix 2.4d).[93]

At first Brutus escaped into the mountains, taking four legions with him, and for a while Antony's men pursued him. But then Lucilius, one of Brutus' officers, risked his life to save his commander, or so the story goes, when he pretended to be Brutus and allowed himself to be captured in his place. The stunt bought Brutus time; and as it happened it turned out well for Lucilius. For when he demanded to be taken to Antony, the latter excused the soldiers who had been duped and spared their captive: 'By the gods, I do not know how I could have dealt with Brutus had he come to me alive', Antony is said to have remarked. And then he embraced Lucilius, put him under guard and later found in him a loyal companion. The story evidently survives to explain how Lucilius came into the service of Antony while remaining a true and loyal follower of Brutus, and as such we might question its foundations in fact. Still it speaks to men's desire to be included in the legend of Brutus and to have their own moments of chivalry recorded for posterity.

Others remained with Brutus to the end. It was getting dark, Plutarch tells us, and having crossed a tree-lined brook, Brutus found a place to retire with just a few close friends and officers. One of those with him was Volumnius, who wrote an important account of Brutus' final moments which Plutarch in turn used to inform his work. Brutus, we are told, at first raised his eyes to the star-studded heavens and quoted a famous verse from Greek literature: 'O Zeus, do not forget who has caused all these woes', runs the line from Euripides' *Medea*, one of the most powerful and enduring of tragedies. Plutarch does not tell us whether he meant Antony or Octavian; Appian is specific on the point that it was Antony. Yet we may suspect otherwise.[94] There is no doubt that in Brutus' mind it was Octavian who was the ultimate threat. 'How I wish you could look into my heart and see how much I fear him!' he had written to Cicero back in the summer of 43 BC.[95] And now, as Brutus reflected on the battles he had fought against his foe, he called the name of each of his comrades who had fallen in the fight to defend him.

As evening progressed and the night closed in, Brutus spoke with his slave Cleitus, who was in tears, Dardanus his shield-bearer, and finally to Volumnius. Speaking in Greek he reminded his friend of their student life together, their philosophical training, before begging Volumnius to help him drive the sword into his body. But Volumnius refused – as did the others. 'It is not the time to delay, but to fly', said one of his companions, to which Brutus recorded the last words directly attested to him by Plutarch: 'By all means we must fly, but with our hands, not our feet', thus signalling his intention to end his life.

Plutarch records that Brutus took each of his friends by the hand and rejoiced that none of them had deserted him; then, he begged them to save themselves before withdrawing from their company, taking only two or three friends with him. Among the friends who stood by Brutus at the end was Strato, with whom he had once studied rhetoric and whom Brutus now placed by his side. In some of our accounts, it was Strato who helped deliver the final blow, as Brutus seems to have wanted: a steady and faithful hand at the last moment. Plutarch had read this version in some of his sources, but he personally preferred the one he relates as the real ending of his hero: Brutus took the sword in both hands, he tells us, and fell upon it: a swift, clean death befitting a philosophical martyr. Moments earlier, Brutus had purportedly celebrated the fact that he was leaving behind him a reputation for virtue (*arete*). When the world judged his death, he is reported to have said, its verdict would be that 'unjust and evil men had killed the just and good'. And thus, he died – in this version at least – not in defeat, but as a moral champion. In so doing, like Cato before him, Brutus eternalised his name as another republican martyr, as a man of virtue and integrity.

Alternative Endings

In the years that followed, as the survivors returned from war and put their stories to paper, this was the version of his life and conduct that Brutus' friends tried to ensure for him: the 'noblest Roman of them all', as Shakespeare would have it. But theirs was not the only side of the story. Some, like Antony and his circle, seem to have treated their dead foe's memory with respect from the beginning. Several sources tell us, for example, how Antony gave orders for Brutus' body to be wrapped in the most expensive of his own robes to make his cremation more honourable; others add that he sent the ashes home to Servilia as a last mark of respect for the family. It was also said that Antony was later furious when he discovered the robe he had provided for Brutus had been stolen. 'Do you not know which man's burial it was that I entrusted to you?' he asked the thief, before having him swiftly executed.[96] For Antony, Brutus was a man not unlike himself – a man of noble ancestry, born into the same troubled generation, which had grown up in the shadows of civil wars and violence. They had shared a similar pattern of education, which instilled respect for the *mos maiorum*, and both men had enjoyed Caesar's favour. There had been enough common ground for Brutus to spare Antony's life when the other conspirators called for his blood, and they had at least tried to work out a compromise solution for the better good of Rome in those first few days after the assassination.

But not so Octavian: at just nineteen he had marched his army on Rome and demanded a consulship. 'He treated the Roman past with breezy insincerity' – as Barry Strauss has put it.[97] Whatever respect for the *res publica* he claimed to have in his later life as Augustus, now, at the age of twenty-one, all Octavian cared about was delivering revenge for Caesar. He demanded Brutus' head – and he got it. Mark Antony might have secured an honourable burial for the rest of the corpse, but Suetonius tells us that Octavian gave orders for Brutus' severed head to be sent back to Rome and there cast at the feet of Caesar's statue: 'he was not moderate in the face of victory', adds the imperial writer.[98] Yet the story does not quite end there. For Dio records that a terrible storm brewed as the ship carrying the head made its return journey from Dyrrachium. There and then the sailors, perhaps fearing that it was bringing them bad luck, threw what was left of Brutus into the sea – a sad and inglorious end for his last remains, if it is true. However, when we remember that Brutus died a proscribed man, the victim of a son seeking revenge for his adopted father's death, such an ending might only be expected. Antony and Octavian, it seems, held different views on how Brutus' body should be treated.

Even before Brutus' body was cold, then, Octavian was attempting to record for posterity an alternative version of the man he knew. Brutus' severed head stood as testament to the disgrace in which he died. From this point of view, he had conspired against and killed a man who had been constitutionally elected by an assembly of the people; he had since plundered Rome's provinces in the east and engaged in a war against the very men who were claiming to restore the *res publica* in their capacities as triumvirs. If Brutus' friends had circulated reports of his dying moments in which the Liberator celebrated the reputation for virtue he left behind him, there were others with a different story to tell. For when Dio researched the material for his *Roman History* he found that Caesar's assassin lamented his blind commitment to the ideal: 'O wretched Virtue, you were but a word! And yet I practised you as a deed', were the words he purportedly quoted from a lost tragedy. 'Only now does it seem you were a slave to Fortune.'[99]

As a revelation of his final disillusionment and self-condemnation, this version presumably reflects the Augustan line which sought to discredit Brutus; far from celebrating his act of martyrdom, his suicide was an act of failure. The 'virtue' upon which Brutus had built his life was an empty and phoney ideal. It was also subordinate and subservient to 'Fortune' – a reminder that divine forces were at play in this conflict. In a similar vein is the story of Brutus' birthday party, shortly before Philippi, when he was said to have quoted Patroclus' dying words to Hector from the *Iliad*: 'But I am destroyed by cruel fate and the son of Leto'. The effect of this story again is to suggest that even Brutus thought himself a loser; he was foolish to think he had the support of Apollo (the son of Leto), whose image he had struck on his coins, and whose name he had purportedly used as a watchword at the second battle of Philippi.[100]

As we have repeatedly seen throughout this chapter, the wrangle over Brutus' reputation generated competing sides to the man, as his friends and enemies alike tried to shape the memory he was to leave behind; already at his death, different 'endings' were being written for Brutus' life. But these competing narratives in the historical material are a blessing rather than a curse. The legend of Brutus, the complexities of his character, and the questions that surround his legacy are all significantly enriched when we trace them back to the beginning, as we shall attempt to do in the next chapter, to the life of Brutus and how he was received by his contemporaries.

CHAPTER 8

DEATH AND LEGEND

The Noblest Roman

This was the noblest Roman of them all:
All the conspirators, save only he
Did that they did in envy of great Caesar.
He only, in a general honest thought
And common good to all, made one of them.
His life was gentle, and the elements
So mixed in him that nature might stand up
And say to all the world, 'This was a man!'

— Shakespeare, *Julius Caesar*, 5.5.69–76

In one of the most famous lines of the play – second only perhaps to *Et tu, Brute?* or 'Friends, Romans, countrymen' – Shakespeare has Mark Antony call Brutus 'the noblest Roman of them all'. Nor is the sentiment entirely fictitious. In several places in his *Life of Brutus* Plutarch emphasises that even his enemies respected Brutus: 'in fact Antony once said, and many men heard it', he tells us, 'that in his opinion Brutus was the only man to have slain Caesar because he was driven by the splendour and nobility of the deed, while the rest conspired against the man because they hated and envied him'.[1] The words were not uttered over Brutus' dead body, as in Shakespeare, and it is highly doubtful that Antony ever credited Caesar's assassin with any particular distinction. Yet the sentiment captures a feeling about Brutus which seems to have been there from the beginning.

But why, we might ask, was Brutus alone singled out as the 'noble conspirator'? As we saw in Chapter 4, there had been many causes stirring the hearts of Caesar's assassins, and we can readily assume that different reasons had weighed heavily on different men. A clue to their individual ambitions can perhaps be teased out from the correspondence of Cicero, who always framed his appeals to his friends in the terms that mattered to them. Thus, to Decimus Brutus he talked of his *dignitas* and the people's love for him, while he promised to include Trebonius in his writings. Towards Brutus and Cassius, however, he took a different stance.[2] Upon them, he pinned his hopes for the restoration of the *res publica*, and in so doing he contributed greatly to the development of their posthumous reputations. 'Our *heroes*', Cicero called them, using the Greek word which elevated them to a place in legend, our 'tyrant-slayers' (*tyrannoctoni*) and 'Liberators' (*liberatores*). 'Forever will they be famous', he predicted, 'as well as blessed in the knowledge of what they did.' There was no doubt about it in Cicero's mind: the murder of Caesar was a 'great and glorious deed'.[3]

As we shall see more clearly in what follows, Cicero's after-the-event interpretations of the assassination have had immeasurable influence on all generations of political thinkers who have grappled with the question of how to act in the face of tyranny. Yet his voice is only one of the many contemporary responses we can recover, and a close reading of his correspondence is particularly illuminating for the light it sheds on the ancient reactions towards Caesar's death. For as we have seen in earlier chapters, opinions on Brutus, his character and conduct were not unanimous in their assessment of him; nor were they in the later legend that developed. In this chapter, then, it will serve us well to glance over some of the key themes in Brutus' afterlife, as well as the conflicting judgments that have been cast upon his personality and motivations.

Others have written more fully on Brutus' reputation from antiquity to the modern day, as well as on the perennial interest in him as an agent of political murder.[4] My aim in what follows is more limited: in dealing with the main questions that arise out of a study of Brutus, I will discuss the principal resonances of his life across a spectrum of time periods. Because the focus is on key themes and debates rather than the chronological development of Brutus' reception, we shall find ourselves shifting through various centuries and intellectual movements; dates are hence provided in brackets for new or less familiar authors we encounter along the way. In so doing I will seek to explain how some of the preconceptions of Brutus that are prominent in popular imagination came into existence. But I will also illustrate how those exact same debates bring us closer to understanding how Brutus was respected, feared and judged in his own day.

All the Conspirators, Save Only He

That Brutus was somehow unique among the conspirators is a response that started during his lifetime and has continued until the present day; thus, the immediate reception of Brutus' historical personality must start with the intellectual legacy which Brutus himself created. In his pamphlets *On the Dictatorship of Pompey* (*De Dictatura Pompei*) and *For T. Annius Milo* (*Pro T. Annio Milone*), both composed in 52 BC, Brutus had argued that servitude was intolerable and that murder in defence of one's country was justifiable. His coins, circulated first in the 50s and then between 43 and 42 BC, had carried the message that Brutus was devoted above all to the *libertas* of the Roman people. In his philosophical works, all of which were composed in the period after Pharsalus and before the Ides of March (i.e. between 47 and 45 BC), he debated questions of practical ethics, personal obligations and good conduct. Another work sadly lost to us is the speech Brutus delivered and later published from the *contio* on the Capitoline Hill on 17 March 44 BC, in which he justified the assassination of Caesar to the people of Rome.

Even though we do not have full access to these works today, what is clear is that in the years both before and after the assassination Brutus had singled himself out as a man who acted upon an ideal code of conduct, one which he had partly inherited, partly shaped for himself. Hence his reputation as a man of virtue first and foremost stemmed from the works in which he engaged in the philosophical and political debates of his times. But Brutus had also engaged in other literary activities, which give a further insight into his character. Pliny the Younger tells us he wrote poetry in his youth; he composed an epitome of Polybius' *History*, as well as summaries of the annals of Fannius and Caelius.[5] He engaged in debates about the best style of oratory, and here Brutus seems to have come across as particularly exceptional, to judge from Tacitus' comment in his *Dialogue on Oratory* (*Dialogus de Oratoribus*), composed towards the end of the first century AD, in which he wrote: 'In my opinion, Brutus alone among them laid bare the convictions of his heart frankly and ingeniously, with neither ill-will nor spite.'[6]

Shakespeare is unlikely to have known these words – 'with neither ill-will nor spite' – when he too spared Brutus from any charge of malice. Yet Tacitus' observation on Brutus' oratory does reflect the kind of reactions towards Brutus more generally by the time Plutarch came to write his *Life of Brutus*. For as the biographer notes at the onset, 'even those who hated him because of his conspiracy against Caesar have tended to attribute whatever was noble in the deed to Brutus, and to direct at Cassius the more distressing features of what happened'.[7] And, as we have already seen, Antony had been heard to distinguish between Brutus and the rest of the conspirators, who had only acted because 'they hated and envied' Caesar. When Plutarch's evaluation fell into the hands of the Bard, it was inevitable that the magic of Shakespeare's verse once more gave expression to this ancient viewpoint: 'All the conspirators save only he / Did that they did in envy of great Caesar'.

Thus, when we meet Shakespeare's Brutus in his orchard at the beginning of the second act of *Julius Caesar*, before the assassination has taken place, he has already determined on his course of action: 'It must be by his death', he claims, before listing the reasons that have led him to this conclusion. In the previous scenes we have seen something of the 'servile fearfulness' of Caesar's regime, anxieties over his ambitions to be king, as well as his punishment of the tribunes who were meant to be inviolable.[8] And, by this time, Cassius has also cajoled his friend with thoughts of glory and fame: why should the name of Caesar sound greater than that of Brutus, he asks.[9] But as the soliloquy of Brutus reveals, it is neither the past spurring him on, nor thought for his own eternal reputation. Brutus' concern is what will happen if Caesar becomes king: 'How that might change his nature, there's the question.'[10]

The philosophical reasoning might remind us of the Platonic thinking we earlier mapped against Brutus' motives for the assassination, as well as Plutarch's insistence that philosophical discourse was used as a means for recruiting further conspirators. But the most famous justification of Caesar's death came not from Brutus, but from Cicero's treatise *On Duties* (*De Officiis*), in which he indirectly presented Caesar as a tyrant and a would-be king, and then not so subtly extolled the assassins' actions as combining virtue with expediency. 'For just as limbs are amputated if they show signs of being bloodless and near lifeless, and thus harm the other parts of the body', he argued, 'so those fierce and barbarous beasts in human form must, as it were, be cut off from the common body of humanity.'[11] The wicked tyrant, in other words, must be removed; or as Shakespeare would have it, 'it must be by his death'.

That is not to say that Shakespeare was advocating tyrannicide; far from it. His tragedy rather forces us to consider slightly different questions, such as how to distinguish the just ruler from the tyrant, or envious murderers from noble conspirators and patriotic assassins.[12] It is significant in *Julius Caesar* that in Brutus' eyes the dictator is not a tyrant *yet*. But in using the example of Caesar and Brutus as a vehicle through which to explore these anxieties, Shakespeare was tapping into a tradition that stretched as far back as the twelfth-century humanist John of Salisbury (*c.* 1115–80), who kept a copy of Cicero's *On Duties* in his personal library. In his *Policraticus*, John of Salisbury not only defended tyrannicide as a just and right course of action; but like Cicero before him, he considered it a moral duty. 'Brutus aroused civil strife in order that the city might be freed from servitude', he wrote. The assassination of Caesar may have caused a series of 'lamentable wars', but in the practice of liberty he was exemplary.[13]

Yet, even in this moral defence of tyrannicide, there is a hint of the problem that was to plague later thinkers, as much as it did the contemporaries who tried to justify Caesar's assassination: Brutus had killed Caesar because he could not bear 'to sustain a lord [*dominus*], even a very gentle one', writes John, in a comment he may have picked up and adapted from Cicero's correspondence with Cassius.[14] For Caesar's *clementia* was so well attested and confirmed by his contemporaries that it was difficult to reconcile with the image of a tyrant. Thus, Thomas Aquinas (1225–74), who in his earlier career had read and approved of Cicero's defence of the assassins in *On Duties*, seems to have shifted his position on the question by the time he came to write *On the Government of Princes* (*De Regimine Principium*) in 1267. Although he still conceded that action against tyrants could be permitted under certain circumstances and to authorised persons, a mild tyrant, he added, ought to be tolerated: for the overthrowing of a tyrant, he reflected, may give rise to graver perils.[15]

And this is the dilemma for Shakespeare too, who never offers his own verdict on the rightness or wrongness of Brutus' decision. To be sure, his Cassius laments the degeneration of republican politics under Caesar, the plebeians unequivocally declare that Caesar was a tyrant, and Caesar provides the firmest evidence of all when he arrogantly asserts 'always I am Caesar'. Yet Cassius is presented as a scheming and deceptive villain, the plebeians change their mind and call for vengeance, and time and again we are called to question the nature of Caesar's tyranny. He may well come across as unstable, arbitrary, hubristic, and fearful of plots, especially in Act I of the play. At the same time, however, he is as kind towards his friends in life as he is generous towards the people in his will. He is physically weak, old and vulnerable.[16] Here is not the place to draw comparisons with Elizabeth I – Virgin Queen, Gloriana, advancing in years and in the latter stages of her long reign when *Julius Caesar* was first performed in 1599.[17]

But there is one certain outcome in Shakespeare's mind, for all his ambiguity over the rights and wrongs of tyrannicide: if a ruler should be usurped, civil war would follow.

For the Common Good of All

That Brutus' role in – and motives for – the assassination of Caesar came to be seen as such a decisive moment in his life is no surprise: conspiracies fascinated the Romans, and their writings in turn provided ample material for the study of Caesar's death in later ages. Even if some of our first writers did look to assess Brutus' works on their own merits – as works of philosophy and oratory or even as letters for imitation – others used his writings to answer questions which had been prominent from the start. Propositions such as 'Should Marcus Brutus have accepted the gift of his life from the divine Caesar?' and 'What reasoning did Brutus employ in killing Caesar?' had thus become topics for debate as rhetorical exercises by the middle of the first century AD according to Seneca the Younger (*c.* 4 BC–AD 65).[18] While the latter question focused on the philosophical arguments that could be advanced in justification of Caesar's assassination, the former reflects a dilemma which plagued ancient minds. For as Plutarch tells us, the fact that Brutus had been honoured by Caesar and was spared along with all the friends for whom he pleaded, added to the charge of ingratitude that was brought against him.[19] In other words, the question facing his contemporaries and earliest critics was: should Brutus have put his friendship and obligation to Caesar ahead of his country?[20]

Cicero, as we have already seen, was clear on this point in his treatise *On Duties*, as he was (more subtly) in another philosophical treatise he published slightly earlier the same year, *On Friendship* (*De Amicitia*) – a dialogue in which his characters are made to tackle head on the issue of what to do when political morality and friendship collide.[21] But he also expressed the same point in particularly blunt terms in the autumn of 44 BC, when he wrote to Matius – a man who had been a loyal friend to Caesar and was still grieving his death:

> It will not escape such a learned man as yourself that if Caesar was a despot, which seems the case to me, your duty can be debated in one of two ways. Either (and this is the line I generally take) that your loyalty and kindness towards a friend you still hold dear even after he is dead is commendable, or there is the line taken by several others: that the freedom of one's country should come before the life of a friend.[22]

Matius, however, was not convinced. And his response to his critics, whom he knew included Cicero and almost certainly Brutus too,[23] survives to provide a powerful and eloquent counter-argument:

> I know the criticisms people have levelled against me since Caesar's death. They find it a fault in me that I bear the loss of a friend gravely and resent that a man I loved has been destroyed. They say that one's country should come before friendship – as though they have proved that his loss was beneficial to the *res publica*. But I shall not make a clever defence. I confess that I have not attained to that level of philosophical thinking. It was not Caesar I followed in the civil war, but a friend. And although I did not like what he was doing, still I did not desert him.

So there we have it: friendship first. Matius' concession that he 'did not like what he [Caesar] was doing' hints at the fact he felt some moral reservations over siding with the dictator. But as the rest of the letter continues, he adds: 'I have no doubt that even those who despise me because of my loyalty to Caesar would prefer friends like me than like themselves.'[24] Brutus, or so the implication goes, was an unfaithful friend.

Yet for all his claims not to have attained Cicero's heights of philosophical reasoning, Matius' letter makes it abundantly clear that he *was* taking a very sophisticated stand on the question. For nowhere does he explicitly reject Cicero's thesis that one's country should come before friendship; rather, he hints that in the case of Caesar's assassination it was not applicable: 'They say that one's country should come before friendship – as though they have proved that his loss was beneficial to the *res publica*', he argues. As this exchange shows, then, there were any number of ways in which the question over Caesar's death could be figured, even by those living at the time. The competing demands of friendship and country was one; another was the extent to which Caesar *was* a tyrant, or how far his elimination *was*, to paraphrase both Matius and Shakespeare, for the common good of all. After all, even if Brutus had joined the conspiracy in 'a general honest thought', still he led the plot which set in motion an even more catastrophic sequence of events – as Shakespeare's audience well knew by the time the eulogy was delivered over Brutus' dead body.[25]

To the ancient mind, however, the dilemma rested above all on the question of ingratitude; hence stories soon emerged to make the betrayal of Brutus appear even greater than it was: Caesar's special attention towards, and perhaps even paternity of Brutus, as well as Brutus' own acceptance of political honours from the dictator.[26] We have already seen this point of view expressed by Plutarch, and a few hints at this idea appear in Shakespeare, too. Yet the belief that Brutus was a traitor to his friend was the predominant motif in medieval writings, and especially in the work of the Florentine poet Dante Alighieri (1261–1321), who famously placed Brutus and Cassius, together with Judas Iscariot, in the lowest circle of hell, where they were to be eternally chewed in Lucifer's jaws. For all its gore and terrifying evocation, the passage is worth quoting at length:

> Each mouth devoured a sinner clenched within,
> Frayed by the fangs like flax beneath a brake;
> Three at a time he tortured them for sin.
>
> But all the bites the one in front might take
> Were nothing to the claws that flayed his hide
> And sometimes stripped his back to the last flake.
>
> 'That wretch up there whom keenest pangs divide
> Is Judas called Iscariot,' said my lord,
> 'His head within, his jerking legs outside;
>
> As for the pair whose heads hang hitherward:
> From the black mouth the limbs of Brutus sprawl –
> See how he writhes and utters never a word;
>
> And strong-thewed Cassius is his fellow-thrall.
> But come; for night is rising on the world
> Once more; we must depart; we have seen all.'[27]

In Dante's *Inferno*, then, these three men are the worst sinners of all time, for all had attacked God's will. Thus Brutus' sin was more than a betrayal of a friend's trust or the iniquity of assassination. In killing Caesar, whom Dante identified as a quasi-prototype for all contemporary monarchs, and perhaps even as a forerunner of the Holy Roman Emperors of his day, Brutus, Dante believed, was resisting God's 'historical design'. From this point of view, the assassination had been doomed to fail from the start.[28]

We have seen something of this idea already in the works of Plutarch, Appian and Dio; hence the omens and the portents both after the assassination of Caesar and before the battle of Philippi. 'Power could no longer be retained in the hands of many', wrote Plutarch, 'and a monarchy was necessary.'

In other words: heaven had ordained that Octavian should have the victory at Philippi as he alone could be sole master.[29] But it is perhaps significant that Dante's knowledge of Brutus came not through Plutarch but from his readings of Lucan, Appian and especially Virgil. Through Virgil we have already traced the contemporary feelings of fear after the Ides, as well as the hopes for Octavian after Philippi. More pervasive in the *Aeneid*, however, is the view that Augustus' rule was divinely sanctioned; from Jupiter's prophecy in Book 1, to the revelation of the future history of Rome in Book 6, Augustus is 'the man promised to you', 'born of the gods', 'who will establish again a Golden Age', and an 'Empire without end'. That is not to say that Virgil was a mouthpiece for Augustan propaganda; far from it. However, his poetry does reflect themes that were being promoted in Augustus' portraits, statues and coins – all with the same, consistent message: his authority and military success were backed by the will of the gods (Plate 11).[30]

According to this line of thought, then, Brutus had got it wrong – even the Stoic Seneca thought so when he composed his work *On Benefits* (*De Beneficiis*) in the mid-first century AD. He listed three counts against him. First, he claimed Brutus was wrong to fear the name of king when Stoic teaching argued that the best form of government was under a good king. Second, he wrongly supposed that liberty could exist in an oligarchy which privileged a small few at the expense of the many. And last of all, he was perhaps naïve to think that the ancient constitution could be restored when all its former customs had been lost. 'How forgetful he seems to have been, both of human nature and of the history of his own country, in supposing that when one despot was destroyed another of the same temper would not take his place', Seneca exclaimed.[31]

As Ronald Syme rightly pointed out in his classic book *The Roman Revolution* in 1939: to judge Brutus because he failed is simply to judge from the results.[32] What is more, to do so undermines both the fight the Liberators *did* put up, as well as the one which continued long after Philippi under the leadership of Sextus Pompeius. But still, we should perhaps take seriously and return to Matius' contemporary criticism – that the Liberators and their supporters were speaking 'as though they have proved that his loss was beneficial to the *res publica*' – for it reminds us that there is another point of view to engage with here: Caesar may have stretched the republican institutions to breaking point, but was it not possible that he had in view a constitutional arrangement that might be acceptable in the future? That seems to have been the view of some of Caesar's friends at least: 'for if a man with his [Caesar's] genius could not find a way out', Matius had asked of Cicero shortly after the assassination, 'who will find one now?'[33]

To be sure, if Caesar did have a coherent programme for government in mind, there is no surviving description of it. Still, however, that the death of Caesar was not a 'common good to all' is an impression that has been created and passed down by some of the most influential historians to have written on the topic of Roman history. Take Theodor Mommsen's monumental *History of Rome*, published in 1854–56, for example, whose account spans from the city's origins through to the end of the Roman Republic. For, in choosing to end his three-volume work with the reforms Caesar had passed two years before his assassination, Mommsen not only influenced a generation of readers to believe that Caesar had some sort of solution to the problem of how to deal with Rome's growing empire; he cast a damning verdict on Brutus, whose role in the political life of the Roman Republic is noticeable only by its absence.

On this verdict, Caesar was a man of vision, while Brutus failed to see that the *res publica* for which he fought was already beyond remedy. But Mommsen did not need to make the point explicit, for Wilhelm Drumann (1786–1861), a man by whom Mommsen had been greatly influenced, had already argued that there was a perceivable gap between Brutus' ideas and reality.[34] In more recent times, the idea has been stated and restated: Brutus was 'a Messiah looking for a cause', in Graham Wylie's 1998 assessment of the conspiracy: his 'lofty idealism' might have impressed his intellectual peers, 'but he was quite incapable of understanding or leading ordinary men'.[35]

The naïve Brutus is perhaps there behind the criticism of Matius, too, and he is certainly there, although with a different slant, in the later criticisms Cicero had to make of the assassination as a 'deed carried out with the courage of men and the policy of children'.[36] By the time of Seneca in the early imperial period, the 'ending' had of course been written: Octavian, while claiming to be restoring rule to the Senate and the people of Rome, established himself as the *princeps* (the 'first citizen'), and changed his name to Augustus – the man we call the first Roman emperor. And once the new system of the principate was entrenched it was presumably easy for later writers to look back and think that Caesar's assassins had just been ideologically resisting the inevitable direction of history.

Gentle in Life

If some remembered Brutus for the civil war with its needless loss of life into which he threw his country, for his own part Brutus had advertised and was evidently keen to cultivate a reputation for *clementia*. Thus, as we saw from his own correspondence with Cicero, the problem of what to do with Gaius Antonius had vexed him for the most part of 43 BC, while the friends who later wrote of his Lycian campaign took pains to emphasise Brutus' lack of cruelty. The point was made by Velleius too (born *c.* 19 BC–after AD 30), one of our earliest sources for Brutus' reception. For in telling us that Cassius, contrary to his usual behaviour, once 'surpassed even Brutus' clemency', he gives us a profound hint about how the two men were remembered. The implication need hardly be spelled out: Brutus was famed for his *clementia* while it was not a virtue routinely associated with Cassius.[37]

It is the very same distinction we see made by Plutarch, only he uses the Greek term *praos* to denote this aspect of Brutus' character: 'He was a remarkably gentle [*praos*] and broad-minded man, free from all anger, hedonism and greed, direct in his opinion and unyielding in defence of the honourable and just.'[38] The translation of 'gentle' here, the word which informed Shakespeare's thinking on Brutus' character in the eulogy,[39] hardly does justice to the importance of this virtue as a quality of the ideal statesman in ancient political thought. Gentleness (*praotés*) was one of the most esteemed qualities in Plutarch's reckoning: it was the ability to check one's anger, ambitions and passions – all virtues far removed from the stereotypical image of a tyrant. In Plutarch, there is no hint that Brutus' dedication to clemency could be more negatively interpreted as a sign of military weakness – a point to which we shall come soon. Before then, however, let us first put Brutus' claims to *clementia* under the spotlight and imagine how they must have seemed to his opponents.

Insofar as *clementia* was linked to the more general concept of *humanitas* (or *philanthropia*, in the Greek), it also conveyed a sense of moral obligation and a kindliness of attitude. Yet there was nothing loyal in Brutus' treatment of Caesar; in fact, he had killed the man who had spared his life. We have seen that point of view already expressed by numerous writers – and presumably Augustus himself in his lost autobiography had treated Brutus' memory even less liberally. Far from being benevolent and clement, then, from a different partisan perspective, he could be impugned as a parricide who had killed 'the father of the country', and as a cut-throat killer, as well as a cruel bandit who had fleeced the cities of Lycia in preparation for war. These are all assessments which have made their way into the later historians, and through them into the traditions which question the motives and morality of Caesar's assassination.[40] But the foundations were first set by Antony, when he erected a statue of Caesar on the *rostra* in the Forum and inscribed upon its base: 'To Father and Benefactor'. The result, as Cicero already saw it in early October 44 BC, was that Brutus and

Cassius were being judged 'not only as assassins [*sicarii*], but even as parricides [*parricidae*]'.[41]

Of these two charges, the last has had a particularly powerful afterlife in the reception history of Brutus in two different ways. Early on, some turned the accusation of parricide into a literal charge against Brutus, believing that he could have been the actual son of Caesar. Appian had certainly come across this speculation in his research for the *Civil Wars*, although his language makes it clear that he placed little trust in its reliability: 'It was thought [*enomízeto*]', he says cautiously at the first telling of the accusation, and then 'it was said [*légetai*]' when he recalls how Caesar wanted Brutus' life spared at Pharsalus.[42] The idea, of course, was to prove irresistible for later playwrights. Thus, in *La Mort de César* (1736), the French Enlightenment writer Voltaire makes Brutus' dilemma a conflict between his patriotic duty and his Caesarian bloodline, the fact of which is revealed to him shortly before the assassination. And while Shakespeare noticeably avoids any such suggestion of paternity in *Julius Caesar*, in *Henry VI, Part 2* almost the last words of Suffolk before his murder are: 'Brutus' bastard hand / Stabb'd Julius Caesar'.[43] In this case, the death of the dictator is one of several examples – 'of great men [who] oft die by vile bezonians' – used by Suffolk to console himself on his own ignominious demise; Suffolk's general point is that the great Caesar was killed by the base felon Brutus.

For others, however, what was more telling against Brutus and Cassius was the fact they had killed the *parens patriae*: the title conferred upon the dictator in early 44 BC as part of the honours recognising his generous *clementia*. It signified that Caesar was hence the paternal type of autocrat, not the tyrannical one, as even writers like John of Salisbury and Thomas Aquinas, who had both approached the topic of the assassination through Cicero's *On Duties*, had to admit. Thus, the parricide argument was a neat and effective counter to those who would call Caesar's murder a tyrannicide – a juxtaposition of ideas which was particularly developed by the Italian humanist Coluccio Salutati, who paid close attention to the assassination of Caesar in his treatise *On Tyranny* (*De Tyranno*, written in 1400). In this work, he argued that Dante was right to put Brutus and Cassius in the lowest pits of hell: 'those killers of Caesar did not kill the tyrant', he concluded, 'but killed the father of the land and the most merciful and legitimate ruler of the world'.[44] What this reveals about Antony is that, when he set up his statue base and inscribed it 'To Father and Benefactor', he well knew what he was doing – as did Cicero; for at some point after Caesar's death, and presumably under the direction of his young heir, the Senate voted to call the Ides of March the 'Day of the Parricide' (*Parricidium*).[45] That the assassins should not be remembered as tyrannicides was hence an effective strategy and it lent weight to Antony's other favourite charge against Caesar's murderers: that they were little more than cut-throat assassins (*sicarii*).

In the early imperial age at Rome, this charge would be superseded by the accusation that Brutus and Cassius were 'parricides' and 'bandits' (*latrones*), to reflect on their plunder of the Greek cities in the east. Indeed, as we saw in the Introduction, this was the accusation current at the time Cremutius Cordus was prosecuted in AD 25. However, that the Liberators were regarded as cold-blooded murderers can be seen in the Greek historians, starting with Nicolaus and continuing through to Appian and Dio, who translate the Latin *sicarii* into the corresponding term *sphageis*, which also means something like 'butchers' or 'throat-cutters'.[46] A hint of the same idea may also be traced in the *Satires* of Horace (*Satires* 1.7), Brutus' contemporary, who makes a joke about Brutus' reputation as a 'king-slayer', based on an event in 43/42 BC to which he represents himself as a witness. The occasion was a dispute (possibly fictitious) at Clazomenae, about 20 miles west of Smyrna, where Brutus was called upon to arbitrate between the Greek businessman, Persius Hybrida, and a proscribed Italian man called Rupilius Rex. We are not told what the quarrel was about, and the brevity of Horace's satire has left it subject to several interpretations.[47] Yet at the end Persius turns to Brutus to make a telling pun on Rex's name: 'For god's sake, Brutus, you are used to finishing off kings; why don't you cut this King's throat? Believe me, this job is yours.' And then the piece curiously ends, with no clever comeback forthcoming from a speechless Brutus.

When we consider the dynamics of the fight for public and military support in the years 43–42 BC, we should thus take the strength of Antony's partisan rhetoric seriously. That Brutus was a cut-throat killer rather than a tyrannicide was a damning accusation, which reflects the general abhorrence accorded to acts of conspiracy. So far, however, the only defence we have seen has come from the pen of Cicero, whose works *On Duties* and *On Friendship* were rushed out soon after the assassination to give expression to the idea that the murder was a noble and virtuous deed. Yet for his part Brutus also had a message to convey, only he chose a different medium which has often been overlooked in this connection: the iconography of his famous coin (Plate 1), and specifically the threatening image of the two daggers, which thus merits further attention.

We have already noted the legend referring to the Ides of March, as well as the *pileus* (the cap of liberty) in the centre. However, it is the two daggers that are of interest here, for they are representative of the sort used in military contexts – *pugiones* (or *pugio*, in the singular). On closer inspection, they are slightly different: the one on the left has a cross-shaped hilt, while the one on the right is decorated with two flat discs. Barry Strauss has even suggested that the cross-shaped dagger was rare and that it may in fact be a representation of Brutus' actual sword, which would have hence been distinctive.[48] However, the main point must surely be that the *pugio* was a weapon associated with soldiers, not assassins, who instead preferred the curved dagger called a *sica* (hence the word *sicarii*). And *this* was the thrust of Brutus' defence: Caesar had been no father to his country but a *dominus* who cast all citizens into a state of abject slavery. As the image of the cap reinforces, the Ides of March was part of an ongoing fight for *libertas*. Yet, as the daggers reveal, it was a campaign being waged by Roman soldiers. Brutus' message on this coin was thus a simple one, and it would have been instantly clear even to those – or we might say especially to those – unversed in philosophy: that is, the troops among whom these coins were circulated.

What, then, of Brutus' *clementia*? The life that was 'gentle'? As in the tradition that developed around Brutus' afterlife, Shakespeare has presented us with an enigma: a man who defies and transcends categorisation – 'the elements so mixed in him'. There are inherent contradictions in the fact that Brutus, who killed Caesar after accepting his clemency, was later accused of showing too much clemency towards Gaius Antonius. For his part, Plutarch praised Brutus' philanthropy and (perhaps rightly to the modern mind) approved that he had not killed a fellow citizen, against Cicero's urging to the contrary. Others linked Brutus' clemency to his weaknesses as a military leader and especially his susceptibility to bad advice, or 'group-think' as modern psychologists might call it.[49] Later, as we know, Gaius Antonius was executed; Brutus waged a bitter campaign in the east; he offered to his soldiers the cities of Thessalonica and Sparta to plunder; he had the captives in his camp killed and twice led his forces out to war. Yet amidst all these apparent anomalies, there is one clear consistent thread in the reception history of Brutus: his *virtus* – the quality he either vaunted or rejected in his dying moments, depending on which version you read. But what did it *mean* for Brutus to be remembered as a man of virtue?

This Was a Man!

When Antony ends his eulogy of Brutus with the exclamation 'This was a man!', we can detect a carefully orchestrated climax on the part of Shakespeare. Though it may have been said of his classical learning that Shakespeare only had 'small Latin and less Greek',[50] his knowledge of the ancient languages was enough to know that the Latin word for 'man' was *vir*, and from that came the Latin word *virtus* (the ancestor of English 'virtue'). Thus, while the word *virtus* implied manliness, courage and might, it also denoted a moral state towards which a man should strive: a 'manly excellence' – a vital connection between virtue and manhood which was rarely forgotten in Brutus' day.

We can fairly imagine that not all of Shakespeare's audience would have picked up on the point for themselves: that what made Brutus a 'man' was the nobility of purpose which had driven him to join and then lead the conspiracy. But then again, they did not need to; for in the line which immediately follows Antony's 'This was a *man*!', Shakespeare has Octavius say of Brutus: 'According to his *virtue* let us use him, / With all respects and rites of burial' (my italics). In this way, Brutus in *Julius Caesar* is recognised by his opponents as having acted in accordance with the benchmarks by which Brutus and his contemporaries liked to be judged in the first century BC. But what about Brutus' *virtus* in the ancient sources? What did the Augustan and early imperial writers have to say about that?

The first thing to note is that mention of Brutus' *virtus* is nearly always more complex than it initially appears: Velleius argued that the 'rashness [*temeritas*] of a single deed deprived him of all his virtues [*virtutes*]', while Valerius Maximus remarked that: 'Marcus Brutus murdered his own virtues before committing the parricide of the *parens patriae*.'[51] The former casts doubt on Brutus' philosophical integrity insofar as the *temeritas* with which Brutus acted was the exact opposite of the *virtus* he purported to hold so dear: his moral claim to virtue was hence an apparition which was easily shattered.[52] Valerius, too, hints at a weakness in Brutus' moral position because, in Stoic thought at least, true *virtus* was immune to physical assault of all types: for Brutus to murder his *virtus* was hence a paradox, unless it was only a phoney sort of *virtus*.[53] But what is more significant is that both historians drew a link between Brutus' loss of virtue and his downfall. Or, as the late-republican poet Horace was to put it in one of his *Odes* (2.7): '*virtus* was shattered' at Philippi.

What precisely Horace meant by this comment has been a matter of lively debate. Taken positively, it may seem to suggest that Brutus was the last representative of *virtus* and the only commander at Philippi to embody it.[54] After all, we may remember that Horace had been one of the young men to join Brutus at Athens, and he had risen through the ranks to become a military tribune by the time of Philippi. Yet nowhere does Horace express any great affection for Brutus, who appeared only as a silent and unfathomable presence in the Clazomenae *Satire* we saw above (*Satires* 1.7). What is more, after Brutus' death, Horace surrendered to the triumvirs and later returned to Rome where, having first secured employment as an office clerk, he discovered his vocation as a poet.[55] By the time he wrote the first three books of *Odes* in 23 BC, he was safe and forgiven in the regime Augustus had established. Could it be possible, then, that Horace's *Odes* 2.7 was intended to reflect negatively on Brutus? There are two potential criticisms against Brutus' *virtus* to consider here.

The first regards Brutus' military *virtus*, for the ancient sources routinely painted him as an incompetent general: the catastrophic decision to fight the first battle of Philippi had been urged by Brutus; his discipline of the troops on the day was poor; his decision to fight the second battle of Philippi had been equally short-sighted; when compared with Cassius, all agree that Brutus was no match.[56] But in the opening stanza of this poem, which purports to welcome the return home of a former republican comrade in arms (an unknown man by the name of Pompeius), Horace appears to make the point more explicit still:

> O Pompeius, often led, with me, to the edge
> of doom, when Brutus was head of our army
> who has made you a Roman again and restored you
> to the Gods of the country and the Italian sky.

Not once but *often* Brutus led his men into extreme peril; when contrasted against the unnamed saviour of line three, who has restored Pompeius to Rome (we are surely meant to think of Augustus here),[57] we are forced to confront the question of whose military legacy (whose *virtus*) was the greater: the man who imperilled or the man who saved Rome's citizens?

Before we get there, however, let us also consider the second potential criticism levelled against Brutus. For ever since the ancient scholiast Porphyrio commented that the significance of the phrase 'shattered *virtus*' rested on the fact that 'Brutus and Cassius publicly prided themselves above all on their virtue', some have thought that Horace specifically attacks Brutus' philosophical *virtus* in the third stanza, where he reminds Pompeius:

> With you I experienced Philippi, and that swift flight,
> My little shield indecorously left behind,
> when virtue was shattered, and menacing men
> shamefully bit the dust.

The argument runs that the *virtus* boasted by Brutus was a brittle ideal, which snapped in the face of defeat. That the republicans were arrogant and menacing men, who were eventually forced to submit to the triumvirs, just as Appian also pictured it in his *Civil Wars.*[58] More than anything else, it will be noted that this sentiment almost exactly recalls the version of Brutus' death in which he too criticised his commitment to the ideal: 'O wretched Virtue, you were but a word!' By this estimation, Brutus had failed to live up to the *virtus* he so publicly preached; his was a pale imitation of 'virtue', the affectation of which was quickly 'shattered' (*cum fracta virtus*).

But a closer look at the rest of the stanza, quoted above, does not seem to support the conclusion that Horace is delivering a personal attack on Brutus.[59] Rather, another way of reading this poem is to focus on how Horace is gently nudging Pompeius into the admission that they were *all* wrong to share and follow Brutus' cause, in what is essentially a political apology. Thus, we can note how Horace tempers the reproach of Philippi by including himself and Pompeius in its purview. As is appropriate to the poetic context, the experience is described using a literary motif: the throwing away of one's shield in battle.[60] But in so doing Horace makes it clear that he, as well as the rest of the idealistic young men who followed Brutus, realised the futility of the republican ideal of *virtus*: it was simply not worth fighting for any more.[61]

In all of this, however, we have still not explained why it was so important that Brutus be denied his *virtus*. Why did Horace have to admit he had been disillusioned? I would like to suggest that a clue might be found in the nexus binding *virtus*, service to the state, and the old aristocracy of republican Rome. As Carlos Noreña has explained in a study of imperial ideals, for centuries the Roman aristocracy had perpetuated its standing partly via an 'exclusionary ideology' in which rank, status, achievements and virtue were represented as something that could be inherited and passed down through the generations.[62] *Virtus* was hence an individual quality, one which bestowed glory on the man who attained it. But in the last generation of the Roman Republic, the competition for personal supremacy had brought men into civil conflicts of unprecedented scale: 'to the edge of doom', as Horace puts it in the opening lines of this poem.

In his lifetime, Brutus had engaged in something like the old concept of *virtus* when he commissioned the family tree and boasted of his own ancestry, or when he wrote the funeral speech for his father-in-law Appius, or the eulogy of his uncle Cato. Brutus' *virtus* had also caused him to emulate his ancestors by plotting to kill Caesar. But under Augustus the aspect of *virtus* celebrated most was the ethical concept that looked to the protection of Rome's citizens.[63] In January 27 BC, four years before the *Odes* were published, the Senate and people of Rome had honoured Augustus with a golden shield on which *virtus* was inscribed – along with *clementia* ('clemency'), *pietas* ('piety') and *iustitia* ('justice'): it was even referred to as the 'shield of virtue' (the *clipeus virtutis*). One point of *Odes* 2.7 must surely be that, for men like Horace and Pompeius, the past is behind them and they must recognise the futility and the dangers of the republican *virtus* for which they fought. Now it was time to look ahead and accept the political reality, to find peace and tranquillity in the new state, where real *virtus* could finally flourish.

Brutus, Liberty and the Republic

A tragic suicide, a eulogy and the promise of an honourable burial later, and Shakespeare's *Julius Caesar* ends – by focusing not on the tragedy of Caesar, the eponymous hero of the play, but on the death of Brutus, 'the noblest Roman of them all'. One of the first questions critics ask, then, is: 'Who is the tragic hero of the play?' Is it Caesar, around whom so much of the action of the play revolves, or Brutus, who speaks more lines than any other character and whose death marks the climax? A popular response to this problem today is to see the play as deliberately ambiguous; the only certainty, as we have seen, is the very real danger of civil war after the assassination of a ruler. But in raising questions over the nature of Caesar's rule, the motives of the conspirators, and the justifiability of the act, Shakespeare both reflected and contributed to a debate that preoccupied the best political thinkers from antiquity through to the Middle Ages and Renaissance, and that remains of relevance today: the value we place on liberty versus tyranny.[64]

Brutus had minted images of Libertas on his coins; he had published speeches attacking Pompey's power and championing the legitimacy of political murder; he had played a leading role in the assassination of Caesar and afterwards styled himself as a 'Liberator' of Rome. Brutus thought it unbearable to serve as another man's slave, and he meant it. The lot of the slave was to live under a master's control, never knowing what would happen next, and to be subject to someone else's arbitrary power. The Liberators' cry for *libertas* is often more negatively represented as the response of an aristocratic elite which begrudged any attempt to curb its power, status or ambition; and to some extent it was. But, as modern political thinkers such as Quentin Skinner have pointed out, there is another way of looking at past ideas of freedom: under Caesar's perpetual dictatorship, they had lost the markers of status that defined them as free men.[65] Worse still, Rome had lost its status as a free and self-governing nation – a *res publica* in which magistrates were elected annually, and the rule of law was greater than the will of one man. When Octavian later continued where Caesar had left off and established himself as Augustus, he was more careful about how he presented his power, but the effect was essentially the same. Under these circumstances, it was only to be expected that few would venture to commemorate Brutus too loudly as a champion of freedom.[66]

One important exception, however, is Lucan's epic *Civil War* (*Pharsalia*), written during the reign of Nero (AD 54–68). Admittedly, in the poem as it survives, Brutus plays only a minor role, and he is overshadowed by Cato, who appears as the epitome of virtue and moral rectitude. But the epic was incomplete at the time of Lucan's death in AD 65 and it is clear that he envisaged a greater part for Brutus in the unfinished portions, which looked likely to include an account of Caesar's assassination. For in a particularly dramatic scene in the seventh book, Lucan describes an imaginary scene from the battle of Pharsalus, in which Brutus approaches Caesar with a view to killing him, but the poet interjects:

> O glory of Rome, last hope of the Senate, final descendant of a family so famed throughout history, don't rush so recklessly into the enemy's midst, nor bring on fatal Philippi ahead of time, you will perish in a Thessaly of your own. Nothing do you achieve here, intent on Caesar's throat: not yet has he attained the citadel, or surpassed the peak of human law, controlling everything; he has not yet earned from destiny a death so noble. Let him live and let him rule, so he may fall victim to the dagger of Brutus.[67]

These lines reveal quite clearly that the message on Brutus' posthumous reputation was mixed. There is a hint that he is on his way towards earning a reputation as a political failure, hence Brutus extinguishes rather than lives up to the great name of the Junii Bruti; and worse still there are signs of the moral damnation to come in his potentially reckless behaviour, which is again characterised by *temeritas*. What we also notice in these lines is that it is the *death* of Caesar which will be noble, rather than the conspirator who is to slay him. But still we see that Lucan perceived Caesar as a tyrant and Brutus as a rightful defender of liberty. When this double-sided picture came into the hands of later writers, there was consequently one of two ways in which it could be reinterpreted: by focusing on either the positives or the negatives of Lucan's presentation.

Thus, when Dante was inspired by Lucan to take up the characters of Cato and Brutus in his own poem, he took the former as the epitome of virtue and moral rectitude (much like Lucan's Cato), but largely condemned the latter by recycling some of the stereotypes that surrounded Brutus in the first and second centuries AD, where the assassination was largely censured as an act of ingratitude or political short-sightedness. As we saw earlier, it was Brutus who had thus earned a place in hell with Cassius and the traitor Judas. However, an alternative way of looking at the assassination emerges from the point of view of Brutus as a defender of Liberty in the tradition of Cato. An early example can be found in Juvenal, who flourished in the periods of Trajan (AD 98–117) and the early part of Hadrian's rule (AD 117–38), and who used Brutus and his uncle as shorthand for the types of good men once found in the world. More intriguing still are the *Meditations* of the emperor Marcus Aurelius (AD 121–80), who included Brutus among those who inspired the ideal of a monarchy that cherished the liberty of the subject.[68] In contrast to Dante's valuation, then, other Renaissance writers tended to view Brutus' actions more sympathetically. From this perspective, it was Brutus who came to symbolise the tradition of ancient republicanism through the ages, and his name and image became a potent memory in times of political unrest.

Other Brutuses hence spring up across Europe, such as the unknown author of the *Defences against Tyrants* (*Vindiciae contra Tyrannos*), published under the pseudonym Stephanus Junius Brutus in sixteenth-century France, or the so-called 'British Brutus', Algernon Sidney, who was executed in 1683 for allegedly plotting against Charles II, in part because of ideas he expressed in his work *Discourses Concerning Government*. To these we can add a Florentine Brutus: Lorenzino de' Medici, who murdered his cousin the Duke Alessandro in 1537 and went on to strike a medal in imitation of the coin of Brutus. And Lucien Bonaparte, too, adopted the name Brutus at the outbreak of the French Revolution in 1789.[69] In this latter period, it was the name of Lucius Junius Brutus, as much as the younger Marcus, which was used to invoke revolutionary feeling and eventually undermine the foundations of the Bastille. But it did not matter much. The Brutus myth generally took on new life and fervour with the result that, in 1793/94 in Paris alone, some 300 children were registered with the name of Brutus.[70]

This at last returns us to the idea expressed in my preface: that the name of Brutus pops up even in the most unexpected of places: in a Freudian dream, in Gulliver's travels, or in the murky streets of Dickensian London.[71] And when it does, it is as if we are looking at only one side of his famous coin – the symbols of liberty, the military resistance to tyranny, the Ides of March. It was these ideals which led Donato Giannoti – a former secretary of state at Florence and a fervent upholder of republicanism – to persuade Michelangelo to attempt a portrait of Brutus in 1539 (Plate 12). But the bust only survives in an unfinished state. For the story goes that when Michelangelo tried to put a face to the Liberator, he found not a noble conspirator but an unjust oppressor. He laid the bust aside in disgust and could never be prevailed upon to complete it.[72] When we encounter Brutus today in modern representations on TV, stage and film, the Brutus we see is predominantly the product of Shakespeare. Thus, when he appears, he is more of a troubled soul than a public symbol, and the result is often sympathetic: a tragic hero akin to Hamlet. Best known, perhaps, is James Mason's appearance as the romantic idealist Brutus in Joseph Mankiewicz's 1953 film *Julius Caesar*. But different takes on the Shakespearean play have also proved possible, such as the cold-blooded and neurotic Brutus played by John Wood in Trevor Nunn's 1972 adaptation, or Anton Lesser's masterly presentation of Brutus as an unsympathetic intellectual in Deborah Warner's 2005 production. More recently, we have seen Tobias Menzies on our screens as a youthful Brutus caught on the horns of a dilemma in HBO's *Rome* (2005–7); in this series, he has been detached from his Shakespearean role, yet still the image of Brutus is conditioned more by specific portrayals of him than by any factual evidence or his own utterances.[73]

In this connection, it is significant that the decision on how to present Brutus is still guided by the way his role in the assassination has been perceived. For the same questions surround Brutus from whichever angle we approach him: was he a noble and constant patriot or a cold and traitorous murderer? Should he have placed his country over his friendship and obligations to Caesar? Did the assassination of Caesar help or hinder peace? As a 'mild tyrant', should Caesar have been tolerated by Brutus? However, as we have repeatedly seen, the problems in reaching a definitive answer were there from the start, and when a historical figure has been so variously interpreted, it is unlikely that any study of him can claim finality on the topic. It is not my intention, then, to offer my own judgment on Brutus or his legacy. But what we can aim to do, as I shall attempt in the conclusion to this book, is to reshape the question from 'What should we think of Brutus?' to 'What did his contemporaries think of Brutus?' And from there, we might be able to start seeing the man emerge from behind his legend.

CONCLUSION

THE MANY FACES OF BRUTUS

> I do love and have always loved your talents, interests and your habits. Every day my heart grows warmer, not only with a desire to be with you, enjoy your conversation and listen to your learned discourse, but also because you have a marvellous reputation for incredible virtues, which though they look disparate are harmonised by your prudence. For what is as different as severity and kindliness? Yet who was ever thought of as more upright or more charming than you? What is as difficult as to be loved by all in settling a multitude of disputes? Yet you manage to send away even those you decide against in friendly and satisfied mind. The result is that, although you do nothing simply to please, everything you do still manages to gain favour.
>
> — Cicero, *Orator*, 33–4

The more we look at the evidence for Brutus' life and how it shaped his later legend, the less sure we may feel at making definitive statements about the historical man: a detailed study only demonstrates that there were many sides to Brutus, and that he drew a wide variety of responses from those who knew him. As Cicero wrote in his treatise *Orator*, which he dedicated to Brutus in 46 BC, he had an array of talents and attributes, not all of which appear immediately compatible. Yet of all the words that have been used to describe him in the various sources, two appear to stand out as suitable irrespective of the verdict drawn on his role in the assassination of Caesar: he was a man of *noble* birth, and he *conspired* in the plot to kill the dictator of Rome. It may not seem much to go on, but the tag 'noble conspirator' does provide a convenient peg upon which to hang a final verdict; not least because it represents and connects the two major phases of his life and career – his political profiling as he made the climb up the ladder of honours, and his military campaigns in the fights for freedom which started on the Ides of March. What is more, for both these spheres of activity we have direct access to Brutus through his coins and letters to help us keep our eyes on the man himself.

As we have seen, the political career of Brutus coincided with and contributed to the turbulent last decades of the Roman Republic; indeed, by 59 BC many thought the *res publica* was either already dead, or at least terminally ill. But Cicero had been heard to say that 'what was now wanted was a Servilius Ahala or a Brutus', referring to the need for a champion of liberty to expel or exterminate the three-headed monster which was plaguing Rome in the form of Pompey, Caesar and Crassus.[1] At precisely that time, Quintus Servilius Caepio Brutus – our Brutus under his official name – was beginning to build something of a reputation for himself at Rome.

At first, there are only traces of the splash he was making. 'Quintus Caepio – I mean, this Brutus', Cicero could comment to Atticus in a letter discussing the alleged plot to kill Pompey in which Brutus was bitterly implicated. But the ripples started to spread further when Brutus minted coins advertising his descent from those legendary republican heroes. Now that we are familiar with the coin Brutus minted after the Ides of March, we may note the staggering similarity between the appearance of the younger Brutus (Plate 1) and the portrait he grafted onto his famous ancestor (Plate 4). With the same steely expression of determination, the original Brutus looks ahead to the ejection of the Tarquins and the establishment of the republican constitution, as well as his own position as a magistrate in a Rome free of kings. In years to come, the younger Brutus would strike the same pose in the fights for freedom that followed on from the assassination of Caesar. But in the immediate term, he had given a face to the name by which he wanted to be recognised.

Even before he held the quaestorship, then, Brutus was engaging in a conscious strategy of what today we would call 'self-fashioning': that is, the process of constructing an identity and public persona according to a set of approved social standards. Yet, although Brutus' claim to fame and nobility offered him great scope for the future, there was always a more threatening aspect to such a heritage. Use it well and he could promote his career exponentially by success at the polls. However, by building and advertising his own identity as a continuum of the attitude that made his ancestors famous, Brutus had also established the benchmark by which his behaviour and conduct would be judged.

Thus, Cicero was the first to criticise him when he fell short of that ideal in 45 BC: 'what of that family tree I saw . . . what of Ahala and Brutus?'[2] And here we have the first contemporary criticism of Brutus: it was not implausible to argue a lack of political constancy, especially when we remember that he fought for the man who had killed his father, before accepting pardon from the man he would go on to kill. But then he assassinated the dictator and he re-branded himself as a 'Liberator'. It meant Cicero could now publicly boast that Brutus had lived up to the nobility expected of him: his ancestors had spurred him on – 'a happy day for the *res publica*' and 'a glorious one for the assassins'.[3]

There is no doubt, however, that in his short life Brutus was an eminent man in his own right, as a politician, orator and author of philosophical treatises and other literary pamphlets. His outspoken views and productivity in these fields soon found Brutus admirers, but he also received criticism, both among his peers and from the generations that followed. This was partly because, despite his own achievements in his early career, most of Brutus' public offices were granted to him by the favour of Caesar, who had shown an interest in the young man from early on. It was probably with the support of Caesar that he was elected to the prestigious pontifical college, of which Caesar was the *pontifex maximus*. And, although he rejected a generous invitation to serve on Caesar's staff in the 50s BC, he was later appointed as governor of Cisalpine Gaul and then to the urban praetorship – again because of the dictator's favour. We have anecdotal evidence to suggest that he administered all of these duties conscientiously: thus, he was considered diligent in Cisalpine Gaul, and observant of the law as urban praetor. Yet his shady business transactions in Salamis and the legal loopholes he jumped through to secure a morally questionable investment are fully exposed by Cicero to leave a question mark over Brutus' provincial activities.

As a politician and orator, Brutus was active in the law courts, notably when he defended Appius Claudius, and a hint in Cicero's *Brutus* suggests that he had begun to appear quite regularly in the *contiones* of the Forum during his urban praetorship. After the assassination of Caesar, Brutus continued to make public appearances for a while, and he tried at least to influence the people to his side. In this connection, we know that he possessed a certain substance (*gravitas*), exuded a natural authority (*auctoritas*), and had the ability to speak his mind freely and forcefully. But Cicero, for all his public praise, admitted to Atticus that he found Brutus' oratory rather lacklustre and dispassionate; later readers of his texts seem to confirm the impression, although we must bear in mind the possibility that Brutus could have been more impressive in person than he was in his publications.

We can only access Brutus' philosophical treatises and literary pamphlets through fragments and titles, yet these are enough to see how Brutus established a reputation for himself as a man of moral fibre. They fall broadly into three main groups: one, the speeches and pamphlets he composed in the 50s BC which celebrated ideas such as liberty over slavery, as well as justifiable homicide; two, the more private, inward-looking treatises composed after he had made his reconciliation with Caesar; and three, the speeches and edicts he published in his final fight for freedom against the rise of Caesarism, especially as personified by Antony. Consequently, we might be tempted to draw a verdict on the conduct of his life based on his intellectual rigour and ethical interests. His family mattered to him, especially the women in his life: his mother Servilia, his sisters, and later his wife Porcia. On the other hand, the ease with which he divorced his first wife Claudia and celebrated the death of her uncle Clodius reminds us that political considerations still counted for a lot with Brutus.

The eulogy he composed in memory of Cato was also formative on how Brutus was judged. Again, however, it worked both to his credit and detriment. Cicero was offended by it because Brutus had not given him due recognition for the exposure and execution of the conspirators who had joined Catiline's alleged coup d'état. Caesar thought it was less well written than the equivalent *Cato* published by Cicero. These points are probably less important than the fact that, by its publication, as well as by his marriage to Cato's daughter, Brutus firmly pitched himself on the side of his uncle, who was already being upheld as a republican martyr. When Brutus later followed Cato's lead in committing suicide rather than facing his enemies and the loss of freedom, the similarity was enough for people to see the younger man as a conscious imitator of his more illustrious relative. This may in part be true of the last year of Brutus' life, when he led a republican revival and gave up his life fighting for his ideals. Yet it masks the point that Brutus had not always agreed with his uncle's way of operating, and had noticeably taken a different life decision after the battle of Pharsalus, from which Brutus was among the first to escape and defect.

In the words and deeds of Brutus after the Ides of March we see a different strand emerge in his personality; or, more appropriately, we should say a return of the fiercely outspoken championing of freedom he had demonstrated in his youth. Up until this point his 'nobility' had rested on his name and hereditary status, as well as the high moral qualities he had put down in writing. In leading the conspiracy against Caesar, however, Brutus added a nobility of purpose; he became famed in his own right. In his own representation of it, he fought for the liberation of Rome, and pursued a policy of peace, national tranquillity and clemency. Yet from a different partisan perspective he was little more than an unscrupulous killer who had propelled his country into a state of civil war. Far from being a Liberator, he showed signs of becoming worse than the man he killed, and it is often seen as entirely ironic that Brutus was among the first men after Caesar to put his own portrait on a Roman coin.

Brutus' letters from this period, and especially his correspondence with Cicero, almost certainly provide the fullest impression of Brutus' multi-faceted personality. Before the assassination of Caesar, and especially in the period after the first civil war at Pharsalus, Cicero's friendship with Brutus had been important to him. Whatever their differences – and there were many – their experiences as ex-Pompeians in a world dominated by Caesar gave them a common bond; their mutual friend Atticus reinforced the strength of that tie; and their literary relationship, expressed in the numerous works they dedicated to each other, had publicly and formally advertised their friendship (*amicitia*). But the assassination – the slaughter of a tyrant – added a new dimension: Brutus and his 'glorious deed' were now central to the survival of the *res publica*. Cicero both marvelled at what Brutus and Cassius had done and despaired at what they failed to accomplish in the days and months that followed.

In this period, Brutus resurfaces first to obtain favours from Cicero, who was effectively directing the republican campaign in Italy, then to ask (and ignore) his advice, and finally to criticise Cicero's policy towards Octavian. By the end of the surviving correspondence, Brutus and Cicero had disagreed on almost every point about how affairs were being conducted in their respective arenas, yet still Brutus managed to impose his will on Cicero, even to the point that the latter went back on his own policy to protect Lepidus' children as a favour to Brutus. Throughout the collection, Brutus appears as having clearly expressed views on the political situation, as possessing an unshakeable sense of confidence in his own rightness, and as fighting for what he believes is the just course of action; at the same time, in his heart he fears he might be moved by the appeals of his enemies, he appears reluctant to inflict penalties, and he hopes to avoid civil war at any cost.

In all, Brutus emerges as a human being possessing some of the most admirable virtues, and a concomitant share of the corresponding vices, of his day. At times, he could seem arrogant, outspoken and rude – or, to put it another way, he was confident, candid and frank. It is easy to view him as demanding and humourless, or more positively as a man of purpose and gravity. He made his money by questionable means, but whereas others indebted themselves to get on the ladder, his wealth enabled him to start his career as an independent operator. We can criticise his side-switching and lack of constancy, or see a shrewd political player. No plain imitator of Cato, he nevertheless championed his connection when it served his purposes to do so. We have seen the extent to which we can push the question of the assassination; whether he betrayed a friend or remained a patriot to his country has been a subject of enduring philosophical interest. Likewise, questions over the justifiability and consequences of political murder are of perennial importance.

To return to the man, however, it is easy to mock his military failures or otherwise appreciate them as a sign of his magnanimity. He had weaknesses and flaws, as well as talents and abilities. We have now flipped his famous coin and seen both sides – and more: more than the image he constructed, and more than the ideals and the cause for which he claimed to fight. From the contemporary sources, Brutus appears more vibrantly as a man than he does anywhere else. But if at the end of this study there are questions that cannot be answered, we should be grateful that we can get so close as to be perplexed by the man of whom Cicero said: 'you have a marvellous reputation for incredible virtues, which though they look disparate are harmonised by your prudence'.[4] The point is expressed with Cicero's usual hyperbole, but the essence is clear: even to those who knew him in life, Brutus was an enigma.

APPENDIX 1: KEY DATES

88 BC	Sulla's first consulship; his march on Rome.
87	Sulla in the east (first war against Mithridates); Marius and Cinna occupy Rome.
86	Marius' seventh consulship and death.
	Domination of Cinna (until 84).
85	? Birth of Brutus to mother (Servilia) and father (the elder Brutus).
84	Sulla returns to Italy.
82	Sulla institutes proscriptions; he is appointed dictator.
81	Sulla's reforms; he abdicates dictatorship.
	Pompey's first triumph (12 March).
80	Sulla's second consulship.
78	Consulship of M. Lepidus.
	Death of Sulla.
	Rise of Lepidus.
77	Pompey receives *imperium* to assist against M. Lepidus and the elder Brutus.
	The elder Brutus put to death on Pompey's orders.
71	Pompey's second triumph.
70	First joint consulship of Pompey and Crassus.
69	? Brutus' *tirocinium fori.*
67	Pompey given extraordinary command against the pirates.
66	Pompey given another extraordinary command against Mithridates.
63	Cicero's consulship; Catilinarian conspiracy and the rise of Cato.
	Caesar elected *pontifex maximus.*
62	Pompey returns to Rome.
	Servilia marries Decimus Junius Silanus.
61	Pompey's third triumph.
59	Consulship of Caesar and Bibulus.
	Coalition between Pompey, Caesar and Crassus (the 'First Triumvirate'); Pompey marries Julia, the daughter of Caesar.
	Vettius affair; Brutus implicated in alleged plot to kill Pompey.
	? Brutus adopted, formally becomes known as Quintus Servilius Caepio Brutus.
	Death of Decimus Junius Silanus; ? affair between Servilia and Caesar starts.
58	Tribunate of Clodius.
	Brutus accompanies Cato to Cyprus.
	Exile of Cicero (recalled in 57).
	Caesar in Gaul (remains until 49).

56	Brutus returns to Rome (possibly in February). Conference of Luca; renewal of coalition between Pompey, Caesar and Crassus.
55	Second joint consulship of Pompey and Crassus.
54	Death of Julia, the daughter of Caesar and wife of Pompey. Brutus' marriage to Claudia, the daughter of Appius Claudius Pulcher. ? Brutus mints coins in his capacity as *triumvir monetalis*.
53	Battle of Carrhae; death of Crassus. Cassius leads survivors of Carrhae to Syria (remains there until 51). Anarchy on the rise at Rome. ? Brutus appointed quaestor; refuses to serve under Caesar in Gaul. Brutus accompanies Appius Claudius to the province of Cilicia.
52	Murder of Clodius by Milo (18 January); sole consulship of Pompey. Brutus writes pamphlets *On the Dictatorship of Pompey* and *For T. Annius Milo*. Pompey's marriage to Cornelia.
51–50	Descent into civil war; attempts to remove Caesar from the command of Gaul. Cicero governor of Cilicia; discovers and disapproves of Brutus' money-lending activities in the province. ? Brutus elected *pontifex*.
50	Attempts to supersede Caesar continue in the Senate. Brutus defends Appius Claudius on charges of *ambitus* (electoral bribery) and *maiestas* (treason). The consul C. Marcellus entrusts the defence of the *res publica* to Pompey.
49	The Senate pass an emergency decree (7 January) prompting Caesar to march his army to Rome. Pompey and the republicans first evacuate Rome and later leave Italy (17 March). Caesar assumes the dictatorship. Brutus serves as a legate to Publius Sestius in Cilicia before joining Pompey at Dyrrachium in late 49 or early 48.
48	Death of Appius Claudius; Brutus composes a eulogy for him. Battle of Pharsalus and defeat of the republicans (9 August). Brutus defects immediately and is welcomed by Caesar. Pompey murdered in Egypt.
47	Brutus in Tarsus, Cilicia; he speaks on behalf of King Deiotarus at Nicaea (August); he works for reconciliation after the civil war. Caesar returns to Rome (September); then leaves to fight the Pompeians regrouped in Africa.
47–46	Brutus publishes works *On Virtue, On Duties* and *On Endurance.*
46	Brutus appointed to govern Cisalpine Gaul. Caesar defeats the republicans at Thapsus (6 April); Cato commits suicide at Utica. Cicero composes a eulogy for Cato.
45	Brutus composes a eulogy for Cato; Caesar and Hirtius write *Anti-Catos.* Pompeians defeated at Munda in Spain (17 March). Brutus returns to Rome (end of March); he divorces Claudia and marries Porcia, the daughter of Cato and widow of Bibulus. Caesar returns from Spain.
44*	Brutus assumes office as urban praetor. Caesar accepts title of *dictator perpetuo* ('dictator for life'). Festival of the *Lupercalia* (15 February). Ides of March: assassination of Caesar. Funeral of Caesar; Octavian named as heir and arrives in Italy. Antony takes control but restores an uneasy peace. Brutus and Cassius leave Rome on or before 13 April; Brutus leaves Italy late August; Cassius follows later.

	Antony makes an allocation of provinces; leaves Rome for Cisalpine Gaul (28–29 November).
	Rivalry between Antony and Octavian.
	Cicero delivers his *Third Philippic* to the Senate (20 December) and prepares ground to wage a war against Antony.
43*	Cicero continues to call for war; forms a new republican alliance including Octavian against Antony; delivers and publishes the rest of his *Philippics*.
	Brutus and Cassius re-emerge, each at the head of an army, in Macedonia and Syria respectively.
	Antony besieges Decimus Brutus at Mutina in two battles (14/15 and 21 April).
	Antony, Dolabella and supporters are declared *hostes* (27 April).
	Antony defeated and retreats but soon regains strength; Lepidus defects to his cause, as do other provincial governors.
	Octavian marches on Rome and demands consulship; elected consul (19 August).
	Lex Pedia passed to try assassins; Brutus and Cassius convicted in absence (late August–September).
	Lex Titia formalises the 'Second Triumvirate' – an alliance between Antony, Octavian and Lepidus (27 November).
	Proscriptions initiated.
42*	Brutus and Cassius prepare for war in the east.
	Lepidus consul in Rome.
	Antony and Octavian raise troops and sail across the Adriatic.
	Two battles fought at Philippi (3 and 23 October); deaths of Brutus and Cassius.

* These years are treated to a much more detailed breakdown in Appendix 2.

APPENDIX 2: AFTER THE ASSASSINATION – CHRONOLOGY AND SOURCES

1. Approximate Sequence of Events (March–August 44 BC)

Panic spreads after the assassination of Caesar but, with the cooperation of Antony, the Liberators at first manage to continue in their posts as praetors. For as long as all sides stick to the terms of the amnesty agreement, there is some level of stability. But as pressure mounts upon Antony to avenge Caesar's murder, life at Rome becomes impossible for the Liberators. The arrival of Octavian exacerbates the situation further and cracks begin to appear in the fragile foundations of the amnesty agreement. Antony arranges for Brutus and Cassius to leave Rome but his offer only insults them. After a bitter and public exchange of edicts, Brutus finally leaves Italy in August; Cassius follows him in either September or October.

15–16 March	Mass exodus from Senate meeting; Antony, whom the assassins had agreed to spare, flees from the scene (Cic. *Phil.* 2.88). Brutus possibly attempts but fails to give a speech either to the Senate (Plut. *Caes.* 67) or to the people (Cass. Dio 44.21).
	Liberators gather on Capitoline Hill, having picked up a retinue of supporters along the way (App. *B. Civ.* 2.119; Cass. Dio 44.14).
	Cicero urges conspirators to call a Senate meeting on Capitoline Hill but they refuse (Cic. *Att.* 14.10.1 = SB 364); instead they send an emissary to Antony (Cic. *Phil.* 2.89); Lepidus occupies the Forum (Cass. Dio 44.22).
17 March*	Bacchus' Day (festival of *Liberalia*): the Senate meet at the temple of Tellus.
(* Plut. *Brut.* 19 wrongly dates meeting to 16 March.)	An amnesty is agreed for the assassins; Caesar's acts are validated and title of 'dictator' abolished (Cic. *Phil.* 1.4.31, 2.89; Cic. *Att.* 14.11.1 = SB 365, 14.2 = SB 366; Cass. Dio 44.22–34).
	Contio held by Brutus on Capitoline Hill (Cic. *Att.* 15.1A2 = SB 378); Atticus warns against state funeral for Caesar (Cic. *Att.* 14.14.3 = SB 368).
	Brutus dines with Lepidus and Cassius with Antony (Cass. Dio 44.34.7).

c. 20 March	Caesar's funeral; will opened; riots, raids and attacks on houses of conspirators (Cic. *Phil.* 2.91; Cic. *Att.* 14.10.1 = SB 364; App. *B. Civ.* 2.143; Cass. Dio 44.35–50; Suet. *Iul.* 83.5; Plut. *Brut.* 20).
Late March–mid-April	Confirmation of provinces assigned to Decimus Brutus (Cisalpine Gaul), Trebonius (Asia) and Tillius Cimber (Bithynia) (App. *B. Civ.* 3.2.4–5, 6.18; Cic. *Att.* 14.10.1 = SB 364, 14.3.2 = SB 367); Appian (*B. Civ.* 3.2) is probably wrong to suggest Brutus and Cassius were due to get Macedonia and Syria.
	Caesar's heir and adopted son, Octavian, arrives in Italy in early April; he seems to have gone first to Rome (Cic. *Att.* 14.5.3 = SB 359; Nic. Dam. 108; Vell. Pat. 2.59.5–6; Plut. *Brut.* 22.3; App. *B. Civ.* 3.9–12, 28); cf. Toher (2004).
	Octavian arrives at Naples on 18 April (Cic. *Att.* 14.10.3 = SB 364). He visits Cicero at Puteoli (Cic. *Att.* 14.11.2 = SB 365, 14.12.2 = SB 366).
April–May	Brutus and Cassius remain outside Rome. They write to Antony with concerns over his proposed legislation on 1 June (Cic. *Fam.* 11.2.1 = SB 329).
5 June	Senate passes a decree giving Brutus and Cassius grain commission in Asia and Sicily respectively (Cic. *Att.* 15.9.1 = SB 387; cf. 15.5.2 = SB 383 and 15.11.1 = SB 389).
8 June	Conference of Brutus' family and friends is held at Antium to discuss whether he and Cassius should accept grain commission (Cic. *Att.* 15.11 = SB 389).
25 June	Brutus leaves Antium, possibly under the guise of preparing for grain commission (Cic. *Att.* 15.24 = SB 401; cf. 15.11.2 = SB 389).
6–13 July	Games of Brutus (*ludi Apollinares*) are held on his behalf by Gaius Antonius (Cic. *Att.* 16.1.1 = SB 409, 16.2.3 = SB 412, 16.14.1= SB 425); mixed reactions towards Brutus (App. *B. Civ.* 3.23).
	Cicero meets Brutus at Nesis; while there, they receive a letter from Sextus Pompeius. Brutus also seems better prepared for a journey than Cicero had thought but he is in no hurry (Cic. *Att.* 14.4 = SB 358).
Late July–early August	[1 August?] Assignment of Crete and Cyrene to Brutus and Cassius respectively (Cic. *Phil.* 2.31).
	Brutus and Cassius issue an edict; they prepare to leave Italy (Cic. *Att.* 16.7.1 = SB 415). Antony issues a hostile reply, to which they send a counter-reply on 4 August (Cic. *Fam.* 11.3 = SB 336).

2. Brutus in the East (August 44–July 43 BC)

During this period, Brutus leaves Rome, re-emerges at the head of an army and is given command over Macedonia, Illyricum and Greece. He corresponds with Cicero and we can follow him as he heads east from Dyrrachium towards Asia in pursuit of Dolabella. The period is unified by his focus on building a stronghold in the east but is interrupted by the change of events at Rome when Octavian, as consul, has the lex Pedia *passed. From this point on, the programme of revenge against the assassins has started and Brutus' military preparations step up pace.*

44 BC

17 August	Cicero meets Brutus at Velia (Cic. *Att.* 16.7.1 = SB 415); some time afterwards, towards the end of August, Brutus leaves Italy (Cic. *Phil.* 10.8).
September–November	Brutus arrives in Greece, where he and Cassius (possibly in the latter's absence) are granted exceptional honours (Plut. *Brut.* 24.1; Cass. Dio 47.20.4). Brutus attends lectures at Athens and recruits young men (Plut. *Brut.* 24.3); meanwhile he sends Herostratus to initiate discussions with Hortensius over the future handover of Macedonia (Plut. *Brut.* 24.1–2; cf. Vell. Pat. 2.62.3–4, App. *B. Civ.* 3.24 and Cass. Dio 47.21.1).
28 November	Antony allocates praetorian provinces, awarding Macedonia to his brother Gaius (Cic. *Phil.* 3.24–6, 5.23–4, 13.19; App. *B. Civ.* 3.46); consequently, Brutus starts to plan his march to Macedonia (see discussion in Ch. 6).
December–January 43	Brutus heads north to Thessaly, gathers soldiers and arms, and marches to Macedonia (Cic. *Phil.* 10.13; Plut. *Brut.* 25.1–4; Cass. Dio 47.21.3–7). Marcus Appuleius (Cic. *Brut.* 1.7.2; Cic. *Phil.* 10.24, 13.32) and Antistius Vetus (Cic. *Ad. Brut.* 2.3.5 = SB 2, 1.11.1 = SB 16; Plut. *Brut.* 25.1) transfer substantial amounts of money to Brutus, following the cessation of their quaestorships (cf. Vell. Pat. 2.62.3; App. *B. Civ.* 4.75).

43 BC

January	Brutus enters Macedonia and prevents Gaius Antonius from taking control; he takes Gaius hostage (Cic. *Phil.* 10.13, 11.26; [Livy], *Per.* 118; Plut. *Brut.* 25.3, 26.3–5; App. *B. Civ.* 3.24, 3.79, 4.75; Cass. Dio 47.21.1–7; Vell. Pat. 2.62.3, 69.3–4).
Early–mid-February	Brutus' letter stating he has taken over Macedonia from Gaius Antonius, as well as the Illyrian legions from Publius Vatinius, reaches Rome; Cicero delivers his *Tenth Philippic* and proposes an extraordinary command for Brutus (Cic. *Phil.* 10.25–6).
1 April	Brutus' letter to the Senate reaches Rome (Cic. *Brut.* 2.5.1 = SB 5); letter from Gaius Antonius ('proconsul') is also read out, much to the dismay of Brutus' friends, who declare Brutus' letter a forgery (2.5.3–4 = SB 5) because it is too lenient in tone. Brutus writes to Cicero from Dyrrachium (Cic. *Brut.* 2.3 = SB 2) commenting on the death of Trebonius (2.3.1), his own capture of Gaius Antonius (2.3.2), and the successes of Cassius in Syria (2.3.3). He approves of Cicero's *Philippics* (2.3.4) and ends with a request for money and men (2.3.5), before commending the performance of the younger Marcus Cicero, who is with him (2.3.6).
c. 7 May	Brutus writes to Cicero, again from Dyrrachium (Cic. *Brut.* 1.4 = SB 10); he has not yet heard about the battle of Mutina on 21 April and the deaths of Hirtius and Pansa (cf. 1.3a = SB 7); nor does he know that Antony and his followers have been pronounced *hostes* (ibid.). He disagrees with Cicero's hardened attitude towards Gaius Antonius (1.4.2) and criticises his policy towards Octavian (1.4.3).

Early May	Until now, Brutus has stayed in Apollonia and Dyrrachium but changes his plans upon hearing of Antony's escape and Decimus' breaking free from Mutina (Cic. *Brut.* 1.2.2 = SB 14). When he next writes to Cicero (see below), he is on the move, in pursuit of Dolabella's cohorts. Meanwhile, Brutus has reported Gaius Antonius' attempts to stir up a mutiny (1.2.3).
15 and 19 May	Brutus writes to Cicero twice from his camp in Candavia (Cic. *Brut.* 1.4a = SB 10, 6 = SB 12) with a new tone of urgency. He now reprimands Cicero for honouring Octavian excessively and says he will hold him to blame if anything goes wrong (1.4a.1–3). Having expressed his fear at the rumour that Octavian is seeking the consulship (1.4a.3), he alludes to the (false) report that Cicero has been elected consul (1.4a.4). Brutus has sent the younger Cicero ahead to Macedonia with a force of cavalry (1.4a.4); he tells the elder Cicero that he will next meet the younger Cicero at Heraclea (1.6.2).
29 May	Brutus' brother-in-law, Lepidus, joins Antony (Cic. *Fam.* 10.23.2 = SB 414); the next day Lepidus writes a letter of apology to the Senate (Cic. *Fam.* 10.35 = SB 408; cf. *Ad Brut.* 1.13.1 = SB 20). In later letters, Brutus expresses concern over the fate of Lepidus' (and his sister's) children and asks for Cicero's support in protecting them. At first reluctant to help, Cicero eventually pleads the children's cause in the Senate (Cic. *Ad Brut.* 1.12.1–2 = SB 21, 1.15.11–12 = SB 23). Spinther writes to Cicero to report that he has recently seen Brutus in Macedonia and his entry into Asia has been delayed; Cassius is expected to arrive to deal with Dolabella soon (Cic. *Fam.* 12.14 = SB 405).
Mid-June	Having previously lent support to Brutus' plan to pursue Dolabella (Cic. *Ad Brut.* 1.2.1–2 = SB 14), Cicero starts urging Brutus to return to Italy (Cic. *Ad Brut.* 1.10.1, 4–5 = SB 17); his plea becomes more insistent in later letters (Cic. *Ad Brut.* 1.9.3 = SB 18, 1.12.2 = SB 21, 1.14.2 = SB 22, 1.15.12 = SB 23).
Mid-to-late June	Brutus' wife Porcia dies (Cic. *Ad Brut.* 1.9.1 = SB 18). Cassius' campaign against Dolabella has meanwhile begun (Cic. *Fam.* 12.13 = SB 419).
25 July	Servilia hosts a second meeting to which Cicero is invited (Cic. *Ad Brut.* 1.18.2 = SB 24), this time to discuss whether Brutus should return to Italy.
27 July	Cicero's last extant letter to Brutus (Cic. *Brut.* 1.18 = SB 24); he expresses his hope that he might still be able to control Octavian (1.18.3) in the course of reviewing everything that has gone wrong in the war to date (1.18.2–5).
July–August	Brutus makes his first journey to Asia (?) ([Brut.] *Ep. Gr.* 1–2, 7–10, 51–8, 61–2). Cassius defeats Dolabella in Syria; starts to move against Egypt ([Livy], *Per.* 121; App. *B. Civ.* 4.57–64; Cass. Dio 47.30). Octavian marches his army from Cisalpine Gaul to Rome, arriving some date after 27 July (Cass. Dio 46.43.5–45; App. *B. Civ.* 3.89–94).

19 August	Octavian elected consul after marching on Rome (Tac. *Ann.* 1.9; Cass. Dio 46.45.3; App. *B. Civ.* 3.94). Shortly afterwards, *lex Pedia* is passed, under which Brutus and the assassins are incriminated (Vell. Pat. 2.69.5; Plut. *Brut.* 27.4–5; Suet. *Aug.* 10.1; App. *B. Civ.* 4.27; Cass. Dio 46.48, 47.12.2).

3. War in the East (October 43–October 42 BC) – Overview

It is hard to recover details for this period with any precision, not least because our sources for Brutus' activities are mixed and sometimes conflicting. In Section 4, below, I have attempted to separate out the independent accounts. In what follows I have listed the key events and sources for the entire period.

43 BC

October (?)	Death of Decimus (App. *B. Civ.* 3.97–8; Cass. Dio 46.5.3; cf. Plut. *Brut.* 28.1).
27 November	*Lex Titia* formalises the agreement under which Antony, Octavian and Lepidus enter office as triumvirs (App. *B. Civ.* 4.2–3); on the promulgation of this law, see Lintott (1999a), 40; Lintott (2008), 445.
7 December	Death of Cicero (Tac. *Dial.* 17; Sen. *Suas.* 6.17; Plut. *Cic.* 47–9, *Ant.* 20.3–4; App. *B.Civ.* 4.19–20; Cass. Dio 47.8.3–4; [Livy.], *Per.* 120; [Ps.-Asc.] *Vir. Ill.* 81.6).
Late December–early January 42	Brutus has Gaius Antonius executed (Plut. *Brut.* 28.1; Plut. *Ant.* 22.6; Cass. Dio 47.24.4); fearing a revolt, he rushes back to Macedonia, passing through Thrace and taking territories (Cass. Dio 47.25.1); his troops hail him as *imperator*. Brutus crosses into Asia for a second time (Plut. *Brut.* 28.3; Cass. Dio 47.25.1–2; cf. [Livy], *Per.* 121–2; he equips a fleet in Bithynia and Cyzicus and settles the affairs of the cities (cf. [Brut.] *Ep. Gr.* 33, 35–40, 41–2, 47–50, 59–68). Cassius agrees not to go to Egypt as planned, but meets Brutus at Smyrna to co-ordinate strategy (Plut. *Brut.* 28.3–6, 30.1; App. *B. Civ.* 4.63–5; Cass. Dio 47.32.1–3; [Livy], *Per.* 122). Brutus circulates coins (Cass. Dio 47.25.3); they bear his image, title, Libertas and Apollo (as well as other religious symbols), and celebrate Ides of March and his Thracian victory: see *RRC* 501/8; Laignoux (2012); and Hollstein (1994).

42 BC

January–April	Brutus campaigns successfully in Lycia, laying siege to city of Xanthus (Vell. Pat. 2.69.6; App. *B. Civ.* 4.76–80; Cass. Dio 47.34.1–6; Plut. *Brut.* 30.3–31.7; [Brut.] *Ep. Gr.* 11–12 [Rhodians], 43–4 [Myrians]). Cassius occupies Rhodes (Vell. Pat. 2.69.6; Val. Max. 1.5.8; Plut. *Brut.* 30.3, 32.4; App. *B. Civ.* 4.65–74; Cass. Dio 47.33.1–4; Oros. 6.18.13; cf. *RRC* 505/1–3). After Xanthus, Brutus secures loyalty of other Lycian cities (Plut. *Brut.* 32.1–4; App. *B. Civ.* 4.81–2; Cass. Dio 47.34.4–6; [Brut.] *Ep. Gr.* 11, 25).

Mid-July	Brutus and Cassius meet again, at Sardis; they are hailed *imperatores* by their troops; they quarrel but are reconciled and hasten into Macedonia (Plut. *Brut.* 34.1–8; Cass. Dio 47.35.1).
August–September	Brutus and Cassius march towards Philippi; on the way, they engage in a preliminary skirmish with an advance troop, led by Norbanus, but the Liberators drive the enemy back into Macedonia and occupy best positions at Philippi. (Plut. *Brut.* 38.1; App. *B. Civ.* 4.87, 106; Cass. Dio 47.35–6).
	Antony and Octavian cross the Adriatic and arrive at Philippi. Octavian encamps against Brutus; Antony faces Cassius (Plut. *Brut.* 38.4; App. *B. Civ.* 107; Cass. Dio 47.36–7).
c. 3 October	First battle of Philippi; Brutus defeats Octavian's side but Antony's side overpowers that of Cassius; Cassius takes his own life (Plut. *Brut.* 38.5–44.2; App. *B. Civ.* 109–15; Cass. Dio 47.38–45).
23 October	Second battle of Philippi (Plut. *Brut.* 44.3–53; App. *B. Civ.* 114–38; Cass. Dio 47.47–9); Brutus is defeated and takes his own life (Plut. *Brut.* 50–4; App. *B. Civ.* 4.129–38; Cass. Dio 47.49).

4. Detailed Breakdown of Main Sources for January–October 42 BC

4a. The Siege of Xanthus

Plutarch 30.6–31.7	**Appian 4.76–80**	**Dio 47.34.1–3**
30.6: Brutus lays siege to Xanthus.	4.76: Facing opposition from Xanthians, Brutus and his men trap them within their own walls and lay siege to city.	47.34.1: Brutus besieges Xanthus.
30.7: Xanthians are foiled in an attempt to escape city by swimming underwater across a river.		
30.8: Xanthians make a sally by night and set fire to siege engines; caught by the Romans, they are driven back to their walls. Flames spread to city; Brutus orders men to help put out fire.	4.77: Brutus tricks Xanthians, who make a night expedition and set fire to siege engines, thinking the Romans have withdrawn. Upon an agreed signal, the Romans attack. City guards shut the gates, sacrificing men trapped outside city.	47.34.2: Xanthians make a sally, hurling fire onto Brutus' siege engines, and throwing arrows and javelins. Brutus' troops push back and make an unexpected counter-attack.
	4.78: The remaining Xanthians make a second sally; 2,000 Romans burst into city, but many are killed by falling portcullis; others take refuge in temple and are trapped within city walls.	47.34.3: Romans push the Xanthians back within the walls and break into city alongside them.

31.1: Lycians 'possessed by a dreadful and indescribable impulse to madness'.		
31.2: Xanthians attack enemy but in process add fuel to the flames tearing through the city.		
31.3: Distressed, Brutus is eager to help; he calls on Xanthians to save their city.		
	4.78: Brutus is anxious for the safety of his men.	
	4.79: With the help of local allies, Brutus' men manage to open city gates and release portcullis; frenzied attack on Xanthus.	
31.4: Xanthians kill their families and hurl themselves onto lit pyres or from the walls in mass suicide.	4.80: After the capture of the city, Xanthians start killing their loved ones.	47.34.3: When the Romans attack, Xanthians set fire to city and commit mass suicide.
31.5: One woman is seen hanging with her dead baby still attached to her body.		
31.6: Brutus bursts into tears and offers prizes to help save Lycians.	4.80: Brutus, mistaking cries of suicidal Xanthians for Roman pillaging, orders his army to stop. He takes pity on Xanthians and offers terms, but remaining citizens build funeral pyres onto which they throw themselves.	
31.7: 150 men 'did not escape such preservation'.	4.80: Brutus only manages to capture 150 male citizens, some freewomen and slaves.	

4b. *After Xanthus: Brutus Pacifies the Rest of Lycia*

Plutarch 32.1–4	**Appian 4.81–2**	**Dio 47.34.4–6**
32.1: Hesitant to attack Patara, Brutus releases some prisoners of war.	4.81: Brutus surrounds Patara and orders inhabitants to obey him in everything, or meet the same fate as Xanthians. He gives them a day to think.	47.34.4: Brutus invites Patarans to conclude an alliance but they refuse to obey; Brutus tries to negotiate by sending them some captive Xanthians to whom the Patarans are related.

32.2: These prisoners – the wives and daughters of prominent men – praise Brutus as a man of 'the greatest moderation' and 'most just'. They persuade Patarans to surrender the city.	4.81: After Brutus moves his troops forward, Patarans decide to surrender city.	47.34.5–6: With Patarans still resilient, Brutus stages an auction of other prominent Xanthians to force a surrender. When that does not work, he releases most of his captives anyway; Patarans surrender, deeming Brutus a virtuous man (characterised by *arete*).
33.3: The rest of the Lycians then come and surrender.		
33.4: Brutus' goodness and kindness exceed their hopes.		
33.4: Whereas Cassius compelled Rhodians to hand over all their gold and silver, and fined city an additional 500 talents, Brutus only exacts 150 talents from Lycians, and inflicts no further punishments or injury.	4.81: Brutus neither kills nor banishes anybody. He gives orders for all the city's silver and gold to be delivered to him, along with each citizen's private holdings.	47.34.6: Brutus only imposes a fine.
	4.81: One slave testifies that his master has hidden gold; Brutus crucifies slave and lets master keep his gold unpunished.	
	4.82: Working for Brutus, Lentulus collects money from inhabitants of Myra.	47.34.6: People of Myra surrender; in a short time, Brutus secures control of other districts.
	4.82: A Lycian confederation sends ambassadors to Brutus; they offer to form a military league.	
	4.82 Brutus imposes taxes; restores free Xanthians to their city; orders Lycian fleet to sail to Abydus to meet Cassius, coming from Ionia.	

4c. From Sardis to the End of the First Battle of Philippi

Omens, prophecies and religious observances in italics

Plutarch 34–42	Appian 4.82–138	Dio 47.35–49

34.1–8: Brutus and Cassius meet at Sardis; they quarrel and make up.		47.35.1: Brutus and Cassius meet in Asia; they are reconciled and hasten into Macedonia.
35.1–6: Brutus reminds Cassius of need for justice; 'such were the principles of Brutus'.		
36.1–37.6: *Brutus sees apparition.*	[cf. App. *B. Civ.* 4.134.]	
37.7: *Omen of two eagles.*	[cf. App. *B. Civ.* 4.101.]	
38.1: Brutus and Cassius begin march through Macedonia.	4.87: Octavian and Antony send advance force under Norbanus and Decidius to intercept Brutus and Cassius on road to Philippi, who take the long route to avoid them. [cf. App. *B. Civ.* 4.101–104.]	47.35.2–5: Brutus and Cassius find that Norbanus and Decidius have occupied whole country as far as Mount Pangaeum and were encamped near Philippi ('This city is situated near Pangaeum and Symbolon'). Forced to take longer route, Brutus and Cassius nevertheless arrive at Philippi. Norbanus and Saxa retreat.
[cf. Plut. *Brut.* 38.2–3, for mention of Symbolon.]		
	4.88: Brutus and Cassius review troops; summary of republican troops.	
[cf. Plut. *Brut.* 39.1–2.]		[cf. Cass. Dio 47.38.4 and 47.40.7–8.]
	4.89: Brutus and Cassius perform *a lustration* for army and pay soldiers.	
	4.90–100: Cassius addresses troops.	
	4.101–104: With army in good spirits, Brutus and Cassius dismiss assembly; *omen of two eagles*; detailed account of how Brutus and Cassius bypass Norbanus and Decidius.	

	4.105: By 'astonishing act of audacity' Brutus and Cassius advance to Philippi.	
	4.106: Brutus and Cassius encamp on two hills, 8 stades (1 mile) apart and 18 stades (just over 2 miles) from Philippi.	47.35.6: Description of Brutus' and Cassius' conjoined camps.
38.2–3: Brutus and Cassius encounter Norbanus near Symbolon and compel him to withdraw and abandon his positions. They would have captured his forces had they not heard Antony was approaching.	4.106: Brutus and Cassius do not advance against the retreating army of Norbanus because they hear Antony is approaching.	47.36.1–2: Brutus and Cassius drive others out of Symbolon; Norbanus and Saxa choose not to offer battle; having retreated west they send urgent summons to Antony and Octavian.
38.3: Octavian delayed by sickness.	4.106: Octavian left behind at Epidamnus (Dyrrachium) as he is ill.	47.36.3–37.2: Flashback and digression to cover journey of Antony and Octavian from Rome; Antony hastens ahead to Philippi leaving Octavian behind ill.
	4.106: Brutus and Cassius build fortification from camp to camp, with gate in the middle; a river (Ganga/Gangites) flows alongside the fortification; behind it is the sea from where they can access their reserves on the island of Thasos; their triremes are anchored at Neapolis, 70 stades (just under 9 miles) away.	[cf. Cass. Dio 47.35.6, for description of camp.]
	4.107: Narrative follows Antony, who pitches his camp 'with great audacity' only 8 stades (1 mile) from Brutus and Cassius; comparison of respective camps.	
38.4: Ten days later Octavian arrives.	4.108: Cavalry skirmishes and missile throwing between camps; Octavian arrives; triumviral army prepares for battle; comparison of forces on each side.	47.37.3–5: Suspicious of Antony, Octavian hastens to Philippi, although still ill; some sallies and counter-sallies between opposing sides.

[cf. Plut. *Brut.* 39.8 for preliminary skirmishes.]		
	4.108: Nothing done for several days.	47.37.5: No battle for some time, despite Octavian and Antony wanting to engage in swift combat.
	4.108: Octavian and Antony cut off from supplies.	47.37.6: Octavian and Antony have stronger forces but are not as well supplied (their fleet is fighting Sextus Pompeius and they are not 'masters of the sea').
		47.38.1: Octavian and Antony worried that Sextus Pompeius might take Italy in their absence and then come to Macedonia.
[cf. Plut. *Brut.* 39.1–6 where Brutus and Cassius delay war because of omens.]	4.109: Brutus and Cassius delay war.	47.38.2–6: Brutus and Cassius 'being friends of the people and because they were contending with citizens, they took thought for the latter's interests no less than those of their own men, and desired to afford safety [*soteria*] and freedom [*eleutheria*] to all'. Thus they delay war.
[cf. Plut. *Brut.* 41.1 for Antony's work on marshes.]	4.109: For ten days, Antony's men secretly build causeway through marsh to reach Cassius' camp; Antony sends column of troops in by night. When Cassius realises, he builds a cross-fortification.	
	4.110: Antony notices Cassius' cross-fortification at midday and leads his army against fortifications.	
[cf. Plut. *Brut.* 39.7–9 where Cassius wants to delay; Brutus wants to hasten attack.]	4.110: Brutus' soldiers see attack and charge unbidden.	47.38.2–5: Troops of Brutus and Cassius annoyed that, after *lustration*, they have not engaged in battle yet; Brutus and Cassius reluctantly agree to join battle.

38.5: 'Roman forces of such size had never before encountered one another.'	[cf. App. *B. Civ.* 4.137–8.]	47.39.1–5: Digression on scope and size of battle and its contribution to fall of the *res publica.*
38.5–7: Splendour of Brutus' troops: 'most of their armour was covered with silver and gold, with which Brutus had lavishly supplied them.'		
39.1–6: Each side *performs lustration* and pays troops (Brutus and Cassius pay their men lavishly). *It is taken as a bad sign when lictor presents Cassius with an upside-down wreath as well as, before this, the sign of victory. Carrion birds hover over camp; swarms of bees force soothsayers to shut area for fear of generating superstition.*	[cf. App. *B. Civ.* 4. 134.]	47.40.1–8: Portents at Rome; portents at Macedonia include: *bees at Cassius' camp; during lustration of the camp, someone set the garland on Cassius' head the wrong way; a boy fell down while carrying sign of victory; omen of vultures over republicans' heads.*
[cf. Plut. *Brut.* 41.7 for *dream of the physician.*]		47.41.1–4: No bad omens for Octavian or Antony; *dream of Octavian's physician in which Minerva commands him to lead Octavian out of camp and into the line of battle.*
39.7–8: Cassius wants to delay war; Brutus wants to hasten the attack (to restore liberty sooner; to relieve mankind of expenses of war; because his horsemen had been successful in preliminary skirmishes).		47.42.1–2: Both sides arm themselves and draw up in battle order.
39.9–10: Council of war: majority side with Brutus' proposal to engage in battle the next day.		
40.1–4: Republicans have supper the night before battle; Cassius expresses anxiety.		
40.5–12: Signal for battle (a scarlet tunic) displayed; Brutus and Cassius discuss plans and battle strategy; Brutus asks for command of right wing, which he leads out with Messalla.		47.42.3–5: Battle speeches on both sides: Brutus' men speak of freedom (*eleutheria*) and democracy (*demokratia*); freedom from tyrants and

		masters; benefits of equality and excesses of monarchy: 'giving instances of the working of each system separately they besought them to strive for one and avoid the other'.
		On the other side: Antony and Octavian urge their army to exact vengeance upon the assassins and talk of rewards (property, hegemony and cash).
[cf. Plut. *Brut.* 41.4 for watchword.]		47.43.1–3: Brutus' watchword is 'freedom' (*eleutheria*); the other side had a watchword too.
	4.110: Battle has begun; Brutus' soldiers also charge Octavian's army and storm their camp (although Octavian himself is absent; cf. Dio 41.3–4).	47.43.2–3: They join battle simultaneously.
41.1: Soldiers of Antony labour to create a passage through marshes.	4.111: Antony continues his charge and breaks through cross-fortification to reach Cassius' camp.	47.44.1–45.1: General battle description.
41.2–3: Octavian's forces surprised by Brutus' charge.	[cf. App. *B. Civ.* 4.110 for the lack of defence made by Octavian's men, which is suggestive of surprise attack.]	
41.4–6: Brutus carries tickets with watchword to his officers, and rallies troops; only some of his men hear watchword, the rest charge without waiting. Some disorder throws the legions out of line but some (including Messalla's men) breach Octavian's lines and storm camp.		
41.7–8: Octavian absent because of *dream of his physician*; his life is saved but many of his men are killed (including 2,000 Spartan auxiliaries).		[cf. Cass. Dio 47.41.1–3 for *dream*.]

42.1–4: The rest of Brutus' men cut three of Octavian's legions to pieces; some counter-fighting but in the end Brutus is entirely victorious, as Cassius is completely defeated.	4.112: Antony's men easily take camp and Cassius' men scatter; Brutus defeats Octavian's left wing; Antony defeats Cassius. Cassius' side lose 8,000; Octavian's double that.	47.45.2–3: Brutus forces Octavian to yield ground; Cassius defeated by Antony. The result practically the same for each, because they have been partly defeated and partly victorious.
[On the numbers, see Plut. *Brut.* 45.1: 8,000 dead among Cassius' side and double that on Octavian's.]		
42.5: 'One thing alone brought ruin to their cause – Cassius thought Brutus dead.'	4.113: Cassius hastens up hill to Philippi but dust of battle prevents him from seeing properly.	47.45.4: Troops scatter and this, combined with dust of battle, make it difficult to know the outcome.
		47.46.2–3: Octavian's *dream* seems confirmed.
42.6–8: Brutus, surprised not to see Cassius' tent still towering above others, or any other tents in camp, goes to assist Cassius.		
43.1–9: Death of Cassius: having withdrawn to a plain, from where he cannot see much of battle, he mistakes troop of Brutus' horsemen for enemies. Thinking them in pursuit of him, he sends centurion Titinius to reconnoitre. When Titinius is delayed, Cassius thinks he has been captured by enemy. At which point he offers his neck to Pindarus. (When Titinius later returns, blaming himself for his slowness, he kills himself.)	4.113: Death of Cassius: believing Brutus has been defeated, Cassius has Pindarus kill him; also gives alternative version (centurion Titinius takes too long to report information; centurion also kills himself).	47.46.3–5: Death of Cassius: having escaped to 'a different spot', he thinks, one, that Brutus has been defeated, and two, that a party of victors is coming in pursuit of him. Having sent centurion to find out what is happening, Cassius orders Pindarus to kill him when centurion doesn't return. (Centurion later kills himself.)
44.1–2: Brutus hears of Cassius' death when already near his camp. He mourns 'last of the Romans' and has Cassius' body sent to Thasos for burial.	4.115: Brutus mourns 'last of the Romans' and has Cassius secretly buried.	47.47.1: Brutus sends Cassius' body to Thasos.

4d. The Second Battle of Philippi (3–23 October 42 BC)

Omens, prophecies and religious observances in italics

Plutarch 44.3–53	**Appian 4.114–38**	**Dio 47.47.2–47.49**
44.3: Brutus takes thought for Cassius' soldiers, promises them 2,000 drachmas.	4.114: Brutus puts Cassius' camp in order.	47.47.2: Brutus wins over Cassius' men with gift of money; he establishes camp in Cassius' quarters.
44.4: Brutus wins confidence of troops, who hail him as only commander of the four not defeated in battle.		
44.5–6: Brutus' victory would have been complete had his men not pillaged the enemy camp.	[cf. App. *B. Civ.* 4.117 where Brutus chides his men for preferring plunder to killing men they had defeated.]	
45.1: The losses on both sides.	[cf. App. *B. Civ.* 4.112; Appian again refers to numerical victory of republicans in Brutus' speech at 4.117.]	
45.2–3: Antony offers battle the next day but Brutus refuses; there were many prisoners of war in Brutus' camp.	4.114: The enemy offer battle but retreat; Brutus mocks them.	
45.4: Of the captives, Brutus puts to death all slaves.		*[cf. Cass. Dio 47.48.3 for prodigies.]*
45.6–9: Denunciation and execution of two captives: Volumnius the actor and Saculio the jester.		
46.1–5: Brutus distributes promised rewards to soldiers and, having chided them for forgetting watchword, offers them cities of Thessalonica and Sparta as plunder if successful in next campaign; similarities and differences between Brutus and Antony and Octavian.	[cf. App. *B. Civ.* 4.117 for rebuke, and 4.118 for rewards to soldiers.]	
47.1–3: General plight of Antony and Octavian; a large force carrying provisions to them from Italy is defeated by Brutus' ships; Antony and Octavian keen to engage in battle quickly again.		

47.4–6: On the same day as Brutus' naval victory, disaster as Brutus proceeds to second battle (yet Brutus ignorant of success at sea).	4.115–16: Simultaneous battles on land and sea. Murcus and Ahenobarbus victorious on republican side.	
47.7–9: Government of Rome no longer a democracy; Octavian destined to be sole ruler. This fact explains Brutus' change of fortune.		
	4.117: Brutus addresses troops; he prefers a strategy of attrition.	47.47.3: Brutus resists battle but conducts night raids to confuse enemy; even diverts a river into their camp.
	4.118: Brutus promises legionaries 1,000 denarii; 'some people believe he promised to let them plunder Thessalonica and Sparta.'	
	4.119–20: Antony's speech to soldiers; rewards to soldiers.	
	4.121–3: Antony keeps offering battle, while Octavian makes moves to cut republicans off from supplies. Antony and Octavian feel pressure from lack of supplies, especially when news of their naval defeat reaches them.	47.47.4–5: Antony and Octavian running short of supplies; force sailing to supply them is destroyed by Murcus. They are eager for decisive engagement.
		47.48.1: As Brutus is unwilling to join battle with them, Antony and Octavian have pamphlets thrown into republican camp urging Brutus' men either to defect or to force battle.
48.1–5: *Second appearance of apparition to Brutus; omen of bees on standard; omen of Ethiopian.*	*[cf. App. B. Civ. 4.128, 134, for omens.]*	
	4.123–4: Brutus continues to resist battle but his army and officers disagree. 'I seem to be conducting my campaign like Pompeius Magnus, no longer giving the orders, but receiving them.'	

49.1–3: Brutus stations forces but delays because suspicious of some of them; Camulatus defects to other side.	4.124–5: Brutus is suspicious that his army will become disaffected and desert him. Forced by these concerns as well as his by his officers, Brutus leads men out to battle.	47.48.2: A contingent of German troops defect to Brutus; but others defect to Antony and Octavian from Brutus' side. These desertions drive Brutus to despair and prompt him to join battle.
[cf. Plut. *Brut.* 45.4–9, for Brutus' treatment of captives.]		47.48.3: Brutus puts to death majority of captives against his will.
	4.125–7: Battle exhortations on both sides. Fate of Rome to be decided.	
[cf. Plut. *Brut.* 48.2–3, above, for omens.]	4.128: *Omen of two eagles.*	47.48.4: *Prodigy of two eagles.*
49.4: Partly from anger, partly from fear of further treachery, Brutus engages in battle.	4.128: Battle commences; generic description of fighting; Octavian's soldiers break enemy line and rout Brutus' men.	
49.5: Wing under Brutus' command is victorious.		
49.6: Other wing is too stretched and gives flight.		
49.7–8: Left exposed, the triumviral army envelops Brutus.	4.129: Antony and Octavian divide up final work: latter mounts a guard on the camp while Antony rampages 'with magnificent energy'. He sends cavalry in pursuit of fugitives.	47.48.4: Brutus defeated.
49.9–10: Son of Cato dies fighting 'among the bravest and noblest young men'.	[cf. App. *B. Civ.* 4.135 on the lives of young men lost.]	

4e. The Death of Brutus

Omens, prophecies and religious observances in italics

50.1–9: Lucilius tries to save Brutus by pretending to be him.	4.129: Some of Antony's men chase after Brutus but they are tricked by Lucilius; Antony consoles his men and later befriends Lucilius.	47.48.5: Victors pursue Brutus' men as they flee.
51.1: Flight of Brutus; surrounded by a few friends; 'O Zeus, do not forget the author of these ills!'	4.130: Brutus escapes into mountains with four legions; 'O Zeus, do not forget the author of these ills!' ('referring of course to Antonius').	

51.2: Brutus recalls all his comrades who have died trying to defend him, especially Labeo and Flavius.	[cf. App. *B. Civ.* 4.135 on death of Labeo.]	
51.3–4: Water 'is all drunk up'.		
51.5–6: Brutus reckons he has not lost many men. Statyllius proposes cutting through enemy forces to ascertain safety of camp; death of Statyllius.	4.131: Brutus meets with his officers, who refuse to fight ('heaven unhinged them').	47.49.1: Brutus tries to break through enemy into his camp, but is unsuccessful and denounces virtue.
52.1–3: Brutus tries to persuade friends to kill him but they refuse: 'By all means, we must fly; not with our feet, however, but with our hands.'		
52.4: Brutus clasps friends by hands and blames Fortune.		
52.5: Brutus reflects on his reputation for virtue.		
52.6–8: Brutus retires with Strato and falls on his sword.	4.131: Brutus urges Strato to kill him.	47.49.2: Brutus orders one of his companions to kill him.
	4.132–3: Eulogy of Brutus and Cassius; summary of their achievements.	
	4.134: Divinely sanctioned fate of the assassins; *list of omens and prodigies.*	
53.1–3: Strato and Messalla reconciled with Octavian.		
53.4: Antony gives Brutus an honourable burial and sends ashes to Servilia.	4.135: Antony gives Brutus an honourable burial and sends ashes to Servilia.	47.49.2: Antony gives Brutus' body a burial but sends his head to Rome; the head is lost at sea during a storm.
53.5–6: Death of Porcia.	4.135–6: Brutus' men (about 14,000) reconciled with Antony and Octavian; deaths of others, including Cato's son Cato, and Labeo; Porcia's suicide.	47.49.3: At Brutus' death, many of his men transfer their allegiance when an amnesty is offered to them; Porcia's suicide.
[cf. Plut. *Brut.* 38.5 on the scale of the battle.]	4.137–8: Magnitude and importance of the victory.	[cf. Cass. Dio 47.39.1–5 on the scale of the battle.]

ENDNOTES

Abbreviations

Classical sources

Abbreviations employ the conventions of the *Oxford Classical Dictionary* (2012), ed. S. Hornblower, A. Spawforth and E. Eidinow, 4th edn (Oxford), xxvii–liii; for works not included in the *OCD* I have adopted abbreviations of a similar style. For convenience, I list here the principal abbreviations and editions used. Square brackets indicate spurious or questionable authorship.

For Cicero's letters, I have given the traditional numerations as well as Shackleton Bailey's: e.g. Cic. *Att.* 14.14 (SB 368), or Cic. *Ad Brut.* 1.15 (SB 23).

App. *B. Civ.*	Appian (1913). *Bella Civilia* (*Civil Wars*), trans. H. White, *Roman History*, 4 vols, Loeb Classical Library (Cambridge, MA).
[Aur. Vict.] *Vir. Ill.*	[Aurelius Victor] (1911). *De Viris Illustribus* (*On Famous Men*), ed. F. Pichlmayr (Leipzig).
[Brut.] *Ep. Gr.*	[Brutus] (1959). *Epistole Greche* (*Greek Letters*), ed. L. Torraca (Naples).
Caes. *B. Civ.*	Caesar (2016). *Bellum Civile* (*Civil War*), trans. C. Damon, Loeb Classical Library (Cambridge, MA).
Cass. Dio	Cassius Dio (1916–17). *Roman History*, trans. E. Cary, 9 vols, Loeb Classical Library (Cambridge, MA).
Cic. *Ad Brut.*	Cicero (2002). *Epistulae ad Brutum* (*Letters to Brutus*), trans. D.R. Shackleton Bailey, Loeb Classical Library (Cambridge, MA).
Cic. *Att.*	Cicero (1999). *Epistulae ad Atticum* (*Letters to Atticus*), trans. D.R. Shackleton Bailey, 4 vols, Loeb Classical Library (Cambridge, MA).
Cic. *Brut.*	Cicero (1939; rev. edn 1962). *Brutus* or *De Claris Oratoribus* (*On Famous Orators*), trans. G.L. Hendrickson, Loeb Classical Library (Cambridge, MA).
Cic. *Fam.*	Cicero (2001). *Epistulae ad Familiares* (*Letters to Friends*), trans. D.R. Shackleton Bailey, 3 vols, Loeb Classical Library (Cambridge, MA).
Cic. *Off.*	Cicero (1913). *De Officiis* (*On Duties*), trans. W. Miller, Loeb Classical Library (Cambridge, MA).
Cic. *Orat.*	Cicero (1939; rev. edn 1962). *Orator*, trans. H.M. Hubbell, Loeb Classical Library (Cambridge, MA).
Cic. *Phil.*	Cicero (2009). *Orationes Philippicae* (*Philippics*), trans. D.R. Shackleton Bailey, rev. J.T. Ramsey and G. Manuwald, 2 vols, Loeb Classical Library (Cambridge, MA).
Hor. *Carm.*	Horace (2004). *Carmina* (*Odes*), trans. N. Rudd, Loeb Classical Library (Cambridge, MA).
Hor. *Sat.*	Horace (1926). *Satires*, trans. H.R. Fairclough, Loeb Classical Library (Cambridge, MA).

Joseph. *AJ*	Josephus (1943). *Jewish Antiquities*, trans. R. Marcus and A. Wikgren, books 14–15, Loeb Classical Library (Cambridge, MA).
Jul. Obs.	Julius Obsequens, in Livy (1959), trans. A.C. Schlesinger, vol. 14, Loeb Classical Library (Cambridge, MA).
Livy	Livy (1919). *Ab Urbe Condita* (*History of Rome*), trans. B.O. Foster, 14 vols, Loeb Classical Library (Cambridge, MA).
[Livy], *Per.*	[Livy] (1959). *Periochae* (*Summaries*), trans. A.C. Schlesinger, vol. 14, Loeb Classical Library (Cambridge, MA).
Luc. *Phars.*	Lucan (1928). *Pharsalia* (*The Civil War*), trans. J.D. Duff, Loeb Classical Library (Cambridge, MA).
Nic. Dam.	Nicolaus of Damascus (1923–). *Die Fragmente der griechischen Historiker*, ed. F. Jacoby (Berlin).
Plut. *Brut.*	Plutarch (1918). *Brutus*, trans. B. Perrin, Loeb Classical Library (Cambridge, MA).
Plut. *Caes.*	Plutarch (2011). *Caesar*, trans. C. Pelling, Clarendon Ancient History Series (Oxford).
Suet. *Iul.*	Suetonius (1914). *Divus Iulius* (*The Deified Julius*), trans. J.C. Rolfe, Loeb Classical Library (Cambridge, MA).
Tac. *Ann.*	Tacitus (1931). *Annales* (*Annals*), trans. C.H. Moore, Loeb Classical Library (Cambridge, MA).
Val. Max.	Valerius Maximus (2000). *Memorable Doings and Sayings*, trans. D.R. Shackleton Bailey, 2 vols, Loeb Classical Library (Cambridge, MA).
Vell. Pat.	Velleius Paterculus (1924). *History of Rome*, trans. F.W. Shipley, Loeb Classical Library (Cambridge, MA).
Verg. *Aen.*	Virgil (1999–2000). *Aeneid*, trans. H.R. Fairclough, rev. G.P. Goold, 2 vols, Loeb Classical Library (Cambridge, MA).
Verg. *Ecl.*	Virgil (1999). *Eclogues*, trans. H.R. Fairclough, rev. G.P. Goold, Loeb Classical Library (Cambridge, MA).
Verg. *Georg.*	Virgil (1999). *Georgics*, trans. H.R. Fairclough, rev. G.P. Goold, Loeb Classical Library (Cambridge, MA).

Journals and other serial publications

Anc. Soc.	*Ancient Society.*
AHB	*Ancient History Bulletin.*
AJN	*American Journal of Numismatics.*
AJPh	*American Journal of Philology.*
CJ	*Classical Journal.*
Cl. Ant.	*Classical Antiquity.*
CPh	*Classical Philology.*
CQ	*Classical Quarterly.*
CW	*Classical World.*
G&R	*Greece & Rome.*
GRBS	*Greek, Roman & Byzantine Studies.*
HSCPh	*Harvard Studies in Classical Philology.*
ICS	*Illinois Classical Studies.*
JRA	*Journal of Roman Archaeology.*
JRS	*Journal of Roman Studies.*
PCPS	*Proceedings of the Classical Philological Society.*
RhM	*Rheinisches Museum für Philologie.*
TAPhA	*Transactions of the American Philological Association.*
ZPE	*Zeitschrift für Papyrologie und Epigraphik.*

Works of reference and other works cited by author

CAH	*Cambridge Ancient History.*
Cich. *Röm. Stud.*	C. Cichorius (1922). *Römische Studien: historisches, epigraphisches, literargeschichtliches aus vier Jahrhunderten Roms* (Leipzig).
CIL	*Corpus Inscriptionum Latinarum.*
FRHist	T.J. Cornell et al. (ed.) (2013). *Fragments of the Roman Historians* (Oxford).
GL	H. Keil (ed.) (1857–80). *Grammatici Latini* (Leipzig).
IG	*Inscriptiones Graeciae.*

ILS	H. Dessau (ed.) (1892). *Inscriptiones Latinae Selectae* (Berlin).
LIMC	*Lexicon Iconographicum Mythologiae Classicae.*
Moles–Pelling	J.L. Moles (1979). 'A Commentary on Plutarch's *Brutus*', DPhil thesis, Oxford; rev. ed. C.B.R. Pelling (forthcoming), *Histos.*
MRR	T.R.S. Broughton (1951–52 and 1986). *The Magistrates of the Roman Republic*, 3 vols (New York and Atlanta).
OCD	S. Hornblower, A. Spawforth and E. Eidinow (eds) (2012). *Oxford Classical Dictionary*, 4th edn (Oxford).
ORF	H. Malcovati (ed.) (1966). *Oratorum Romanorum Fragmenta Liberae Rei Publicae*, 3rd edn (Turin).
RAA	F. Münzer (1920). *Römische Adelspartien und Adelsfamilien* (Stuttgart) = *Roman Aristocratic Parties and Families* (*RAPF*), trans. Thérèse Ridley (1999) (Baltimore and London).
RE	A.F. Pauly and G. Wissowa (1893). *Paulys Real-Encyclopädie der classichen Altertumswissenschaft* (Stuttgart).
RRC	M.H. Crawford (1974). *Roman Republican Coinage*, 2 vols (Cambridge).
Stangl	T. Stangl (1964). *Ciceronis Orationum Scholiastae* (Hildesheim).
TLRR	M.C. Alexander (1990). *Trials of the Late Roman Republic* (Toronto).
Tyrrell and Purser	R.Y. Tyrrell and L.C. Purser (1901–33). *The Correspondence of M. Tullius Cicero*, 7 vols, 2nd edn (Dublin and London).

Preface

1. Nelson (2000); on this point I am also indebted to discussions with Charlotte Behr.

Introduction: Brutus and the Biographical Tradition

1. Ancient accounts of the conspiracy are to be found in: Nic. Dam. 58–106; Plut. *Caes.* 60–8, Plut. *Brut.* 8–20; Suet. *Iul.* 76–85; App. *B. Civ.* 2.106–47; Cass. Dio 44.9–19. The various sources have been usefully compiled by Drumann and Groebe (1906), 655–7. Modern narratives are too numerous to list in full. However, lively and accessible versions can be found in Parenti (2003), 167–85; Woolf (2006), 6–18; Tatum (2008), 145–66; Wiseman (2009), 211–15; Alston (2015), 15–30; Strauss (2015), 127–41. The most useful starting point for students is Lintott (2009); a classic is Gelzer (1968), 322–9. For earlier scholarly literature, see the bibliography collected by Bell (1994), 824 n. 2.
2. Plut. *Brut.* 14.6; App. *B. Civ.* 2.115 is similar in its focus on the conspirators in the moments leading up to Caesar's arrival, but the emphasis is different: there the silence of Brutus and Cassius is more matter of fact.
3. Nic. Dam. 84. For Calpurnia's dreams and her attempts to keep Caesar at home, see also Vell. Pat. 2.57.2; Suet. *Iul.* 81.3; Plut. *Caes.* 63.9–10; Cass. Dio 44.17.3. On the time of day, see Suet. *Iul.* 81.4, who adds that Decimus called on Caesar at about the fifth hour (i.e. between ten and eleven in the morning).
4. Suet. *Iul.* 81.4; cf. Plut. *Caes.* 83. On Spurinna's first warnings to Caesar, see Cic. *Div.* (*De Divinatione*) 1.119. On Porcia's collapse and other false alarms, see Plut. *Brut.* 15. More on Spurinna and the circumstances that inspired his prophecy in Ramsey (2000).
5. This account is largely based on Plut. *Brut.* 17 (*). The most important sources for the climactic moment of the assassination besides this are: Nic. Dam. 88–90; Suet. *Iul.* 82; Plut. *Caes.* 66 (*); App. *B. Civ.* 2.117 (*); Cass. Dio 44.19. (An asterisk indicates the accounts which compare Caesar to a wild beast).
6. Suet. *Iul.* 82.2 and Cass. Dio 44.19.5; for Shakespeare's adaptation, see Shakespeare, *Julius Caesar* 3.1.77.
7. On the question of who started the plot, see Cass. Dio 41.14.1 and Plut. *Brut.* 10; on the order of their names ('Brutus and Cassius' or 'Cassius and Brutus') in literature, see Rawson (1986 = 1991). In this paragraph, I have used the term 'Greek historian' to describe both Appian and Dio, even though their subject matter is undeniably Roman. On the distinction followed here, see Gowing (2009) who points to the ways in which Appian and Dio, as Greek writers of Roman history, differ from their Latin counterparts.
8. Woolf (2006), 8–18; for a fuller analysis of the various accounts, see Moles–Pelling on Plut. *Brut.* 17.
9. 'The day of the Republic was past' (Plut. *Brut.* 47.7); on the conspirators' jealousy and hatred, see Cass. Dio 44.1.1.
10. Tac. *Ann.* 4.34; for a full interpretation of this passage see Wisse (2013), with further bibliography.

11. Although the relevant books of Livy have been lost for this period, we do have summaries (the *Periochae*) which seem to support this claim. According to this work, Book 120 included a digression on the 'achievements (*res gestae*) of Brutus' in Greece ([Livy], *Per.* 120), while Book 122 covered his 'successful campaigns against the Thracians' ([Livy], *Per.* 122).
12. The classic study is MacMullen (1966), esp. 1–45.
13. Val. Max. 1.5.7 (referring to Brutus) and 1.8.8 (referring to Cassius); 'sin' (*nefas*, in the Latin) is the word specifically used to describe Brutus' participation; for Valerius' view on divine retribution, also see Val. Max. 1.7.1.
14. 'Heavens above, what a reward . . .' (Vell. Pat. 2.25.5); for his verdict on Brutus elsewhere, see Vell. Pat. 2.57.1, 2.72.1; for the quotation of Valerius Maximus – 'a single deed' – see Val. Max. 6.4.5.
15. Plut. *Comp. Dion et Brut.* 3.3.
16. For Brutus' promises of cities to plunder to his soldiers, see Plut. *Brut.* 46.1.
17. Plutarch mentions these sources at various points in his narrative: see Plut. *Brut.* 13.3, 23.6 (Bibulus); 2.4 (Empylus); 48.2, 51.1–52.7 (Volumnius). For a full attempt to identify Plutarch's sources (where possible), see Moles–Pelling, 27–59.
18. Duff (1999) offers a full investigation of Plutarch's work along these lines.
19. Plut. *Dion* 1.1–2; cf. Plut. *Brut.* 1.3. On the openings of the two *Lives*, see Stadter (1988); Duff (2011), esp. 216–42, *passim.*
20. On the value of Appian as an historical recorder of events, see the collection of essays in Welch (2015); in particular, see Welch's own chapter on Appian's narrative of the civil wars at 277–304.
21. The best treatment of Dio remains that of Millar (1964), but an excellent comparison of the narratives of Appian and Dio for this period is Gowing (1992).
22. I have already treated the evidence and career of Cicero in Tempest (2011), with further references. Since then, see also the fuller discussion of Cicero as author by Manuwald (2015). For the intellectual world of republican Rome, the best survey remains Rawson (1985); although not strictly relevant to the current study, Toner (2017) is nevertheless right to widen the scope of her definition to include the creative and practical approaches to problem-solving exhibited by the Roman non-elite.
23. For an expression of this view, see e.g. Narducci (2002), 402: 'Characterization of the latter [i.e. the interlocutors], particularly that of Brutus, does not appear especially respectful of historical reality.'
24. I have counted the *Letters to Brutus* on Shackleton Bailey's numbering, but omit here numbers 25 and 26 (Cic. *Ad Brut.* 1.16 and 1.17), which are largely believed to be forgeries. It should be noted that there are a further four letters to Brutus from Cicero contained in the collection *Letters to Friends*: Cic. *Fam.* 13.10–13 (SB 277–80).
25. Middleton (1840), 284.
26. Gibbon (1814), vol. 4, 96.
27. Pelling (2002), 301.
28. The ancient evidence for Brutus' date of birth is conflicting and it is hence impossible to fix it with any certainty. Cic. *Brut.* 324 states that Brutus was born ten years after Q. Hortensius Hortalus made his debut appearance as an orator, and since he elsewhere tells us that Hortensius first spoke in the Forum during the consulship of Lucius Crassus and Quintus Scaevola (Cic. *Brut.* 229) – i.e. in 95 BC – it seems reasonable to date Brutus' own entry into the world to 85 BC. If we calculate according to Cicero's chronology, it means that Brutus was almost forty-two years old when he died on 23 October 42 BC, for Brutus' birthday was late in the year (Plut. *Brut.* 24.5–6; App. *B. Civ.* 4.134; Val. Max. 1.5.7). This conclusion is largely supported by Brutus' career on the *cursus honorum* which was regulated by age, yet Velleius states explicitly that Brutus was in his thirty-seventh year (i.e. was thirty-six years old) when he died (Vell. Pat. 2.7.1). According to Velleius' chronology, Brutus was born either in late 79 or in 78 BC. In deciding between the two, our third main piece of evidence ([Livy], *Per.* 124) does not offer much help: for it simply tells us that Brutus was around the age of forty when he died, which means that either Cicero or Velleius could be correct. To suggest that Cicero is a more reliable source on the matter by virtue simply of his friendship with Brutus – a point most recently expressed by Corrigan (2015), 8 – is, however to miss the point that scholars have debated: namely, whether we can trust the manuscript for Cicero's *Brutus*, who elsewhere in the same work seems to suggest that Brutus may have been younger. For this argument, see Douglas (1966), 229–30, commenting on Cic. *Brut.* 248. Not everyone has been convinced by Douglas' point here; see e.g. Badian (1967). Yet there are several other arguments in favour of the later date: e.g. Plutarch states Brutus was a *meirakion* (i.e. a teenager) when he accompanied Cato to Cyprus in 58 BC (Plut. *Brut.* 3.1) and the argument that Brutus must have been over forty to hold the praetorship in 44 BC is not watertight when we remember that there were other clear violations of the *lex annalis* under Caesar (on which, see Sumner (1971)). Indeed, Nipperdey (1864: 291) maintained that *decem* ('ten') in the manuscript should be emended to *sedecim* ('sixteen') to bring Cicero into line with Velleius; cf. Seeck (1901, 1907) who also suggested *septemdecim* ('seventeen').

Editors who have accepted the emendation *sedecim* include: Wilkins (1903); Martha (1960, Bude series); Douglas (1966), D'Arbela (1968). Yet several scholars have forcefully argued in favour of Cicero's chronology: see e.g. Groebe (1907) who points out that Velleius often gets dates wrong; Badian (1967) who argues against Douglas (1966). More recently, Woodman (1983) commenting on Vell. Pat. 2.7.1 has followed J. J. Paterson in emending thirty-seven (XXXVII) to forty-two (XXXXII), to bring Velleius into line with Cicero. It should also be added in this context that Plutarch's use of *meirakion* is rather erratic in other texts, where he uses it to describe men whom he knew to be much older than their teens or early twenties: thus e.g. of Marius when he was twenty-three to twenty-five (Plut. *Mar.* 3.5); Philopoimen when he was thirty (Plut. *Phil.* 6.13); for further discussion, see Konrad (1994), 37. Recent editors who have restored the text to *decem* include: Jahn and Kroll (1962); Malcovati (1965); Narducci (1995); Coria (2004); Marchese (2011). The consensus is certainly not universal, but in the absence of any decisive arguments to refute the traditional dating of Brutus' birth to 85 BC, I have accepted it for now. For extensive discussions and emails on this point, I am grateful to Jaap Wisse.

29. For a more detailed look at the problem, see Pelling (1990).
30. Thus e.g. Dettenhofer (1992), 100.

Chapter 1: Becoming Brutus

1. The 'virtue' of Brutus is ubiquitous in our sources (see the overview of his presentation in our sources on pp. 6–7). For the idea that he was the only conspirator who was spurred on by the nobility of the deed, see Plut. *Brut.* 29.7. For the statue at Mediolanum, which probably dated from Brutus' governorship of Cisalpine Gaul in 46–45 BC, see Plut. *Comp. Dion et Brut.* 5.2 (Augustus' reaction to it, which he turned into a positve display of acceptance) and Suet. *Gram. et Rhet.* 30.5 (for the anecdote of the orator, Gaius Albucius Silus, who invoked it as part of a rhetorical appeal); on this last passage, see Kaster (1995), 324.
2. For its recognition in his own lifetime, see e.g. Cic. *Fam.* 9.14.5 (SB 326), Cic. *Orat.* 33.
3. On the representations of Brutus which survive from antiquity, some real and some hypothesised, see Nodelman (1987).
4. His 'leading man looks', Strauss (2015), 16; 'at once young and old', Bossier (1897), 309; 'not easy to think of him as the bold and inspiring leader', Toynbee (1978), 62–3.
5. Plin. *Ep.* 3.10.6; on Roman portraiture and its interpretation, see, for example, Borg (2012).
6. Cass. Dio 47.25.3; on the symbolism of the *pileus*, see Arena (2012), 32–4; on the representation of Libertas on Brutus' coinage more generally, see Clark (2007), 149–53; for the reminder of the importance of reading the two faces of a coin as a coherent whole, see Wallace-Hadrill (1986), 66–87, esp. 69. For the coin, see *RRC* 508/3; further discussion of its message in Wallman (1989), 37–8.
7. Livy 1.59–60; on the legend of Lucius Brutus, see especially Wiseman (2008), 293–305, with additional bibliography and references. A reprinted version of this chapter, together with a useful critical addendum by the editors, can be found in Richardson and Santangelo (eds) (2014), 129–46.
8. On the development of the office of consulship, see Urso (2011), which examines evidence other than Livy to argue that the first use of the term 'consul' may have occurred as late as 449 BC. See also Wiseman (1995), 103–10, who argues that the consulship as a power-sharing device only originated in 397 BC; ideas repeated in Wiseman (2008 = 2014).
9. Livy 2.1.9–10; I say that this moment was 'used to explain' the hatred Rome felt towards kings because their fear of monarchs was more likely a result of Rome's interaction with Hellenistic monarchies in the east: see Erskine (1991).
10. The concept of the *res publica* in Roman political thought and vocabulary is much harder to define than this simplified summary suggests; for a comprehensive treatment of the problem, see Hodgson (2017). In this book, I shall use the term Republic to refer to the historical period, and the Latin *res publica* to refer to the institutions and style of government that gave shape to the ideal.
11. A useful introduction to republican institutions and governance can be found in Pina Polo (2017).
12. On this point see Arena (2012), 42, 74–8.
13. Useful treatments of early Roman history and the sources for studying in can be found in Cornell (1995, 2005); also see Oakley (2004); on the veracity (or otherwise) of the Lucius Brutus legend and its development, see, most recently, Richardson (2011), with further references.
14. The Roman playwright Accius, whose patron was Decimus Junius Brutus Callaecus (consul in 138 BC), wrote a *Brutus*, which depicted the overthrow of the Tarquinii and concomitant establishment of the *res publica*. On the performance history and for further discussion, see Flower (1995), 175–6.
15. Plut. *Brut.* 1.1; cf. Gregory (1994), 85, with further references.
16. The classic discussion of funeral customs and aristocratic power is Flower (1996).

17. The event is recorded by Cic. *De Or.* 2.225; there are good discussions of the passage at Flower (1996), 152–3 and Lentano (2008), 889–90.
18. On the influence of Brutus' legendary ancestry upon his career and self-promotion, see the ideas variously discussed by MacMullen (1966), 7–10; Flower (1996), 88–9; Welwei (2000), 53–4 and (2001); Gotter (2000), 330–3; Treggiari (2003); Walter (2003); Lentano (2007), 127–34, (2008), 891–5.
19. For the story of Ahala, see Cic. *Cat.* 1.1, Livy 4.13–14; for discussions, see Lintott (1999b), 55–6 and, fuller, at Lintott (1970), esp. 13–18; also see Smith (2006).
20. On Brutus' family tree, see Nep. *Att.* 18.3 and Cic. *Att.* 13.40.1 (SB 343), where he describes it using the Greek word *philotechnēma*, meaning 'arranged artistically'; Cicero refers to the busts (*imagines*) of Brutus and Ahala at Cic. *Phil.* 2.26.
21. See Wiseman (1987) for the general importance of the aristocratic house as a visible expression of a man's standing.
22. Plut. *Brut.* 1.6–8 (which also records the creative attempt of Posidonius to circumvent the problem of Lucius' sons; cf. Dion. Hal. *Ant. Rom.* 5.18. It is worth noting, however, that the taunt may date to the period before the dictator's death. We can infer from the fact that this story was known to Posidonius – a philosopher and historian who lived *c.* 135–51 BC, and who tried to defend Brutus' heritage by explaining that the original Brutus had a third son, from whose line the Junii Bruti descended – that it was also familiar to at least some of Brutus' contemporaries, at the time Posidonius was writing; for a fuller discussion of the question, see Richardson (2011), who traces the claim back to Quintus Aelius Tubero. This may suggest that there were many who were doubting Brutus' self-advertisement in the years prior to Caesar's assassination in 44 BC, and that these claims probably resulted from Brutus' bold coins minted when he was a moneyer in *c.* 55/54 BC (on which see Chapter 2).
23. Thus Cicero (at Cic. *Brut.* 62) berates the fact that history was becoming quite distorted as a result.
24. On the electoral value of ancestry, see [Q. Cicero], *Comm. Pet.* 53; for the general idea that *imagines* reminded men to emulate their ancestors, see Val. Max. 5.8.3.
25. Livy 2.5.8.
26. Of fundamental importance for understanding the nature of Rome's constitutional development is Flower (2010).
27. The estimated figure comes from Crawford (1992), 2.
28. The fragment of Sulla's memoirs (21.20.1) is preserved in Prisc. *GL* 2.476K (= *HRR* vol. 1); cf. Smith (*FRHist* I, 282–6).
29. Detailed treatments and discussion of Sulla's programme of reforms can instead be found in Hantos (1988); Christ (2002); Keaveney (2005); Santangelo (2007). The extent to which Sulla's reforms represented a complete departure from previous constitutional arrangements has been well documented by Flower (2010), 117–34. Recent analyses of the reforms and their effects can be found in Steel (2013), 107–17, 126–31; Steel (2014b). On his motives, see Steel (2014a), with further references.
30. On the numbers of senators in the Senate, however, see the important arguments advanced by Santangelo (2006, 2007) who concludes that there may have been as few as 150 senators left in the Senate by 82 BC; hence he suggests a new Senate of about 450 members, which is considerably lower than traditional estimates.
31. Hawthorn (1962), 55, who uses the reforms to illuminate the causes for corruption in the post-Sullan period.
32. On the impact of Sulla's reforms on political competition, see Wiseman (1971); for a more general introduction to the competition culture in Roman political life, see Wiseman (1985).
33. Lucr. 2.13; this line and the passage to which it belongs are discussed further by Wiseman (1985), 12–13.
34. The number of quaestors before the increase to twenty is not clear in our sources, but it was somewhere between eight and twelve; see Harris (1976).
35. Cic. *Cluent.* 154.
36. On the profits from war, see Rosenstein (2011); on the parameters for accruing wealth in the provinces, see Blösel (2016).
37. On the fear of failure – of *dolor repulsae* – and its consequences see the comments of Tatum (2007), 110; cf. Yakobson (1999) for a fuller discussion of elections and electioneering.
38. Discussion of the terms *nobilis* (singular) and *nobiles* (plural) has been a matter of intense scholarly debate depending on whether one sees the consulship as the office that ennobled a family, or just the higher offices generally; for a useful overview see Van der Blom (2010), 35–41. For the emphasis placed on the consulship as a marker of 'nobility' in the late Republic, see Flower (1996, 2010).
39. On the possible career paths for aspiring politicians in the late Republic, see Van der Blom (2016).
40. For discussion of the revolt, see Christ (2002), 141–2. For new analyses of the political inclinations and motives of Lepidus in 77 BC, see Santangelo (2014) and Burton (2014).

41. Very little is known about the elder Marcus Junius Brutus before he was appointed legate in 77 BC. We can perhaps infer that he was a man of some military ability, since Lepidus had entrusted to him the command of Gaul, yet we know of no prior military experience on his part. He had, however, been a tribune of the plebs in 83 BC and he played an active part in civil and administrative affairs (see e.g. Cic. *Leg. Agr.* 2.89, 92 and 98; cf. Cic. *Quinct.* 29, 63, 65).
42. On the revolt of Lepidus and the death of Brutus' father, see Val. Max. 6.2.8; Plut. *Pomp.* 16.2–5; [Livy], *Per.* 92; App. *B. Civ.* 2.16.111; Oros. 5.22.17.
43. On the nickname and some of Pompey's victims, see Val. Max. 6.2.8, cited above.
44. A good sketch of Servilia with further references can be found in Hallett (1984), 49 ff.
45. The evidence for dating Brutus' adoption around 59 BC comes from Cic. *Att.* 2.24.3 (SB 44), where Cicero refers to Brutus as *Caepio hic Brutus* ('this Caepio Brutus'), seemingly drawing attention to him using the demonstrative *hic*. What Cicero means by this phrase has been the subject of much debate, but it may point to the fact that Brutus' adoption by Q. Servilius Caepio was recent enough for Cicero to comment on the new form of his name. Another explanation could simply be that Cicero uses it to distinguish between Marcus Brutus and another Caepio. That Brutus continued to use this name, at least in an official capacity, can be seen in an inscription erected by the people of Oropus in 43 BC: *IG* 7.383 = *ILS*, 9460; cf. Cic. *Fam.* 7.21 (SB 332), Cic. *Phil.* 10.25, where Cicero refers to him as Q. Caepio. On the controversy surrounding Brutus' name and his adoption, see Geiger (1973), esp. 148 ff.
46. Thus Cic. *Dom.* 35. Modern treatments of adoption in the ancient world include Gardner (1998) and Lindsay (2009).
47. For a different opinion, see Clarke (1981), 12, who flirts with the idea that Cato influenced Brutus' education. However, this is speculation. As it will become clear over the next two chapters, there is no firm evidence to support the popular belief that Cato exerted a strong influence over Brutus until a much later period.
48. On Staberius Eros, see Suet. *Gram. et Rhet.* 13.1; cf. Kaster (1995), 165–70. For the influence of Eros on Brutus, see Balbo (2013), 316 n. 15; the anecdote about Cassius and Faustus comes from Plut. *Brut.* 9.1–4.
49. [Aur. Vict.] *Vir. Ill.* 82.
50. These cases were in defence of one, Marcus Fonteius; two, P. Oppius; three, Aulus Caecina. Of these speeches, only the speech *Pro A. Caecina* survives in full. The speech *Pro M. Fonteio* is incomplete, while we only have a handful of fragments left of *Pro P. Oppio*; see Crawford (1994), 23–32. For other trials, the standard work of reference is *TLRR*.
51. Discussions of Brutus' oratory and his oratorical career can be found in Filbey (1911) and Balbo (2013).
52. On the role of rhetoric and oratory in Roman education, see *i.a.* Bonner (1977); Steel (2006), 63–78; Corbeill (2010); Bloomer (2011).
53. On the role of these orators in the rhetorical instruction of Cicero's (and hence by extension Brutus') day, see Weische (1972), esp. 134–44.
54. Brutus' comments on Demosthenes' *On the Crown* appear at Quint. *Inst.* 9.4.63; his opinion of Isocrates is referred to by Cicero at Cic. *Orat.* 40. On Brutus' iambic rhythms, see Quint. *Inst.* 9.4.75–6; on the use of the iambic trimeter, from the time of Archilochus (seventh century BC) up into the medieval period, see Kerkhecker (1999). For Aristotle's view that iambic rhythm was the one closest to natural speech, see Arist. *Poet.* 1449a; cf. Arist. *Rhet.* 1408b. Brutus' criticisms of Cicero's speech are recorded at Tac. *Dial.* 18.22.
55. On the number of speeches available in Brutus' day, see Cic. *Brut.* 65, where Cicero claims to have found and read more than 150 of them. The fragments in *ORF* 8, M. Porcius Cato; for discussion, see Hölkeskamp (2004), 225–9.
56. On Cato the Younger's use of Cato the Elder as an exemplum see Cic. *Mur.* 66; some discussion in Van der Blom (2010), 154–5.
57. On the place of these three principles within Roman culture and society, see the overview and further reading suggested by Tatum (2008), 23–4.
58. The standard treatment of the *progymnasmata* is Cribiore (2001); a useful introduction is Kennedy (2003). The date at which the *progymnasmata* originated has been a matter of some debate, but a convincing argument dating them to the second century BC has been made by Barwick (1928). Some ancient testimony can be found at Quint. *Inst.* 2.4.41, which names the Hellenistic orator Demetrius of Phalerum as the instigator of the practice.
59. Cic. *Tusc.* 1.7; cf. Suet. *Gram. et Rhet.* 1.3 who records that Cicero declaimed in Greek down to his praetorship in 66 BC, but that he continued exercising in Latin as an older man too. A compelling case for the practical impact of the *progymnasmata* on Cicero's oratory has been made by Frazel (2009). A famous example of the use to which Cicero put his Greek declamations occurs at Cic. *Att.* 9.4.2 (SB 173), which opens Chapter 4 of this book.

60. As mentioned in the main text, our evidence for *progymnasmata* comes from later sources. For a useful overview of the evidence and further discussion of the tyrant and tyrannicide types, see Tomassi (2015).
61. See Daly (1950).
62. Plut. *Brut.* 2.2–3. On the extent to which Plutarch has probably underplayed Brutus' Stoicism, see Moles–Pelling *ad loc.* and Swain (1990), 202–3.
63. Cic. *Acad.* 1.12; on Aristus' succession to the headship of Antiochus' school, see the re-examination of the papyrus evidence (*PHerc.* 1021) by Blank (2007); cf. Hatzimichali (2012), esp. 25–6.
64. Cic. *Brut.* 332; cf. Plut. *Brut.* 2.3–4.
65. On Brutus' poetry, see Tac. *Dial.* 21.6 and Plin. *Ep.* 5.3.5; his collections of art, which included a bronze statue of Demosthenes, are mentioned at Cic. *Orat.* 110, Plin. *HN* 34.82, and Mart. 2.77.4, 14.171. His knowledge of Greek literature is evidenced e.g. in his quotation from Greek tragedy at Plut. *Brut.* 23.6, 24.6, 51.1.
66. On Atticus' financial services to Brutus and his family, see Welch (1996), 463–6.
67. *Etsi es natura politikos*: Cic. *Att.* 4.6.1 (SB 83).
68. On the modified versions of Sulla's laws (the *leges Corneliae*), see Williamson (2005) esp. 367–414. On the effects of these reforms, and especially the creation of a 'two-tiered Senate' see Steel (2014b).
69. The terms *nobiles* and *novi homines* are more difficult than my treatment of them here suggests; for fuller analysis, see Van der Blom (2010), 35–59. For other perspectives on the challenges facing a *nobilis*, see Tatum (1999) esp. 36–38, with further discussion and references.
70. The debate was spearheaded by Millar's seminal article (1986) and later book (1998) on the role of the people in the late republic, to which Hölkeskamp has presented a series of stimulating challenges; the best point of entry to which, as well as to an array of earlier scholarship, is Hölkeskamp (2010); also see Mouritsen (2011) who is surely right to point out that political participation was restricted by the small crowds who could feasibly represent it. Still, however, the importance of the *contio* as a means of mass–elite interaction is hard to overlook; see esp. Morstein-Marx (2004), with further bibliography; for the role of public opinion, see Rosillo-López (2017); cf. Sumi (2005) on the importance of the games and spectacles, and Van der Blom (2016) on oratorical careers. The overriding impression is that, due to the unpredictability of the Roman system and the annually-refreshed pool of competition against which a senator had to contend, the popular vote was not one he could afford to ignore.
71. The scholarship on the topics presented here is vast. For the refutation of 'party politics' in republican Rome, the classic starting point is Taylor (1949); on the terms *optimates* and *populares,* see Robb (2010), usefully summarised in Mouritsen (2017), 112–23. I shall consequently use these terms sparingly in the discussion that follows; in any case, they are only marginally relevant for understanding Brutus' early career, and even less so for the events which led to Caesar's assassination in 44 BC.
72. Steel (2013), 138.

Chapter 2: Independent Operator

1. Also taken from Cic. *Brut.* 331.
2. Fuller surveys of these campaigns and Pompey's career can be found in: Gelzer (1984); Sherwin-White (1984), 186–226; Seager (2002), 53–62; a useful overview of Pompey's extraordinary career is provided by Steel (2013), 236–48.
3. Plut. *Pomp.* 45; cf. App. *Mith.* 116.
4. The bibliography on the 'First Triumvirate' is vast, but useful overviews can be found in Gruen (1974); Seager (2002), 83–4; Baltrusch (2004). Primary sources include: Vell. Pat. 2.44.1–3; Suet. *Iul.* 19.2; Plut. *Caes.* 13, *Pomp.* 47, *Cat. Min.* 31; App. *B. Civ.* 2.8–9; Cass. Dio 37.54–8.
5. Several scholars would maintain that 60 BC was the real 'end of the Republic'. This was certainly the position of the ancient historian C. Asinius Pollio, according to the Roman poet Horace (*Odes* 2.1.1–4), followed in more recent years by Syme (1939), 5–8, 44–86, and Morgan (2000); cf. Flower (2010), 153 who, while dating the end of the traditional republican politics much earlier, also adds that: 'we should take seriously Cicero's feeling of a lost republic in the year 60, especially when taken with the later decision of C. Asinius Pollio.'
6. Cic. *Att.* 2.17.1 (SB 37).
7. Suet. *Iul.* 20.2; on Caesar's sidelining of Bibulus, also see Plut. *Caes.* 14, *Pomp.* 48.4; Cass. Dio 38.6.3–5.
8. Cic. *Att.* 2.19.3 (SB 39); on Pompey's unpopularity, both in and outside Rome, in the months leading up to the Vettius affair, see Cic. *Att.* 2.13.2 (SB 33), 2.14.1 (SB 34), 2.18.2–3 (SB 38), 2.21.3–4 (SB 41), 2.23.2 (SB 43).

9. Cic. *Att.* 2.18.2 (SB 38); for a similar assessment of the general environment, see Cic. *Att.* 2.20.3 (SB 40), 2.21.1–2 (SB 41), 2.22.6 (SB 42). On Cicero's personal situation, another dominant theme of the letters, see Lintott (2008), 171–3.
10. Vettius became particularly notorious in 62 BC, when he gave information against several of Catiline's associates: see Cass. Dio 37.41.2–4 and Suet. *Iul.* 17. That Cicero had received information from Vettius prior to this, in 63 BC, is nowhere made explicit but is based on the implicit evidence of his letter to Atticus, in which he refers to Vettius as 'that informer of mine' (*ille noster index*): Cic. *Att.* 2.24.2 (SB 44). In any case, Vettius was a professional scoundrel and may have been the treacherous informer of Catull. 98; see Forsyth (1979). On informers in the late Roman Republic, more generally, see Lintott (2001–3), esp. 111.
11. The date has been variously interpreted: Taylor (1950) has quite convincingly argued for a date in July 59 BC – but has not persuaded everyone; see e.g. Brunt (1953) and Meier (1961), 96–8, who hold for a date in August. See Taylor (1954, 1968) for attempted rebuttals of these objections. Her argument has won some support – see *i.a.* McDermott (1949); Allen (1950); Gelzer (1968), 90 n. 1.
12. For a fuller reconstruction, see Lintott (2008), 174–5.
13. On the precise legal charges against Vettius, see Lintott (1999b), 119–20.
14. Cic. *Att.* 2.24.3 (SB 44).
15. 'Me he did not mention by name, but said that a certain eloquent ex-consul, the consul's neighbour, had said to him [i.e. to Vettius] that what was now wanted was a Servilius Ahala or a Brutus' (Cic. *Att.* 2.24.3 = SB 44). Whether true or not, Vettius' accusation has the ring of a Cicero-type comment. For Cicero's use of these *exempla* see e.g. Cic. *Cat.* 1.5. On Cicero's evocation of these legendary tyrannicides (or enemies of tyrants) more generally, see Lintott (1999b), 54–8. That Cicero remained under suspicion for some time may be deduced from his attempts to defend himself against the charge at Cic. *Pis.* 76, Cic. *Dom.* 28, Cic. *Sest.* 41.
16. The evidence for the affair, aside from Cicero's jest in this letter (Cic. *Att.* 2.24.3 = SB 44) comes from several sources, e.g. Suet. *Iul.* 50.2, who records that Caesar loved Servilia most of all his mistresses, adding the fact that he bought her a pearl worth 6 million sesterces in the year of his first consulship (i.e. 59 BC). The anecdote that Servilia sent a love letter to Caesar during a Senate meeting in 63 BC is probably a later addition to the story: see Plut. *Brut.* 5.2–4, Plut. *Cat. Min.* 24.1–3.
17. Cic. *Att.* 2.24.2–3 (SB 44); Suet. *Iul.* 20.5; Plut. *Luc.* 42.7–8; App. *B. Civ.* 2.2.12–14; Cass. Dio 38.9. Cicero also makes several allusions to the plot in his later speeches: Cic. *Flacc.* 46 (where, presumably referring to the Vettius affair, he mentions that he was implicated in the plot), and Cic. *Sest.* 132 (where he names Vettius and stresses the attack upon himself). At Cic. *Vat.* 26, Cicero transfers the responsibility from Caesar to Vatinius, in keeping with his rhetorical agenda. The *Scholia Bobiensia* comments on two of these passages and adds the further detail that Caesar was identified as a second target of the attack (Cic. *Sest.* 132 = 139.22–8, Stangl). For a full overview and discussion of the evidence, see McDermott (1949).
18. See Allen (1950) for the suggestion that Caesar intended to check Pompey's power; for the possibility for the affair also to affect the forthcoming elections, see Taylor (1949). Because of the discrepancies in our ancient evidence, a number of modern scholars have attempted to iron out the inaccuracies to discern who was behind the plot and why. Suspicion has fallen on a range of candidates including Caesar (Taylor (1949); McDermott (1949)); Pompey (Marshall (1987), 121–4); and even Clodius (Seager (1965); repeated in Seager (2002), 98–9, *contra* Tatum (1999), 111–12). Others have cautioned against these attempts to solve the mystery on the grounds that the matter is no more clear to us now than it was to Cicero in 59 BC; see e.g. Pocock (1926), 183–5; Gruen (1974), 95–6; Tatum (1999), 112; Kaster (2006), 373.
19. Support for Curio at Cic. *Att.* 2.18.1 (SB 38); hostility towards Pompey at Cic. *Att.* 2.19.3 (SB 39).
20. Cic. *Att.* 2.8.1 (SB 28).
21. These 'youths' (the *iuvenes*) are referred to in several of Cicero's letters, often grouped condescendingly under the label 'those goateed young men', or *barbatuli iuvenes* in the Latin (referring to the popular trend of a chin-strap beard in imitation of the revolutionary Catiline): e.g. Cic. *Att.* 1.14.5 (SB 14), 1.16.11 (SB 16); on the follies of these youths, see 1.16.1 (SB 16), 1.18.2 (SB 18). From 60 BC onwards, however, Cicero speaks of them in warmer tones, suggesting that they have become particularly attentive towards him; see Cic. *Att.* 1.19.8 (SB 19). We cannot assume, however, that Cicero's change in spirit was shared by his contemporaries, and in fact it is more likely that Cato – who had clashed with them on political matters (see Cic. *Att.* 1.14.5 (SB 14)) – was less than forgiving.
22. I omit mention here of the suggestion by Münzer – *RAA* 338–9 = *RAPF* 310–11 – that Brutus was also motivated to kill Pompey because of the latter's recent marriage to Julia. His argument runs that in order for the wedding to take place Julia had to jilt a certain Servilius Caepio (whom he identifies as our Brutus under his official name), to whom she was already betrothed. Ancient sources which mention Pompey's marriage to Julia include Plut. *Pomp.* 47; Plut. *Caes.* 14; Cass. Dio

38.9.1; App. *B. Civ.* 2.14.50; Suet. *Iul.* 21; in particular, see Cic. *Att.* 2.17.1 (SB 37), written in early May 59 BC, which indicates that the marriage was recent. However – contra Potter (1934), 670–2 – there is no evidence to support Münzer's identification of Servilius Caepio with Marcus Brutus. In fact, as other scholars have noted, it seems to rule him out, for Suetonius tells us that this Caepio had recently 'rendered conspicuous service to Caesar in his contest with Bibulus'. And Plutarch adds that, in order to appease the aggrieved man, Pompey offered Caepio his own daughter in marriage. Yet neither of these pieces of information squares with what we know about Brutus' political activity and alliances at the time, and they may be enough to rule Brutus out of Julia's list of suitors. For a fuller discussion and overview, see Geiger (1973), esp. 153.

23. For the joke of Cicero, see Cic. *Att.* 2.1.8 (SB 21); some of the information presented here is loosely based on Tempest (2012). The fullest account of his life is Plut. *Cat. Min.*, which, although highly anecdotal, provides good evidence for Cato's authority and career. For studies of Cato, see Fehrle (1983); Goar (1987); Morrell (2017). Van der Blom (2016), 204–47, further suggests that Cato's filibustering had a pragmatic political purpose, and that it was useful for promoting his own persona and view of the state.
24. On Clodius' motives and actions in appointing Cato, see especially Tatum (1999), 155–6; other accounts of Cato's command can be found in Oost (1955); Badian (1965); Fehrle (1983), ch. 6; Steel (2001), 203–4.
25. For the identification of Canidius with Caninius, see Geiger (1972), accepted by Moles–Pelling on Plut. *Brut.* 3.2 and Morrell (2017), 148.
26. For the full version, see Plut. *Brut.* 3.1–4.
27. Plut. *Cat. Min.* 38–9.
28. See esp. Moles–Pelling on Plut. *Brut.* 3.4.
29. Caesar attacked him on this basis in his *Anti-Cato* according to Plut. *Cat. Min.* 36.3.
30. [Aur. Vict.] *Vir. Ill.* 82.
31. As several scholars have pointed out, he was probably back by February 56 BC when envoys from Salamis arrived in Rome to request the raising of the loan (see pp. 46–7). On the likelihood of foreign embassies being in Rome in the month of February, see e.g. Cic. *Verr.* 2.2.76; cf. Bonnefond (1984), accepted by Morrell (2017), 148 n. 141; on Cato's return, see the chronology offered by Oost (1955), 105.
32. On the office of the moneyer and its dating to Brutus in 54 BC, see *RRC* 598–603. However, other suggestions have ranged from 60 to 50 BC: Sydenham (1952), 150, places it in 60 BC; Evans (1992), 146, has suggested 59 BC, and argues that Brutus' implication in the Vettius affair was a direct consequence of his propagandist activities on the coinage. On the other hand, Cerutti (1993) has dated the coins to 55 BC but his reasons do not seem entirely watertight: he denies an anti-Pompeian message; he downplays Brutus' involvement in the Vettius affair; and he argues that two years needed to lapse between holding the office of moneyer and other elected positions. On this last point, he is wrong: there was no fixed connection between the office of moneyer and the other magistracies on the *cursus honorum*, and indeed some men held the office as late as their praetorship or consulship. Despite this, 55 BC is still possible and so I have not entirely excluded it; cf. the discussion on the date of Brutus' quaestorship at n. 40, below.
33. That coins of this period typically featured the achievements of one's ancestors (whether real or alleged) has been demonstrated by Alföldi (1956), 65–6; see also Luce (1968), 27–8. I say 'in Brutus' day', because it was only after 137 BC that coins were used to commemorate ancestors in this way. For a full list of moneyers using ancestral themes see Flower (1996), 333–8; cf. Hölscher (1982), 270–1; Chantraine (1983), 530–1; Wallace-Hadrill (1986), 74; Howgego (1995), 67; Meadows and Williams (2001), 37–8. Hollstein (1993), 387–91, looks specifically at the period 78–50 BC and tabulates a sharp increase in the 60s and 50s BC.
34. The example of Clodius is instructive here: on the possibility of Clodius as a Liberator, see Arena (2012), 212–13; cf. Tatum (1999), 158, *passim.*
35. For a different interpretation, see Cerutti (1993), who has denied a political motivation to the choice of imagery on Brutus' coinage.
36. For Brutus as Appius' son-in-law, see Cic. *Fam.* 3.4.2 (SB 67).
37. On the marriage connection, also see Cic. *Fam.* 3.10.10 (SB 73); for the dating of it, see Tatum (1991).
38. There are several illuminating comments about Appius at Cic. *Fam.* 3.7.4–5 (SB 71), 8.12.1–2 (SB 98), 5.10a.2 (SB 259). He was caught up in a shameful scandal while consul in 54 BC, but, even then, Cicero admits that Appius emerged unscathed at Cic. *Att.* 4.17.2 (SB 91). For more favourable presentations of him (although these admittedly appear in letters written to Appius himself), see e.g. Cic. *Fam.* 3.10.9 (SB 73); 3.13.2 (SB 76); cf. 2.13.2 (SB 93) for his possession of the advantages of birth, rank, riches, etc.
39. This is the date accepted, among others, by Broughton (*MRR* 2, 229), with references. However, as

so often, trying to pinpoint an exact date for Brutus' tenure of the office is a matter of some controversy. For further discussion, see n. 40, below.

40. [Aur. Vict.] *Vir. Ill.* 82.3. The first thing to note here is that this piece of evidence does not provide a date; only the tantalising detail that Brutus 'went with Appius his father-in-law to Cilicia' – a fact which has given rise to several different hypotheses. Since Appius was in Cilicia from 53 to 51 BC, most scholars have favoured 53 BC as the date of Brutus' quaestorship. The argument runs along the lines that Brutus was appointed quaestor, refused to serve his office under Caesar, and instead held his post under Appius. Yet others have disagreed because the text of the Latin does not say that Brutus turned down the appointment in Gaul and spent his term of office in Cilicia *instead*; it simply notes that he went with Appius to Cilicia as a 'companion' (*socius*); that is, as a member of his entourage. Moreover, editors of the text have quibbled on how best to construct the Latin original; on the problems of the manuscript, see Braccesi (1973), 70 n. 13, who notes that Keil emended the text to *quaestor <Caesari>*, while Sylburg suggested *quaestor <cum Caesare>*. Seeck (1907), 506, accepting *cum Caesare*, suggested that Brutus must have then held the quaestorship in 58 BC. But this cannot be right. More persuasively, Sumner (1971), 365–6, has argued that – if Brutus was born in 85 BC – he was probably first eligible to stand for election in 55, to hold the quaestorship for 54 BC. It is his suggestion that Brutus can either have been quaestor to Appius in 53, or quaestor in 54 and then proquaestor to Appius in 53 BC; either way, the evidence is not as certain as Broughton (*MRR* 2, 229) suggests.
41. Dettenhofer (1992), 107, citing Shatzman (1975), 373, on the economic considerations.
42. As Gelzer (*RE* 10.1 (1917), 977) explains, with further references, Caesar would have selected his quaestors personally, rather than leave the decision to the lot.
43. An expression of this bond can be found at Cic. *Div. Caec.* 61–3.
44. On Caesar's tendency to nurture young men of talent, see Syme (1939), 44–5; Wiseman (1971), 175–7; Dettenhofer (1992), 107.
45. At the very least a man needed to have the 400,000 sesterces necessary to qualify for equestrian status first. There does not seem to have been a separate property qualification for senators in the late Roman Republic, but Augustus later saw that the life of a senator required a good deal of money: see e.g. (varying in details) Tac. *Ann.* 1.75, 2.37; Suet. *Aug.* 41.1. For discussion, see Hopkins (1983), 74–5; on the importance of wealth for a senatorial career and the means of accruing it, see the useful overview, with further references, in Van der Blom (2016), 50–2.
46. On Brutus' early money-lending activities, see the passing remark of Cic. *Q. Fr.* 1.3.7 (SB 3); for an overview of his general financial situation, see Shatzman (1975), 371–4.
47. For such large-scale financial investments in this period, see Andreau (1999), 9–29.
48. For analysis and discussion of Cicero's texts dealing with provincial government and extortion, see Steel (2001).
49. Cic. *Att.* 5.16.2 (SB 109).
50. On Cicero's growing attachment to Brutus, see Cic. *Att.* 5.20.6 (SB 113), 6.1.3 (SB 115).
51. Cic. *Att.* 6.1.5 (SB 115), which also includes the details of Brutus' memorandum.
52. On this outcome, see Cic. *Att.* 6.3.5 (SB 117).
53. Cic. *Att.* 6.1.5 (SB 115).
54. The calculations are those of Lintott (2008), 264.
55. On the history of the loans, see Cic. *Att.* 5.21.10–12 (SB 114); for discussion, see Lintott (2008), 263–5.
56. For the episode and Cicero's reaction, see Cic. *Att.* 6.1.6–7 (SB 115), 6.2.8–9 (SB 116).
57. Cic. *Att.* 6.1.5 (SB 115).
58. Cic. *Att.* 6.1.7 (SB 115).
59. Welch (1996), 463, has suggested that Atticus may have been responsible for Brutus' financial affairs, as he was for several other members of Cato's family. If so, his concern is understandable. For Atticus' agreement on the matter of Scaptius' appointment, see Cic. *Att.* 6.2.8 (SB 116).
60. Thus Hill (2010), 228 n. 1, following Gelzer (*RE* 10.1 (1917), 977), points out that the amount was 'paralleled at the time'. See e.g. the loan to Gytheum in Greece: *SIG* 3, 748; 2, 35ff.
61. Luc. *Phars.* 1.80–2; for a similarly adverse reaction to money-lending as an enterprise, see the earlier work by Cato the Elder: Cato, *Agr. praef.* 1–4. On this episode within the framework of corruption in Roman political life more generally, see Rosillo-López (2010), esp. 989–91.
62. On Cato's assumed disapproval and ignorance of the loan, see Cic. *Att.* 5.21.13 (SB 114); for attempts to put a cap on interest rates to help provincials repay their debts, see Plut. *Luc.* 20, 23.1.
63. Cic. *Att.* 6.1.6 (SB 115).
64. '[U]nrelenting avarice' is the verdict of Gibbon (1814), edited by Sheffield, vol. 4, 103; 'hypocritical' is the word of Clarke (1981), 19; the harsh summary summarised here is by Stockton (1971), 242, in response to the positive appraisals of Brutus made by Syme (1939), 148, 183–4, 320.

65. 'You have my case': Cic. *Att.* 5.21.13 (SB 114). Welch (1996), 464–5, is right to draw attention to the cooling in the relationship between Cicero and Atticus prompted by the Salamis affair. For a rhetorical reading of Cicero's letters on this episode, see Hutchinson (1998), 100–7.
66. *Cic. Att.* 5.17.6 (SB 110), 6.1.7 (SB 115).
67. Cic. *Fam.* 3.11.3 (SB 74).
68. I have discussed the murder of Clodius and the accompanying violence in greater detail at Tempest (2011), 142–50. On how and why Pompey was eventually made sole consul, see Ramsey (2016).
69. The fragment is preserved at Quint. *Inst.* 9.3.95; cf. *ORF* 158.16.
70. On the philosophical tone, see Carvazere (2000), 184; Balbo (2013), 317 n. 22, who explains the 'slogan' with reference to Cic. *Parad.* 1.15.
71. '[N]ot just imbued but even infected by civil blood' – Sen. *Contr.* 10.1.8; Pompey and Caesar as 'king' and 'queen' – Suet. *Iul.* 49.2; cf. *ORF* 158.17.
72. For the expression, see Plut. *Cat. Min.* 47.3; cf. Plut. *Pomp.* 54.4; Asc. *Mil.* 35–6C; Cass. Dio 40.50.4. That it was Cato to whom Pompey owed his appointment may be inferred from the evidence which suggests Pompey later thanked him: Plut. *Cat. Min.* 48.1–3; Plut. *Pomp.* 54.5.
73. Morrell (2017), 250–5, who also traces signs of cooperation through the processes of Milo's trial.
74. For the argument of the prosecution, see e.g. Cic. *Mil.* 7; on the decree of the Senate, ibid. 12; for the common belief that Pompey, too, wanted to secure Milo's condemnation, see ibid. 15. The extent to which Cicero's published speech faithfully represents the version he delivered on the day is a matter of dispute which need not concern us too much here. For an introduction to the debate, see Alexander (2002), 20–2.
75. Asc. *Mil.* 41C; cf. Quint. *Inst.* 3.6.93, 10.1.20.
76. Balbo (2013), 320.
77. On the published status of the speech *For T. Annius Milo*, see Quint. *Inst.* 10.1.23, where Quintilian corrects Cornelius Celsus for saying that Brutus delivered it in court; cf. Lewis (2006), 246: 'Brutus apparently had a penchant for pamphleteering with literary fictions of this kind.' On pamphleteering as a common means for magistrates to get their voices heard *in absentia*, see Rosillo-López (2017), esp. 132–41.
78. As also noted by Clarke (1981), 17; Dettenhofer (1992), 105–10.
79. Broughton (*MRR* 2, 254) has suggested 51 BC as a possibility for Brutus' election to the pontifical college but Taylor (1942) is more cautious in placing it somewhere between 56 and 50.
80. On the role of the *pontifex* and for a general introduction to Roman religion, see Rüpke (2004).
81. The *pontifex maximus* did not traditionally nominate members for election; see Szemler (1972), 21–4. Yet it is difficult not to believe that Caesar had some influence over the candidates who were presented for election; see also Taylor (1942), 405, who speculates on the role of Servilia in securing this result.
82. Cic. *Brut.* 324; on Cicero's 'filiation' of Brutus, see Dugan (2005), 247–8; the point is taken up by Grabarek (2010).
83. Details of the charges are provided by Cic. *Fam.* 3.11.1–3 (SB 74) and 3.12.1 (SB 75); cf. *TLRR*, nos 344 and 345. We do not know the precise charges behind the *maiestas* accusation, but they are perhaps connected in some way to his governorship of Cilicia and Cyprus; [Aur. Vict.] *Vir. Ill.* 82.4, gives the charge as extortion (*repetundae*).
84. Here I disagree with Stewens (1963), 22–3, who sees Brutus' influence as less compared to the eloquence brought by Hortensius and the *auctoritas* by Pompey.
85. Thus Balbo (2013), 320. This seems to be a fair assessment based on the evidence: at Cic. *Brut.* 324 Cicero connects Brutus closely with Hortensius, while at Cic. *Fam.* 3.11.3 (SB 74) he remarks specifically on Pompey and Brutus' cooperation in the *maiestas* trial.
86. Cic. *Fam.* 3.11.1 (SB 74).
87. Van der Blom (2016).

Chapter 3: The Politics of War

1. The evidence is fully discussed by Gruen (1974), 451–60; for a full coverage of the period described here, see Wiseman (1994).
2. On the marriage between Pompey and Cornelia, see Plut. *Pomp.* 55; cf. Vell. Pat. 2.54.2; Luc. *Phars.* 3.21–2. We do not know for certain when the marriage took place, but Plutarch may well be right in placing it after Pompey's appointment to the consulship in March 52 BC (Plut. *Pomp.* 55.1–3); compare, however, Asc. *Mil.* 31C who regards Pompey as Scipio's son-in-law already in 53 BC. On the political nature of Pompey's marriages, see Haley (1985). On Caesar's attempt to save the alliance by offering Pompey his sister's granddaughter, Octavia, see Suet. *Iul.* 27.1.

3. Caes. *B. Gall.* 7.6.1.
4. *Divino tertio consulatu*: Cic. *Att.* 7.1.4 (SB 124).
5. See e.g. Cic. *Att.* 9.1.4 (SB 167): 'he is not fighting for his own cause, or so he says, but for that of the people'.
6. For the threat of prosecution hanging over Caesar, see Suet. *Iul.* 30.3–4. Whether such a threat really existed has been a matter of some debate. For an overview and sceptical assessment of this question, with further bibliography, see Morstein-Marx (2007).
7. Discussions of Pompey's political manoeuvring as regarded Caesar's position from 52 BC onwards can be found in Gruen (1974), 492–3; Morstein-Marx (2007); Steel (2013), 186–95; Stevenson (2015), 114–18.
8. At Cic. *Fam.* 8.1.1 (SB 77), Caelius explains that he has delegated the task of compiling more precise details of senatorial decrees and edicts, as well as the gossip and rumours to a third party; these sadly do not survive, except for the senatorial decree preserved in *Fam.* 8.8 (SB 84). However, Caelius also promised to send his personal commentary on the major political events, and so we do still have a lot of valuable information. These letters are best accessed via Shackleton Bailey's Loeb edition, where they are all grouped together in *Letters to Friends,* vol. 2, nos 77–98.
9. Cic. *Fam.* 8.14.2 (SB 97).
10. Plut. *Caes.* 30.2; Plut. *Pomp.* 58.5.
11. The account presented here is highly condensed. For primary sources, see: App. *B. Civ.* 2.26–33; Plut. *Pomp.* 56–9; cf. Plut. *Caes.* 29–31; Cass. Dio 40.60–6. Fuller overviews, with further references, can be found in Seager (2002), 140–51; Lintott (2008), 433–6; Ramsey (2009), 50–3; Steel (2013), 188–95.
12. Thus Dettenhofer (1992), 115–16.
13. Cic. *Fam.* 8.14.3 (SB 97).
14. For a damning assessment of Pompey's actions and position at the outbreak of the war, see Cic. *Att.* 8.3.3–5 (SB 153); after the war, too, Cicero reflected on the weak and *ad hoc* arrangements on the Pompeian side compared to the resourcefulness of the Caesarians; see Cic. *Att.* 11.9.1 (SB 220). Most narratives of the period stress Pompey's unpreparedness; a positive case, however, was suggested by Fritz (1942) and recently revived by Welch (2012), 43–57.
15. Cic. *Att.* 9.14.2 (SB 182).
16. In the Vettius affair of 59 BC, see pp. 36–9 and, more recently, Caesar had probably assisted in Brutus' election to the pontifical college, see pp. 52–3; on Caesar's probable support for the latter, see Taylor (1942), 405.
17. On the marriages of Brutus' sisters to the Caesarians Servilius Isauricus and M. Lepidus, see Vell. Pat. 2.88.1, 3; Cic. *Att.* 6.1.25 (SB 115), which mention Julia and Lepidus; cf. *RAA* 427 = *RAPF* 362.
18. See especially Cic. *Att.* 9.10.6 (SB 177) where Cicero quotes Atticus as saying: 'Never did I suggest in any letter that if Gnaeus left Italy you should leave with him; or if I did suggest it I was – I won't say inconsistent – out of my mind.'
19. Plut. *Brut.* 4.2–3; there is no explicit evidence either to support or refute this claim. Moles–Pelling *ad loc.* reviews some of the arguments both for and against Plutarch's claim here, but simply concludes that 'it should perhaps be accepted at face value'; not least because he seems to concur with the picture of Brutus as a man who is steadfast in his self-righteousness. I am inclined to think that the demands of the trial might have led the two men to communicate, but this is not a given, either.
20. In addition to Cassius, these would have included C. Valerius Triarius and L. Manlius Torquatus. For Brutus' friendship with these men, see Cic. *Brut.* 266. On their participation in the war, as well as a full list of men who we know for certain fought on Pompey's side, see Shackleton Bailey (1960).
21. Plut. *Brut.* 4.2; an explanation accepted wholesale by Clarke (1981), 20, when he claims that Brutus' 'political principle came before personal feelings'. *Contra* see Dettenhofer (1992), 119, who argues that Plutarch's account reflects philosophical considerations more in vogue in Plutarch's own day than in republican Rome.
22. Luc. *Phars.* 2.234; on the pure fiction of Lucan's account, see Lintott (1971), 489 n. 4.
23. Shackleton Bailey (1960), 253–67, has shown, through an analysis of the sides men took in the civil war, that personal reasons were the major influence on most men's decisions; cf. Dettenhofer (1992), 118, who adds the point that, in Brutus' case, personal ties (*necessitudines*) coincided with his political inclinations (*partium sensus*). For more on *necessitudines*, see Hellegouarc'h (1963), 63–90; Meier (1966), 7–23. On the importance of *necessitudines* as a subset of friendship (*amicitia*), see Brunt (1965).
24. Alföldi (1985), 357, only considers the financial motivations for Brutus' visit; cf. Shatzman (1975),

373. An opposing idea is put forward by Stewens (1963), 17, who, on the basis of the ancient sources which mention the contribution made by Cilicia to the fleet of Pompey (Caes. *B. Civ.* 3.3–4; Cass. Dio 41.63.1; App. *B. Civ.* 2.49, 71), concludes that Brutus was contributing to the war effort. As the two activities are not mutually exclusive, it is possible that Brutus took steps to secure his own position as well as Pompey's, as I have suggested in the main text.

25. If Brutus was among the 200 senators mentioned by Dio as being in Thessalonica at the beginning of the new year (Cass. Dio 41.43.2), that would place Brutus there in early 48 BC; on this point, see Steel (2013), 198.
26. Cic. *Att.* 11.4a (SB 214).
27. Ancient explanations for Brutus' motivations do not tell us much here; Plut. *Brut.* 4.4 simply tells us that, with nothing of importance to do in Cilicia, Brutus travelled to Macedonia when the supreme contest between Pompey and Caesar grew closer. Conversely, the anonymous author Pseudo-Aurelius (*Vir. Ill.* 82.5) records the tradition that Brutus only left Cilicia upon Cato's urgent insistence.
28. Cass. Dio 41.63.5.
29. Dettenhofer (1992), 194, concludes that he was probably only present in the community and not on the battlefield; cf. Clarke (1981), 21, who upholds that Brutus did take an active part in the fighting.
30. For a narrative of what happened, see Caes. *B. Civ.* 3.62–74.
31. Plut. *Brut.* 4.6–8 tells us that he worked on a Latin translation and epitome of Polybius' *Histories*. Brutus' attachment to his literary studies is generally well attested; e.g. Cic. *Orat.* 34, Cic. *Brut.* 22; cf. Quint. *Inst.* 10.7.27. But his behaviour here is also a literary commonplace. For the man devoted to his literary studies, compare Pliny the Younger's description of his own scholarly behaviour in the face of impending disaster (the eruption of Vesuvius) at Plin. *Ep.* 6.16.7. For the point that Brutus is rather characterised as a philosopher, see Moles–Pelling on Plut. *Brut.* 4.8: 'there is a distinct whiff of the wellknown τόπος of the philosopher going about his business imperturbably despite scenes of the utmost chaos around him: one thinks of Socrates at Potidaea, Archimedes at Syracuse, or Cato at Utica'.
32. While arguments from silence should be treated with caution, Dettenhofer (1992), 193, is perhaps right to suggest that the few traces of mention of Brutus in the sources for the civil war imply he was not entrusted with a major military task. Radin (1939), 96, has argued that Brutus was too young and inexperienced but that cannot be right. Many of Brutus' contemporaries occupied prominent positions; e.g. Cassius, who was only slightly older, was put in charge of the fleet.
33. Thus Dettenhofer (1992), 194, who suggests Brutus played no role in the war, other than providing the senatorial side with the 'symbolic value' attached to his name and ancestry.
34. App. *B. Civ.* 2.82 puts the casualties on Caesar's side at 30 centurions and 200 legionaries (although he adds that some accounts recorded 1,200); the number of Pompeians killed was apparently 6,000, although he again adds that some inflated the number to 25,000. For these numbers, Appian relies on the account of Asinius Pollio, which has sadly not come down to us. On Pollio's reliability here, see Morgan (2000), 57, with n. 32.
35. Seager (2002), 167.
36. Plut. *Pomp.* 73–6, Plut. *Cat. Min.* 60–1.
37. Plut. *Brut.* 5.1.
38. Plut. *Brut.* 6.1.
39. Plut. *Brut.* 4.5 (Pompey greets Brutus); Plut. *Caes.* 46.4 (Caesar's pleasure at seeing Brutus).
40. Thus Dettenhofer (1992), 194–7.
41. Schmidt (1889), 169, and Purser (1896), 370, consequently see him as a traitor, while other writers have sought to discredit Plutarch's account or ignore it entirely; cf. Clarke (1981), 21, Gelzer (*RE* 10.1 (1917), 986) and Stewens (1963).
42. Bengtson (1970), 9–10, has also argued that there is no real reason to doubt Plutarch's testimony, although Dettenhofer (1992), 197, has rightly cautioned against accepting the psychoanalytical explanation Bengtson provides for Brutus' actions after Pharsalus: namely that Brutus was under a cloud of deep depression.
43. Plut. *Pomp.* 76.4–6.
44. Caes. *B. Civ.* 3.102.
45. Caes. *B. Civ.* 3.106; cf. Plut. *Pomp.* 77.1 (for the decision to sail to Egypt from Cyprus).
46. For Pompey's death, see Plut. *Pomp.* 77–80; cf. Caes. *B. Civ.* 3.106; App. *B. Civ.* 2.84–6; on Caesar's reaction see Plut. *Caes.* 48.2. Later writers who comment on it include Cass. Dio 42.7.2–8.3 and Lucan 9.1104–6. On the literary tradition of writing about Pompey's death, see Bell (1994).
47. For the suggestion of Greece, see Drumann and Groebe (1908), 29; Gelzer (*RE* 10.1 (1917), 981, has made the argument for Cilicia.
48. As suggested by Schmidt (1889), 170.

49. Plut. *Pomp.* 80.6; Appian has Cassius down as the killer of Theodotus at *B. Civ.* 2.90.
50. Caes. *B. Alex.* 66 for the meeting at Tarsus; for this reconstruction see Dettenhofer (1992), 197–9.
51. Caes. *B. Alex.* 78; cf. Cic. *Deiot.* 8–14, 17, 24, 35–6.
52. Cic. *Att.* 14.1.2 (SB 355); cf. Plut. *Brut.* 6.7–8.
53. Schmidt (1889), 170, reads it as an ironic expression conjuring 'the obstinacy of Brutus'; Gelzer (*RE* 10.1 (1917), 982) suggested that 'Caesar recognized in him a peculiar independence of mind'; Dettenhofer (1992), 197–9, links it to the surprise Caesar experienced at Brutus' unpredictability.
54. Rothstein (1932), 324–34; Dihle (1978).
55. Based, in large part, on Tacitus' verdict of Brutus' speech *For King Deiotarus* (*Pro Rege Deiotaro*), which he groups among others equally 'slow and flat' at Tac. *Dial.* 21.6.
56. See e.g. Cic. *Orat.* 97, where the perfect orator is conceived as the master of 'full [*amplus*], copious [*copiosus*], weighty [*gravis*], ornate [*ornatus*]' style, 'in which there is the greatest force [*vis maxima est*]'; for discussion of Brutus' oratory, see Filbey (1911) and Balbo (2013).
57. Plut. *Cat. Min.* 12.2 records that Deiotarus had been a guest-friend of Cato's father and that Cato renewed the connection when he visited the east in the 60s BC.
58. Pompey offers a comparable case in the ancient world for the deployment of vague expressions; see Van der Blom (2011).
59. Plut. *Brut.* 6.5 (Brutus secured pardon for Cassius); Plut. *Caes.* 62.2–3 (Caesar spared many of Brutus' friends); cf. Cic. *Att.* 11.20.2 (SB 235) where Cicero reports that Caesar was denying the privilege to nobody; on Brutus as the first prominent defector, see also the comments of Gelzer (1968), 243.
60. I have treated this period of Cicero's life more fully at Tempest (2011), 168–71.
61. Cic. *Att.* 11.12.3 (SB 222), 11.13.1 (SB 224).
62. On the growing strength of the Pompeians, see: Cic. *Att.* 11.10.2 (SB 221), 11.11.1 (SB 222), 11.12.3 (SB 223), 11.13.1 (SB 224), 11.14.1 (SB 225). On the perceived weakness of Caesar's position, see: Cic. *Att.* 11.15.1 (SB 226), 11.16.1–3 (SB 227), 11.18.1 (SB 230). For the speculation that many men were re-joining Africa and Cicero's comments on their chances, see Cic. *Att.* 11.15.2 (SB 226).
63. Cic. *Brut.* 11; this 'letter' may be identifiable with the (lost) text of Brutus' *De Virtute* according to Hendrickson (1939), but his arguments have not been accepted by all; see e.g. the comments of Clarke (1981), 138 n. 1; Strasburger (1990), 24; Dettenhofer (1992), 199.
64. On the 'very sweetness' of the letter, see Cic. *Brut.* 330, '*suavissimis litteris*'; on their shared intellectual pursuits, also see Cicero's comments at Cic. *Tusc.* 5.1. On the development of their friendship, see Grabarek (2010).
65. On Brutus' writings, see Gelzer, *RE* 10.1 (1917) 974. References to *On Virtue* at Cic. *Fin.* 1.3.8, Cic. *Tusc.* 5.1 and 30; Sen. *Cons. Helv.* 9.4. The three words from On *Endurance* are quoted by Diomedes, in Keil, *GL* I, 383, 8.
66. Sen. *Cons. Helv.* 8.1, 9.4–7; cf. Cic. *Tusc. Disp.* 5.12.
67. Quotations taken respectively from Sen. *Cons. Helv.* 9.4 and 8.1.
68. Sen. *Cons. Helv.* 9.6–7.
69. *Scias eum sentire quae dicit*: Quint. *Inst.* 10.1.23.
70. On the neutrality of Sulpicius Rufus, see e.g. Cass. Dio 40.59.1; Brutus' own connection with Rufus may have gone back some way, since Cato and Rufus had cooperated on the prosecution of Murena in 63 BC.
71. Cic. *Brut.* 156; since Brutus was indeed one of the *pontifices* – the fifteen priests responsible for overseeing the proper performance of the state religion – it seems plausible to accept Cicero's evidence that this topic formed the gist of Brutus' conversation with Sulpicius.
72. This suggestion, made by Hendrickson (1939), 411, is developed by Dettenhoffer (1992), 199–201.
73. *Ipso legato ac deprecatore*: Cic. *Fam.* 15.15.2 (SB 174).
74. For the expression of this anxiety, the opening lines of Cic. *Brut.* 10–11, composed in the winter 47/46 BC, might prove telling. Yet Cicero's letters also reveal his despondency: see e.g. Cic. *Fam.* 5.21.3 (SB 182); Cic. *Att.* 12.2.1 (SB 238).
75. Cic. *Brut.* 171, Cic. *Fam.* 6.6.10 (SB 234); cf. Plut. *Brut.* 6.10; App. *B. Civ.* 2.111.
76. [Aur. Vict.] *Vir. Ill.* 82.5 suggests he went with pro-consular power (*proconsul Galliam rexit*). But Broughton (*MRR* 2, 301) is probably right to suggest a propraetorship; cf. also Gelzer (*RE* 10.1 (1917), 983). This would bring Brutus' role into line with the position held by Decimus Brutus in Transalpine Gaul (App. *B. Civ.* 2.111).
77. On Brutus' good conduct in Gaul see Cic. *Orat.* 34, Cic. *Fam.* 11.19.2 (SB 399); Plut. *Brut.* 6.10–11.
78. Although five letters survive from Cicero to Brutus (Cic. *Fam.* 13.10–14 = SB 276–81), they are of a very formal nature and yield no further information beyond the name of the quaestor who served under Brutus in Gaul: M. Terentius Varro (Cic. *Fam.* 13.10.1–2 = SB 276). On the date of his return, see p. 74 with n. 97, below.
79. Plut. *Cat. Min.* 65.1, 3–5; 70.3–4 (on the safety of the fleet); reasons for Cato's suicide, as well as his

role in the civil war, have been revisited recently by Welch (2012), 95–9.
80. For the fuller account of Cato's death, see Plut. *Cat. Min.* 66–70; App. *B. Civ.* 2.98–99. A reappraisal of the Plutarchan account can be found in Zadorojnyi (2007).
81. Cic. *Off.* 1.112.
82. Principal texts referring to Cato and suicide are: Cic. *Tusc.* 1.30.74; Sen. *Prov.* 3.14 and Mart. 1.78.8–10. On Roman attitudes towards suicides, as well as the impact of Cato's death in the later development of his legend see e.g. Griffin (1986).
83. Cic. *Att.* 12.4.2 (SB 240).
84. 'I call you to testify that I only dared to write it, and reluctantly at that, because you [Brutus] asked me to. For I want you to share the blame with me so that, if I cannot defend myself against so great a charge, you will take the blame for imposing this excessive task on me – as I blame myself for accepting it': Cic. *Orat.* 35. That Cicero was hiding behind Brutus' name was the observation at least of Aulus Caecina at Cic. *Fam.* 6.7.4 (SB 237).
85. On the death of Appius, see Val. Max. 1.8.10. It is likely that Brutus only composed and did not deliver the eulogy; a five-word fragment, *qui te toga praetexta amicuit* ('who wrapped you in a purple-bordered toga'), is at *ORF* 158.23.
86. As Dettenhofer (1992), 206, puts it, the responsibility for praising Cato was a '*Schwarzer Peter*' – an unwelcome 'card' – which Brutus passed on to Cicero, who was seemingly eager to take it.
87. Cic. *Att.* 12.5.2 (SB 242), '*Cato me quidem delectat*'; for Caesar's displeasure, see Plut. *Caes.* 54.6.
88. Macrob. *Sat.* 6.2.33; on the contents of Cicero's *Cato*, see Kierdorf (1978); for Caesar's compliments on the literary quality, see Cic. *Att.* 13.46.2 (SB 338).
89. *In quo colligit vitia Catonis:* Cic. *Att.* 12.40.1 (SB 283); cf. 12.41.4 (SB 284), 12.44.1 (SB 285), 12.48.1 (SB 289); cf. Plut. *Caes.* 54.3–6. Discussion of these works can be found in Taylor (1949), 170ff; Gelzer (1969), 301–4; Tschiedel (1981); Marin (2009), 163–5.
90. Cicero calls Hirtius' attempt a 'kind of rough draft' for Caesar's *Anti-Cato* at Cic. *Att.* 12.41.4 (SB 283); cf. Cic. *Att.* 12.44.1 (SB 285).
91. I have treated this episode more fully elsewhere: Tempest (2011), 90–100.
92. Cic. *Att.* 12.21.1 (SB 260); later works that may have been influenced by Brutus' *Cato* in their presentation of the senatorial debate include Sall. *Cat.* 52–53.1; Vell. Pat. 2.34–5.
93. Plut. *Brut.* 40.7; Dettenhofer (1992), 205–8, also sees the origins of this extract in Brutus' *Cato*; my only point of disagreement with her analysis is that she concludes that it was written entirely as a 'handshake' with Caesar.
94. On the Platonic/Academic arguments on suicide, see e.g. Soc. *Phaed.* 61B–62D, Soc. *Laws* 873C–D. On the rights and wrongs of Cato's suicide in contemporary debate, see Cic. *Tusc.* 1.74, Cic. *Off.* 1.112. Thus, it is not unthinkable that Brutus expressed his own disapproval. On the possible historicity of this statement, also see Moles–Pelling *ad loc.* which tentatively suggests that the passage in Cicero's *Tusculan Disputations*, in which Cato's suicide is justified as a parallel to that of Socrates, could be a direct reply to Brutus (to whom the work was dedicated).
95. For a different interpretation of the format, see Brozek (1959), who suggests it was a speech, similar in character to Cicero's *Pro Marcello.*
96. See Zadorojnyi (2007), 220–1, on Thrasea Paetus and Manucius Rufus.
97. Cic. *Att.* 12.19.3 (SB 257), 12.27.3 (SB 266).
98. Cic. *Att.* 12.29.1 (SB 268): 'I am not avoiding Brutus . . . but there were reasons why I should not want to be in Rome at the current time': cf. ibid. 12.36.2 (SB 275): 'If you write to Brutus, unless you think otherwise, scold him for not wanting to stay at Cumae.'
99. Cicero took a keen interest in the baby's welfare, but we hear nothing more about his grandchild, who soon died, after a letter to Atticus on 27 March 45 BC; Cic. *Att.* 12.30.1 (SB 270).
100. Cic. *Att.* 12.13.1 (SB 250), 12.14.4 (SB 251).
101. Cic. *Att.* 12.38a.1 (SB 279); cf. Cic. *Ad Brut.* 1.9.1 (SB 18).
102. On the death of Julia, see Cic. *Q. Fr.* 3.6.3 (SB 26); for a good discussion of men's attitudes to death, with reference to Cicero, see Treggiari (1998), 14–23; cf. Treggiari (2007), 136–8.
103. Or so Cicero reports at Cic. *Att.* 13.9.2 (SB 317); cf. 13.10.2 (SB 318).
104. Cic. *Att.* 13.10.3 (SB 318).
105. Thus Bengtson (1970), 13; Clarke (1981), 29–30; a possibility not ruled out by Corrigan (2015), 55.
106. Cic. *Att.* 13.22.4 (SB 329).
107. Compare the observation of Dettenhofer (1992), 208: 'From a political point of view, Brutus had managed to unite the antipodes of the time in the form of Servilia and Porcia in his family. But perhaps he was not aware of it.' ('Politisch gesehen hatte es Brutus jedenfalls fertiggebracht, die Antipoden der Zeit in Gestalt von Servilia und Porcia in seiner Familie zu vereinen. Aber mögli cherweise war ihm das so nicht bewußt.') My interpretation differs here in that Dettenhofer sees the union of the women as an unwitting by-product of the marriage, whereas I am inclined to see it as part of Brutus' wider political strategy.

108. Cicero gives us some evidence for the meeting. At Cic. *Att.* 13.44.1 (SB 336) he suggests that Brutus had been with him at Tusculum in late July, and that he had gone from there to meet Caesar. Brutus was on his way back in mid-August, by which time Cicero was anxious to hear the outcome of the journey; see Cic. *Att.* 13.39.2 (SB 342).
109. On Caesar's reception of Brutus, see Plut. *Brut.* 6.12.
110. Paraphrased and abridged from Cic. *Att.* 13.40.1 (SB 343): '*Itane? nuntiat Brutus illum ad bonos viros? εὐαγγέλια. sed ubi eos? nisi forte se suspendit. hic autem ut fultum est. ubi igitur φιλοτέχνημα illud tuum quod vidi in Parthenone, Ahalam et Brutum? sed quid faciat?*'

Chapter 4: Thinking about Tyrannicide

1. On the certainty of civil war, see Caelius in Cic. *Fam.* 8.14.2 (SB 97) and Cic. *Att.* 7.1.2 (SB 124). On the inevitability of a tyranny afterwards, see Cic. *Att.* 7.5.4 (SB 128).
2. For a philosophical reading of this letter, Cic. *Att.* 9.4.2 (SB 173), see Baraz (2012), 55–7.
3. Cic. *Fam.* 15.18.1 (SB 213); for discussion of this passage, see McConnell (2014), 20–3.
4. Suet. *Iul.* 76.1–2. On the honours Caesar accepted and received, see also – more selectively – Plut. *Caes.* 57–61. Fuller discussion in Jehne (1987), esp. 191–220; Rawson (1994), 438–67; Pelling (2011), 420–59. On the place of such catalogues in the tradition of writing conspiracy narratives, see Pagán (2004), 111–12.
5. Cic. *Fam.* 7.30.2 (SB 265).
6. Suet. *Iul.* 77; his source was a pamphlet by one of Caesar's enemies: T. Ampius Balbus. On the credibility of the sentiments expressed, see Gelzer (1968), 274 n. 3.
7. Cic. *Att.* 14.1.2 (SB 355).
8. See Caes. *B. Civ.* 1.7.2.
9. Suet. *Iul.* 79.2; cf. Plut. *Caes.* 60.3; App. *B. Civ.* 2.108. For a brief overview of the past scholarship regarding what Caesar meant by this, see Deutsch (1928).
10. On these incidents, see (in addition to the sources in n. 9, above): Plut. *Caes.* 60.4–61.10, with commentary by Pelling *ad loc.*; cf. Cic. *Phil.* 13.31; Cass. Dio 44.9.3–10.3.
11. Cic. *Phil.* 2.84–7. The crown, according to Plutarch *Caes.* 61.5, was a diadem – the white strip of cloth which symbolised kingship in the Hellenistic world, with a laurel crown wound around it. Plutarch's account in his life of Caesar says that Antony offered it twice (as does Nic. Dam. 71–5; App. *B. Civ.* 2.109; Cass. Dio 44.11.1–3); however, at Plut. *Ant.* 12, the number of attempts is given as three; cf. also Suet. *Iul.* 79.2, who suggests several occasions ('saepius' in the Latin).
12. I take the phrase 'it is lucky we killed him when we did' from Balsdon (1958); as for the tale of an oracle, even Cicero admits it was false (Cic. *Div.* 2.110).
13. On the date Caesar received his new title, see Meyer (1922), 526, who puts it on 14 February based on the evidence of Cic. *Div.* 1.119; however, I have found no firm evidence to corroborate this inference. The title seems to have been in use by the time of the Lupercalia to judge from a comment by Cicero (Cic. *Phil.* 2.87); but on 26 January the entries of the official calendar, or *fasti*, still refer to him as *dict. IIII*. So it was bestowed upon him at some date between 27 January and 15 February. For the coinage advertising his new title, see, e.g. *RRC* 480/13: a silver denarius of February–March 44 BC, minted by Publius Sepullius Macer. Carson (1957) also presents a useful survey of the coinage in circulation in early 44 BC.
14. Plut. *Caes.* 57.1, with Pelling's note *ad loc.* The allusion is to Plato's *Republic* 8.569b – referring to the moment when a demagogue emerges as tyrant (565c–6d).
15. Pagán (2004), esp. 109–10.
16. E.g. the alleged conspiracies of Deiotarus (Cic. *Deiot.* 5–22) and Cassius, discussed on p. 90.
17. Cic. *Marcell.* 21.
18. On the plot, see Plut. *Ant.* 13.2; Cicero's later accusation of Antony's involvement appears at Cic. *Phil.* 2.34.
19. Suet. *Iul.* 75.5.
20. At Cic. *Phil.* 2.74 Cicero refers to an incident in which Antony allegedly hired someone to attack Caesar in his house; Dolabella's own role in any alleged assassination plot is less clear; see Moles–Pelling on Plut. *Brut.* 8.2.
21. Plut. *Brut.* 8.1.
22. Plut. *Brut.* 8.3; cf. Plut. *Caes.* 62.6.
23. It is extremely unlikely Caesar had any real plans to make Brutus his successor. As the event of his assassination proved, the main beneficiary of his will was his great-nephew and posthumously adopted son, Octavian. I think we can discount the argument advanced by Schmidt (1889) that Brutus had somehow become aware of the dictator's will and hence developed an all-consuming hatred of Caesar; *contra* Schmidt see especially Bengtson (1970), 7–8.
24. The concept of 'backshadowing' is developed by Bernstein (1994), 16; for its applicability to

conspiracy narratives, see Pagán (2004), 117–18. We have already seen the quotation from Plut. *Brut.* 6.7; my point bringing the reference up again here is simply to highlight the proximity of this statement to that of Caesar's alleged remark on Brutus' trustworthiness at Plut. *Brut.* 8.3.

25. For the pro-Liberator tradition and the particularly positive memory of Brutus, see Rawson (1986 = 1991), discussed further at p. 185.
26. For this approach, I draw inspiration from Wiseman (1994), see especially his comments in the introduction, at xii–xiii.
27. On Caesar's calendar reforms, see Plut. *Caes.* 59; further references and bibliography provided by Pelling *ad loc.*; on problems of debt and unemployment, see Cass. Dio 42.51.1–2; cf. Frederiksen (1966), 128–41.
28. I exclude from the discussion here the thousands of slaves who had no claim to liberty at all; on *libertas* as a civic right, see Wirszubski (1950), 1–3.
29. Caes. *B. Civ.* 1.22.5; for discussion of Caesar as a liberator, see Tatum (2008), 140–2; on Caesar's understanding of *libertas,* see Morstein-Marx (2009).
30. This is the basic definition of *libertas* offered by Wirszubski (1950), 15. A fuller discussion and analysis of the concept is that of Arena (2012), which I build upon in the next paragraph.
31. Cic. *Deiot.* 33–4.
32. Nic. Dam. 69; Cass. Dio 44.9.2; Suet. *Iul.* 79.1; Appian, *B. Civ.* 2.108; Plutarch possibly exaggerates at Plut. *Caes.* 61.8, where he mentions several statues.
33. Thus e.g. Dyson (2010), 274, who specifically connects this observation to the appearance of graffiti in the last days of Caesar's dictatorship; for a good discussion arguing for the political nature of the extant evidence at Pompeii, see Milner (2014), esp. 97–136.
34. Suet. *Iul.* 80.3; cf. Plut. *Brut.* 9.6–7; Plut. *Caes.* 62.7; Cass. Dio 44.12.2–3; App. *B. Civ.* 2.112; for discussion of this graffiti in its political context, see Hillard (2013), 112–14, to which the following paragraph is indebted.
35. As Pelling notes on Plut. *Caes.* 62.7, because of the lack of punctuation marks, it is unclear whether these phrases were intended as questions or statements. In any case, he offers interesting parallels to graffiti in Pompeii using similar turns of expression, especially: 'you are asleep' / 'are you sleeping?': *dormis*).
36. Cass. Dio 43.45.3–4; cf. Morstein-Marx (2012), 205–6, on the location of the statue.
37. Cass. Dio 44.12.2.
38. For a thoughtful analysis of popular attitudes towards Caesar, see Jehne (1987), 304–26; Morstein-Marx (2012), 209–13, is more insistent on the idea that popular opinion had turned against Caesar, although he is rightfully mindful of the fact we cannot speak of a unanimous '*plebs*-eye view'.
39. The work was Cicero's *Brutus* published in 46 BC; on the date, see Gelzer (*RE* 10.1 (1917), 983); Robinson (1951); Dettenhofer (1992), 201.
40. Cic. *Brut.* 331.
41. E.g. Strasburger (1990), 30, cited by Dettenhofer (1992), 201.
42. Lintott (2008), 309.
43. Balsdon (1958), 91.
44. Thus Bengtson (1970), 15: 'Es ist wieder eine typische *interpretatio post eventum*.'
45. Winterbottom (2002); on Cicero's possible hopes and fears for the Republic, see Tempest (2013a).
46. Dettenhofer (1992), 201–4, suggests that Cicero perhaps hoped to inspire Brutus to lead the young men of his generation in opposing Caesar's tyranny, and to fulfil the hopes he had once held for him as the *princeps iuventutis*.
47. The argument that Brutus was a Caesarian was put forward already by Purser (1896) but it has not gained much currency in subsequent scholarship.
48. Cic. *Att.* 1.20.3 (SB 20), written in 60 BC.
49. Cic. *Phil.* 2.25.
50. For the application of the phrase *Cherchez la femme* to the Brutus conundrum, see Potter (1934), 673; cf. Balsdon (1958), 92: 'Où est-ce qu'il faut chercher la femme?'
51. Cass. Dio 44.13.1–4, 14.1; Porcia's direct speech at 44.13.3.
52. Plut. *Brut.* 13.2–11; Val. Max. 3.2.15.
53. For arguments for the preference of the Valerius/Plutarch tradition over that of Dio, see e.g. Gelzer (*RE* 10.1 (1917), 989); Dettenhofer (1992), 239–42; Pagán (2004), 119–22.
54. Parker (1998), 168.
55. Cic. *Phil.* 2.26; for the suggestion that this story contributed to Cassius' fame as the first conspirator, as told at Plut. *Brut.* 8.5–10.1; App. *B. Civ.* 2.113, see Balsdon (1958), 82.
56. On Cassius' role in the Parthian war, see Plut. *Crass.* 18–29; Cass. Dio 40, 25–30; Joseph. *AJ* 14.119–20; cf. mention of Cassius in Antioch in 51 BC at Cic. *Att.* 5.18.1 (SB 111), 5.20.3 (SB 113).
57. Caes. *B. Civ.* 3.101.

58. Plut. *Brut.* 7.1–5; cf. App. *B. Civ.* 2.112. Plutarch mentions the same story at Plut. *Caes.* 62.4, although there he suggests that the contest was for the consulship (which is also the version recorded by Vell. Pat. 2.56.3).
59. This argument is made in much fuller detail by Huß (1977).
60. For the dating of Cassius' conversion to Epicureanism to a point shortly after Pharsalus, see the comments of Shackleton Bailey (1977), 378–81, on Cic. *Fam.* 15.16.3 (SB 215), which suggests a date of two or three years before the letter was written in 45 BC.
61. Cic. *Fam.* 15.18.1–2 (SB 213); Dettenhofer (1990) has argued that the philosophical exchange here is also a code for testing Cassius' political allegiances. However, as Griffin (1995), 342–3, has pointed out, Cicero and Cassius normally draw a clear distinction between talking about philosophy and talking about politics.
62. Cic. *Fam.* 15.19.2 (SB 216), written mid-January 45 BC.
63. Cic. *Fam.* 15.19.4 (SB 216).
64. Thus Balsdon (1958), 94 n. 93; cf. Rawson (1986 = 1991), who also traces the interchangeable ways in which the two men are accredited with the deed.
65. Plut. *Brut.* 10.1–7; App. *B. Civ.* 2.113.
66. On the arguments available to Cassius to reconcile his Epicurean beliefs with the idea of tyrannicide, see Sedley (1997), 46; cf. Momigliano (1941), Griffin (1989), Fowler (1989).
67. On Cassius' refusal, see Cass. Dio 44.8.1; for the list of honours, see ibid. 44.2–5.3. At first glance, this story seems incompatible with the account of Nicolaus (at Nic. Dam. 71–5), which has Cassius next to Antony offering the crown to Caesar at the Lupercalia. But not everyone has accepted this evidence. See e.g. Hohl (1941–42), 108, who argues that it is a fabrication, intended to blacken the tyrannicides as 'hypocrites and cowards'; Gelzer (1968), 321 n.2, dismisses the scene as a 'divergent version' more 'in the style of tragic historiography' than a genuine account. Bengtson (1970), 15, is more willing to accept the story of Cassius' involvement and argues that it has important implications for our understanding of the plot: namely, he argues, it links Cassius to the accusation that some of Caesar's men were working to bring about his unpopularity and thus engineer his downfall.
68. Cic. *Phil.* 2.26. Cicero was probably thinking of Spurius Cassius Vicellinus (consul in 502, 496 and 486); he was said to have killed his own son in 485 BC because he was aspiring to be monarch. See Berry (2006), *ad loc.* On Spurius Cassius, see Smith (2006), esp. 49–52.
69. On the importance of glory and being *seen* to be virtuous, see Morstein-Marx (2009), 118–19.
70. Cic. *Brut.* 281; the 'lesson' was delivered under the guise of the example of Curio.
71. Dettenhofer (1992), 242.
72. Even before the civil war was in full swing and while Cicero was still in Italy, Caesar had made it clear that Cicero would have little freedom of expression if he returned to the Senate; Cic. *Att.* 9.18.1 (SB 187). By the end of 45 BC, Caesar no longer talked politics with Cicero at all; see Cic. *Att.* 13.52.1–2 (SB 353). As Cicero later wrote (Cic. *Off.* 2.2), in a description of the Caesarian regime, there was no place for 'counsel' (*consilium*) or 'authority' (*auctoritas*).
73. A point repeatedly emphasised by Dettenhofer (1992), e.g. at 163–4, 250–1, 316–17, 333–4.
74. Plut. *Brut.* 8.3; cf. Plut. *Caes.* 62.6 (see n. 24, above).
75. Varro, preserved in Censorinus, *DN* 14.2, names five stages of life: birth to fifteen (*pueritia*); fifteen to thirty (*adulescentia*); thirty to forty-five (*iuventus*); forty-five to sixty (*seniores*); sixty and upwards (*senes*).
76. On the important role played by philosophy in the formation and justification of the plot, the best analysis remains that of Sedley (1997).
77. Thus Lucullus associated with Antiochus, the founder of the Old Academy; Brutus with Antiochus' brother, Aristus; Cato the Younger with the Stoic Athenodorus; Calpurnius Piso with Philodemus. For further discussion and references, see Barnes (1997), 60–2.
78. Plut. *Brut.* 2.3; Cic. *Brut.* 332.
79. Cicero speaks of Aristus as *his* guest in 46 BC, and there is no suggestion that he had died. Although we cannot pinpoint when he moved to Brutus' estate, it is worth pointing out that he may have had some influence over Brutus in the years of Caesar's dictatorship.
80. I have adapted my summary from Cicero's own description at Cic. *Tusc.* 5.22. For other expressions of the Old Academy's position, see Cic. *Fin.* 5.71, 81. On the topic of Antiochus' philosophical position, see Barnes (1997), Sedley (1997) and the collection of essays in Sedley (2012).
81. Sedley (1997), to whose work the next two paragraphs are particularly indebted.
82. Thus Plato *Pol.* 300e–303b.
83. Plato *Rep.* 8.564a.
84. It is mentioned by the contemporary writer Philodemus, *Index Academica* 6.13, cited by Sedley (1997), 53.
85. For the hint that Caesar's regime was perceived as 'lawless' at the time, see Cic. *Fam.* 4.4.5 (SB

203), in which Cicero appears to suggest to the jurist S. Sulpicius Rufus that the rule of law (*ius*) has been abandoned in favour of 'what Caesar seems to want'.

86. Cic. *Off.* 3.19.
87. The role of Decimus Brutus has been reinvigorated in recent treatments of the conspiracy; see e.g. Bengtson (1970), 15–80; Tatum (2008), 155; Strauss (2015), 81–6. For the ancient evidence in support of his place alongside Brutus and Cassius, see Cic. *Fam.* 12.1.1 (SB 327).
88. I follow Horsfall (1974), 193, in accepting that the conspiracy was probably only finalised towards the end of the month; cf. Yavetz (1983), 190.
89. On Trebonius and the alleged assassination plot, see n. 18 above, where he had hinted at the idea to Antony. In recent months, there was a further reason why Trebonius might have wanted to end the regime of Caesar. Trebonius had been consul in 45 BC when Caesar staged the irregular election of Rebilius (see p. 80). In so doing Caesar had diminished the honour due to the post – and by extension, to Trebonius.
90. Sen. *Ira* 3.30.4; in all, a list of some twenty known conspirators can be compiled from the various sources that mention the assassination, which seems a roughly plausible figure for the total number of accomplices. For a summary list of conspirators, see Lintott (2009), 77; cf. the list of Drumann and Groebe (1906), 627–42, which provides more detail on each of the assassins, as well as their previous political affiliations.
91. Plut. *Caes.* 58.1.
92. Storch (1995) coins the term 'relative deprivation' to cover this emotion.
93. Plutarch records the 'recruitment' mission in detail at Plut. *Brut.* 12.3–8; for the argument in favour of its authenticity and our consequent understanding of the conspiracy, I am indebted to Sedley (1997).
94. Plut. *Ant.* 13.1.
95. Sources for these discussions at: Nic. Dam. 93; Vell. Pat. 2.58.2; Plut. *Brut.* 18.2; Plut. *Ant.* 13.2; App. *B. Civ.* 2.114; Cass. Dio 44.19.1.
96. See Nic. Dam. 81 for the various dates and locations suggested, as well as the manner in which the conspiracy was conducted. A fuller discussion of the planning, which stresses how excellently conceived some of the details were, can be found in Horsfall (1974).
97. The significance of the date has also been noted by Weigel (1992), 41.
98. Nic. Dam. 81; App. *B. Civ.* 2.114.
99. Cass. Dio 44.16.1.
100. Plut. *Caes.* 66; Suet. *Iul.* 82; cf. Nic. Dam. 90, who records thirty-five.
101. Suet. *Iul.* 82; the debt to Cornelius Balbus is made clear at ibid. 81.
102. A readable collection of emperors' death scenes and famous last words can be found in Meijer (2004).
103. Famous last words: Cato (Plut. *Cat. Min.* 70.1); Cicero (Sen. *Decl.* 6.17); Brutus (Plut. *Brut.* 52.3).
104. Plut. *Pomp.* 79.4.
105. In one account (Suet. *Iul.* 87), Caesar had even wished for such a death the night before he was assassinated.
106. Suet. *Iul.* 82.2; Cass. Dio 44.19.5.
107. For the story, see App. *B. Civ.* 2.112.
108. For the fullest treatment, which has been almost universally accepted, see Münzer, *RE* 2A (1923) 1871–21, 'Servilia'. One notable exception is Walter (1938) who dates Brutus' birth to 78 BC, in order to enhance the likelihood that Caesar was Brutus' father. *Contra* Walter, see Gelzer (1938).
109. His first betrothal was to Cosuttia, a woman of equestrian rank – an arrangement which was made while Caesar was still only fourteen or fifteen. However, this marriage never came to fruition as he had to take a patrician wife in order to hold the priesthood to which he had been appointed (*flamen Dialis*). Hence he was betrothed to and subsequently married Cornelia, the daughter of Cinna. See Suet. *Iul.* 1,1; Plut. *Caes.* 1.1.
110. Balsdon (1958), 86–7, is highly speculative when he argues that even the most fertile of men would have found it near impossible to impregnate Servilia within such a fleeting period of time, suggesting that Caesar was not the most fertile of men. But the point that Caesar was largely absent from Rome should not be entirely overlooked.
111. Plut. *Caes.* 66; although note App. *B. Civ.* 2.117 which records that Brutus struck Caesar in the thigh. That the 'groin' version might ultimately be linked to the story of Caesar's paternity of Brutus is also suggested by Pelling (2011), *ad loc.*
112. E.g. *teknon emon* at Hom. *Od.* 1.64 (Zeus to Athena); *phile/philon teknon* at Hom. *Il.* 22.84, *Od.* 2.363, 15.125, 23.26; for a fuller discussion of the the uses of *teknon* in addresses, see Dickey (1996), 65–72. While she observes that *teknon* is often used by fathers in addressing their sons, she also notes that it is the more suitable word for older men addressing non-kin adults.
113. Russell (1980). The only exceptions I have found are Tatum (2008), 112 (where he suggests the

translation, 'See you in hell, punk!'), and Pelling (2011), 482–3, commenting on Plut. *Caes.* 66.12, who also discusses the further alternative provided in n. 114, below.

114. For a comparative case with the second half of the proverb, see Suet. *Galba* 4.1 (where the warning is issued by Augustus to Galba); cf. Cass. Dio 57.19.4 (where the phrase is attributed to Tiberius). The argument presented here is that of Arnaud (1998), accepted by Woodman (2006), 183–4.
115. App. *B. Civ.* 2.112.
116. I am not in the least convinced by, but should not overlook in this connection, an article by Africa (1978), esp. 612–28, which argues that Brutus' attitude towards Caesar was akin to that of a man possessing an Oedipus complex: 'the protective son against a hated father figure'.

Chapter 5: After the Assassination

1. See the similar list of omens and prodigies at Cass. Dio 45.17.2–8; for further discussion of the portents in 44 BC, see Osgood (2006), 19–25, to which I am indebted here.
2. Cic. *Fam.* 12.25.1 (SB 373).
3. For the gloom, see Plin. *HN.* 2.98; further discussion and references in Forsyth (1988).
4. See Ramsey and Licht (1997) for more on the astrological phenomenon.
5. Verg. *Georg.* 1.466–9, 487–8.
6. Verg. *Georg.* 1.479. On Virgil's use of the word *infandum* and other cognate forms, especially in the *Aeneid,* see Commager (1981). For further discussion of portents, see pp. 193–5, where I consider their role more closely in connection to the Pharsalus campaign.
7. Nic. Dam. 91–2; Plut. *Caes.* 67.1, *Brut.* 18.1; cf. App. *B. Civ.* 2.118–19; Cass. Dio 44.20.1–2.
8. Nic. Dam. 96.
9. Cic. *Div.* 2.23.
10. Nic. Dam. 97.
11. Cic. *Phil.* 2.28, 30; had the claim come from Cicero in another context we might have questioned its reliability. However, since Cicero in the *Philippics* is keen to refute Antony on this point, it rather seems to lend weight to the suggestion.
12. Some details on pp. 3–4. An excellent summary of the discrepancies can be found in Woolf (2006), 12–18.
13. Cass. Dio 44.20. 2; on the panic, see the references cited in n. 7, above.
14. The ancient accounts are muddled as to his precise location at the time of the assassination: Plut. *Caes.* 97.2 has him in the Senate; Cass. Dio 44.19.2 places him in the suburbs, performing military drills; App. *B. Civ.* 2.118 thought that he was in the Forum. Given his military role and the imminent campaign against Parthia, I follow Weigel (1992), 44, in believing that he was probably not at the Senate that day.
15. On Lepidus' actions in the aftermath, see Cass. Dio 44.22.2. For the argument that Lepidus' decisive action was crucial for stabilising the situation, see Weigel (1992), 44–5.
16. Suet. *Iul.* 82.4.
17. App. *B. Civ.* 2.119 states they were afraid when the people did not join them in their jubilations after the assassination; Nic. Dam. 94 also presents their departure as an escape.
18. There are differing accounts in our ancient sources. Plut. *Brut.* 18.7–14 has speeches by Brutus and Cinna on 15 March (although he makes no mention of it in his *Life of Caesar*, and has Brutus speak only on 16 March). Nic. Dam. 99–100 also mentions a *contio* speech by Brutus. Appian provides the longest account, attributing speeches to Cinna and Dolabella, as well as to Brutus and Cassius, at *B. Civ.* 2.122. Cass. Dio 44.21.1–22.2 also has Dolabella speak, although he is vaguer about which of the assassins spoke. For a fuller analysis of the various accounts, see Moles–Pelling, 231–43, and Sumi (2005), 76–89. I largely base my description of the events here on the reconstruction of Pina Polo (1989), 308, who identifies two *contiones* on 15 March: the first featuring speeches from Brutus, Cassius and Cinna in the Forum; the second convened by Dolabella as he took up his role as suffect consul.
19. Cass. Dio 44.21.1; on the short shrift given to the assassins by Dio here and in the rest of his work, see Gowing (1992), 230.
20. App. *B. Civ.* 2.122; see the discussion by Morstein-Marx (2004), 152–3.
21. Plut. *Brut.* 18.8–12; Plut. *Caes.* 67; App. *B. Civ.* 2.120–21; Cass. Dio 44.21.2; Nic. Dam. 100.
22. Modern scholars have often taken the lack of positive support as evidence of hostile feeling at the death of Caesar; see e.g. Yavetz (1969), 62–9, (1974), 64. But see now the more measured reading of Morstein-Marx (2004), 150–8, who stresses the difficulty of recovering the (doubtless mixed) feelings of the urban plebs and contional audiences.
23. This argument is well laid out by Pina Polo (2006), followed by *i.a.* Morstein-Marx (2012), 209–13, who links it specifically to the assassins' misreading of public opinion.
24. The *lex Porcia* and the *lex Sempronia.* On these laws as the guardians of freedom, see: Cic. *Rab.*

Perd. Reo 12, *Verr.* 2.5.163; Sall. *Cat.* 51, 22; [Sall]. *Cic.* 5. For discussion, see Wirszubski (1950), 25 and Arena (2012), 50–1.

25. The detail of the insignia is from App. *B. Civ.* 2.121; for a sceptical treatment see Wiseman (2009), 221.
26. App. *B. Civ.* 2.122; Cass. Dio 44.22.1; cf. Cic. *Phil.* 2.84 when Antony, who had previously tried to block Dolabella's appointment, finally succumbed to recognising Dolabella's authority on 17 March.
27. Cic. *Att.* 14.10.1 (SB 364), discussed below.
28. In fact, Münzer has argued for a more general, long-standing relationship between the families of Brutus (the Junii) and Lepidus (the Aemilii); see *RAA* 157–9, 168 n. 1 = *RAPF* 147–9, 156 n. 192.
29. Cic. *Phil.* 2.89.
30. See e.g. Welch (2012), 130, who suggests that Antony came under Cicero's attack 'not because he was one of the greatest villains of Roman history but because he was capable of fighting back on almost equal terms'.
31. Surveys in English include Rice-Holmes (1928), 1–89; Syme (1939), 97–207; Frisch (1946); Rawson (1994), 468–90; Pelling (1996), 1–8; cf. Gotter (1996), 21–41, for a good examination of the events in German.
32. Later historical narratives, such as those of Appian and Dio, tend to streamline these months into a seamless narrative that underemphasises the roles of other individuals; while the biographical treatment of Plutarch explains Brutus' conduct from a moral standpoint largely shaped by the author's own ideas. For the preference of the contemporary evidence over the later accounts, I follow the reasons listed by Balsdon (1958), 80–1, and Osgood (2006), 25–39. Osgood, in particular, uses Cicero's letters to focus on the general uncertainties in the period after Caesar's death; my approach is similar but my aim here is to use a different selection to illuminate Brutus' actions and responses, as well as how they were perceived by his contemporaries.
33. An accompanying table of events and sources can be found in Appendix 2.
34. Quotations are from Cic. *Fam.* 11.1 (SB 325). On the date of the letter, see the varying solutions proposed by How (1926), vol. 2, 479–80 and Shackleton Bailey (1977), 464. But here I incline towards the suggestion of 16 March made by Lintott (2008), 340 n. 6. For the military situation of the assassins, see Drum (2008). For a partial acceptance of Drum's hypothesis, also see Welch (2012), 134.
35. See the discussion on pp. 177–22.
36. Quotations from Cic. *Att.* 14.2 (SB 356). On the policy of Brutus after the assassination, see Wistrand (1981); for Cicero's role in reaching the agreement with Antony, see Cic. *Phil.* 1.1–2, with comments and further references by Ramsey (2003), *ad loc.* Although Cicero nowhere adds the detail of the reconciliation scene in the forum, it occurs repeatedly in other ancient sources: App. *B. Civ.* 2.126; Cass. Dio 44.34.7; Plut. *Ant.* 14.1, *Brut.* 19.1–3; [Livy], *Per.* 116; Zonaras 10.12. Furthermore, that there was a relative period of calm after the assassination appears confirmed by Nep. *Att.* 8.1. He may well be exaggerating when he says that there was a period 'when it seemed the whole state was in the hands of the two Brutuses and Cassius, and when all the citizens turned to them', but it is important evidence nonetheless; see the further discussion by Horsfall (1989), *ad loc.*
37. Quotations from Cic. *Att.* 14.3 (SB 357), sent on 9 April and ibid. 14.5 (SB 359) from 11 April. On the efforts of Brutus and Cassius to secure support from the veterans and people, see App. *B. Civ.* 2.141; Cass. Dio at 44.34.1–2; approval in the municipal towns is reported by Cic. *Att.* 14.6.2 (SB 360).
38. Ancient evidence for Octavian's movements and arrival at Rome can be pieced together from Cic. *Att.* 14.5.3 (SB 359); Nic. Dam. 108; Vell. Pat. 2.59.5–6; Plut. *Brut.* 22.3; App. *B. Civ.* 3.9–12, 28; for the fuller reconstruction of his journey, see Toher (2004); on Caesar's popularity with the people and his celebrity at Rome prior to his arrival, see Sumi (2005), 125–6. Gowing (1992), 59–64, is right to demonstrate that later accounts have been distorted by the knowledge of what happened next; as far as possible this chapter will try to incorporate the rumours of Octavian's behaviour within its stated framework of the contemporary perspective.
39. On the date of Brutus' departure, see Drumann and Groebe (1899), 420; Denniston (1926), 72; on the possible connection between Octavian's arrival and Brutus' departure, see Toher (2004), 181–2.
40. Quotations from Cic. *Att.* 14.6 (SB 360) sent on 12 April and Cic. *Att.* 14.7 (SB 361) sent on 15 April. For more on the activities of 'Marius' (also referred to in the sources as Pseudo-Marius, Amatius or Herophilus), see Nic. Dam. 32; Val. Max. 9.15.1; App. *B. Civ.* 3.3.6–8; [Livy] *Per.* 116.
41. Quotations from Cic. *Att.* 14.10 (SB 364); for Cassius' presumed departure at the same time, see Ramsey (2003), 3. For the departures of Decimus and Trebonius, see Cic. *Att.* 14.13.2 (SB 367), Cic. *Fam.* 12.16.1 (SB 328); further references at *MRR* 2, 328, 330. Cicero's first expression of 'the tyranny lives on' motif, so strong in Cicero's later letters, is at Cic. *Att.* 14.9.2 (SB 363), sent on 17

April. For the description of the funeral in this paragraph, see App. *B. Civ.* 2.146–7; cf. Plut. *Brut.* 20.4–7 and Suet. *Iul.* 84.2, which are very different in tone. On the conflict in our later sources for the funeral, see the sensible assessment of Gotter (1996), 267, who points out that the accounts of Suetonius and Nicolaus reflect a systematic reduction of Antony's role in the Augustan literature. For the firebrands in the contemporary evidence, however, see Cic. *Phil.* 2.90–1. That Appian's account may owe something to dramatic conventions in Livy is suggested by Wiseman (2009). As a final note, we should add that in Plutarch's account (Plut. *Brut.* 21.2), Brutus and Cassius leave Rome immediately after the funeral, as a direct consequence of the popular demonstrations against them. Accordingly, he has Brutus go to his villa in Antium, hoping to return to the city in due course, but never actually returning to Rome. This chronology and account have been followed by some modern treatments of the assassins' movements; see e.g. most recently Corrigan (2015), 106. But scholars have largely treated Plutarch's account sceptically. Moles–Pelling, 279–90, has suggested that Plutarch (or the source he was using) has condensed the chronological timeframe, perhaps for narrative effect. Bengtson (1970), 20–1, does not discuss this point in any detail, but he silently rejects Plutarch's account by accepting that Brutus and Cassius left on 13 April – as Cicero's letters make it quite clear they did. It might, of course, be possible that Brutus went to Antium (which is also mentioned as a destination at Nic. Dam. 49), returned to Rome and then made his final departure in April. For this suggestion, see Gelzer (*RE* 10.1 (1917), 993).

42. Arrival of Octavian: Cic. *Att.* 14.10.3 (SB 364); 'he is completely devoted to me': Cic. *Att.* 14.11 (SB 365); 'His followers were calling him Caesar': Cic. *Att.* 14.12.2 (SB 366).
43. On the question of Caesar's *acta* and Antony's use of them in 44 BC, see Ramsey (1994).
44. Quotations are from Cic. *Att.* 14.2 (SB 366); on the continued ill-feeling between Cicero and Atticus, see e.g. Cic. *Att.* 14.14.2 (SB 368), where Cicero retorts: 'You defend Brutus and Cassius as if I were blaming them'. On the problem of Antony's use of Caesar's acts, as well as the recall of Cloelius, Cic. *Att.* 14.13.6 (SB 367); there is a good discussion of the problem in Mahy (2009), 56–62.
45. Cic. *Fam.* 12.4.1 (SB 363), to Cassius, 2 or 3 February 43 BC; cf. Cic. *Fam.* 10.28.1 (SB 364), to Trebonius.
46. For Lepidus' frame of mind after the Ides, see Cass. Dio 44.22.2 (where he delivers a speech against the assassins to the assembled soldiers) and 44.34.5 (where he favours war); see also Weigel (1992), 44–7.
47. Cic. *Phil.* 1.1; and again at 1.31. Note that in the accounts of Appian (*B. Civ.* 2.142) and Cass. Dio (44.34.4–7) the sons of Lepidus were also sent up, along with Antony's.
48. Cic. *Phil.* 1.32.
49. Cic. *Phil.* 1.3.
50. Quotations from Cic. *Att.* 14.14 (SB 368). On the position of Antony and his political manoeuvring, see Welch (2012), esp. 126–30; Osgood (2006), 33–4, also discusses this letter and Cicero's lack of analysis of the political developments.
51. Cic. *Att.* 14.9.3 (SB 363). On the word 'Caesarism' see Yavetz (1971), esp. 189; it should be noted here only that, although a useful description of the phenomenon that outlived Caesar the man, it is not a word found in our ancient sources.
52. Cic. *Att.* 14.21.2 (SB 375); cf. Cic. *Phil.* 2.101–7. On the date of Antony's departure, see Ramsey (2003), 4.
53. On Lepidus' activities and the need to secure Sextus Pompeius' cooperation, see Weigel (1992), 49–51.
54. Unless otherwise stated, quotations are from Cic. *Att.* 14.15 (SB 369), sent on 1 May; for a similar letter see Cic. *Fam.* 12.1 (SB 327) sent to Cassius on 3 May; Cic. *Fam.* 9.14 (SB 326) for the letter of congratulations sent directly to Dolabella, also preserved at Cic. *Att.* 14.17a (SB 371a). On Cicero's hopes for Dolabella, more generally, see Cic. *Att.* 14.16.1–2 (SB 370), which includes his wish that Brutus may now walk in Rome 'with a crown of gold'; cf. Cic. *Att.* 14.19.5 (372); Cic. *Fam.* 9.14 (SB 326). On the actual events of Marius' execution and the destruction of the altar, see Cic. *Phil.* 1.5, 2.107; cf. App. *B. Civ.* 3.3 and Val. Max. 9.15.1. For the chronology adopted here, see Toher (2004), 181.
55. For the existence of the letter, which we do not possess, see Cic. *Att.* 14.17.4 (SB 371).
56. 'He is contemplating exile': Cic. *Att.* 14.19.1 (SB 372); 'I don't know what he will do in public life': Cic. *Att.* 14.18.3 (SB 373). On his earlier attitude towards exile, see Chapter 3, p. 69.
57. Cic. *Att.* 14.20.5 (SB 374); Boes (1990), 383 n. 418, has suggested that the diminutive form (*vulticulus*) may refer to Brutus' inability to express himself well in his public interventions; I just take it here to mean that the serious countenance of Brutus, as he is thinking about retiring from public affairs, is used against the Epicurean doctrine 'do not get involved in political life' (*me politeuesthai*).
58. On the threat of Sextus Pompeius and worries over the prospect of civil war in these months, see e.g. Cic. *Att.* 14.4.2 (SB 358), 14.8.2 (SB 362), 14.3.2 (SB 367).

59. Gotter (1996), 64. Support for the suggestion of conflict between Lucius and Dolabella can be found at Cic. *Att.* 14.20.2 (SB 374) where Cicero refers to two speeches he had received: 'Lucius Antonius speech from the *contio* is appalling', he wrote to Atticus, 'Dolabella's is splendid.' We can only guess at the contents of each, but Lucius Antonius seems to have been calling for vengeance against the assassins; cf. the report Cicero had received of another 'vile speech' delivered (but not yet published) by Lucius on 18 May: Cic. *Att.* 15.2.2 (SB 379). Dolabella, on the other hand, was still promoting the cause of the Liberators; for this interpretation, also see Sumi (2005), 129; Lintott (2008), 346.
60. Cic. *Att.* 15.2.3 (SB 379); cf. 15.3.2 (SB 380), in which Cicero says this move was blocked by the tribunes.
61. Quotations are taken from Cic. *Att.* 14.20.3 (SB 374).
62. The date for this speech is difficult to pin down with any certainty. Pina Polo (1989), 308–9, puts it on 16 March; *contra* see Mahy (2009), 30, following Gowing (1992), 231–2, who tentatively moves it to later on the 17 March, while Morstein-Marx (2004), 153 n. 179, does not rule out 18 March as a possibility.
63. For the speech, see Cic. *Att.* 14.11.1 (SB 365); for the possible identification of its speaker and subsequent author as one of the Antonii brothers, see Welch (2012), 126. The fast publication and dissemination of speeches, especially *contional*, in 44 BC is the subject of an article by Kelly (2008).
64. Cic. *Fam.* 9.14.7 (SB 326); a copy of the letter is also preserved at Cic. *Att.* 14.17A (SB 371A).
65. Cic. *Att.* 14.20.2 (SB 374); for the possible contents of these speeches, see n. 60, above.
66. Cic. *Att.* 15.1a.2 (SB 378).
67. Even App. *B. Civ.* 2.142, who had earlier accused the assassins of hiring bribed claqueurs, refers to the genuine approval Brutus' speech won for its justness.
68. Cic. *Att.* 15.3.2 (SB 380).
69. The speech attributed to Brutus by Appian can be found at App. *B. Civ.* 2.137–41. Although speeches in Appian needed to be handled cautiously as evidence for what was said on any given occasion, scholars have been more generous in their treatment of this one as a possible reflection of Brutus' published oration; in particular, see Narducci (2007) and Balbo (2011). I am indebted to the latter's analysis of the speech for the summary here.
70. It should perhaps also be noted that, if the speech was delivered after the meeting of the Senate on 17 March as some have suggested (see n. 62, above), then the 'tyrant' argument would not have worked.
71. 'I see you feel the same as me about his little speech': Cic. *Att.* 15.3.2 (SB 380).
72. Quotations from Cic. *Att.* 15.3.1(SB 380). This letter also fixes Antony's return to Rome around 18 May, when Atticus had informed Cicero of this circumstance. For the circumstances of that return and the presence of the veterans, see Cic. *Phil.* 2.108; cf. App. *B. Civ.* 3.5, though we should perhaps take Appian's number of 6,000 veterans cautiously.
73. Cic. *Att.* 14.22.2 (SB 376).
74. 'Antony's plan seems set on war': Cic. *Att.* 15.4.1 (SB 381); 'You say you don't know what our friends ought to do': Cic. *Att.* 15.4.2 (SB 381).
75. Quotations in the following two paragraphs are from Cic. *Fam.* 11.2.1–3 (SB 329). For letter-writing conventions generally, see White (2010), 67–71, although he does not discuss this letter.
76. For a detailed exposition of this idea, see Wistrand (1981).
77. Quotations in this paragraph are from Cic. *Fam.* 11.2 (SB 329).
78. For Hirtius' concerns and Cicero's dismissal of them, see Cic. *Att.* 15.6.3 (SB 386); compare other jokes to suggest that Brutus was not thinking along military lines; e.g. 15.9.1 (SB 387): 'sitting still beside the Eurotas'.
79. Cic. *Phil.* 1.6; cf. 2.108–9.
80. Cic. *Phil.* 8.28: the calculation is based on the idea that Brutus and Cassius were in line to hold the consulships for 41 BC and would then be entitled to a provincial command of up to two years after that; i.e. all four men would then lay down *imperium* in 39 BC.
81. '[A] wretched affair': Cic. *Att.* 15.9.1 (SB 387); 'what duty . . . more sordid?': Cic. *Att.* 15.11 (SB 389).
82. '[B]ankrupt of advice': Cic. *Att.* 15.9.2 (SB 387); 'What a lovingly written letter': Cic. *Att.* 15.10.1 (SB 388).
83. On the question of whether Caesar had allocated provinces to Brutus and Cassius, see Kniely (1974), 37–71.
84. Quotations and paraphrase from Cic. *Att.* 15.11 (SB 389). The phrasing of Cicero's letter does not rule out the possibility that Brutus accepted the grain commission and he explicitly states that Brutus looked set on Asia (Cic. Att. 15.11.2 = SB 389). And so there remains a question mark over Servilia's promise: did she mean it to apply to Cassius' Sicilian post only? The structure of the passages does seem to imply as much, yet as we shall see, it does not look as though Servilia ever managed to have it removed anyway.

85. As we saw in Chapter 3, it was at the *ludi Apollinares* in 59 BC that popular feeling showed itself against Pompey. Further examples are collected by Sumi (2005), 143–4.
86. Sumi (2005), 145.
87. On Brutus' preparations, see Plut. *Brut.* 21.4–6; App. *B. Civ.* 3.23; Cass. Dio 47.20.2 (although he mistakenly writes that Cassius was the sponsor).
88. Cic. *Att.* 16.4.1 (SB 411); cf. 16.1.1 (SB 409).
89. Change of play: Cic. *Att.* 16.5.1 (SB 410); Applause for Brutus: Cic. *Phil.* 1.36–7, 10.8; 'waste the use of their hands by clapping': Cic. *Att.* 16.2.3 (SB 412). App. *B. Civ.* 3.24 adds that there were demonstrations calling for Brutus' recall.
90. '[L]eaving behind peace': Cic. *Att.* 16.3.4 (SB 413); 'Brutus is still at Nesis': Cic. *Att.* 16.3.6 (SB 413).
91. Cic. *Att.* 16.5.3 (SB 410).
92. Cic. *Att.* 16.4.4 (SB 411).
93. This is the argument presented by Ramsey (2001) which offers a convincing alternative to the traditional explanation that Antony sought an alliance later in the month.
94. On the games, the fullest account is Cass. Dio 45.5–7; cf. Nic. Dam. 108 (applause for Octavian); Plin. *HN.* 2.90, Suet. *Iul.* 88 and Plut. *Caes.* 89 (the appearance of the comet); Suet. *Aug.* 10 (the obstruction of Antony). For discussions of the comet, the games and Octavian's use of them, see Ramsey and Licht (1997); Sumi (2005), 150–3.
95. Nic. Dam. 110; on the reconciliation between Antony and Octavian, see ibid. 115–19; cf. Plut. *Ant.* 16; App. *B. Civ.* 3.39; Cass. Dio 45.8.2.
96. Vell. Pat. 2.62.3.
97. Unless otherwise stated, all quotations in this section are from Cic. *Fam.* 11.3 (SB 336).
98. The terms of the initial request Brutus and Cassius made of Antony are not clear in our sources. Some scholars have suggested that the Liberators requested dispensation from their duties to go into voluntary exile: thus Gelzer, *RE* 10.1 (1917), 998; Shackleton Bailey (1977), 475–6. On the contrary, Ramsey (2003), 260–1, commenting on a reference to this earlier edict at Cic. *Phil.* 1.8, prefers to follow Denniston (1926), 76, who believed the Liberators were rather stating their intentions not to take up the grain commission. This last suggestion seems to make better sense because, as we shall see, Brutus seems to have retained his *imperium* and the grain commission does not seem, at this stage, to have been removed from the decree.
99. Quintus wearing a garland: Cic. *Att.* 14.14.1 (SB 368); 'he says he owes everything to Caesar and nothing to his father, and for the future looks to Antony': Cic. *Att.* 14.17.3 (SB 371).
100. Cic. *Att.* 15.19.2 (SB 396); on Quintus' departure, see Cic. *Att.* 15.21.1 (SB 398), 15.22.1 (SB 399).
101. Nep. *Att.* 8.6.
102. For the letter and the meeting, see Cic. *Att.* 16.4.1–2 (SB 411); cf. Cicero's plans for Sextus Pompeius at Cic. *Att.* 14.13.2 (SB 367); for discussion, see Welch (2012), 130–4.
103. Cic. *Att.* 14.22.1 (SB 376).
104. Unless otherwise stated, all quotations in this section come from Cic. *Att.* 16.7 (SB 415).
105. The insistence on Brutus' trip to Asia in the correspondence seems to point to the conclusion that Cicero was expecting him to accept the grain commission; as does his reference to Cassius and Sicily in another letter (Cic. *Att.* 16.4.4 = SB 411) that he could not count Cassius' fleet 'beyond the Sicilian straits'.
106. There is a huge amount of confusion in our sources over which provinces were allotted to whom. The confusion was already there by the time Appian was writing: he mentions a few of the rogue suggestions at App. *B. Civ.* 3.8 but seems convinced that Cassius was to go to Crete and that Brutus was to be governor of Cyrene. That these were the two provinces assigned to the Liberators seems to be the correct report because Cicero also mentions it at Cic. *Phil.* 2.97. But it seems more likely that they were allocated the other way round, because Cicero links Brutus to Crete, which would mean that Cassius was given Cyrene. For other suggestions, see Nic. Dam. 112–13; Plut. *Brut.* 19.3; Cass. Dio 47.21.1. That the provincial assignments were made in the meeting on the Kalends of August is by no means certain either, but it seems the most plausible suggestion. At Cic. *Phil.* 2.31, Cicero mentions that the provinces were assigned immediately after the games of Apollo in July, by which he would mean at the next available meeting of the Senate. For an overview of the debate, see Manuwald (2007), vol. 1, 11–12, with further bibliography.
107. Cic. *Att.* 14.21.3 (SB 375); cf. ibid. 15.4.2 (SB 381).
108. Cic. *Att.* 15.4.3 (SB 382).

Chapter 6: Reviving Republicanism

1. For the reminder of this point, I am indebted to Welch (2012), 178.
2. The allusion is to Hom. *Il.* 6.429ff.; the scene was a popular one in Roman art; for surviving depic-

tions of this scene (at Pompeii and Rome), see *LIMC* 1.1.768–9; for discussion, see Graziosi and Haubold (2010), 49, 51; cf. Lorenz (2008), 49–50.

3. Moles–Pelling on Plut. *Brut.* 23.2 is more prepared to accept its historical plausibility; commenting on the fragment at *FRHist* III, 511, Drummond is more cautious and is, I think, right to suggest the passage may owe a debt to literary conventions.
4. For example, the saying had been a motto of Cicero's from boyhood: Cic. *Q. Fr.* 3.5.4 (SB 25).
5. On Brutus' arrival in Greece, see Plut. *Brut.* 24.1 and Cass. Dio 47.20.4; for the statue base, see *IG* 7.383; discussion in Raubitschek (1957, 1959); see also Habicht (1997), 357–8.
6. Plut. *Brut.* 24.1–2. Here Plutarch differs slightly from the other historians, who all assume that both Brutus and Cassius were intent on war from the beginning; see Vell. Pat. 2.62.3–4, App. *B. Civ.* 3.24.91 and Cass. Dio 47.21.1.
7. Cic. *Phil.*10.9; cf. Clarke (1981), 50. Although Clarke is probably correct to point out that Cicero was still seemingly under the impression that his son was studying philosophy in Athens when he was writing the *De Officiis* (see e.g. Cic. *Off.* 2.45 in which Cicero talks about his son's military exploits as a thing of the past), there is good reason to suppose that Brutus acted earlier, and probably in November; Gelzer (*RE* 10.1 (1917), 1000) suggests some date after 28 November, following news of Antony's allocation of the praetorian provinces, and the transfer of Macedonia to Gaius Antonius (discussed on pp. 147–8). Gotter (1996), 201–2, is less committal on dates but also suggests a point in time around November, and certainly before the latter part of December.
8. Cic. *Att.* 15.11.1 (SB 389).
9. Cic. *Fam.* 11.3.4 (SB 336); for a similar attitude expressed elsewhere, see the edict Brutus and Cassius sent to Antony in May 44, preserved at Cic. *Fam.* 11.2.3 (SB 329).
10. For Brutus' recruitment of the younger Cicero, see Plut. *Cic.* 45.3. Cic. *Off.* 2.45 refers to his son's military experience at Pharsalus; on the general successes of the younger Cicero under Brutus, see Plut. *Brut.* 26.4. On the recruitment of Horace, see Hor. *Sat.* 1.6.47–48, *Ep.* 2.2.46–56 and Suet. *Hor.* 1.
11. Just as Syria may have been the province reserved for Cassius by Caesar, it is possible that Macedonia was the province Caesar had planned for Brutus; see Kniely (1974), 37–71.
12. Cic. *Phil.* 10.1.
13. See e.g. Cic. *Fam.* 12.4.2 (SB 363), the letter Cicero wrote to Cassius on 2 or 3 February 43 BC: 'Rumour reports that you are in Syria but nobody knows the origin of that report. As for Brutus, the news seems surer insofar as he is nearer Italy.' Cicero was still unsure of Cassius' whereabouts or his forces at the end of the month; see Cic. *Fam.* 12.7.2 (SB 367).
14. Cic. *Phil.* 10.11.
15. I can find no evidence to support the view of Syme (1939), 126, still peddled in many recent works on the period – e.g. Richardson (2012), 26, and Corrigan (2015), 132 – that Brutus and Cassius were actually deprived of their provinces. On the contrary, a close reading of the relevant passage (esp. Cic. *Phil.* 3.25) suggests that Antony only sought to distribute the remaining provinces to which a governor had not yet been allocated by 28 November; on this point, see Manuwald (2006), summarised at Manuwald (2007), vol. 2, 416–17.
16. On Gaius Antonius' appointment, see Cic. *Phil.* 3.24–6. See Stroh (1983) on the provincial lots of 28 November and their implications. To opponents of Antony, the legal basis for Gaius' command seemed questionable and threatening; however, recent scholarship has emphasised the technical correctness of the process Antony followed. On the legality of Mark Antony's procedure, see the review of literature in Manuwald (2007), vol. 1, 417; on the scholarly consensus, see e.g. Welch (2012), 136–7.
17. *Pace* Gelzer (*RE* 10.1 (1917), 1000) and, more recently, Gotter (1996), 201–2. This reconstruction does not preclude the possibility, suggested by Plutarch (Plut. *Brut.* 24.2), that Herostatus had made informal overtures earlier; on this point, see Moles–Pelling *ad loc.*
18. In addition to the accounts at Plut. *Brut.* 25.1–4 and Cass. Dio 47.21.3–7, specific details are provided by the more contemporary evidence of Cic. *Phil.* 10.13 (defection of the legion to Cicero's son and the taking of cavalry).
19. Cic. *Phil.* 3.37–9; Manuwald (2007), vol. 2, 836.
20. As Brutus later tells Cicero, Antistius had in fact donated 2 million sesterces to the cause; Brutus' letter can be found in the collection of Cic. *Ad Brut.* 1.11.1 (SB 16). At Cic. *Phil.* 10.24 Cicero only mentions that Brutus praised M. Appuleius in his letter; the reason of his donation becomes clear at ibid. 13.32; mention of Appuleius' services can also be found at Cic. *Ad Brut.* 1.7.2 (SB 19). A precise date is impossible to arrive at, but Plutarch locates the meeting with Appuleius and Antistius before Brutus' annexation of Macedonia.
21. The role Vatinius played in either resisting Gaius or assisting Brutus is muddled in our later sources. Cass. Dio 47.21.5–7 records that Publius Vatinius came to Gaius' aid by seizing the city of Dyrrachium; but he adds that the latter was swiftly defeated when his men, with whom he was unpopular, joined Brutus' troops. Conversely, Cic. *Phil.* 10.13 – possibly in response to information

from Brutus – praises Vatinius and suggests he opened the gates of Dyrrachium to Brutus willingly; however, it would also suit Cicero's rhetorical purposes to gloss this incident and deflect criticism from Brutus' actions. Plut. *Brut.* 25.3 records only that Gaius Antonius was marching to Dyrrachium to join forces with Vatinius' men, but does not state whether or not he had the consent of the governor.

22. Plut. *Brut.* 25.4–26.2; see Moles–Pelling *ad loc.*
23. Cf. Cic. *Phil.* 11.27: 'he [Brutus] flew [*advolavit*] into Macedonia'.
24. For the phrase 'as his own Senate', I have adapted words Cicero uses to describe both Brutus and Cassius at Cic. *Phil.* 11.27: *Nam et Brutus et Cassius multis iam in rebus ipse sibi senatus fuit.*
25. Cic. *Phil.* 10.25–6.
26. For Cicero's success, see Cic. *Phil.* 11.26; although Woodman (1983), 177–8, has argued that Brutus did not receive his command until 27 April, Cicero's language in this passage seems to suggest Brutus' command was agreed upon when he delivered this speech in late February. Cf. Welch (2012), 160 n. 78, who argues the same point from different evidence: namely, Cic. *Ad Brut.* 2.4.4 (SB 4), sent on 12 April, which suggests Brutus could raise money from the *civitates* because of the senatorial decree.
27. For a different opinion, see Girardet (1993) who has argued for the impossibility of an absolute *imperium maius* in the Republic; according to this line of thinking, Brutus did not possess *imperium maius* in 43 BC. For a recent review of the problem with further bibliography, see Kirbihler (2013). A clear discussion of the nature of the command is at Drogula (2015), 327–32. However, his confidence in the suggestion that Brutus and Cassius did each receive *imperium maius* should be read cautiously, as I have tried to suggest in the main text; on Drogula, see the review by Day (2016).
28. The extent to which the consul Pansa also influenced the course of the debate is not clear; see the summary in Mahy (2009), 166–7.
29. Cic. *Phil.* 11.27.
30. In Plutarch's account (Plut. *Cic.* 43.5–6) Cicero arrived back in Rome the day before the Senate meeting, but in Cicero's own statements, he delivered his first *Philippic* on the day after his return; see Cic. *Fam.* 12.25.3–5 (SB 373). This should be taken to suggest that Cicero arrived back in Rome early on the morning of 1 September. On the chronology, see Ramsey (2003), 9, 111, followed by Manuwald (2007), vol. 1, 19, who reviews the scholarship and evidence at 19 n. 53.
31. Cicero evidently called the speeches 'his Philippics' when he sent copies of them to Brutus; for Brutus approved and replied: 'I am now willing to let them be called the *Philippics*, as you jokingly suggested in one of your letters'; see Cic. *Ad Brut.* 2.3.4 (SB 2).
32. Cic. *Phil.* 2; cf. Cic. *Fam.* 12.2.1 (SB 344).
33. 'To Father and Benefactor': Cic. *Fam.* 12.3.1 (SB 345); as traitors to their country: ibid. 12.3.2 (SB 345); no room in the *res publica*: ibid. 12.23.3 (SB 345).
34. As he states himself in a letter to Cornificius at Cic. *Fam.* 12.22.1 (SB 346).
35. Cic. *Fam.* 12.3.1 (SB 345). Scholarship is divided on the question of when Cassius left Italy; for the suggestion that it was soon after Brutus' departure, see Cic. *Phil.* 10.8; for arguments in favour of the position adopted here, see Gelzer, *RE.* 10.1 (1917), 999; Gotter (1996), 196.
36. Cic. *Fam.* 12.2.3 (SB 344).
37. For an expression of his despondency along these terms, see Cic. *Fam.* 12.22.2 (SB 346).
38. Cic. *Fam.* 12.23.2 (SB 347).
39. Cic. *Att.* 16.8.1 (SB 418); on Octavian's efforts to recruit the soldiers and veterans, see App. *B. Civ.* 3.40–8; Cass. Dio 45.12–13.
40. Cic. *Att.* 16.9 (SB 419).
41. Cassius' appeal to Cicero can be gleaned from Cicero's letter to him at Cic. *Fam.* 12.2.2 (SB 344).
42. Octavian's remark is repeated by Cicero at Cic. *Att.* 16.15.3 (SB 426).
43. See e.g. Cic. *Fam.* 11.5.2–3 (SB 353) and 11.7.2–3 (SB 354).
44. For a full introduction to the speech, its content and importance, see Manuwald (2007), vol. 2, 295–462.
45. Cic. *Phil.* 3.37–9.
46. According to Cic. *Phil.* 5.5 and 5.7, the only senator who spoke to defend Antony was Lucius Varius Cotyla.
47. Already in October, Cicero had started to recognise Octavian's position as Caesar's heir by calling him Caesar Octavianus: see Cic. *Fam.* 12.23.2 (SB 347). In the third *Philippic*, however, he is more regularly and publicly referred to by his Caesarian name than hitherto: see. e.g. Cic. *Phil.* 3.3, 7, 12, 14, 15, 27, 30, 38.
48. Cic. *Phil.* 10.9.
49. There is not room to discuss the point here, but it should be noted that Cicero had, however, been communicating with Decimus Brutus in Gaul. Although the actions of Marcus Brutus against Gaius Antonius look deceptively similar to those of Decimus Brutus against the other Antony,

there were significant differences which are deliberately obfuscated by Cicero. See Mahy (2009), 172–4 for a good overview.

50. Later commentators referred to the twenty-six letters in our collection as belonging to the ninth and presumably last volume of a lengthy correspondence between Cicero and Brutus over the years. On the existence of nine volumes, see the comments on the survival of the collection by Watt (1958), 164, and Shackleton Bailey (1980), 14. A further five letters written to Brutus can be found in Cic. *Fam.* 13.10–4 (SB 277–80), 11.17 (SB 435). In the count of Brutus' letters, I have excluded two letters – Cic. *Ad Brut.* 1.16–17 (SB 25–6) – the authenticity of which has been heavily debated. My investigation into their authorship is part of a larger current project on Brutus' *pseudepigrapha*, which argues that they are rhetorical exercises of a later date and not the handicraft of Brutus. For divergent opinions see: Shackleton Bailey (1980), 10–14, and Moles (1997), with further references.
51. Cic. *Ad Brut.* 2.4.4 (SB 4), in response to Brutus' request at ibid. 2.3.5 (SB 2).
52. Cic. *Ad Brut.* 2.4.4 (SB 4).
53. In this paragraph, I have largely paraphrased the observations of Bengtson (1970), 28–9.
54. For the letter dated 10 April, see Cic. *Att.* 4.4.2 (SB 358). On the glory earned by Brutus and Cassius, see Cic. *Att.* 14.11.1 (SB 365); cf. ibid. 14.12.2 (SB 366), 14.14.3 (SB 368).
55. On the 'Caesarian party' see Cic. *Ad Brut.* 2.4.5 (SB 4).
56. Cicero responds to the letter of Lepidus at Cic. *Phil.* 13.7–10, 49 (delivered to the Senate on 20 March 43 BC).
57. Cic. *Ad Brut.* 2.3.2 (SB 2).
58. Brutus had probably captured Gaius Antonius in (early) March; see Moles–Pelling on Plut. *Brut.* 26.5.
59. Cic. *Ad Brut.* 2.4.3 (SB 4).
60. For further discussion of Cicero's reaction to the letter of Brutus, see the discussion by Ortmann (1988), 288–90.
61. Quotations and references in this paragraph are taken from Cic. *Ad Brut.* 2.5.1, 3–4 (SB 5).
62. On the news and circumstances of Trebonius' death, see: Cic. *Phil.* 11.1, 15, 12.25, 13.22–3; App. *B. Civ.* 4.58; Cass. Dio 47.29. For further references and discussion, see Manuwald (2007), 45. On the possible date, see Mahy (2009), 177–8.
63. Cic. *Ad Brut.* 2.5.5 (SB 5).
64. After all, as Brutus had confessed to Cicero back in his first communication on the topic in April 43, he was personally moved by Gaius' entreaties (Cic. *Ad Brut.* 2.3.2 (SB 2)). As in the case of Mark Antony, Brutus evidently held out some hope that he could reform Gaius and bring him round to his side. But Brutus' motivation for keeping Gaius alive has been variously interpreted. For the idea of personal obligation after the *ludi*, see Rice-Holmes (1928), 50 n. 3; hope of truce with Antony, see Gelzer, *RE* 10.1 (1917), 1003; Clarke (1981), 54.
65. Cic. *Ad Brut.* 1.2a.2 (SB 6).
66. When Brutus wrote this letter on 7 May, Cicero's letter (Cic. *Ad Brut.* 1.3a (SB 8)) reporting that Antony and his supporters had been pronounced *hostes* had either not yet reached Brutus; or, if it had, Brutus was not convinced that the Senate had formally declared Gaius *hostis*. Cicero's language on this point is deliberately vague.
67. Cic. *Ad Brut.* 1.4.2 (SB 10); in this letter, Brutus is replying to the argument expressed by Cicero in his letter, Cic. *Ad Brut.* 1.3 (SB 7). The two letters should be read together for a fuller comparison.
68. The mutiny is revealed in a lost letter, to which Cicero replies at Cic. *Ad Brut.* 1.2.3 (SB 14); on an early short-lived mutiny, see Cass. Dio 47.23.2 (although this is not to be confused with the mutiny he goes on to describe at length at Cass. Dio 47.23.3–25).
69. On Cicero's exile, see my introduction to the event and the sources for it in Tempest (2011), 120–2.
70. Cicero gives the details of the Senate meeting at Cic. *Ad Brut.* 1.5.1–2 (SB 9); for the ratification of all three commands, see Cass. Dio 46.40.3, with discussion by Welch (2012), 163–4.
71. In fact, Woodman (1983), 132–4, has argued, not unreasonably, that Brutus' command was also only ratified at this time (i.e. 27 April 43 BC), and not in the senatorial debate after Cicero's *Tenth Philippic*. While I maintain that the balance of probability falls on the earlier date – based largely on the way Cicero talks of the Senate's decree, which allowed Brutus to collect revenue from the Greek communities, at Cic. *Ad Brut.* 2.4.4 (SB 4) – his opinion merits attention. In any case, the fact that the Senate now decreed commands for Cassius and Sextus Pompeius still upholds his idea of 'pro-republican feeling'.
72. Cic. *Ad Brut.* 1.5.2 (SB 9).
73. For Cassius' letter, see Cic. *Fam.* 12.12 (SB 387).
74. Cic. *Ad Brut.* 1.2.2 (SB 14).
75. On the deaths of Hirtius and Pansa, see Cic. *Fam.* 11.9. 1 (SB 380); cf. Cic. *Ad Brut.* 1.3a (SB 8), written *c.* 27 April 43 BC.

76. That Antony was urging Octavian to form an alliance is evidenced in Cicero's *Thirteenth Philippic* (13.22–48); for a full discussion, see Ramsey (2010), esp. 163–4.
77. Cic. *Phil.* 3.3.
78. Cic. *Ad Brut.* 1.3.1 (SB 7).
79. Thus Cass. Dio (47.22.3): 'For a while he was sending letters to [Octavian] Caesar . . . urging him both to resist Antony and to be allied with Brutus personally.' But, since this line is immediately followed by the curious statement that Brutus also planned to sail to Italy in the summer of 43 BC – a point which seems entirely at odds with his actual intentions and movements – perhaps we should treat it with caution. On the speciousness of this line, see the comments of Gelzer, *RE* 10.1 (1917), 1004.
80. At Plut. *Brut.* 22.4 Brutus is alleged to have argued that Cicero's policy was akin to choosing a gentle form of despotism; he was amazed that Cicero feared the perils of civil war more than he dreaded a shameful and inglorious peace. He even accused Cicero of requesting for Octavian to be established as tyrant as a reward for driving out the tyranny of Antony. 'Our ancestors', Brutus purportedly wrote, 'could not endure even gentle despots.' For Plutarch's insistence that the criticisms appear in Brutus' earliest letters, see Plut. *Brut.* 23.1.
81. The letters are at Cic. *Ad Brut.* 1.16 (SB 25) and 1.17 (SB 26). Although Moles (1997) has made a quite compelling case for the authenticity of these letters, I am still of the opinion that they are the products of the pseudepigraphic tradition.
82. Cic. *Ad Brut.* 1.4.2–3 (SB 10).
83. Cic. *Ad Brut.* 1.4.1–2 (SB 10).
84. Cic. *Ad Brut.* 1.4a.3 (SB 11).
85. Manuwald (2007), vol. 1, 80, 89, tentatively suggests that Cicero may have sent Brutus the *Third Philippic* as well.
86. Cic. *Ad Brut.* 2.3. 4 (SB 2).
87. Cic. *Ad Brut.* 1.8.1 (SB 15).
88. Recommendations for: Glyco: Cic. *Ad Brut.* 1.6.2 (SB 12); Flavius: Cic. *Ad Brut.* 1.6.4 (SB 12); Bibulus: Cic. *Ad Brut.* 1.7 (SB 19).
89. Thus, also Gelzer, *RE* 10.1 (1917), 1006; Bengtson (1970), 30.
90. For Lepidus' own explanation of his actions, and appeal for peace, see Cic. *Fam.* 10.35 (SB 408). However, earlier reports of his allegiance to Antony had already given Cicero reason to doubt Lepidus' loyalty: see C. Asinius Pollio's letter to Cicero at Cic. *Fam.* 10.31.4 (SB 368), as well as Cicero's own appeal to Lepidus at ibid. 10.27.1–2 (SB 369), written on 20 March.
91. Praise of Lepidus at Cic. *Phil.* 5.38–41.
92. Criticisms of Lepidus at Cic. *Ad Brut.* 2.2.1 (SB 3), 1.10.12 (SB 17); cf. Cic. *Fam.* 12.8.1 (SB 416).
93. Quotations from Cic. *Ad Brut.* 1.13.1–2 (SB 20).
94. Quotation and paraphrases from Cic. *Ad Brut.* 1.12.1–2 (SB 21).
95. Later sources for Porcia's death, which have her swallowing coals in a bid to take her own life, include: Plut. *Brut.* 53.5, Plut. *Cat. Min.* 73.6; App. *B. Civ.* 4.136; Cass. Dio 47.79.3; Val. Max. 4.6.5; Mart. 1.42. It is possible that both versions can be reconciled: i.e. Porcia may have taken her own life when her illness had reached an advanced and terminal stage. For the suggestion that she died from a plague, which apparently struck Rome at about this time (Cass. Dio 45.17.8), see Tyrrell and Purser on Cic. *Ad Brut.* 1.9.
96. Quotations in this paragraph are all taken from Cic. *Ad Brut.* 1.9.1–2 (SB 18).
97. For the complaint about the brevity of Brutus' letter, see Cic. *Ad Brut.* 1.14.1 (SB 22); his thoughts on the war and the necessity of Brutus' return are at ibid. 1.14.2.
98. As White (2010), 162, has emphasised in his study of epistolary relations.
99. Cic. *Ad Brut.* 1.15.13 (SB 23).
100. Cicero's calls for Brutus to return to Italy, and his support for Brutus' decision not to do so in early May, can be traced in the letters Cic. *Ad Brut.* 1.3.2 (SB 7), 1.5.2 (SB 9), 1.2.2 (SB 14). Appeals to return intensify from mid-June 43: see Cic. *Ad Brut.* 1.10.1, 4–5 (SB 17), 1.9.3 (SB 18), 1.12.2–3 (SB 21), 1.14.2 (SB 22), 1.15.12 (SB 23), 1.18.1–5 (SB 24).
101. 'Hurry, I beg you' . . . 'Urge Cassius': Cic. *Ad Brut.* 1.10.4 (SB 17); the 'tottering and almost collapsing *res publica*': Cic. *Ad Brut.* 1.18.2 (SB 24).
102. Cic. *Ad Brut.* 1.14.2 (SB 22).
103. Cic. *Ad Brut.* 1.10.3 (SB 17) for Cicero's concerns over the messengers and letters spurring on Octavian.
104. Cic. *Fam.* 12.14.1 (SB 405).
105. The letters from Spinther are at Cic. *Fam.* 12.14 (SB 405) and 12.15 (SB 406); the confident prediction comes at Cic. *Fam.* 12.15.7 (SB 406).
106. Cic. *Fam.* 12.13.4 (SB 419); on the identity of this other Cassius – who may or may not have been one of Caesar's assassins – see Shackleton Bailey (1977), vol. 2, 562. Parmensis only mentions that

Dolabella has the support of the peoples of Tarsus and Laodicea; cf. Cass. Dio 47.30.4, who adds that Cleopatra, Caesar's former lover, was supplying him with ships and money from Egypt.

107. On the death of Dolabella, see App. *B. Civ.* 4.60–2; Cass. Dio 47.30; [Livy], *Per.* 121.
108. Details at Cass. Dio 47.22.4–25.3.
109. On Messalla, see the excellent introduction to his life and the fragments of his works in Drummond (*FRHist* I, 61).
110. Quotations from Cic. *Ad Brut.* 1.15 (SB 23), my italics.
111. Cic. *Ad Brut.* 2.5.5 (SB 5).
112. Nearly all modern accounts include mention of the need for the triumvirs to gain resources to plan and execute the war against Caesar's assassins; the added importance of instilling terror has recently been brought to my attention by Welch (2012), 174–5, following Hinard (1985), 262–4.
113. On the existence of such 'proscription literature' and its use by later historians, see Osgood (2006), 64–81; Welch (2009), 195–9.
114. Plut. *Cic.* 46.3–5 records a more favourable picture: in his account, Octavian struggled for two days against Antony and Lepidus before finally giving Cicero up on the third day of their negotiations.
115. The quotation from Livy is recorded by Sen. *Suas.* 6.22.
116. Tatum (2008), 172.
117. Plut. *Brut.* 28.2; for a fuller discussion of the mixed scholarly reactions only summarised here, see Moles–Pelling *ad loc.*
118. Wiseman (2009), 128.
119. See Flower (2010) for the argument that the *res publica* was never a single, monolithic constitution; her analysis clearly reveals the difference that existed between the *res publica* after Sulla's constitutional arrangements and the 'republics' of earlier generations. As for Cicero's lifetime, he was born in 106 BC – a year after Marius' first consulship. For the fundamental differences that had occurred at that point between the idealised *res publica* and the *res publica* of Cicero's day, see Flower (2010), 61–79.
120. Cic. *Att.* 14.20.3 (SB 374).
121. Cic. *Att.* 2.1.8 (SB 21).

Chapter 7: Brutus' Last Fight

1. Numbers provided by App. *B. Civ.* 4.88; cf. App. *B. Civ.* 4.108 for the revised figure before Philippi.
2. On the scale of the casualties, which may have reached up to 50,000 dead, see Brunt (1971), 487–9; it is emphasised by all our major writers for this period: Plut. *Brut.* 38.5; App. *B. Civ.* 4.137–8; Cass. Dio 47.39.1–5.
3. On autobiographies and memoirs for this period, see the overview in Geiger (2011).
4. On the pardon and promotion of Dellius, as well as Augustus' policy of sparing those who had fought against him, see Sen. *Clem.* 10.1. On Dellius' writings, see Pelling (2002), 38–9; Tatum (2011), 183–4.
5. A good overview of these issues can be found in Citroni (2000).
6. Aug. *Res. Gest.* 2; the best introduction to the *Res Gestae,* complete with the Latin text, translation and commentary, is Cooley (2009).
7. On the origins and appearance of these words, see Welch (2015).
8. Cic. *Ad Brut.* 1.2.3 (SB 14) refers to an attempted mutiny by Gaius which was quickly suppressed in late April or early May; this seems to concur with Dio's comment (Cass. Dio 47.22.4–23.2) that an attempt of Gaius was foiled and he was stripped of his praetorian insignia before being placed under a guard. The main difference in our sources is that Plut. *Brut.* 26–9 then only describes one attempt to rescue Gaius from captivity, whereas App. *B. Civ.* 3.79 and Cass. Dio 47.22.4–25.3 both hint at several. For an analysis of the differences in these sources, see Moles–Pelling on Plut. *Brut.* 26–9.
9. Elsewhere Cass. Dio 47.24.3–6 reports that L. Gellius Publicola also formed a separate plot against Cassius and adds that he was spared because of the intervention of Publicola's mother. The plots and sparing of Publicola, however, seem to have been of greater importance than the brief mentions in Dio suggests; the fact that the event makes it into the summary of Livy's lost book for this period suggests that the narrative occupied a position of some importance ([Livy], *Per.* 122).
10. The main sources for Gaius' death are Cass. Dio 47.24.4 and Plut. *Brut.* 28.1. I have inclined towards the version of Plutarch here, partly because Plutarch adds that Brutus sent the command to Hortensius in Macedonia, which is consistent with the detail he provides at Plut. *Ant.* 22.6: namely, that Antony later took his revenge by killing Hortensius on his brother's tomb. On this point, Dio is less committal; he simply states that Gaius' guard killed him, 'either on his own responsibility or following instructions from Brutus'.
11. Cass. Dio 47.25.1.

12. App. *B. Civ.* 4.75.
13. Laignoux (2012) has drawn attention to the prominent use of sacerdotal instruments and other religious imagery on the Liberators' coins; Hollstein (1994) has argued that Brutus and Cassius used Apollo as a means of communicating the restored *libertas* of the *res publica*.
14. Dion. Hal. 4.69, Livy 1.1; for the importance of Apollo in republican propaganda, see Gosling (1986).
15. On Brutus' summons, which prevented Cassius from completing a planned expedition against Egypt, see the competing narratives of Plut. *Brut.* 28.3–7; App. *B. Civ.* 4.63; cf. Welch (2012), 176–7, for an analysis of the differences. On the meeting of Brutus and Cassius, see Plut. *Brut.* 28.7 and Cass. Dio 47.32.1–2. On the general tendency of Brutus, Cassius and their supporters to see themselves as friends, see Osgood (2006), 101.
16. Welch (2012), 163–202, on what she calls the 'republican triumvirate'.
17. For the emphasis on the naval policy and the cooperation with Sextus Pompeius, see Welch (2012), 178–9; for a different opinion, see Bengtson (1970), 36, who sees this decision as a fundamentally strategic error and essentially a 'raid, which served to fill the empty coffers of the assassins'. His argument rests on the (flawed) assumption that the republicans had nothing to fear from Rhodes and Lycia; but he may be right in drawing attention to the waste of time this caused the Liberators when they could have been focusing on fortifying their base around Philippi; for a similar opinion, see Pelling (1996), 7.
18. Thus App. *B. Civ.* 4.52 on the role of Cornificius and Pompeius; Welch (2012), esp. 178–82, offers a more thorough appreciation of these men's roles in the campaign and adds the name of Murcus to Appian's summary; we should perhaps not overlook Lucius Tillius Cimber, the governor of Bithynia, who came to Cassius' aid in the campaign against Dolabella and continued to provide naval support thereafter.
19. Narrative accounts which give fuller emphasis to Cassius' activities for this period can be found in Rice-Holmes (1928), 75–80; Magie (1950), 421–6; Corrigan (2015), 175–6.
20. Many scholars have pointed out that Appian, as well as Dio, uses the activities of Brutus and Cassius in the east as a 'foil' to the atrocities of the proscriptions; see e.g. Rawson (1986), 115, on Dio, followed by Gowing (1992), 169, on Appian. Others have (also rightly) pointed out that Appian is largely sympathetic to Cassius; see e.g. Gabba (1956), 182–4. However, the picture presented by Appian is nowhere uniform and when he adds his own comments, it is clear he was not a personal supporter of the assassins; thus Gowing (1992), 164; Welch (2015), esp. 278–80. I believe this is what is happening in the programmatic statement here. Although, as we shall see, the narrative tends to paint a sympathetic picture, because of the nature of Appian's source material, his own verdict was more complex.
21. The accounts of Xanthus are at Plut. *Brut.* 30.6–31.7; App. *B. Civ.* 4.76–80; Cass. Dio 47.34.1–3.
22. App. *B. Civ.* 2.112; on this point, see also Gowing (1992), 171.
23. On the tragic colouring of this passage, see Pelling (2016), 122–3.
24. Hdts. *Hist.* 1.176, also mentioned at App. *B. Civ.* 4.80; for the development of the motif of the captured city, which is rooted in the literary memory of the fall of Troy, see e.g. Paul (1982); Kraus (1994).
25. These stories appear respectively at Diod. Sic. 17.28.1–5 and 18.22.4–7.
26. The story features in Appian's account of the Punic Wars at App. *Pun.* 133, where he also alludes to Polybius as a source; on the crying general, see Hau (2016), 53–4.
27. Vell. Pat. 2.72.
28. Verg. *Aen.* 6.851–3.
29. For an historical reading of the *Aeneid,* which stresses its debt to contemporary discourse see e.g. Marincola (2010).
30. Points at which direct comparisons occur are Plut. *Brut.* 1.4, 7.1–5, 8.5–7, 9.5–6, 16.4, 20.1, 28.3–6, 29.2–7, 30.2, 30.3–4, 32.3–4, 35, 39.7–8, 40.1–2, 46.3.
31. On the use of such rhetoric by Antony from another perspective, see Welch (2015), esp. 280–5.
32. Extracts from letter taken respectively from Joseph. *AJ* 14.309–10, 11.
33. Joseph. *AJ* 14.271–6.
34. For Josephus' use of Nicolaus generally, see Toher (2003); on this passage, see Schürer (1885/1973), 277 n. 40.
35. The sources in the following discussion are: Plut. *Brut.* 32.1–4; App. *B. Civ.* 4.81–2; Cass. Dio 47.34.4–6.
36. The summary of Appian in this paragraph, as well as the next, is based on App. *B. Civ.* 4.81.
37. On the 'canon', or better the 'topoi' (commonplaces), of virtues in the discourse on leadership, the Roman tradition owed much to Hellenistic ideas of rulership. A good treatment of the development of these virtues can be found in Murray (2007); I have already discussed their application to the Roman political climate of the late Republic in Tempest (2013b).

38. This point has also been made by Moles–Pelling commenting on Plut. *Brut.* 32 who treats the question of Plutarch's sources far more fully than I have attempted here.
39. On the 'corrective' nature of Appian and Dio, see Gowing (1992), 172 n. 30, with further bibliography.
40. Scholars have endlessly debated the authenticity of this collection. While some scholars have defended their attribution to Brutus and believe they are genuine products of his penmanship – e.g. Gelzer (*RE* 10.1 (1917), 1010, followed by Bengtson (1970), 4 – historical errors and inconsistencies have led others to dismiss the collection as a forgery, either in full – e.g. Marcks (1883); Rawson (1986); Moles (1997) – or in part – e.g. Westermann (1851); Smith (1936); [Brut.] *Ep. Gr.* (Torraca). On the use of letters in the schools, see the later evidence of Philostratus of Lemnos, who begins his short tract on epistolography by recommending model letters for this purpose (Philostratus II, 238 K. = Hercher, *Ep. Gr.*, nr. IV, translated at Malherbe (1988), 42–3). My arguments here are part of a larger project (together with Tasos Aidonis) to produce the first English translation of the letters of Pseudo-Brutus.
41. On the potential for using the Greek letters in this way, I follow Rawson (1986), 107: 'one cannot help suspecting that the picture of Brutus continually ordering towns to provide money, arms and men as rapidly as possible, and accompanying his orders with undisguised threats, is indeed the picture most provincials retained of him'. On the possibility the letters contain evidence of important historical value, see also the approach of Magie (1950), 422.
42. 'The Xanthians ignored my kindness': [Brut.] *Ep. Gr.* 25; 'I slaughtered the Xanthians who rebelled against us': ibid. 11.
43. See e.g. [Brut.] *Ep. Gr.* 27, 28 on the fate of the Xanthian exiles.
44. [Brut.] *Ep. Gr.* 25.
45. Compliments for their brevity at Plut. *Brut.* 2.3. In his introduction to the later collection of Brutus' *Letters*, the editor Mithridates (*Ep. Gr. praef.*) also comments on their brevity, and adds 'forcefulness' and 'the stamp of a leader's genius'.
46. Plut. *Brut.* 34.2; cf. Cass. Dio 47.35.1 who puts it in almost the exact same words: 'all the suspicions they were harbouring between them as a result of slanderous accusations, as is often the case in such conditions, they brought forward and discussed in private'. But Dio's account is short, and the source of the 'slanderous accusations' comes from the mouths of others; a point which suppresses the mutual doubts and disagreements Brutus and Cassius seem to have shared against each other. Plutarch alone details their quarrel in any depth.
47. Plut. *Brut.* 34.2–3; the quotation from the *Iliad* is from Hom. *Il.* 1.259.
48. In fact, Brutus is said to have called Favonius a *haplokuna* and a *pseudokuna*, often translated as 'a mere dog' and 'a false Cynic'. On the problems of these terms, see Moles–Pelling *ad loc.* (Plut. *Brut.* 34.4).
49. For the reliability of this passage as evidence for the men's historic personalities, see the comments of Moles–Pelling *ad loc.* on Favonius: 'a revealing and closely observed portrait of Favonius'. Furthermore, Cassius' humour is revealed by a number of sources, not least Cicero at Cic. *Fam.* 15.18.1 (SB 213), 15.19.1 (SB 216).
50. Plutarch's text names this friend as Lucius Pella, although there is a strong chance the text should read Lucius [Livius] Ocella; thus Cich. *Röm. Stud.* 253–7, accepted by Moles–Pelling *ad loc.* (Plut. *Brut.* 35.1). For L. Livius Ocella see *MRR* 2, 464.
51. Shakespeare, *Julius Caesar*, 4.3.18–28.
52. In fact, Caesar's failure to control his associates formed a significant part of Plutarch's analysis at Plut. *Caes.* 51.3; cf. Plut. *Ant.* 6.7.
53. Plut. *Brut.* 35.6.
54. On the two appearances of the apparition, see Plut. *Brut.* 36.7, 48.1. Plutarch's account of the first apparition has parallels at App. *B. Civ.* 4.134 and Flor. 2.17.8; Val. Max. 1.7.7 has a similar story about Cassius of Parma, upon which the story of Brutus' ghost was probably modelled (see n. 56, below). Aside from Plutarch, the second apparition also appears at App. *B. Civ.* 4.134.
55. Omen of the eagles at Plut. *Brut.* 37.7; App. *B. Civ.* 4.101; for the signs during the lustration ceremony, see (with varying details) Plut. *Brut.* 39.1–6; Cass. Dio 47.40.7–8; Jul. Obs. 39.5, 70; Flor. 2.17.7. For the omens at Rome, see Cass. Dio 47.40.1–6.
56. If anything of the sort did happen, it belonged not in the legend of Brutus, but in the stories of Cassius of Parma (another of Caesar's assassins). To this Cassius there appeared a 'man of huge proportions, black in colour, with an unkempt beard and shaggy hair' who announced himself, in Greek, to be Cassius of Parma's 'evil demon' (Val. Max. 1.7.7). This, at any rate, is the story told by the Roman writer Valerius Maximus, which appears to have provided a model for the version in Plutarch's *Brutus*. What this means is that Plutarch or one of his sources did not entirely fabricate the event; however, it was appropriated from another tradition, and then adapted to Brutus' legend for special effect.

57. Plut. *Brut.* 48.1–4; for commentary and discussion, with further bibliography, see Drummond (*FRHist* III, 509–10).
58. For bees as a sign of individual military success, see Plin. *HN.* 11.55; for their negative forecast, see e.g. Verg. *Aen.* 7.59, where bees land on the sacred laurel of Latinus; Livy 21.46 records how bees predicted calamity for the Romans battling against Hannibal; at Tac. *Ann.* 12.64.1 a swarm of bees which settled on the Capitol is listed among the prodigies that signalled a change of circumstances for the worse. Moles–Pelling *ad loc.* (Plut. *Brut.* 48.1–4) cites the evidence of Artemidorus, which explains why bees signify confusion, wounds, sickness and death. For discussion of bee swarm prodigies in military camps, see MacInnes (2000), esp. 63–4; on the imagery of bees more generally, with further references, see Xenophontos (2013).
59. The prodigies appear in our main narratives at: Plut. *Brut.* 39.1–6; Cass. Dio 47.40.1–8; App. *B. Civ.* 4.134 (although Appian does mention the omen of the two eagles prior to the battle narrative at ibid. 4.101).
60. Descriptions of the camp at App. *B. Civ.* 4.106; Cass. Dio 47.35.6; on the plan to block the triumvirs from gaining access to the supply route, see App. *B. Civ.* 4.86. For an illustrated introduction to Philippi, see Sheppard (2008).
61. The numbers are given by App. *B. Civ.* 4.88, 108: on the legionaries he claims that each side had nineteen legions but that Brutus' and Cassius' were not at full strength; Brunt (1971), 485–8, has hence suggested that the number should be reduced to seventeen legions for the Liberators' side. The figures given here are based on the idea that a legion would consist of roughly 5,000 men. For other estimates, see Pelling (1996), 8; Goldsworthy (2010), 252; and Strauss (2015), 218.
62. For the figures of the payout, see App. *B. Civ.* 4.100; at App. *B. Civ.* 4.120 Appian tells us that Antony and Octavian offered a considerably higher sum (5,000 denarii to each legionary, 25,000 to centurions and 50,000 to the tribunes), but it was dependent on a victory as they did not have the money to hand.
63. Plut. *Brut.* 38.5–39.2; according to Plin. *HN* 33.12.39, a letter of Brutus' survived in which he expressed his disapproval of military tribunes wearing gold brooches. But it was quite customary for armies to display their treasures; see e.g. Nisbet and Hubbard (1978) commenting on Hor. *Carm.* 2.1.10, with further examples. If Pliny is drawing on a genuine source, there is nothing contradictory here; Brutus may not have liked it, but he allowed it.
64. Plut. *Brut.* 40.3. On the imagery and its similarity to the famous expression of Caesar, *alea iacta est* ('the die is cast'), see Moles–Pelling *ad loc.* For a discussion of the fragment of Messalla (*FRHist* 61 F 1) and the nature of his work, see Drummond (*FRHist* I, 466–71, III, 546–7), with further bibliography.
65. Scholars have argued that this dialogue is fictional. And, indeed, it is unthinkable that such a conversation would take place – as Plutarch has it – on the very morning of a battle and in the presence of friends. For the dialogue as 'no doubt fictional', see e.g. Sedley (1997), 52 n. 65; for the suggestion that it could not have taken place at the time Plutarch describes, see Moles–Pelling on Plut. *Brut.* 40.5–9.
66. Plut. *Brut.* 50.7–9; on the possibility of a suicide pact, see also Flor. 2.17.14: 'neither of them should survive the battle'.
67. On this passage and its debt to the martyrological tradition, see MacMullen (1966), 76.
68. I have developed the idea that the discussions in Plutarch represented a 'contingency plan' from the suggestion of Drummond, on Messalla (*FRHist* I, esp. 469): 'they [Brutus and Cassius] perhaps anticipated Antony's attack and determined that, should it materialise, they would take advantage of Octavian's less experienced forces (and the incapacity of their commander) to launch their own offensive. In Plutarch, and perhaps already Messalla, this contingency plan has then become a firm decision to fight that day'. It should be added here that Dio largely concurs with Plutarch in presenting an organised battle, complete with rallying speeches by the commanders on each side and a watchword – *eleutheria*, the Greek word for *libertas*. But his account descends into a general description of fighting which does little or nothing to elucidate the chain of events that followed, which is why I have omitted it from the discussion; references will, however, appear in endnotes still.
69. I have taken the initial idea that the two accounts can quite easily be explained in tandem from the note in Moles–Pelling on Plut. *Brut.* 40.1–6: 'some of the discrepancies between P. and Appian are probably to be explained in terms not only of difference of source, but also of difference of perspective, arising from the fact that P.'s main source obviously gives a "Republican-eye-view" and Appian's a Caesarian'.
70. Plut. *Brut.* 39.1–6 (where they delay war because of the omens); App. *B. Civ.* 4.109 (where they are pursuing Cassius' bloodless strategy); Cass. Dio 47.38.2–6 (where ethical motives are adduced to explain the delay).
71. The date for the first battle is tentative and based on a working-back from the more secure dating of the second battle; for which the Praenestine *Fasti* give 23 October. For a different interpretation, which dates the two battles to 23 October and 16 November respectively (on the basis of Suet. *Tib.*

5), see Moles–Pelling on Plut. *Brut.* 41.1–43.9 and 47.5, with further bibliography.

72. This paragraph is largely a paraphrase of Plut. *Brut.* 41.4–6.
73. See Moles–Pelling on Plut. *Brut.* 41.3. Although the interpretation offered in my account differs slightly from his suggestion that 'Antony actually initiated hostilities, unaware of the fact that Brutus and Cassius had decided to respond.'
74. App. *B. Civ.* 4.111; on the plan to take advantage of Octavian's side's inexperience, see Schmitthenner (1958), 54.
75. For the reaction of Octavian's forces, compare Plut. *Brut.* 41.2–3 with App. *B. Civ.* 4.110.
76. On this point, see Plut. *Brut.* 44.5–6; cf. the speech put into Brutus' mouth at App. *B. Civ.* 4.117, where he chides his men for preferring plunder to killing the men they had defeated.
77. Plut. *Brut.* 53.4–9; other accounts present pretty much the same story. See e.g. Vell. Pat. 2.70.2–3; Val. Max. 6.8.4, 9.9.2; Plut. *Caes.* 69.3; Plut. *Ant.* 22.4; App. *B. Civ.* 4.113; Cass. Dio 47.46.3–5; [Livy], *Per.* 124; Flor. 2.17.13, [Ps.-Aur.] *De Vir. Ill.* 83.6–7.
78. On the numbers of the dead, see Plut. *Brut.* 45.1; App. *B. Civ.* 4.112; cf. Cass. Dio 47.45.2–3 who plays down the disaster and calls the result 'practically the same for each'.
79. On the distortion of this fact in our sources, compare Gowing (1992), 111, 212.
80. Plin. *HN* 7.148; other reports of Octavian's absence from battle can be found at: Vell. Pat. 2.70.1; Val. Max. 1.7.1; Plut. *Brut.* 41.7–8; Plut. *Ant.* 22.2; Suet. *Aug.* 13.1; App. *B. Civ.* 4.110; Cass. Dio 47.41.3–4; Flor. 2.17.9; Oros. 6.18.15.
81. The detail is from Plut. *Brut.* 52.6, 54.1.
82. App. *B. Civ.* 4.117–18; it is instructive to compare the speech of Brutus with that of Cassius at ibid. 4.90–100.
83. Cass. Dio 47.47.3.
84. On the promise and Plutarch's reaction, see Plut. *Brut.* 46.1–2; cf. App. *B. Civ.* 4.118. On the support given to the triumvirs by Thessalonica, cf. Plin. *HN* 4.17, who records that it was granted the status of a 'free city' as a result; for Sparta's support, see Plut. *Brut.* 41.8, where Plutarch records the numbers killed fighting for the triumvirs. On Brutus' villa containing the 'Eurotas' and the 'Persike Stoa', see Cic. *Att.* 15.9.1 (SB 387).
85. Plut. *Brut.* 45.4–5; cf. Cass. Dio 47.48.3 who is less detailed and more apologetic in tone.
86. Plut. *Brut.* 45.6–9; for the more sinister interpretation followed here, see Moles–Pelling *ad loc.* For a different interpretation see Affortunati (2004), 112, who reads the anecdote as an example of Brutus' complex relationships with his subordinates and his inability to stand up to them.
87. App. *B. Civ.* 4.123–4; it is impossible to know whether it was Brutus, Cassius, both or neither, who said these words. Cassius' words were reported at Plut. *Brut.* 40.3; for discussion, see Moles–Pelling *ad loc.*
88. Plut. *Brut.* 48.5; cf. App. *B. Civ.* 4.134.
89. Some modern scholars have suggested that Brutus' fear that Antony might be successful might have been an additional factor prompting him to engage in battle. See e.g. Pelling (1996), 8, with further references.
90. Details of the encounter at Plut. *Brut.* 49–52; App. *B. Civ.* 125–31; Cass. Dio 47.48.5–49.1.
91. Plut. *Brut.* 49.9; Vell. Pat. 2.71.2. The story of Lucilius that follows occupies Plut. *Brut.* 50.1–9; cf. App. *B. Civ.* 4.129.
92. Prop. 2.1.27–9.
93. The death scene followed here is that of Plut. *Brut.* 51. Other accounts can be found at: Vell. Pat. 2.70.4–5; Plut. *Caes.* 69.14; App. *B. Civ.* 4.130–1; Cass. Dio 47.49.1–2; Flor. 2.17.14; [Livy], *Per.* 124; Eutr. 7.3.2; Oros. 6.18.16; [Aur. Vict.] *De Vir. Ill.* 82.6. Of these, the accounts of Plutarch, Appian and Dio are the only ones of any real value for ascertaining details of the historical event.
94. For a fuller analysis of this question, see Moles (1983a), 772–3, who argues for the identification with Octavian; Drummond (*FRHist* III, 510) points out, however, that 'Brutus might easily excoriate Antony, the senior partner in the Second Triumvirate, for taking Octavian's part. Nor can the possibility that Volumnius invented the story be entirely excluded'.
95. Cic. *Ad Brut.*1.4a.3 (SB 11).
96. For Antony's reaction, see Plut. *Brut.* 53.4, Plut. *Ant.* 22.4; cf. Val. Max. 5.1.11; App. *B. Civ.* 4.135.
97. Strauss (2015), 226.
98. Suet. *Aug.* 13.1. Some scholars have doubted the second tradition; for an expression of this view see e.g. Osgood (2006), 96 n. 119: 'the different version . . . should be attributed to a hostile and inaccurate source'. However, there is no reason why the two versions need be incompatible. In fact, Dio's slightly longer account (at Cass. Dio 47.49.2) gives an example, already from antiquity, of how the two stories could produce an integrated reading: Antony did give Brutus a proper burial, he says, *except* for the head which was sent to Rome.
99. Cass. Dio 47.49.2; cf. Flor. 2.17.11.
100. Plut. *Brut.* 24.4–5; App. *B. Civ.* 4.134. The original quotation is from Hom. *Il.* 16. 849 although its interpretation has been variously debated. For discussion of the passage in Plutarch, see Moles

(1983a), 249–56, although Moles is less willing than I am to see this passage used as material 'turned against' Brutus for ominous effect in the later writers. As Gosling (1986), *contra* Moles, has pointed out, Apollo was invoked as a protective deity by both sides of the war; thus Val. Max. 1.5.7 adds that 'Apollo' was also the watchword for the Caesarians at Philippi. It is also well known that Octavian later took over and cultivated Apollo as his protector; see e.g. Gurval (1995), 8. It would hence make sense to deprive Brutus of this claim after Philippi. For Brutus' coins, see *RRC* 503–4, 506.

Chapter 8: Death and Legend

1. Plut. *Brut.* 29.7; the context for the utterance is not provided by Plutarch.
2. Decimus Brutus' *dignitas* at Cic. *Fam.* 11.8.1 (SB 360); for the promise to Trebonius, see Cic. *Fam.* 12.16.4 (SB 328).
3. See e.g. *heroes* at Cic. *Att.* 14.4.2 (SB 358); *tyrannoctoni* at Cic. *Att.* 14.15 (SB 369), 14.6.2 (SB 360); *liberatores*, 'famous' and 'blessed' at Cic. *Att.* 14.12.2 (SB 366); 'great and glorious deed', Cic. *Att.* 14.11.1 (SB 365); cf. Cic. *Phil.* 2.114.
4. On Brutus' reception through the ages, see Clarke (1981) and Rawson (1986 = 1991); Woolf (2006) treats the topic of political assassination. Because there is so much overlap with the reception history of Caesar, much of relevance can also be found in the works of Gundolf (1928); Wyke (2006, 2007/2008); Pelling (2006, 2011).
5. His poetry: Plin. *Ep.* 5.3.5; cf. Tac. *Dial.* 21: His summary of Polybius: Plut. *Brut.* 4.8, *Suda* s.v. B § 561; Epitomes of Fannius and Caelius: Cic. *Att.* 12.5B (SB 316), 13.8 (SB 313).
6. Tac. *Dial.* 25.
7. Plut. *Brut.* 1.4; the comment may have been a *topos* of encomiastic literature, as Moles–Pelling points out *ad loc.*; however, as Rawson (1986 = 1991), 507, has pointed out, the roots for the comment may go back to Cicero's own presentation of the two men in his correspondence.
8. 'Servile fearfulness' from Shakespeare, *Julius Caesar* 1.1.76; kingly ambitions from the same play at 1.2.79–80, 'I do fear the people / Choose Caesar for their king'; for Caesar's treatment of the tribunes, 1.2.284–5; for the historical episodes behind these events in Shakespeare, see Chapter 4.
9. '"Brutus and Caesar": what should be in that 'Caesar'? Why should that name be sounded more than yours?': Shakespeare, *Julius Caesar* 1.2.141–2.
10. Shakespeare, *Julius Caesar*, 2.1.13; on Brutus' lack of envy towards Caesar or any other personal motivation, compare his earlier statement at 1.2.161.
11. Quotation from Cic. *Off.* 3.32; cf. 3.19 for tyrannicide as an act which combines 'virtue and expediency'. Other references to Caesar, tyranny and tyrannicide at ibid. 1.26; 2.23, 27, 84; 3.84.
12. On a date of June 1599 for the production (at latest September), as well as the historical context, see Daniell (1998), 7–38.
13. Quotation from John of Salisbury, *Policraticus* 7.25, in Nederman (1990). On John of Salisbury's use of Classical antiquity in his works, see the comprehensive overview by Hermand-Schebat (2014).
14. Cic. *Fam.* 15.19.4 (SB 216), discussed at p. 91; on John of Salisbury's knowledge of the second half of the *Ad Familiares*, see Hermand-Schebat (2014), 199–202. Although Hermand-Schebat does not make the connection between Cassius' letter and the text of the *Polycraticus*, he does provide sufficient other examples which lend strength to my suggestion of direct acquaintance here.
15. Aquinas, *De Regimine Principum* 1.7 = Dyson (2002), 17; for his earlier attitude compare his *Scripta Super Libros Sententiarum* II, Dist. 44, quaest. 2.2 = Dyson (2002), 73.
16. Cassius laments at Shakespeare, *Julius Caesar* 1.2.150–2, 1.3.108–11; the people proclaim Caesar tyrant at 3.2.70; 'For always I am Caesar', see 1.2.211. Cassius presented as scheming villain at 1.2.307–21; people change their mind about Caesar after Antony's speech at 3.2.109ff.; for Caesar's kindness to friends, see e.g. 2.2.126–7 when he warmly invites Brutus and the other conspirators to share wine; his generosity in his will is recorded at 3.2.233–45.
17. On this, see Shapiro (2005), who stresses several themes shared by Julius Caesar and its contemporary context.
18. A paraphrase of Sen. *Ben.* 20.1–2; for an interesting discussion of Seneca's treatment of Brutus see Lentano (2009).
19. Plut. *Comp. Dion and Brut.* 3.4; see also Rawson (1986), esp. 102–3 = (1991), 489–90, and Pelling (2006), 7–8.
20. On this question and the difficult problem of *amicitia*, see Brunt (1965); Konstan (1997), 122–37.
21. See esp. Cic. *Amic.* 33–55; on the connection between this treatise and the letter to Matius discussed in what follows, see MacKendrick (1989), 218–20; Griffin (1997); Lintott (2008), 359–66.
22. Cic. *Fam.* 11.27.8 (SB 348). For Cicero's views on tyranny and tyrannicide elsewhere, see n. 11, above.
23. The exchange of letters makes it clear that Matius knew that Cicero was involved in the criticism of him; for the further suggestion that Brutus was equally guilty, compare Cicero's remark in a letter

to Atticus, sent earlier in the summer of 44 BC, that Matius was distressed at Brutus' suspicions of him, too: Cic. *Att.* 14.5.1 (SB 359).

24. Cic. *Fam.* 11.28.8 (SB 349).
25. On this legacy, see Osgood (2006); on the representation of it in Shakespeare, see Brittin (1959).
26. See Rawson (1986), 103–4 = (1991), 400–1; that ingratitude features little in Shakespeare's play is the observation of Pelling (2011), 73–4.
27. Dante, *Inferno* 34.54–69 (trans. D.L. Sayers).
28. For this interpretation, see Piccolomini (1991), 2–5.
29. Quotations and paraphrase from Plut. *Brut.* 47.7; for the general idea that the fall of the Republic was preordained, see Plut. *Comp. Cimon and Lucull.* 1.1; Plut. *Pomp.* 5.4–5, 75.5; Plut. *Caes.* 28.6, 57.1, 60.1, 66.1, 69.2–3, 69.6–13. For discussion, see Swain (1989), esp. 288–92.
30. '[T]he man promised to you', 'born of the gods', 'who will establish again a Golden Age' (Verg. *Aen.* 6.791–5); an empire 'without end' (Verg. *Aen.* 1.279). The meaning of the *Aeneid* and its political message has been vigorously debated. A useful entry point into these discussions is Schmidt (2001); for further discussion of Augustus' divine authority in the poem, see Grebe (2004). On the topic of Augustus' use of images, the classic text is Zanker (1988).
31. Sen. *Ben.* 2.20; on the unfairness of Seneca's first point, see Griffin (1976), 202–6; on this passage, more generally, see Griffin (2013), 199–200, with further references.
32. Syme (1939), 4, 57–9, 148, 183, 205.
33. Cic. *Att.* 14.1.1 (SB 355).
34. Mommsen (1910); cf. Drumann and Groebe (1908), 21–48.
35. Wylie (1998), quotations taken from pages 170, 178.
36. Cic. *Att.* 14.21.3 (SB 375); cf. ibid. 15.4.2 (SB 381).
37. For Brutus' own references to his *clementia* as well as Cicero's recognition of it, see Cic. *Ad Brut.* 2.5 5 (SB 5), 1.2a.2 (SB 6), 1.15.10 (SB 23); for the quotation, see Vell. Pat. 2.59.6; cf. App. *B. Civ.* 3.79.
38. Plut. *Brut.* 29.3; for Brutus' *praotés* in the rest of the *Life,* see ibid. 6.10 (government of Cisalpine Gaul), 18.4–5 (his insistence on sparing Antony), 26.6 (his treatment of Gaius Antonius), 41 (his distress at the mass suicide of Lycians), 32 (his merciful treatment of Patara), 45.4–5 (his attempt to save his captives); on the importance of *praotés* in Plutarch's *Lives* more generally, see Martin Jr (1960); for its importance in the *Brutus* specifically, see Moles–Pelling, 71–3.
39. I disagree with Clarke (1981), 121, who does not see a Plutarchan echo in these last three lines of Antony's soliloquy. For North's translation and use of 'gentle', see North (1579 = 1928), 7.138: 'bicause he was a marvellous lowly and gentle person'; cf. the marginalia 'Brutus gentle and fayer condicions'.
40. See the overview provided on pp. 5–11.
41. Cic. *Fam.* 12.3.1 (SB 345).
42. App. *B. Civ.* 2.112; for further discussion, see p. 102; cf. Plut. *Brut,* 5.1–2, who uses the verb *légetai* to introduce an entire section on the nexus of relationships between Servilia, Caesar and Brutus.
43. Shakespeare, *Henry VI, Part 2* 4.1.136–7.
44. Salutati, *Tyranno*, 53, cited and discussed by Piccolomini (1991), 54; for further discussion, also see Clarke (1981), 88.
45. Suet. *Iul.* 88; in talking of the honours bestowed upon Caesar after his death he adds: 'it was decided that the hall (*curia*) in which he was killed, be walled up, that the Ides of March be named Day of Parricide (*Parricidium*), and that never should the Senate do business on that day'.
46. The point is made by Welch (2015), 283.
47. There is much more to be said about this satire and so I have restricted myself to the immediate point of throat-slitting here, which I do not believe has been made in this context before. For other readings of the poem and its meaning, all of which endorse a political reading in varying degrees, see Henderson (1994); Gowers (2002); Connor (2005), 134–5.
48. Strauss (2015), 130–1, to whose description of the swords I am indebted here; cf. Strauss (2015), 221.
49. Cic. *Ad Brut.* 2.5.5 (SB 5); cf. the discussion by Dowling (2006), esp. 34–7. On 'group-think' and military incompetence a classic discussion is that of Dixon (1976), esp. 399–400.
50. The remark was made by Ben Jonson in his commendatory poem, 'To the memory of my beloved, the author, Mr. William Shakespeare', in *Mr. William Shakespeare's Comedies, Histories and Tragedies* (London, 1623). As one of Yale's reviewers has pointed out to me, Jonson probably meant 'even if you had only small Latin and less Greek' (thus meaning that Shakespeare in fact had a good deal more). That would not change the interpretation here, but it does help emphasise that Shakespeare really did understand the force of the connection between *vir* and *virtus.*
51. Vell. Pat. 2.72.1; Val. Max. 6.4.5.
52. On *temeritas* as the opposite of wisdom and virtue, see Cic. *Acad. Post.* 42, 45; Cic. *Off.* 2.8. On corresponding virtues and vices, also see Cic. *Cat.* 2.25.

53. For the Stoic paradox, see the discussion by Moles (1987b), 64–5, although he uses it to argue a rather different point.
54. Thus e.g. Clarke (1981), 78: 'Whatever Brutus' faults and inadequacies he had a moral elevation that no other Roman leader at the time had. Virtue was shattered at Philippi'.
55. For these details, see Hor. *Ep.* 2.2.49–52; Hor. *Sat.* 2.6.36; Suet. *Hor.* On the life of Horace, also see Günther (2013).
56. Brutus' responsibility for the first battle: Plut. *Brut.* 39.8; poor discipline: Plut. *Brut.* 41.4; App. *B. Civ.* 4.110; decision to fight the second battle: Plut. *Brut.* 56.2; App. *B. Civ.* 4.124. Comparisons between Brutus and Cassius at: Vell. Pat. 2.71.1–2; App. *B. Civ.* 4.123. See Moles (1987b), 60–1.
57. *Pace* West (1998), 50–1.
58. On the arrogance of the republicans, see App. *B. Civ.* 2.125; on their submission, see ibid. 2.135.
59. This is the conclusion of Nisbet and Hubbard (1978), 106–21; Moles (1987b); Gaskin (2013), esp. ch. 7.
60. On Horace's originality in the use of this literary *topos*, which is crafted to reflect on the political experiences of Horace and Pompeius, see Smith (2015).
61. For other attempts to blend the lines between the positive and negative readings, see Citroni (2000) and Osgood (2006), 101–3. My own interpretation differs slightly in its focus on what *virtus* meant and why Brutus' *virtus* in particular was challenged. But this only adds an extra dimension to the poem and does not rule out other ideas.
62. On the shift in meaning of *virtus* see Noreña (2011), 78–9.
63. The transformation of the concept is more complex than this summary suggests: see esp. McDonnell (2006), 385ff, but this is one of the main ways in which *virtus* changed in its usage.
64. For the relevance of *Julius Caesar* to this debate, see Miola (1985); on the reaction to Shakespeare's play and the responses of his early critics, see Woolf (2006), esp. 171–3.
65. For an extended discussion of this idea, see Skinner (1998).
66. See Clarke (1981), 81–5, for a brief survey; Rawson (1986 = 1991) provides a fuller overview.
67. Luc. *Phars.* 7.588–96. This is a famous passage. It is commented upon by both Clarke (1981), 83 and Piccolomini (1991), 12–13.
68. M. Aur. *Med.* 1.14.
69. *Vindiciae contra Tyrannos* is discussed by Clarke (1981), 87, and Woolf (2006), 170. On Algernon Sidney, see Clarke (1981), 92–3; Skinner (1998), *passim*. On Lorenzino de' Medici, see Dall'Aglio (2015), 14–17. On Lucien Bonaparte, see Roberts (2014), 54.
70. On the French Revolution, see Murphy (1987).
71. Miss Pross comes across 'The Good Republican Brutus of Antiquity' in Dickens, *A Tale of Two Cities*, ch. 8; Brutus appears in the land of Glubbdubdrib in Gulliver's travels (part 3, ch. 7): 'I was struck with a profound veneration at the sight of Brutus, and could easily discover the most consummate virtue, the greatest intrepidity and firmness of mind, the truest love of his country, and general benevolence for mankind, in every lineament of his countenance.' Brutus appears in a Freudian dream in Freud (1900), *PFL* 4.551–2.
72. The story is derived from the dialogue of Gioanotti.
73. For a fuller survey of Brutus on stage, see Ripley (1980); more recent appearances on TV have been discussed by Bataille (2009) and on film by Richards (2008), esp. 64–6, 157; an analysis of Brutus in HBO's *Rome* is in Chiu (2015), who looks at the influence of Plutarch and Shakespeare on his presentation.

Conclusion: The Many Faces of Brutus

1. Cic. *Att.* 2.24.3 (SB 44); I take the term 'three-headed monster' from App. *B. Civ.* 2.9, who in turn says he took it from the contemporary Roman writer Varro.
2. Cic. *Att.* 13.40.1 (SB 343).
3. Cic. *Phil.* 2.26–7.
4. Cic. *Orat.* 33, quoted in full at the top of the chapter.

BIBLIOGRAPHY

Affortunati, M. (2004). *Plutarco: Vita di Bruto, Introduzione e Commento Storico* (Frankfurt am Main).

Africa, T.F. (1978). 'The Mask of an Assassin: A Psychohistorical Study of M. Junius Brutus', *Journal of Interdisciplinary History* 8.4, 599–626.

Alexander, M.C. (1990). *Trials in the Late Roman Republic, 149 BC to 50 BC* (Toronto).

— (2002). *The Case for the Prosecution in the Ciceronian Era* (Ann Arbor).

Alföldi, A. (1956). 'The Main Aspects of Political Propaganda on the Coinage of the Roman Republic', in R.A.G. Carson and C.H.V. Sutherland (eds), *Essays in Roman Coinage Presented to Harold Mattingly* (Oxford), 63–95.

— (1985). *Caesar in 44 v. Chr., Bd 1: Studien zu Caesars Monarchie und ihren Wurzeln* (Bonn).

Allegri, G. (1977). *Bruto usario nell'epistolario ciceroniano* (Florence).

Allen, W. (1937). 'On the Importance of the Young Men in Ciceronian Politics', *CJ* 23, 357–9.

— (1950). 'The Vettius Affair Once More', *TAPhA* 81, 153–62.

Alston, R. (2015). *Rome's Revolution: Death of the Republic and Birth of the Empire* (Oxford).

Andreau, J. (1999). *Banking and Business in the Ancient World* (Cambridge).

Arena, V. (2012). *Libertas and the Practice of Politics in the Late Roman Republic* (Cambridge).

Arnaud, P. (1998). '"Toi aussi, mon fils, tu mangeras ta part de pouvoir" – Brutus le Tyran?', *Latomus* 57, 61–71.

Badian, E. (1965). 'M. Porcius Cato and the Annexation and Early Administration of Cyprus', *Journal of Roman Studies* 55, 110–21.

— (1967). 'Review: Cicero: *Brutus* ed. A.E. Douglas (and other works)', *JRS* 57, 223–30.

— (1970). *Lucius Sulla: The Deadly Reformer* (Sydney).

Balbo, A. (2011). 'Riflessi dell'oratoria reale nei discorsi sulla morte di Cesare: il caso di Bruto', *I Quaderni del Ramo d'Oro* 4, 152–67.

— (2013). 'Marcus Junius Brutus the Orator: Between Philosophy and Rhetoric', in C. Steel and H. van der Blom (eds), *Community and Communication: Oratory and Politics in Republican Rome* (Oxford), 315–28.

Balsdon, J.P.V.D. (1958). 'The Ides of March', *Historia* 7.1, 80–94.

Baltrusch, E. (2004). *Caesar und Pompeius* (Darmstadt).

Baraz, Y. (2012). *A Written Republic: Cicero's Philosophical Politics* (Princeton).

Barnes, J. (1997). 'Antiochus of Ascalon', in M. Griffin and J. Barnes (eds), *Philosophia Togata II: Plato and Aristotle at Rome* (Oxford), 51–96.

Barwick, K. (1928). 'Die Gliederung der Narratio in der rhetorischen Theorie und ihre Bedeutung für die Geschichte des des antiken Romans', *Hermes* 63, 261–87.

Bataille, S. (2009). 'How Many Times Shall Caesar Bleed in Sport: Recent Roman TV Productions and the Shakespearean Legacy', in S. Hatchuel and N. Guerrin (eds), *Shakespeare on Screen* (Rouen), 225–38.

Bell, A.A. (1994). 'Fact and *Exemplum* in Accounts of the Deaths of Pompey and Caesar', *Latomus* 53, 824–36.

Bengtson, H. (1970). *Zur Geschichte des Brutus* (Munich).
Bernstein, M.A. (1994). *Foregone Conclusions: Against Apocalyptic History* (Berkeley).
Berry, D.H. (2006). *Cicero's Political Speeches* (Oxford).
Blank, D. (2007). 'The Life of Antiochus of Ascalon in Philodemus' History of the Academy and a Tale of Two Letters', *ZPE* 162, 87–93.
Bloomer, M. (2011). *The School of Rome: Latin Studies and the Origins of Liberal Education* (Berkeley).
Blösel, W. (2016). 'Provincial Commands and Money in the late Roman Republic', in H. Beck, M. Jehne and J. Serrati (eds), *Money and Power in the Roman Republic*, Collection Latomus (Brussels), 68–81.
Boes, J. (1990). *La Philosophie et l'action dans la correspondance de Cicéron* (Nancy).
Bonnefond, M. (1984). 'La *Lex Gabinia* sur les ambassades', in C. Nicolet (ed.), *Des ordres à Rome* (Paris), 61–99.
Bonner, S.F. (1977). *Education in Ancient Rome: From the Elder Cato to the Younger Pliny* (Berkeley and Los Angeles).
Borg, B.E. (2012). 'Recent Approaches to the Study of Roman Portraits', *Perspective* 2, 315–20; available online at http://perspective.revues.org/137 (last accessed 19 June 2017).
Bossier, G. (1897). *Cicero and His Friends*, trans. A.D. Jones (New York).
Bowman, A.K., E. Champlin and A. Lintott (eds) (1996). *CAH X*, 2nd edn (Cambridge).
Braccesi, L. (1973). *Introduzione al De Viris Illustribus* (Bologna).
Braund, D. (1984). *Rome and the Friendly King* (New York).
Braund, S. (2009). *Seneca, De Clementia* (Oxford).
Brenk, F.E. (1977). *In Mist Apparelled: Religious Themes in Plutarch's* Moralia *and* Lives, *Mnemosyne* suppl. 48 (Leiden).
Brennan, T.C. (2000). *The Praetorship in the Roman Republic I–II* (Oxford).
Brittin, N.A. (1959). 'Shakespeare and the Conflict between Tyranny and Liberty', *Estudios Generales* 6.12 (Puerto Rico), 75–90.
Broughton, T.R.S. (1951–52 and 1986). *The Magistrates of the Roman Republic*, 3 vols (New York and Atlanta).
Brozek, M. (1959). 'Cycerona memoryal polityczny do Cezara', *Meander* 14, 477–86.
Brunt, P.A. (1953). 'Cicero: *Ad Atticum* 2.24', *CQ* 3.1–2, 62–4.
— (1965). '*Amicitia* in the late Roman Republic', *PCPS* n.s. 2, 1–20.
— (1971). *Italian Manpower, 225 BC–AD 14* (Oxford).
— (1988). *Fall of the Roman Republic* (Oxford).
Burton, P. (2014). 'The Revolt of Lepidus (cos. 78 BC) Revisited', *Historia* 63.4, 404–21.
Carson, R.A.G. (1957). 'Caesar and the Monarchy', *G&R* 4.1, 46–53.
Cavarzere, A. (2000). *Oratoria a Roma: Storia di un genere pragmatico* (Rome).
Cerutti, S. (1993). 'Brutus, Cyprus and the Coinage of 55 BC', *AJN* 5–6, 69–87.
Chantraine, H. (1983). 'Münzbild und Familiengeschichte in der römischen Republik', *Gymnasium* 90, 530–45.
Cichorius, C. (1922). *Römische Studien: historisches, epigraphisches, literargeschichtliches aus vier Jahrhunderten Roms* (Leipzig).
Chiu, A.C. (2015). 'A Touch Too Cerebral: Eulogizing Caesar in Rome', in M.S. Cyrino (ed.), *Rome Season Two: Trial and Triumph* (Edinburgh), 13–24.
Christ, K. (2002). *Sulla: Eine römische Karriere* (Munich).
Citroni, M. (2000). 'The Memory of Philippi in Horace and the Interpretation of Epistle 1.20.23', *CJ* 96.1, 27–56.
Clark, A.J. (2007). *Divine Qualities: Cult and Community in Republican Rome* (Oxford).
Clarke, M.L. (1981). *Brutus: The Noblest Roman* (London).
Commager, S. (1981). 'Fateful Words: Some Conversations in *Aeneid* 4', *Arethusa* 14.1, 101–14.
Connor, C. (2005). 'Epic Allusions in Roman Satire', in K. Freudenburg (ed.), *The Cambridge Companion to Roman Satire* (Cambridge), 123–45.
Cooley, A.E. (2009). *Res Gestae Divi Augusti: Text, Translation, and Commentary* (Cambridge).
Corbeill, A. (2002). 'Ciceronian Invective', in J.M. May (ed.), *Brill's Companion to Cicero: Oratory and Rhetoric* (Leiden), 197–217.
— (2010). 'Rhetorical Education and Social Reproduction in the Republic and Early Empire', in W. Dominik and J. Hall (eds), *A Companion to Roman Rhetoric* (Oxford), 69–82.
Cornell, T.J. (1995). *The Beginnings of Rome: Italy and Rome from the Bronze Age to the Punic Wars* (London).
— (2005). 'The Value of the Literary Tradition Concerning Archaic Rome', in K.A. Raaflaub (ed.), *Social Struggles in Archaic Rome: New Perspectives on the Conflicts of the Orders* (Oxford), 47–74.
Cornell, T.J. et al. (2013). *The Fragments of the Roman Historians*, 3 vols (Oxford).

Corrigan, K. (2015). *Brutus: Caesar's Assassin* (Barnsley).
Cowan, E. (2009). 'Marius' in Nicolaus of Damascus. Some Implications from Chronology', *Athenaeum* 97.1, 159–68.
Crawford, J.W. (1994). *M. Tullius Cicero: The Fragmentary Speeches* (Atlanta).
Crawford, M.H. (1974). *Roman Republican Coinage*, 2 vols (Cambridge).
— (1992). *The Roman Republic*, 2nd edn (London).
Cribiore, R. (2001). *Writing, Teachers, and Students in Graeco-Roman Egypt* (Princeton).
Dall'Aglio, S. (2015). *The Duke's Assassin: Exile and Death of Lorenzino de' Medici*, trans. D. Weinstein (London and New Haven).
Daly, L.W. (1950). 'Roman Study Abroad', *AJPh* 71, 40–58.
Daniell, D. (1998). *William Shakespeare: Julius Caesar*, The Arden Shakespeare (New York).
Day, S. (2016). 'Fred K. Drogula, *Commanders and Command in the Roman Republic and Early Empire*', *Bryn Mawr Classical Review* (28 June); available online at http://bmcr.brynmawr.edu/2016/2016-06-28.html (last accessed 10 June 2017).
Denniston, J.D. (1926). *M. Tulli Ciceronis In M. Antonium Orationes Philippicae Prima et Secunda* (Oxford).
Dessau, H. (1892). *Inscriptions Latinae Selectae* (Berlin).
Dettenhofer, M.H. (1990). 'Cicero und C. Cassius Longinus: Politische Korrespondenz ein Jahr vor Caesars Ermordung (Cic. *Fam.* 15,16–19)', *Historia* 39.2, 249–56.
— (1992). *Perdita Iuventus. Zwischen den Generationen von Caesar und Augustus* (Munich).
Deutsch, M.E. (1928). 'I am Caesar, Not Rex', *CPh* 23.4, 394–8.
Dickey, E. (1996). *Greek Forms of Address: From Herodotus to Lucian* (Oxford).
Dihle, A. (1978). 'Cicero *Ad Atticum* 14.1.2', *HSCPh* 82, 179–86.
Dixon, N.F. (1976). *On the Psychology of Military Incompetence* (London).
Douglas, A.E. (1966). *M. Tulli Ciceronis Brutus* (Oxford).
Dowling, M. (2006). *Clemency and Cruelty in the Roman World* (Ann Arbor).
Drogula, F.K. (2015). *Commanders and Command in the Roman Republic and Early Empire* (Chapel Hill).
Drum, M. (2008). 'Cicero's Tenth and Eleventh *Philippics*: The Republican Advance in the East', in T. Stevenson and M. Wilson (eds), *Cicero's Philippics: History, Rhetoric and Ideology*, *Prudentia* 37–38, 82–94.
Drumann, W. and P. Groebe. (1899). *Geschichte Roms*, vol. 1, 2nd edn (Leipzig).
— (1906). *Geschichte Roms*, vol. 3, 2nd edn (Leipzig).
— (1908). *Geschichte Roms*, vol. 4, 2nd edn (Leipzig).
Duff, T.E. (1999). *Plutarch's Lives: Exploring Virtue and Vice* (Oxford).
— (2011). 'The Structure of the Plutarchan Book', *Classical Antiquity* 30.2, 213–78.
Dugan, J. (2005). *Making a New Man: Ciceronian Self-fashioning in the Rhetorical Works* (Oxford).
Dyson, R.W. (2002). *Aquinas, Political Writings*, Cambridge Texts in the History of Political Thought (Cambridge).
Dyson, S.L. (2010). *Rome: A Living Portrait of an Ancient City* (Baltimore).
Epstein, D.F. (1987). 'Caesar's Personal Enemies on the Ides of March', *Latomus* 46, 566–70.
Ercole, F. (1914). *Coluccio Salutati, Tractatus de Tyranno* (Berlin).
Erskine, A. (1991). 'Hellenistic Monarchy and Roman Political Invective', *CQ* 41.1, 106–20.
Evans, J. de Rose. (1992). *The Art of Persuasion: Political Propaganda from Aeneas to Brutus* (Ann Arbor).
Evans, R. (1983). 'The *Consulares* and *Praetorii* in the Roman Senate at the Beginning of Sulla's Dictatorship', *Athenaeum* 61, 521–8.
Fehrle, R. (1983). *Cato Uticensis* (Darmstadt).
Filbey, E.J. (1911). 'Concerning the Oratory of Brutus', *CPh* 6.3, 325–33.
Flower, H.I. (1995). '*Fabulae Praetextae* in Context: When Were Plays on Contemporary Subjects Performed in Republican Rome?', *CQ* 45.1, 170–90.
— (1996). *Ancestor Masks and Aristocratic Power in Roman Culture* (Oxford).
— (2010). *Roman Republics* (Princeton).
Forsyth, P.Y. (1979). 'Order and Meaning in Catullus 97–99', *CW* 72.7, 403–8.
— (1988). 'In the Wake of Etna, 44 BC', *Cl. Ant.* 7.1, 49–57.
Fowler, D. (1989). 'Lucretius and Politics', in M. Griffin and J. Barnes (eds), *Philosophia Togata I: Essays on Philosophy and Roman Society* (Oxford), 120–50.
Frazel, T.D. (2009). *The Rhetoric of Cicero's In Verrem* (Göttingen).
Frederiksen, M.W. (1966). 'Caesar, Cicero and the Problem of Debt', *JRS* 56, 1–2, 128–41.
Freud, S. (1900). *The Interpretation of Dreams*, vol. 4 (repr. 1976), Penguin Freud Library (Harmondsworth).
Frisch, H. (1946). *Cicero's Fight for the Republic* (Copenhagen).
Fritz, K. von. (1942). 'Pompey's Policy Before and After the Outbreak of Civil War of 49 BC', *Transactions of the American Philological Association* 73, 145–80.

Gabba, E. (1956). *Appiano e la storia delle guerre civili* (Florence).
Gardner, J.F. (1998). *Family and* Familia *in Roman Law and Life* (Oxford).
Gaskin, R. (2013). *Horace and Housman* (New York).
Geiger, J. (1972). 'Canidius or Caninius', *CQ* 22.1, 130–4.
— (1973). 'The Last Servilii Caepiones of the Republic', *Anc. Soc.* 4, 143–56.
— (2011). 'The Augustan Age', in G. Marasco (ed.), *Political Autobiographies and Memoirs in Antiquity* (Leiden), 233–66.
Gelzer, M. (1917). 'M. Iunius Brutus (53)', *RE* 10.1, 973–1020.
— (1938). 'Review: *Brutus et la fin de la république* by Gérard Walter', *Gnomon* 15.5, 279–80.
— (1968). *Caesar: Politician and Statesman*, trans. Peter Needham (Oxford).
— (1969). *Cicero: ein biographischer Versuch* (Wiesbaden).
— (1984). *Pompeius*, 2nd edn (Munich).
Gibbon, E. (1814). *Miscellaneous Works of Edward Gibbon, Esq. with Memoirs of his Life and Writings, Composed by Himself: Illustrated from his Letters, with occasional Notes and Narrative, by the Right Honourable John, Lord Sheffield*, 5 vols (London).
Girardet, K.M. (1993). 'Die Rechtsstellung der Caesarattentäter Brutus und Cassius in den Jahren 44–42 v. Chr.', *Chiron* 23, 207–32 = (2007) in *Rom auf dem Weg von der Republik zum Prinzipat* (Bonn), 283–314.
Goar, R.J. (1987). *The Legend of Cato Uticensis from the First Century* BC *to the Fifth Century* AD (Brussels).
Goldsworthy, A. (2010). *Antony and Cleopatra* (London and New York).
Gosling, A. (1986). 'Octavian, Brutus and Apollo: A Note on Opportunist Propaganda', *AJPh* 107, 586–9.
Gotter, U. (1996). *Der Diktator ist tot! Politik in Rom zwischen den Iden des März und der Begründung des Zweiten Triumvirats*, Historia Einzelschriften 110 (Stuttgart).
— (2000). 'Marcus Iunius Brutus – oder: Die Nemesis des Namens', in K.-J. Hölkeskamp and E. Stein-Hölkeskamp (eds), *Von Romulus zu Augustus: Große Gestalten der römischen Republik* (Munich), 328–39.
Gowers, E. (2002). 'Blind Eyes and Cut Throats: Amnesia and Silence in Horace *Satires* 1.7', *CPh.* 97.2, 145–61.
Gowing, A. (1992). *The Triumviral Narratives of Appian and Cassius Dio* (Ann Arbor).
— (2009). 'The Roman *Exempla* Tradition in Imperial Greek Historiography: The Case of Camillus', in A. Feldherr (ed.), *The Cambridge Companion to the Roman Historians* (Cambridge), 332–47.
Grabarek, G.P. (2010). 'Men of Letters: The Oratorical and Philosophical Relationship between Cicero and Brutus', PhD diss., Indiana University.
Graziosi, B. and J. Haubold (2010). *Homer: Iliad, Book VI* (Cambridge).
Grebe, S. (2004). 'Augustus' Divine Authority and Vergil's *Aeneid*', *Vergilius* 50, 35–62.
Gregory, A.P. (1994). '"Powerful Images": Responses to Portraits and the Political Use of Images in Rome', *JRA* 7, 80–99.
Griffin, M.T. (1976). *Seneca: A Philosopher in Politics* (Oxford).
— (1986). 'Philosophy, Cato, and Roman Suicide: II', *G&R* 33.2, 192–202.
— (1989). 'Philosophy, Politics and Politicians at Rome', in M. Griffin and J. Barnes (eds), *Philosophia Togata I: Essays on Philosophy and Roman Society* (Oxford), 1–37.
— (1995). 'Philosophical Badinage in Cicero's Letters to his Friends', in J.G.F. Powell (ed.), *Cicero the Philosopher* (Oxford), 325–46.
— (1997). 'From Aristotle to Atticus: Cicero and Matius on Friendship', in M. Griffin and J. Barnes (eds), *Philosophia Togata II: Plato and Aristotle at Rome* (Oxford), 86–109.
— (2013). *Seneca on Society: A Guide to* De Beneficiis (Oxford).
Groebe, P. (1907). 'Das Geburtsjahr des M. Brutus', *Hermes* 42, 304–14.
Gruen, E. (1974). *The Last Generation of the Roman Republic* (Berkeley).
Gundolf, F. (1928). *The Mantle of Caesar*, trans. Jacob Wittner Hartmann (London).
Günther, H.-C. (2013). 'Horace's Life and Work', in H.-C. Günther (ed.), *Brill's Companion to Horace* (Leiden), 1–62.
Gurval, R.A. (1995). *Actium and Augustus* (Ann Arbor).
Habicht, C. (1997). *Athens from Alexander to Antony* (Cambridge, MA).
Haley, S. (1985). 'The Five Wives of Pompey the Great', *G&R* 32.1, 49–59.
Hallett, J.P. (1984). *Fathers and Daughters in Roman Society: Women and the Elite Family* (Princeton).
Hantos, T. (1988). *Res publica contituta: Die Verfassung des Dictators Sulla* (Wiesbaden).
Harris, W.V. (1976). 'The Development of the Quaestorship, 267–81 BC', *CQ* 26, 92–106.
Hatzimichali, M. (2012). 'Antiochus' Biography', in D. Sedley (ed.), *The Philosophy of Antiochus* (Cambridge), 9–30.
Hau, L. (2016). *Moral History from Herodotus to Diodorus Siculus* (Edinburgh).

Hawthorn, J.R. (1962). 'The Senate after Sulla', *G&R* 9.1, 53–60.
Hellegouarc'h, J. (1963). *Le Vocabulaire latin des relations et des partis politiques sous la République* (Paris).
Henderson, J. (1994). 'On Getting Rid of Kings: Horace, Satire 1.7', *CQ* 44, 146–70 = (1998). *Fighting for Rome: Poets and Caesars, History, and Civil War* (Cambridge), 73–107.
Hendrickson, G. (1939). 'Brutus De Virtute', *AJPh* 60.4, 401–13.
Hermand-Schebat, L. (2014). 'John of Salisbury and Classical Antiquity', in C. Grellard and F. Lachaud (eds), *A Companion to John of Salisbury* (Leiden), 180–214.
Hill, G. (2010). *A History of Cyprus*, vol. 1 (Cambridge).
Hillard, T. (2013). 'Graffiti's Engagement: The Political Graffiti of the Late Roman Republic', in G. Sears, P. Keegan and R. Laurence (eds), *Written Space in the Latin West, 200 BC–AD 300* (London), 105–22.
Hinard, F. (1985). *Les Proscriptions de la Rome républicaine*, Collection de l'École française de Rome, 83 (Rome).
Hodgson, L. (2017). *Res Publica and the Roman Republic: 'Without Body or Form'* (Oxford).
Hohl, E. (1941–42). 'Das Angebot des Diadems an Cäsar', *Klio* 34, 92–117.
Hölkeskamp, K.-J. (2004). *Senatus Populusque Romanus. Die politische Kultur der Republik – Dimension und Deutungen* (Stuttgart).
— (2010). *Reconstructing the Roman Republic: An Ancient Political Culture and Modern Research* (Princeton).
Hollstein, W. (1993). *Die stadtrömische Münzprägung der Jahre 78–50 v. Chr. zwischen politischer Aktualität und Familienthematik. Kommentar und Bibliographie, Quellen und Forschungen zur Antiken Welt* 14 (Munich).
— (1994). 'Apollo und Libertas in der Münzprägung des Brutus und Cassius', *Jahrbuch für Numismatik und Geldgeschichte* 44, 113–33.
Hölscher, T. (1982). 'Die Bedeutung der Münzen für das Verstandnis der politischen Repräsentationskunst der späten römischen Republik', in T. Hackens and R. Weiller (eds), *Actes du 9ème Congrès International de Numismatique, Berne, Septembre 1979* (Louvain-la-Neuve), 269–82.
Hopkins, K. (1983). *Death and Renewal: Sociological Studies in Roman History*, vol. 2 (Cambridge).
Hornblower, S., A. Spawforth and E. Eidonow (2012). *Oxford Classical Dictionary*, 4th edn (Oxford).
Horsfall, N. (1974). 'The Ides of March: Some New Problems', *G&R* 21.2, 191–9.
— (1989). *Cornelius Nepos: A Selection, Including the Lives of Cato and Atticus* (Oxford).
How, W.W. and A.C. Clark (1926). *Cicero: Select Letters* (Oxford).
Howgego, C. (1995). *Ancient History from Coins* (London).
Huß, W. (1977). 'Die menschlichen und politischen Beziehungen zwischen Brutus und Cassius', *Würzburger Jahrbücher für die Altertumswissenschaft* 3, 115–25.
Hutchinson, G. (1998). *Cicero's Correspondence: A Literary Study* (Oxford).
Jehne, M. (1987). *Die Staat des Dictators Caesar* (Cologne and Vienna).
Kaster, R.A. (1995). *C. Suetonius Tranquillus: De Grammaticus et Rhetoribus* (Oxford).
— (2006). *Cicero: Speech on Behalf of Publius Sestius* (Oxford).
Keaveney, A. (2005). *Sulla: The Last Republican*, 2nd edn (London and New York).
Kerkhecker, A. (1999). *Callimachus' Book of Iambi* (Oxford).
Keil, H. (1857–80). *Grammatici Latini*, 3 vols (Leipzig).
Kelly, D. (2008). 'Publishing the *Philippics*, 43–42 BC', in T. Stevenson and M. Wilson (eds), *Cicero's Philippics: History, Rhetoric and Ideology*, Prudentia 37–38 (Auckland), 37–8.
Kennedy, G. (2003). *Progymnasmata: Greek Textbooks of Prose Composition and Rhetoric* (Atlanta).
Kierdorf, W. (1978). 'Cicero's Cato – Überlegungen zu einer verlorenen Schrift Ciceros', *Rheinisches Museum für Philologie* 121, 167–84.
Kirbihler, F. (2013). 'Brutus et Cassius et les impositions, spoliations et confiscations en Asie mineure durant les guerres civiles (44–2 AC)', in M. C. Ferriès (ed.), *Spolier et confisquer dans les mondes grec et romain* (Savoie), 345–66.
Kniely, E.-M. (1974). *Quellenkritische Studien zur Tätigkeit des M. Brutus im Osten (44–42 v.Chr.)* (Wien).
Konrad, C.F. (1994). *Plutarch's Sertorius: A Historical Commentary* (Chapel Hill).
Konstan, D. (1997). *Friendship in the Classical World* (Cambridge).
Kraus, C.S. (1994). 'No Second Troy: Topoi and Refoundation in Livy, Book V', *TAPhA* 124, 267–89.
Laignoux, R. (2012). 'Le monnayage de Brutus et Cassius après la mort de César', in N. Holmes (ed.), *Proceedings of the XIVth International Numismatic Congress (Glasgow 2009)* (Glasgow and London), 785–93.
Lentano, M. (2007). *La Prova del sangue: Storie di identità e storie di legittimità nella cultura latina* (Bologna).
— (2008). 'Bruto o il potere delle imagini', *Latomus* 67, 881–99.
— (2009). 'Il debito di Bruto. Per un'antropologia del nome proprio nella cultura romana', *Materiali e discussioni per l'analisi dei testi classici* 23, 59–89.

Lévy, C. (2012). 'Other Followers of Antiochus', in D. Sedley (ed.), *The Philosophy of Antiochus* (Cambridge), 290–306.
Lewis, R.G. (2006). *Asconius: Commentaries on Speeches by Cicero* (Oxford).
Lindsay, H. (2009). *Adoption in the Roman World* (Cambridge).
Lintott, A. (1970). 'The Tradition of Violence in the Annals of the Early Roman Republic', *Historia* 19, 12–29.
— (1971). 'Lucan and the History of the Civil War', *CQ* 21.2, 488–505.
— (1999a). *The Constitution of the Roman Republic* (Oxford).
— (1999b). *Violence in Republican Rome*, 2nd edn (Oxford).
— (2001–3). '*Delator* and *Iudex*: Informers and Accusers at Rome from the Republic to the Early Principate', *Accordia Research Papers* 9, 105–22.
— (2008). *Cicero as Evidence: A Historian's Companion* (Oxford).
— (2009). 'The Assassination', in M. Griffin (ed.), *A Companion to Julius Caesar* (Oxford), 72–82.
Lorenz, K. (2008). *Bilder machen Räume: Mythenbilder in pompeianischen Häusern* (Berlin).
Luce, T.J. (1968). 'Political Propaganda on Roman Republican Coins: Circa 92–82 BC', *American Journal of Archaeology* 72, 25–39.
MacInnes, D. (2000). '"Dirum ostentum": Bee Swarm Prodigies at Roman Military Camps', in C. Deroux (ed.), *Studies in Latin Literature and Roman History* 10, 56–69.
MacKendrick, P. (1989). *The Philosophical Books of Cicero* (London).
MacMullen, R. (1966). *Enemies of the Roman Order: Treason, Unrest and Alienation in the Roman Empire* (Cambridge, MA).
Magie, D. (1950). *Roman Rule in Asia Minor* (Princeton).
Mahy, T. (2009). 'After the Daggers: Politics and Persuasion after the Assassination of Caesar', PhD diss., University of St Andrews.
Malherbe, A.J. (1988). *Ancient Epistolary Theorists*, SBL Sources for Biblical Study 19 (Atlanta).
Malcovati, H. (1966). *Oratorum Romanorum Fragmenta Liberae Rei Publicae*, 3rd edn (Turin).
Manuwald, G. (2006). 'Ciceros Attacke gegen die Provinzerlosung unter Antonius (zu. Cic. *Phil.* 3.24–26)', *Klio* 88, 167–80.
— (2007). *Cicero, Philippics, 3–9*, 2 vols (Berlin).
— (2015). *Cicero* (London).
Marcks, L.F. (1883). *Symbola critica ad epistolographos graecos*, Diss. Bonn.
Marin, P. (2009). *Blood in the Forum: The Struggle for the Roman Republic* (London and New York).
Marincola, J. (2010). 'Eros and Empire: Virgil and the Historians on Civil War', in C.S. Kraus, J. Marincola and C. Pelling (eds), *Ancient Historiography and its Contexts: Studies in Honour of A.J. Woodman* (Oxford), 183–204.
Marshall, B. (1987). 'The Engagement of Faustus Sulla and Pompeia', *Anc. Soc.* 18, 91–101.
Martin Jr, H. (1960). 'The Concept of Praotes in Plutarch's *Lives*', *GRBS* 3, 65–73.
— (1961). 'The Concept of Philanthropia in Plutarch's *Lives*', *AJPh* 82.2, 64–175.
McConnell, S. (2014). *Philosophical Life in Cicero's Letters* (Cambridge).
McDermott, W.C. (1949). 'Vettius Ille, Ille Noster Index', *TAPhA* 80, 351–67.
McDonnell, M. (2006). *Roman Manliness:* Virtus *and the Roman Republic* (Cambridge).
Meadows, A. and J. Williams. (2001). 'Moneta and the Monuments: Coinage and Politics in Republican Rome', *JRS* 91, 27–49
Meier, C. (1961). 'Zur Chronologie und Politik in Caesars ersten Konsulat', *Historia* 10, 68–98.
— (1966). *Res publica amissa* (Wiesbaden).
Meijer, F. (2004). *Emperors Don't Die in Bed* (London and New York).
Meyer, E. (1922). *Caesars Monarchie und das Principat des Pompeius* (Stuttgart/Berlin).
Middleton, C. (1840). *The Life and Letters of Marcus Tullius Cicero* (London).
Millar, F. (1964). *A Study of Cassius Dio* (Oxford).
— (1986).'Politics, Persuasion and the People before the Social War (150–90 BC)', *JRS* 76, 1–11.
— (1998). *Crowd in Rome in the Late Republic* (Ann Arbor).
Milner, K. (2014). *Graffiti and the Literary Landscape in Roman Pompeii* (Oxford).
Miola, R.S. (1985). 'Julius Caesar and the Tyrannicide Debate', *Renaissance Quarterly* 38, 271–89.
Moles, J.L. (1979). 'A Commentary on Plutarch's Brutus', DPhil thesis, Oxford; rev. ed. C.B.R. Pelling (forthcoming), *Histos*.
— (1983a). 'Fate, Apollo, and M. Junius Brutus', *AJPh* 104, 249–56.
— (1983b). 'Virgil, Pompey, and the Histories of Asinius Pollio', *CW* 76.5, 287–8.
— (1987a). 'The Attacks on L. Cornelius Cinna, Praetor in 44 BC', *RhM* 130.2, 124–8.
— (1987b). 'Politics, Philosophy, and Friendship in Horace *Odes* 2.7', *Quaderni Urbinati di Cultura Classica* 25.1, 59–72.
— (1997). 'Plutarch, Brutus and Brutus' Greek and Latin Letters', in J. Mossman (ed.), *Plutarch and His Intellectual World* (London), 141–68.

Momigliano, A. (1941). 'Review of Benjamin Farrington: *Science and Politics in the Ancient World*', *JRS* 31, 149–57.

Mommsen, T. (1910). *History of Rome*, trans. W.P. Dickson, Everyman's Library (London).

Morgan, L. (2000). 'The Autopsy of C. Asinius Pollio', *JRS* 90, 51–69.

Morrell, K. (2017). *Pompey, Cato and the Governance of the Roman Empire* (Oxford).

Morstein-Marx, R. (2004). *Mass Oratory and Political Power in the Late Roman Republic* (Cambridge).

— (2007). 'Caesar's Alleged Fear of Prosecution and His "Ratio Absentis" in the Approach to the Civil War', *Historia* 56.2, 159–78.

— (2009). '*Dignitas* and *Res Publica*: Caesar and Republican Legitimacy', in K.J. Hölkeskamp (ed.), *Eine politische Kultur (in) der Krise? Die 'letzte Generation' der römischen Republik*, Schriften des Historischen Kollegs Kolloquien 73 (Munich).

— (2012). 'Political Graffiti in the Late Roman Republic: Hidden Transcripts and Common Knowledge', in C. Kuhn (ed.), *Politische Kommunikation und öffentliche Meinung in der antiken Welt* (Heidelberg), 191–217.

Mouritsen, H. (2011). *Plebs and Politics in the Late Roman Republic* (Cambridge).

— (2017). *Politics in the Roman Republic* (Cambridge).

Münzer, F. (1920). *Römische Adelspartien und Adelsfamilien* (Stuttgart) = *Roman Aristocratic Parties and Families* (1999), trans. T. Ridley (Baltimore and London).

— (1923). 'Servilia (101)', *RE* 2A, 1817–21.

Murphy, M. (1987). 'Citizen Brutus: Rome, Sparta and the French Revolution', *Omnibus* 13; available online at: https://archive.org/details/omnibusmagazine (last accessed 19 June 2017).

Murray, O. (2007). 'Philosophy and Monarchy in the Hellenistic World', in T. Rajak et al. (eds), *Jewish Perspectives on Hellenistic Rulers* (Berkeley), 13–38.

Narducci, E. (2002). '*Brutus*: The History of Roman Eloquence', in J. May (ed.), *Brill's Companion to Cicero: Oratory and Rhetoric* (Leiden), 401–25.

— (2007). 'Cesare iure caesus: per la storia di una formulazione (da Cicerone a Svetonio, e un passo del De beneficiis di Seneca)', *Athenaeum* 95, 119–29.

Nederman, C.J. (1990). *John of Salisbury, Policraticus*, Cambridge Texts in the History of Political Thought (Cambridge).

Nelson, J. (2000). 'Writing Early Medieval Bibliography', *History Workshop* 50, 129–36.

Nipperdey, K. (1864). 'Vorläufige Bemerkungen zu den kleinen Schriften des Tacitus (Fortsetzung)', *RhM* 19, 270–92.

Nisbet, R.G.M. and M. Hubbard (1978). *A Commentary on Horace Odes, Book II* (Oxford).

Nodelman, S. (1987). 'The Portrait of Brutus the Tyrannicide', *Occasional Papers on Antiquities* 4: *Ancient Portraits in the J. Paul Getty Museum*, vol. 1, 41–86.

Noreña, C.F. (2011). *Imperial Ideals in the Roman West: Representation, Circulation, Power* (Cambridge).

North, T. (trans.) (1579). *Plutarch's Lives of the Noble Grecians and Romans*, vol. 7; (1928) repr. by The Shakespeare Head Press (Oxford).

Oakley, S.P. (2004). 'The Early Republic', in H.I. Flower (ed.), *The Cambridge Companion to the Roman Republic* (Cambridge), 15–30.

Oost, S.I. (1955). 'Cato Uticensis and the Annexation of Cyprus', *Classical Philology* 50, 98–112.

Ortmann, U. (1988). *Cicero, Brutus und Octavian - Republikaner und Caesarianer: Ihr gegenseitiges Verhältnis im Krisenjahre 44/43 v. Chr.* (Bonn).

Osgood, J. (2006). *Caesar's Legacy: Civil War and the Emergence of the Roman Empire* (Cambridge).

Pagán, V.E. (2004). *Conspiracy Narratives in Roman History* (Austin).

Parenti, M. (2003). *The Assassination of Julius Caesar: A People's History of Ancient Rome* (New York and London).

Parker, H.E. (1998). 'Loyal Slaves and Loyal Wives: The Crisis of the Outsider-within and Roman *Exemplum* Literature', in S. Joshel and S. Murnaghan (eds), *Women and Slaves in Greco-Roman Cultures: Differential Equations* (New York), 152–73.

Paul, G.M. (1982). 'Urbs Capta: Sketch of an Ancient Literary Motif', *Phoenix* 36, 144–55.

Pelling, C.B.R. (1989). 'Plutarch: Roman Lives and Greek Culture', in M. Griffin and J. Barnes (eds), *Philosophia Togata I: Essays on Philosophy and Roman Society* (Oxford), 199–232.

— (1990). 'Childhood and Personality in Greek Biography', in C.B.R. Pelling (ed.), *Character and Individualization in Greek Literature* (Oxford), 214–22.

— (1996). 'The Triumviral Period', in *CAH X*, 2nd edn (Cambridge), 1–69.

— (2002). *Plutarch and History* (London and Swansea).

— (2006). 'Judging Julius Caesar', in M. Wyke (ed.), *Julius Caesar in Western Culture* (Oxford), 3–26.

— (2011). *Plutarch Caesar: Translated with Introduction and Commentary* (Oxford).

— (2016). 'Tragic Colouring in Plutarch', in J. Opsomer, G. Roskam and F.B. Titchener (eds), *A Versatile Gentleman: Consistency in Plutarch's Writing* (Leuven), 89–100.

Piccolomini, M. (1991). *The Brutus Revival: Parricide and Tyrannicide during the Renaissance* (Carbondale and Edwardsville).

Pina Polo, F. (1989). *Las contiones civiles y militares en Roma* (Zaragoza).
— (1995). 'Procedures and Functions of Civil and Military *Contiones* in Rome', *Klio* 77, 203–16.
— (1996). *Contra arma verbis. Der Redner vor dem Volk in der spaten romischen Republik* (Stuttgart).
— (2006). 'The Tyrant Must Die: Preventive Tyrannicide in Roman Political Thought', in F. Marco Simón, F. Pina Polo and J. Remesal Rodríguez (eds), *Repúblicas y cuidadanos, modelos de participación cívica en el mundo antiguo* (Barcelona), 71–101.
— (2017). 'SPQR: Institutions and Popular Participation in the Roman Republic', in P.J. du Plessis and C. Ando (eds), *The Oxford Handbook of Roman Law and Society* (Oxford), 85–97.
Pocock, L.G.A. (1926). *A Commentary on Cicero in Vatinium* (London).
Potter, F.H. (1934). 'Political Alliance by Marriage', *CJ* 29.9, 663–74.
Purser, L. (1896). 'Marcus Brutus as Caesarian', *Hermathena* 9.22, 369–84.
Radin, M. (1939). *Marcus Brutus* (New York, London and Toronto).
Ramsey, J. (1994). 'The Senate, Mark Antony, and Caesar's Legislative Legacy', *CQ* 44.1, 130–45.
— (2000). '"Beware the Ides of March!": An Astrological Prediction?', *CQ* 50.2, 440–54.
— (2001). 'Did Mark Antony Contemplate an Alliance with His Political Enemies in July 44 BCE?', *CPh* 96.3, 253–68.
— (2003). *Cicero: Philippics I–II* (Cambridge).
— (2009). 'The Proconsular Years: Politics at a Distance', in M. Griffin (ed.), *A Companion to Julius Caesar* (Oxford), 37–56.
— (2010). 'Debate at a Distance: A Unique Rhetorical Stategy in Cicero's *Thirteenth Philippic*', in D.H. Berry and A. Erskine (eds), *Form and Function in Roman Oratory* (Cambridge), 155–74.
— (2016). 'How and Why Was Pompey Made Sole Consul in 52 BC?', *Historia* 65, 298–324.
Ramsey, J. and A Licht. (1997). *The Comet of 44 B.C. and Caesar's Funeral Games* (Atlanta).
Raubitschek, A.E. (1957). 'Brutus in Athens', *Phoenix* 11.1, 1–11.
— (1959). 'The Brutus Statue in Athens', *Atti del terzo Congresso internazionale di epigrafia greca e latina, Rome, 4–8 settembre 1957* (Rome).
Rawson, E. (1985). *Intellectual Life in the Late Roman Republic* (Baltimore).
— (1986). 'Cassius and Brutus: The Memory of the Liberators', in I.S. Moxon, J.D. Smart and A.J. Woodman (eds), *Past Perspectives* (Cambridge), 101–19; repr. in Rawson (1991), 488–507.
— (1991). *Roman Culture and Society: Collected Papers* (Oxford).
— (1994). 'Caesar: Civil War and Dictatorship', in *CAH IX*, 2nd edn, 424–67.
Rice-Holmes, T. (1928). *The Architect of the Roman Empire, 44 BC–27 BC* (Oxford).
Richards, J. (2008). *Hollywood's Ancient Worlds* (London and New York).
Richardson, J. (2011). 'L. Junius Brutus the Patrician and the Political Allegiance of Q. Aelius Tubero', *CPh* 106, 155–60.
Richardson, J. and F. Santangelo (eds) (2014). *The Roman Historical Tradition* (Oxford).
Richardson, J.S. (2012). *Augustan Rome, 44 BC to AD 14: The Restoration of the Republic and the Establishment of the Empire* (Edinburgh).
Ripley, J. (1980). *Julius Caesar on Stage in England and America, 1599–1973* (Cambridge).
Robb, M.A. (2010). *Beyond Populares and Optimates: Political Language in the Late Republic*, Historia Einzelschriften 213 (Stuttgart).
Roberts, A. (2014). *Napoleon the Great* (London).
Robinson, E.A. (1951). 'The Date of Cicero's Brutus', *HSCPh* 60, 137–46.
Rosenstein, N. (2011). 'War, Wealth and Consuls', in H. Beck, A. Duplá, M. Jehne and F. Pina Polo (eds), *Consuls and Res Publica: Holding High Office in the Roman Republic* (Cambridge), 133–58.
Rosillo-López, C. (2010). 'La Gestion des profits illégaux par les magistrats pendant la République romaine (IIe-Ier siècle av. J.-C.)', *Latomus* 69.4, 981–99.
— (2017). *Public Opinion and Politics in the Late Roman Republic* (Cambridge).
Rothstein, M. (1932). 'Caesar über Brutus', *RhM* 81, 324–34.
Rüpke, J. (2004). 'Roman Religion', in H.I. Flower (ed.), *Cambridge Companion to the Roman Republic* (Cambridge), 213–29.
Russell, J. (1980). 'Julius Caesar's Last Words: A Reinterpretation', in B. Marshall (ed.), *Vindex Humanitatis: Essays in Honour of John Huntley Bishop* (Armidale), 123–8.
Santangelo, F. (2006). 'Sulla and the Senate: A Reconsideration', *Cahiers du Centre Gustave-Glotz* 17, 7–22.
— (2007). *Sulla, the Elites and the Empire: A Study of Roman Politics in Italy and the Greek East* (Leiden).
— (2014). 'Roman Politics in the 70s BC: A Story of Realignments?', *JRS* 104, 1–27.
Schmidt, E. (2001). 'The Meaning of Vergil's Aeneid: American and German Approaches', *CW* 94, 145–71.
Schmidt, O.E. (1889). 'M. Iunius Brutus', in *Verhandlungen der Vierzigsten Versammlung deutscher Philologen und Schulmänner in Görlitz* (Leipzig), 165–85.
Schmitthenner, W.C.G. (1958). 'The Armies of the Triumviral Period', DPhil thesis, Oxford.

Schürer, E. (1885). *The History of the Jewish People in the Age of Jesus Christ*, vol. 1; (1973) rev. and ed. G. Vermes and F. Millar (Edinburgh).
Seager, R. (1965). 'Clodius, Pompeius and the Exile of Cicero', *Latomus* 24.3, 519–31.
— (2002). *Pompey the Great*, 2nd edn (Oxford).
Sedley, D. (1997). 'The Ethics of Brutus and Cassius', *JRS* 87, 41–53.
— (2012). (ed.). *The Philosophy of Antiochus* (Cambridge).
Seeck, O. von. (1901). 'Des Geburtsjahr des Marcus Brutus', *RhM* 56, 631–4.
— (1907). 'Noch einmal das Geburtsjahr des M. Brutus', *Hermes* 42, 505–8.
Shackleton Bailey, D.R. (1960). 'The Roman Nobility in the Second Civil War', *CQ* 10.2, 253–67.
— (1977). *Cicero: Epistulae ad Familiares* (Cambridge).
— (1980). *Cicero: Epistulae ad Quintum Fratrem et M. Brutum* (Cambridge).
Shapiro, J. (2005). *1599: A Year in the Life of William Shakespeare* (London).
Shatzman, I. (1975). *Senatorial Wealth and Roman Politics* (Brussels).
Sheppard, S. (2008). *Philippi 42 BC: The Death of the Roman Republic* (Oxford).
Sherwin-White, A.N. (1984). *Roman Foreign Policy in the East 168 BC to AD 1* (Norman).
Skinner, Q. (1998). *Liberty before Liberalism* (Cambridge).
Smith, C. (2006). '*Adfectatio Regni* in the Roman Republic', in S. Lewis (ed.), *Ancient Tyranny* (Edinburgh), 49–64.
Smith, J.L. (2015). 'Horace *Odes* 2.7 and the Literary Tradition of *Rhipsasia*', *AJPh* 136.2, 243–80.
Smith, R.R. (1936). 'The Greek Letters of M. Junius Brutus', *CQ* 30, 194–203.
Stadter, P.A. (1988). 'The Proems of Plutarch's *Lives*', *ICS* 13, 275–95.
Stangl, T. (1964). *Ciceronis Orationum Scholiastae* (Hildesheim).
Steel, C.E.W. (2001). *Cicero, Rhetoric and Empire* (Oxford).
— (2006). *Roman Oratory* (Cambridge).
— (2013). *The End of the Roman Republic, 146–44 BC: Conquest and Crisis* (Edinburgh).
— (2014a). 'Rethinking Sulla: The Case of the Roman Senate', *CQ* 64.2, 657–68.
— (2014b). 'The Roman Senate and the Post-Sullan *Res Publica*', *Historia* 63, 323–39.
Stevenson, T. (2015). *Julius Caesar and the Transformation of the Republic* (London and New York).
Stewens, W. (1963). *Brutus als Politiker*, Diss. Zürich.
Stockton, D. (1971). *Cicero: A Political Biography* (Oxford).
Storch, R.H. (1995). 'Relative Deprivation and the Ides of March: Motive for Murder', *AHB* 9, 45–52.
Strasburger, H. (1990). *Ciceros philosophisches Spätwerk als Aufruf gegen die Herrschaft Caesars*, ed. G. Strasburger (Hildesheim).
Strauss, B. (2015). *The Death of Caesar* (New York).
Stroh, W. (1983). 'Die Provinzverlosung am 28. November 44', *Hermes* 11, 452–8.
Sumi, G. (2005). *Ceremony and Power: Performing Politics in Rome between Republic and Empire* (Ann Arbor).
Sumner, G.V. (1971). 'The Lex Annalis under Caesar (continued)', *Phoenix* 25, 357–71.
Swain, S. (1989). 'Plutarch: Chance, Providence, History', *AJPh* 110, 272–302.
— (1990). 'Plutarch's Lives of Cicero, Cato, and Brutus', *Hermes* 118 192–203.
Sydenham, E.A. (1952). *The Coinage of the Roman Republic* (London).
Syme, R. (1939). *The Roman Revolution* (Oxford).
Szelmer, G.J. (1972). *The Priests of the Roman Republic* (Brussels).
Tatum, W.J. (1991). 'The Marriage of Pompey's Son to the Daughter of Ap. Claudius Pulcher', *Klio* 73, 122–9.
— (1999). *The Patrician Tribune: Publius Clodius Pulcher* (Chapel Hill and London).
— (2004). 'Elections in Rome', *CJ* 99, 202–36.
— (2007). '*Alterum est tamen boni viri, alterum boni petitoris*: The Good Man Canvasses', *Phoenix* 61, 109–35.
— (2008). *Always I Am Caesar* (Malden, Oxford and Victoria).
— (2011). 'The Late Republic: Autobiographies and Memoirs in the Age of the Civil Wars', in G. Marasco (ed.), *Political Autobiographies and Memoirs in Antiquity: A Brill Companion* (Leiden), 161–87.
Taylor, L.R. (1942). 'Caesar's Colleagues in the Pontifical College', *American Journal of Philology* 63.4, 385–412.
— (1949). *Politics in the Age of Caesar* (Berkeley and Los Angeles).
— (1950). 'The Date and Meaning of the Vettius Affair', *Historia* 1, 45–51.
— (1954). 'On the Date of *Ad Atticum* 2.24', *CQ* 4, 181–2.
— (1968). 'The Dating of Major Legislation and Elections in Caesar's First Consulship', *Historia* 17, 173–93.
Tempest, K. (2011). *Cicero: Politics and Persuasion in Ancient Rome* (London and New York).
— (2012). 'Cato, Marcus Porcius (Cato the Younger)', *The Encyclopedia of Ancient History* (Oxford).

— (2013a). 'An Ethos of Sincerity: Echoes of Cicero's *De Re Publica* in the *Pro Marcello*', *G&R* 60.2, 262–80.
— (2013b). 'Hellenistic Oratory at Rome: Cicero's *Pro Marcello*', in C. Kremmydas and K. Tempest (eds), *Hellenistic Oratory: Continuity and Change* (Oxford), 295–318.
Toher, M. (2003). 'Julius Caesar and Octavian in Nicolaus', in F. Cairns and E. Fantham (eds), *Caesar against Liberty? Perspectives on his Autocracy* (Cambridge), 132–56.
— (2004). 'Octavian's Arrival in Rome, 44 BC', *CQ* 54.1, 174–84.
Tomassi, G. (2015). 'Tyrants and Tyrannicides: Between Literary Creation and Contemporary Reality in Greek Declamation', in E. Amato and F. Citti (eds), *Law and Ethics in Greek and Roman Declamation* (Berlin), 247–67.
Toner, J. (2017). 'The Intellectual Life of the Roman Non-Elite', in L. Grig (ed.), *Popular Culture in the Ancient World* (Cambridge), 167–88.
Torraco, L. (1959). *Epistole greche* (Naples).
Toynbee, J.M.C. (1978). *Roman Historical Portraits* (London).
Treggiari, S. (1998). 'Home and Forum: Cicero between "Public" and "Private"', *TAPhA* 128, 1–23.
— (2003). 'Ancestral Virtues and Vices: Cicero on Nature, Nurture and Presentation', in D. Braund and C. Gill (eds), *Myth, History and Culture in Republican Rome: Studies in Honour of T.P. Wiseman* (Exeter), 139–64.
— (2007). *Terentia, Tullia and Publilia: The Women of Cicero's Family* (London).
Tschiedel, H.J. (1981). *Caesars 'Anticato': eine Untersuchung der Testimonien und Fragmente*, Impulse der Forschung 37 (Darmstadt).
Tyrrell, R.Y. and L.C. Purser (1901–33). *The Correspondence of M. Tullius Cicero*, 7 vols, 2nd edn (Dublin and London).
Urso, G. (2011). 'The Origin of the Consulship in Cassius Dio's *Roman History*', in H. Beck, A. Duplá, M. Jehne and F. Pina Polo (eds), *Consuls and* Res Publica*: Holding High Office in the Roman Republic* (Cambridge), 41–60.
Van der Blom, H (2010). *Cicero's Role Models: The Political Strategy of a Newcomer* (Oxford).
— (2011). 'Pompey in the Contio', *CQ* 61.2, 553–73.
— (2016). *Oratory and Political Career in the Late Roman Republic* (Cambridge).
Van Oort, R. (2016). *Shakespeare's Big Men: Tragedy and the Problem of Resentment* (Toronto).
Wallace-Hadrill, A. (1986). 'Image and Authority in the Coinage of Augustus', *JRS* 76, 66–87.
Wallman, P. (1989). *Triumviri rei publicae constituendae: Untersuchungen zur politischen Propaganda im Zweiten Triumvirat (43–30 v. Chr.)* (Frankfurt).
Walter, G. (1938). *Brutus et la fin de la République* (Paris).
— (1939). *Brutus et la fin de la République* (Paris).
Walter, U. (2003). 'Ahn Macht Sinn. Familientradition und Familienprofil im republikanischen Rom', in K.-J. Hölkeskamp, J. Rüsen, E. Stein-Hölkeskamp and H.T. Grütter (eds), *Sinn (in) der Antike: Orientierungssyteme, Leitbilder und Wertkonzepte im Altertum* (Mainz), 255–78.
Watt, W.S. (1958). *M. Tulli Ciceronis Epistulae* (Oxford).
Weigel, R.D. (1992). *Lepidus: The Tarnished Triumvir* (London).
Weinstock, S. (1971). *Divus Julius* (Oxford).
Weische, A. (1972). *Ciceros Nachahmung der attischen Redner* (Heidelberg).
Welch, K. (1995). 'Antony, Fulvia and the Ghost of Clodius', *G&R* 42, 182–219.
— (1996). 'T. Pomponius Atticus: A Banker in Politics?' *Historia* 45.4, 450–71.
— (2009). 'Alternative Memoirs: Tales from the "Other Side" of the Civil War', in C. Smith and A. Powell (eds), *The Lost Memoirs of Augustus* (Swansea), 195–223.
— (2012). *Magnus Pius: Sextus Pompeius and the Transformation of the Roman Republic* (Swansea).
— (2015). 'Programme and Narrative in *Civil Wars* 2.118–4.138', in K. Welch (ed.), *Appian's Roman History: Empire and Civil War* (Swansea), 277–304.
Welwei, K.-W. (2000). 'Lucius Junius Brutus – ein fiktiver Revolutionsheld', in K.-J. Hölkeskamp and E. Stein-Hölkeskamp (eds), *Von Romulus zu Augustus: Große Gestalten der römischen Republik* (Munich), 48–57.
— (2001). 'Lucius Iunius Brutus: Zur Ausgestaltung und politischen Wirkung einer Legende', *Gymnasium* 108, 123–35.
West, D. (1998). *Horace Odes II: Vatis Amici* (Oxford).
Westermann, A. (1851). *Commentatio de Epistolarum Scriptoribus Graecis* (Leipzig).
White, P. (2010). *Cicero in Letters: Epistolary Relations of the Late Republic* (Oxford).
Williamson, C. (2005). *The Laws of the Roman People: Public Law in the Expansion and Decline of the Roman Republic* (Ann Arbor).
Winterbottom, M. (2002). 'Believing the *Pro Marcello*', in J.F. Miller, C. Damon and K.S. Myers (eds), *Vertis in Usum: Studies in Honor of E. Courtney* (Munich), 24–38.

Wirszubski, C. (1950). *Libertas as a Political Idea at Rome during the Late Republic and Early Principate* (Cambridge).
Wiseman, T.P. (1971). *New Men in the Roman Senate 139 BC–14 AD* (Oxford).
— (1985). 'Competition and Co-operation', in T.P. Wiseman (ed.), *Roman Political Life, 90 BC–AD 69* (Exeter), 3–19.
— (1987). '*Conspicui postes tectaque digna deo*: The Public Image of Aristocratic and Imperial Houses in the Late Republic and Early Empire', in *L'Urbs: espace urbain et histoire (Ier siècle av. J.-C. – IIIe siècle ap. J.-C.), Actes du colloque international de Rome (8–12 mai 1985)* (Rome), 393–413.
— (1994). 'Caesar, Pompey and Rome, 59–50 BC', in J.A. Crook, A. Lintott and E. Rawson (eds), *CAH IX*, 2nd edn (Cambridge), 368–423.
— (1995). *Remus: A Roman Myth* (Cambridge).
— (2008). *Unwritten Rome* (Exeter).
— (2009). *Remembering the Roman People: Essays on Late-Republican Politics and Literature* (Oxford).
Wisse, J. (2013). 'Remembering Cremutius Cordus: Tacitus on History, Tyranny and Memory', *Histos* 7, 299–361.
Wistrand, E. (1981). *The Policy of Brutus the Tyrannicide* (Göteborg).
Woodman, A.J. (1983). *Velleius Paterculus: The Caesarian and Augustan Narrative (2.41–93)* (Cambridge).
— (2006). 'Tiberius and the Taste of Power: The Year 33 in Tacitus', *CQ* 56, 175–89.
Woolf, G. (2006). *Et Tu, Brute: The Murder of Caesar and Political Assassination* (London).
Wyke, M. (2006). (ed.) *Julius Caesar in Western Culture* (Oxford).
— (2007/2008). *Caesar: A Life in Western Culture* (London and Chicago).
Wylie, G. (1998). 'The Ides of March and the Immovable Icon', in C. Deroux (ed.), *Studies in Latin Literature and Roman History*, vol. 9 (Brussels), 167–85.
Xenophontos, S. (2013). 'Imagery and Education in Plutarch', *CPh* 108.2, 126–38.
Yakobson, J. (1999). *Elections and Electioneering in Rome: A Study in the Political System of the Late Republic* (Stuttgart).
Yarrow, L.M. (2005). *Historiography at the End of the Republic: Provincial Perspectives on Roman Rule* (Oxford).
Yavetz, Z. (1969). *Plebs and Princeps* (Oxford).
— (1971). 'Caesar, Caesarism and the Historians', *Journal of Contemporary History* 6.2, 184–201.
— (1974). '*Existimatio, Fama,* and the Ides of March', *HSCPh* 78, 35–65.
— (1983). *Julius Caesar: Man, Soldier and Tyrant* (London).
Zadorojnyi, A.V. (2007). 'Cato's Suicide in Plutarch', *CQ* 77.1, 216–30.
Zanker, P. (1988). *The Power of Images in the Age of Augustus*, trans. Alan Shapiro (Ann Arbor).

INDEX